Expanding the Linguistic Landscape

Full details of all our publications can be found on http://www.multilingual-matters.com, or by writing to Multilingual Matters, St Nicholas House, 31–34 High Street, Bristol BS1 2AW, UK.

Expanding the Linguistic Landscape

Linguistic Diversity, Multimodality and the Use of Space as a Semiotic Resource

Edited by
Martin Pütz and Neele Mundt

MULTILINGUAL MATTERS
Bristol • Blue Ridge Summit

DOI https://doi.org/10.21832/PUTZ2159

Library of Congress Cataloging in Publication Data
A catalog record for this book is available from the Library of Congress.
Names: Pütz, Martin, 1955- editor. | Mundt, Neele, 1989- editor.
Title: Expanding the Linguistic Landscape: Linguistic Diversity,
   Multimodality and the Use of Space as a Semiotic Resource/Edited by
   Martin Pütz and Neele Mundt.
Description: Bristol; Blue Ridge Summit: Multilingual Matters, [2019] |
   Includes bibliographical references and index.
Identifiers: LCCN 2018029635| ISBN 9781788922159 (hbk : alk. paper) |
ISBN 9781788922142 (pbk : alk. paper) | ISBN 9781788922166 (pdf) |
ISBN 9781788922173 (epub) | ISBN 9781788922180 (kindle)
Subjects: LCSH: Multilingualism. | Applied linguistics.
Classification: LCC P115 .E94 2019 | DDC 410.72—dc23 LC record available at
   https://lccn.loc.gov/2018029635

British Library Cataloguing in Publication Data
A catalogue entry for this book is available from the British Library.

ISBN-13: 978-1-78892-215-9 (hbk)
ISBN-13: 978-1-78892-214-2 (pbk)

Multilingual Matters
UK: St Nicholas House, 31–34 High Street, Bristol BS1 2AW, UK.
USA: NBN, Blue Ridge Summit, PA, USA.

Website: www.multilingual-matters.com
Twitter: Multi_Ling_Mat
Facebook: https://www.facebook.com/multilingualmatters
Blog: www.channelviewpublications.wordpress.com

The policy of Multilingual Matters/Channel View Publications is to use papers that are natural,
renewable and recyclable products, made from wood grown in sustainable forests. In the
manufacturing process of our books, and to further support our policy, preference is given to
printers that have FSC and PEFC Chain of Custody certification. The FSC and/or PEFC logos
will appear on those books where full certification has been granted to the printer concerned.

Typeset by Nova Techset Private Limited, Bengaluru and Chennai, India.
Printed and bound in the UK by Short Run Press Ltd.
Printed and bound in the US by Thomson-Shore, Inc.

Contents

Preface

This collection of 12 chapters has its origins in the 37th International LAUD Symposium (Linguistic Agency University of Duisburg), held on 4–6 April 2016 at the University of Koblenz-Landau in Landau, Germany. It contributes to the expanding field of the study of language and public space, with a particular focus on the late-modern globalised city. The conference theme, 'Linguistic Landscapes and Superdiversity in the City', was concerned with the analysis of multimodal signs in urban spaces as well as the emplacement of different codes in multilingual inscriptions in public space. The papers concentrated on various aspects pertaining to linguistic landscape research such as theoretical and methodological considerations, pedagogy, multimodality, semiotic assemblages, power relations and superdiversity in the city. The event brought together a number of eminent scholars as well as younger colleagues who were engaged in a vibrant exchange of ideas, research results and theoretical advances in interdisciplinary approaches to the study of linguistic landscapes.

There are numerous aspects of linguistic landscape research that we do not touch upon in this introduction. Our purpose here is to provide some of the insightful accounts of recent research findings in a variety of areas that the vast field of linguistic landscapes encompasses. Overall, this collection of selected chapters provides a multifaceted view of key themes in linguistic landscape research today and offers directions for where the future of this research area may be heading.

We owe a debt of gratitude to a large number of people who have contributed to the volume. First of all, many thanks are due to the participants in the symposium for the stimulating discussions in a very pleasant atmosphere, and to the contributors of the present volume, who have responded with alacrity and professionalism to all the requests that have been made of them. Our deep gratitude must also go to those who made this publication possible: to all colleagues and linguistic experts who kindly agreed to act as referees and who reviewed the chapters, offering valuable advice both to the contributors and to the editors.

Thanks to the generous support of the DFG (German Research Foundation), the University of Koblenz-Landau, the Paul and Yvonne Gillet Foundation (Edenkoben), the Faculty of Cultural and Social Sciences and the Friends and Supporters of the University of Koblenz-Landau (Landau Campus), many internationally well-known scholars were able to participate in the symposium and contributed to its great success. We are also grateful to the organising staff of the symposium, in particular to our colleague Monika Reif as well as to student helpers Evelyn John, Fabian Glass, Tim-Oliver Paul and Alexander Frankenfeld for their enthusiasm and kind assistance.

Finally, abundant appreciation goes to our publisher Multilingual Matters, in particular to Editorial Director Anna Roderick for her professional expertise and assistance throughout this venture, and whose support was crucial to the emergence of the present book.

Martin Pütz and Neele Mundt

Contributors

Seraphim Alvanides is Associate Professor at Northumbria University in Newcastle, UK. He is an urban social geographer, with expertise in quantitative methods and geographical information science. He is associate editor of the *Journal of Transport and Health* and editorial board member of the *Journal of Urban Analytics and City Science*. Seraphim is fascinated by sociolinguistics and is currently exploring innovative methods for visualising and mapping linguistic landscapes.

Isabelle Buchstaller is Professor of English Linguistics at the University of Duisburg-Essen. Her research focuses on variationist sociolinguistics, including the element of contact in linguistic change. Isabelle has published widely on ongoing changes in the area of morphosyntax, including her monograph *Quotatives: New Trends and Sociolinguistic Implications* (Wiley, 2014). Her work has appeared in *Language in Society*, the *Journal of Sociolinguistics*, *Language Variation and Change* and *American Speech*. She is a co-editor of the *Routledge Studies in Language Change* series.

Sabine Diao-Klaeger is Professor of French Linguistics at the University of Koblenz-Landau, Landau Campus. She has published on the French language in Burkina Faso and in the area of sociostylistics, and is conducting research on discourse markers in language contact situations and in French as an L2. She is also active in teaching and research on language variation and interactional linguistics.

Christine Domke is Professor of Social Communication at Fulda University of Applied Sciences. She holds a PhD in linguistics from the University of Bielefeld and finished her *habilitation* (postdoctoral degree) in public communication in cities, railway stations and airports at the Chemnitz University of Technology in 2012. Her research interests include pragmatics and media linguistics, organisational communication and semiotic landscapes.

Durk Gorter is Ikerbasque Research Professor at the University of the Basque Country, Spain. He is the head of the Donostia Research Group on Education and Multilingualism (DREAM). He conducts research on multilingual education, European minority languages and linguistic landscapes. He has published extensively on those themes.

Ying-hsueh Hu is an associate professor at the Department of English, Tamkang University, Taiwan. She has researched and taught extensively on topics relating to sociolinguistics and cognitive linguistics (CL). In recent years, she has focused on the issues of identity and culture in the context of learning English as an international language. She is also active in developing materials for teaching Chinese as a foreign language from a CL perspective.

Adam Jaworski is Chair Professor of Sociolinguistics at the School of English, the University of Hong Kong. His latest book is *The Elite Discourse: The Rhetorics of Status, Privilege and Power* (with Crispin Thurlow, Routledge, 2017). With Brook Bolander he co-edits the Oxford University Press book series, *Oxford Studies in Sociolinguistics.*

Karsten Legère is Professor Emeritus (University of Gothenburg) and has been a visiting professor of the University of Vienna since 2011. As a linguist/Africanist he specialises in Bantu languages and recently also on Southern Nilotic Akie (as part of a project funded by the Volkswagen Foundation), with expertise in language endangerment and documentation, sociolinguistics as well as language policy, especially with regard to African language empowerment. He is the author and editor of a number of academic publications, editorial consultant of various Africa related linguistic journals, peer-reviewer, external examiner, WOCAL Board Member and so on. The Akie material (DoBeS collection, Max Planck Institute for Psycholinguistics, Nijmegen) is recognised by UNESCO as 'Memory of the World'.

David Malinowski is Assistant Professor in the Department of Linguistics and Language Development at San José State University. With a background in language and literacy education, multimodal communication and technology-enhanced learning, he teaches and conducts research on language teacher development and place-based language learning. David holds a master's in TESOL from San Francisco State University, a PhD in education from the University of California at Berkeley, and is an associate editor for the journal Linguistic Landscape.

Irina Moore is a senior lecturer in linguistics at the University of Wolverhampton, UK, where she teaches morphology, psycholinguistics and Russian. Her research interests include, among other areas, theory of translation, language teaching methodology, TESOL and comparative psycholinguistics. She is also interested in the sociolinguistics of the post-Soviet space. She has published a number of works on the linguistic rights of minorities, and identity issues, language removal and repositioning in Kazakhstan and Lithuania.

Neele Mundt is a lecturer in English linguistics at the University of Koblenz-Landau, Germany. She works in the field of applied linguistics with a focus on English in central Africa. She spent one year in Yaoundé, Cameroon, where she collected her field data, which also focus on linguistic landscapes. Her research interests include sociolinguistics, multilingualism and second language development in Africa.

Alastair Pennycook, FAHA, is Distinguished Professor of Language, Society and Education at the University of Technology Sydney and Adjunct Professor at the University of Oslo. He is the author of numerous award-winning books, including *Metrolingualism: Language in the City* (with Emi Otsuji), *Language and Mobility: Unexpected Places*; *Language as a Local Practice*, *Global Englishes and Transcultural Flows* and *The Cultural Politics of English as an International Language* (Routledge Linguistics Classic).

Martin Pütz is Full Professor of English linguistics at the University of Koblenz-Landau (Landau Campus) where he regularly organises linguistics conferences (International LAUD Symposia). His research interests include sociolinguistics, applied cognitive linguistics and multilingualism in Africa. He is one of the co-editors of the book series *Duisburg Papers on Research in Language and Culture* (Peter Lang); one of his recent publications includes *Endangered Languages and Languages in Danger* (2016, with co-editor Luna Filipović).

Tove Rosendal is a researcher in African languages at the University of Gothenburg in Sweden, where she obtained her PhD in 2010. Tove Rosendal is working within the field of sociolinguistics in African countries, especially on language policy issues and linguistic landscape studies in multilingual societies. She has conducted projects in Uganda and Rwanda, in addition to projects on language contact between Swahili and Ngoni in rural Tanzania.

Ulrich Schmitz is Emeritus Professor of Linguistics, German Language and Language Teaching at the University of Duisburg-Essen, Germany. His research focuses on contemporary German language, language in mass media and digital media. Recently, he has worked on multimodality with special regard to relations between text and image.

Elana Shohamy is teaching and researching various aspects of multilingualism at Tel Aviv University, Israel within the framework of critical sociolinguistics. Her specific areas include the social, political and power dimensions of language tests; issues of multilingual language policy within engaged language policy, language rights, equality and language maintenance; language learning of immigrants and asylum seekers and linguistic landscape. Elana served as the editor of *Language Policy* (2005–2013) and currently edits the journal *Linguistic Landscape*. Elana is the winner of the 2010 International Language Testing Association (ILTA) lifetime achievement award.

Haci-Halil Uslucan is Professor of Modern Turkish Studies at the University of Duisburg-Essen and the Head of the Center for Turkish Studies and Research on Integration in Essen. He studied Psychology, Philosophy and Comparative Literature at the Free University Berlin. His main research areas are intellectual development, juvenile violence, parenting in diverse cultural contexts, Islam and social integration, psychological health and migration. He is a member and the Vice Director of the German Council on Integration and Migration.

Evelyn Ziegler studied German and English leading to the degree of 'Staatsexamen für das Lehramt an Gymnasien' at the University of Heidelberg. After obtaining her PhD in German linguistics at the University of Heidelberg, she worked as a research associate at the universities of Freiburg and Marburg (*Forschungsinstitut für Deutsche Sprache – Deutscher Sprachatlas*). During these years, she has developed a strong research interest in the domains of sociolinguistics, language variation, multilingualism and language attitudes. In 2008, she was appointed Professor of German Sociolinguistics at the University of Duisburg-Essen.

Rosalie Zongo was born in the Ivory Coast. After her high school diploma, she studied linguistics at the Université Joseph Ki-Zerbo of Ouagadougou. After her master's degree in 2013, she started her PhD studies and since 2015 has been a PhD student at the University of Koblenz-Landau. Her PhD thesis is entitled 'Morphosyntaxe du Ninkaré/Eléments de contact entre le Ninkaré et le Français'.

Multilingualism, Multimodality and Methodology: Linguistic Landscape Research in the Context of Assemblages, Ideologies and (In)visibility: An Introduction

1 Linguistic Landscapes: Purposes, Aims and the Concept of Multilingualism

This volume is intended to be a contribution to the rapidly growing field of research into linguistic landscapes (LL),[1] which draws on the convergence of methods and theoretical frameworks typically associated with language(s), visual multilingualism and public space. In this vein, the dynamic and gradually developing 'branch of sociolinguistics' (Blommaert, 2013: 2) of linguistic landscapes is generally and traditionally perceived as the study of the visible representation of multiple languages in a globalised world. This introduction is not meant to provide an overview of the genesis, development and prospects of LL research (to this purpose see Shohamy (Chapter 1) and, for example, Gorter, 2013). Instead, it focuses on some of the major LL concepts discussed in the volume, along with a brief overview of the various chapters in the book.

Generally, the book seeks to provide a forum for theoretical, methodological and empirical contributions to research on language(s), multimodality and public space,[2] which – it is hoped – will advance new ways of understanding the socio-cultural, ideological and historical role of communication practices and 'experienced' lives in a globalised world. We have chosen to call this book *Linguistic Landscapes* (as has been the case with many other volumes in the past, e.g. Backhaus, 2007; Blackwood *et al.*, 2016; Blommaert, 2013; Shohamy & Gorter, 2009a, 2009b; Shohamy *et al.*, 2010), viewing LL as a metaphor and expanding it to include the whole set of 'semiotic assemblages' (Pennycook, Chapter 4) of discursive modalities: imagery, non-verbal communication, silence, tactile and aural communication, graffiti, smell and so on. For the purpose of the present book, the area of LL will be conceptualised and widened as *multimodal* signage similar to the concept laid out by Shohamy (2015: 168), who touches upon the issue of the boundaries of LL as follows:

> Does an expanded meaning of 'language' need to be limited to words? Is a movement, a dance, food, bodies not languages, that provide and send meanings to others? The term 'language' needs to be expanded to all these other devices which take place in the 'practiced', 'conceived' and 'lived' spaces.

In multilingual and multicultural communities, people and passers-by are surrounded by a multitude of languages and language contact phenomena (such as code-switching, code-mixing and borrowing) as well as visual imagery which appear in public places. LL data in principle can be found across all physical spaces where people leave visible and non-verbal signs which all communicate meanings and intentions in one way or another. Examples include signposts; photographs and videos; billboards; public roads and safety signs; slogans and commercials; lighting and printed materials; names of buildings, streets, shops and areas of major tourist attractions; instructions, warning notices and prohibitions; graffiti; tattoos; and cyber space[3] – in short, 'live' documentations and reflections of the physical environment of the late-modern, globalised urban space. It is therefore particularly appropriate to introduce the concept of the LL as an 'environmental print' (Huebner, 2006) or a perspective of cities as 'texts' (Dagenais *et al.*, 2009). Nowadays, the linguistic and communicative spaces of people are becoming increasingly diverse, and the LL of individuals or sign initiators are not simply defined through physical space, but also through 'electronic space, global travel, media awareness and usage, popular culture, as well as the virtual space of the Internet' (Bolton, 2012: 30).

In particular, the contributions to this volume attempt to capture and comprehend the history, motives, uses, causes, ideologies, communication practices and conflicts of diverse forms of languages as they may be observed in public spaces of the physical environment. Accordingly, the book is anchored in a variety of theories, methodologies and frameworks, from economics, politics and sociology to linguistics and applied linguistics, literacy and education, cultural geography and human rights. It offers interdisciplinary perspectives, whereby 'physical space' is viewed as a significant extension of the traditional scope of sociolinguistic study, thereby becoming a 'diagnostic of social, cultural and political structures inscribed in the linguistic landscape' (Blommaert, 2013: 3).

In LL studies, the focus has traditionally been on a quantitative account of multiple languages and signage in public places as well as the social meanings and indexicalities associated with them such as power, language policy/planning and social justice. The theme of the ideological significance of public signage is also taken up by some contributors/chapters in the book (particularly in Part 3, i.e. power relations, acts of resilience and diachronic changes). They explore the dynamics of the LL as a site of conflict, exclusion and dissent, and focus on sociohistorical, economic, political and ideological issues, as reflected in mass protest demonstrations and official, top-down signage. Before we start discussing some of the major thematic fields dealt with in the book, a few words about the notion of

multilingualism are in order. The term has been paramount in numerous LL studies and has been defined differently depending on the goals and objectives of the
case study under scrutiny.

The following definition of the notion of multilingualism is certainly in line with
a view of multilinguality as we find it in the early phase of LL studies:

> The term/concept of multilingualism is to be understood as the capacity of societies,
> institutions, groups and individuals to engage on a regular basis in space and time
> with more than one language in everyday life. (Franceschini, 2009: 33)

A more comprehensive view and one that is rather in agreement with a *translanguaging* perspective is put forward by Aronin and Singleton (2012), who highlight the
three principal components of multilingualism, that is, user, language and environment; the latter is strongly associated with *material culture* and is particularly suited
to a semiotic framework focusing on the way in which multilinguals interact with
their physical and material environments. Nevertheless, the multiple forms of 'languages' constitute one of the essential characteristics of LL in ethnically diverse communities. Not surprisingly, the counting of languages on signage turned out to be
one of the methodological highlights in the early phase of LL research. However, in
order to challenge the idea of languages as discrete, countable entities, the concept
of translanguaging has now been suggested as a (new) approach to multilingualism
(Gorter & Cenoz, 2015).[4] Originally, the concept of translanguaging was described
as 'the act performed by bilinguals of accessing different linguistic features or various modes of what are described as autonomous languages, in order to maximize
communicative potential' (García, 2009: 140), that is, the deployment of a speaker's
full linguistic repertoire that transcends boundaries of defined languages and language modalities (Otheguy *et al.*, 2015: 281). A more realistic picture of multilingualism in relation to LL therefore should be conceived in terms of translanguaging (see
also Pennycook, Chapter 4), which refers to a holistic view of LL engaging with
space, place, bodies, languages and senses. In other words, translanguaging can be
construed as a social semiotic process that differs from code-switching and other
language contact phenomena, and assumes that bilinguals/multilinguals have only
one complex linguistic repertoire from which they select features that are sociocul-
turally appropriate. It entails movement between different languages or, as Gorter
and Cenoz (2015: 57) put it, 'multilinguals navigate between their languages in social
interactions, while they use all their linguistic resources'. Hence, the LL field, originally limited to the analysis of monolingual or multilingual signage, here emphasises
a holistic view (in line with an *expanded* LL), which proposes 'that the linguistic
landscape itself is a multilingual and multimodal repertoire, which is used as a communication tool to appeal to passers-by' (Gorter & Cenoz, 2015: 63). In order to
move beyond current terms such as multilingualism and multiculturalism, Otsuji and
Pennycook (2010) coined the term *metrolingualism*, which describes readers and
writers as interactants of the urban space where 'people of different and mixed backgrounds use, play with and negotiate identities through language' (Otsuji &
Pennycook, 2010: 245).

2 Linguistic Landscapes, Semiotic Assemblages and Multimodality

During the past 20 years since the early stages of the LL field of study (Landry & Bourhis, 1997), the notion of LL has undergone a number of definitions and conceptualisations from purely language-related matters to semiotic conceptions of communication (with a focus on visualisation) and finally to multimodality as an interdisciplinary and all-encompassing approach that understands communication and representation to be more than one language or language variety. Various LL researchers have alluded to the seminal work by Landry and Bourhis (1997: 23), who conceive of LL as 'the visibility and salience of languages on public and commercial signs in a given territory or region'. Certainly, their definition 'contains the seeds of the development of the field of linguistic landscape' (Gorter, 2013: 193) and provided the basis of LL as a sociolinguistic tool even though Landry and Bourhis did not study language or textual information per se, but rather focused on social psychological aspects of bilingual development and ethnolinguistic vitality as a concept in sociolinguistic research.

Although the boundaries of the field of LL studies cannot be drawn precisely, in its early phase the field was focused on the analysis of language(s) displayed on signs in public space and on the respective methods (mainly quantitative in nature) and techniques of data collection and analysis. Rather critically, Blommaert (2016: 1–2) refers to the first wave of studies as being marked by 'a synchronic, static and quantitative approach to hypostatized "languages" in a given physical arena', deploring the lack of an ethnographic-historical approach 'in which signs are seen as traces of multimodal communicative practices within a socio-politically structured field which is historically configured' (Blommaert, 2016: 2). In the opening paper of the journal *Linguistic Landscape* (2015, Vol. 1, No. 1/2), Barni and Bagna (2015) report on a 'critical turn' in LL in a sense that linguistic objects (i.e. shop signs) were now seen as situated in sociocultural and historical space: their sign-users or authors (both instigators and recipients) were assigned a more active role in LL analysis and an advancement of different and more sophisticated methods has come to the fore. This more qualitative analysis of LL is in line with 'expanding the scenery of the linguistic landscape' (Shohamy & Gorter, 2009a, 2009b) by taking 'images, photos, sounds (soundscapes), movements, music, smells (smellscapes), graffiti, clothes, food, buildings, history' (Shohamy, 2015: 153–154) under one single multimodal umbrella. Thus, *semiotic landscapes* are considered as discursively constructed space (Jaworski & Thurlow, 2010), that is, places are considered not as mere geographically defined areas but as symbolic representations of social, cultural and political values. In this respect, Pennycook (2017, and Chapter 4) speaks of LL as semiotic assemblages, which 'allows for an understanding of how different trajectories of people, semiotic resources and objects meet at particular moments and places, and thus helps us to see the importance of things, the consequences of the body, and the significance of place alongside the meanings of linguistic resources' (Pennycook, 2017: 269).

From a semiotic perspective, therefore, Jaworski (Chapter 5) explores the manifestation and thematisation of *silence* or non-verbal communication in the commercial semiotic landscape of Hong Kong. The issue of non-verbal communication has only recently come to the attention of scholars working in the area of LL studies. Similarly, Jaworski's (2015) analysis of language objects (i.e. Robert Indiana's LOVE sculpture) in urban landscapes (here, Philadelphia) suggests a broadening of LL objects from language and multilingualism, thus making up the spatial repertoire or the sociosemiotics of public place. Therefore, *semiotic landscape* can be considered as an alternative, more encompassing term, for LL that emphasise a wider focus for the studies inherent in this volume. Semiotic signage and multimodality describe communication practices in terms of the textual, aural, linguistic, spatial and visual resources – or modes – used to compose meaningful messages. Thus, the notion of multimodality is clearly related to the question of LL boundaries, which is certainly one of the most debated areas of research since the beginning stages of the LL field. For example, taking Cape Town's tattooing culture as an illustration, Peck and Stroud (2015) argue in favour of extending LL studies to encompass the body as a corporeal landscape, that is, the materiality of the body as a mobile and dynamic space captured by the concept of *skinscape*, thereby bringing the *body* into the analytical repertoire of LL research.

3 Methodology and Educational Perspectives on Linguistic Landscapes

From a methodological perspective, the book is a major step towards an all-encompassing account of collecting signage and audio-material (see Gorter and Hu, this volume). Methods in LL research have mainly been *quantitative*, which means counting and ranking languages in various public places and possibly comparing cities and urban agglomerations of diverse geographical areas using statistical and demographic analysis. Such areas were often seen to represent language presence and ethnolinguistic vitality in urban spaces, especially in settlements of immigrant communities (see Backhaus, 2007; Barni & Bagna, 2010; Gorter, 2006b). Thus, researchers collect data about the status and distribution of languages on monolingual and multilingual signs so that they can supply relevant data about a sociolinguistic or language policy situation. In this vein, many LL publications can report quantitative-distributive results (e.g. see Ben-Rafael & Ben-Rafael, 2015). Research into LL draws on the general repertoire of available traditional methods in sociolinguistics and the sociology of language, but its main innovation is in the typical method of collecting large numbers of photographs, made possible by affordable digital technology (Gorter, Chapter 2).

From a rather more *qualitative* methodological perspective, researchers conduct in-depth enquiries into the significance and meanings of signs to deepen our understanding, guided by theoretical concepts such as ideologies, identities, language policy, literacy, minority languages or multilingualism (Aiestaran *et al.*, 2010). Qualitative data may be based on telephone conversations between researchers, sign instigators and passers-by, along with introspective interviews conducted after these interactions (see especially the chapter by Ziegler *et al.*, Chapter 12). Thus, this expansion in scope has, for the most part, moved away from quantitative methods in favour of more in-depth ethnographic approaches focusing on observed natural language use, participant observation, sociolinguistic questionnaires, informal interviews, attitude studies and historical documentation, and so on. Likewise, 'walking tours' of local language users and passers-by capture impressions and reactions to the LL (Garvin, 2010). Some of the ethnographically orientated studies include, for example, a material ethnography of multilingualism (Stroud & Mpendukana, 2009), a semiotic ecology of LL (Banda & Jimaima, 2015), the materiality of the body as a mobile and dynamic space (Peck & Stroud, 2015) or tourists' discursive and embodied performances (Thurlow & Jaworski, 2014). One of the most vigorous proponents of an ethnographic approach to LL studies is Blommaert and associates (e.g. Blommaert & Maly, 2016). Making reference to the originator and founder of the ethnography of communication, Dell Hymes and his tradition of linguistic anthropology with a focus on ethnography as the main type of sociolinguistic investigation, Blommaert (2016: 2) suggests an ethnographic approach to LL studies 'in which signs are seen as traces of multimodal communicative practices within a socio-politically structured field which is historically configured' or, as Maly (2016: 707) suggests, 'within ethnography, language is understood as the architecture of social behaviour'. Paramount is the notion of indexicality, which means looking at deeper levels of meaning connected to the signs that can explain what they refer to in addition to their referential meaning (Blommaert & Maly, 2016).

Besides quantitative and qualitative methods, some authors in the book (e.g. Buchstaller & Alvanides, Chapter 10) developed methods for capturing the interplay between linguistic, social and geographical spaces through georeferencing photographs, coding them for a range of parameters and visualising the spatial and the contextual information with the use of static and interactive maps. They systematically explore the issue of *geosemiotics* (Scollon & Scollon, 2003), which offers 'an integrative view of these multiple semiotic systems which together form the meanings which we call place' (Scollon & Scollon, 2013: 12), that is, an approach to cross-cultural communication that seeks to investigate how language(s) and signs make meaning in relation to where (and when) they are physically located in the world.

The advancement and spread of digital technology also has an influence on the educational perspectives on LL and the second language learning classroom. For some language educators, much of the interest in public displays of language is grounded in the potential of particular LL for the teaching and learning of second or foreign languages (Chern & Dooley, 2014). Malinowski (Chapter 3), for example, elaborates on an interdisciplinary approach to pedagogical practice and teaching LL as a translational space. Generally, the textual elements found in the LL are considered to be a source of input in the second language acquisition process because learners are confronted with the target language in the outside world, that is, in urban quarters and public spaces (Cenoz & Gorter, 2008: 273). Since the LL reflects authentic language use in diverse ways, it can offer valuable tools for literacy learning and language pedagogy, inside and outside of school settings. Brief surveys of LL studies on teaching/learning perspectives are provided by Cenoz and Gorter (2008), Malinowski (2015) and recently Huebner (2016: 6–7). Owing to limitations of space we will not go into a detailed review of such studies, but would like to briefly focus on a few recent LL learning projects on education.

Situated in a Caribbean context, Hewitt-Bradshaw (2014), for example, discusses LL signage in Creole language environments and presents a range of visual and printed texts from various sources which are used to develop students' critical language awareness and to increase their linguistic and communicative skills. Through illustrations of the use of Jamaican Creole on a T-shirt, for example, Hewitt-Bradshaw demonstrates that the notion of identity of a Creole speaker can be asserted, negotiated and debated in the classroom. By means of a graphic image (graffiti) on a wall, the lexical and semantic choices and their implications can be explored and then critically discussed. At times, incorrect spellings such as 'TAXI STAN' (Creole deletion of consonant cluster) on a sign on a transport shelter provides a rich source for linguistic exploration and discussion in classrooms. This way of targeting students' language awareness and identity formation can make them conscious of linguistic features of their landscape that they may have previously taken for granted. In other words, children are confronted on a daily basis with a multitude of public signage, so their landscape provides an ideal educational tool to develop their literacy. Furthermore, the use of city signs and urban symbols can reveal an abundance of characteristics pertaining to the culture and history of a place, providing excellent material for language learning in 'real-life' situations. LL can therefore be used as a tool to develop students' critical literacy as well as their language skills and pragmatic competence. From the perspective of bilingual education, Dressler (2015) investigates signage and sign-making practices in a Canadian bilingual elementary public school (German-English) using a nexus analysis (Scollon & Scollon, 2003)

> which sheds light on the convergence of (1) the historical body of social actors in which teachers are primarily responsible for sign making, (2) an interaction order in which teachers practice organic sign placement and (3) discourses in place which include the promotion of bilingualism. (Dressler, 2015: 128)

The general aim of Dressler's study was to explore the degree to which a school offering a bilingual programme promotes the acquisition of two languages through signage. The 'most theoretical and practical articulation of the intersection of LL and language teaching and learning' (Huebner, 2016: 6) is the position paper by Malinowski (2015). Based on work by Trumper-Hecht (2010), Malinowski reinterprets Lefebvre's (1991) triadic paradigm of conceived, perceived and lived spaces for the language classroom (see also Malinowski, Chapter 3), and suggests a tentative framework for structuring L2 learning activities in the LL.

4 Linguistic Landscapes and Acts of Resilience: Language Policy, Ideology and the Invisibility of Languages

In the past, LL research has been engaged with a number of studies that focused on minority/regional language situations, illuminating the interrelationships between official and non-official languages, power constellations, visibility, marginalisation and contestations in the city; see, for example, the papers on (1) LL as sites of protest, conflict and exclusion in Rubdy and Ben Said (2015); (2) signage on protests and identity construction in Blackwood *et al.* (2016); (3) language policy, globalisation and resistance in the context of minority languages in Gorter *et al.* (2012); and (4) the spatial dynamics of discourse in global protest movements (Martín Rojo, 2016). These volumes also demonstrate that the LL approach is particularly suitable for highlighting and interpreting the dynamics of minority language situations, the particular characteristics of sign actors (both initiators and receivers), the struggles and protests of language users, and ultimately the loss and survival of endangered languages.

In this vein, from the perspective of language policy, sociopolitical change and emplaced signage, the visibility of minority or local languages in the LL is vitally important for the promotion and maintenance of such languages/varieties in diverse multilingual settings. To underline this point, the Universal Declaration of Linguistic Rights (1996), Art. 50.1 gives any language the right to be *visible* in the LL (quoted from Marten *et al.*, 2012: 7):

> All language communities have the right for their language to occupy a pre-eminent place in advertising, signs, external signposting, and in the image of the country as a whole.

Part 3 in this book, that is, 'Expanding Linguistic Landscape Studies: Power Relations, Acts of Resilience and Diachronic Changes' (Chapters 8–12 by Legère & Rosendal, Diao-Klaeger & Zongo, Buchstaller & Alvanides; Moore and Ziegler *et al.*) focuses on the dynamics of the LL as a site of conflict, exclusion and dissent often arising from mechanisms of linguistic inequality, language policy, dominance and the ethnolinguistic struggles endangered by them. Strongly associated with the issue of minority languages, official language policies and power constellations in multilingual communities is the issue of *ideology*. That the LL can be an important space for ideological debates is shown by Shohamy (2015), who even conceives of LL as a mechanism of language policy. She demonstrates how LL can be used as a tool, for example, for the revival of a language such as Hebrew, and also suggests a multimodal approach (texts, images, location, history, environment and so on) that is needed to capture and contextualise the full meaning of, for instance, a commemoration site in Tel Aviv. For example, Waksman and Shohamy (2010) showed that during the centennial of the city of Tel Aviv, a certain section of the population felt excluded and therefore were engaged in contesting, objecting and resenting the top-down policy exerted by the governmental agency. In order to understand the relative power and status of different languages in a multilingual city, it is advisable to categorise signs in terms of top-down/bottom-up, as suggested by Ben-Rafael *et al.* (2006). It is generally assumed that language use and signage in the LL falls into one of two categories: *top-down* (text dispersed from an official source) and *bottom-up* (created by shop owners, private businesses, advertisements, graffiti and so on). However, research into the social and cultural characteristics of events and actors has shown that this straightforward dichotomy into top-down and bottom-up is perhaps too simplistic and should be replaced by a more nuanced view suggesting varying degrees of how official and unofficial language use can actually be (see also the critique by Kallen, 2009: 273).

So far in previous studies, research on LL in Africa has largely been underrepresented. Sub-Saharan Africa especially is a large and heterogeneous part of a continent with conflicting policies and a multitude of situations with multifaceted landscapes in urban areas. Most LL studies on African spaces deal with acts of resistance, periods of crises or linguistic *warscapes* defined as LL that 'actors create in situations of war and which in some way reflects an experience of war' (Mc Laughlin, 2015: 213). Issues of policy and the ideological significance of public signage with reference to the globalisation of English is a theme that has attracted LL researchers dealing with multilingual signage in, for example, African cities and even rural areas (Banda & Jimaima, 2015). Owing to the fact that sub-Saharan Africa is still highly underrepresented in LL studies (especially compared to Europe and Asia), the chapters on Rwanda, Uganda, Tanzania and Africa in general (Legère & Rosendal, Chapter 8) as well as on francophone Burkina Faso (Diao-Klaeger & Zongo, Chapter 9) in Part 3 are welcome additions to this research paradigm. Therefore, making reference to a few earlier studies concerning LL in Africa is in order. The visibility of (minority) languages or their absence from the LL in diverse, multilingual settings as de facto language policy, for example, is examined in a case study on two minority languages in Southern Ethiopia (Mendisu *et al.*, 2016). The assumption that visibility necessarily indexes vitality and the underlying 'dilemma of visibility' with respect to local African languages in the Ethiopian context constitutes one of the major concerns in their study. As is the case in many African states, in Ethiopia there is a lack of 'coherency' between a territory's official language policy (top-down) and emplaced signage as linguistic practice (Mendisu *et al.*, 2016: 117–118).

From an ethnographic perspective, Juffermans (2015) is concerned with LL in the state of Gambia, focusing on the stated language policy regulations in urban public space. The overwhelming use of English is interpreted with regard to its communicative function rather than its symbolic one in the sense that it reflects the government's top-down policy. At the same time, the overall absence or invisibility of local African languages and the preponderance of images rather than textual information indexes a high rate of illiteracy among the inhabitants. Generally, Juffermans (2015) prefers the term *local languaging* (instead of language(s)), that is, conversing in a multitude of languages and emphasising the fluidity and dynamics of language in order to better comprehend what happens linguistically in public spaces such as in The Gambia. Also, from the viewpoint of language contestation and acts of resilience contextualised in a language policy paradigm, is Woldemariam and Lanza's (2012) analysis of LL embedded in a tension between different Christian religions in the Ethiopian capital, Addis Ababa. Here, the LL serves as a 'platform' for evangelisation, protest and conflict so that the public place becomes an arena for religious groups to exercise influence and attempts to convert new church members. Interestingly enough, their study on 'religious wars' methodologically also makes use of Scollon and Scollon's (2003) nexus analysis which touches upon several discourses on politics, national identity and power.

Finally, with reference to LL in sub-Saharan Africa, a significant step in LL research has been to consider the visual positioning and functional arrangement of languages on individual multilingual signs, as has been demonstrated by Reh (2004) in a study on Uganda, East Africa. Although in her paper a reference to the term 'linguistic landscape' is non-existent, her model of multilingual signage clearly falls into this category. The model is exemplified on the basis of stationary multilingual written text as observed in the LL of a Ugandan town. As the model does not only have relevance for Africa, but to the majority of LL situations worldwide, a brief explication is in order (but see also the critique by Pavlenko & Mullen, 2015: 124). Reh (2004) suggested four types of relationship between message content and the languages used in signage: (1) duplicating multilingual writing, which presents the same content in each language; (2) fragmentary multilingualism, where 'the full information is given only in one language, but in which selected parts have been translated into an additional language' (p. 10); (3) overlapping multilingual writing, which describes a unit of signage 'if only part of its information is reported in at least one more language, while other parts of the text are in one language only' (Reh, 2004: 12); and (4) complementary multilingual writing in which different parts of the overall information are each rendered in a different language (Reh, 2004: 14).

5 Superdiversity in the City: Contact, Attitudes and Perceptions

In order to account for demographic, sociopolitical, cultural and linguistic changes, especially those found in diverse ethnic communities, sociologist Steven Vertovec has introduced the term *superdiversity* to address the changing nature of global migration:

> Such a condition is distinguished by a dynamic interplay of variables among an increased number of new, small and scattered, multiple-origin, transnationally connected, socio-economically differentiated and legally stratified immigrants who have arrived over the last decade. (Vertovec, 2007: 1024)

Since then, the concept has started to impact the areas of sociolinguistics (e.g. Blommaert, 2013) and anthropology (e.g. Arnaut, 2016) to a considerable extent. Vertovec (2007) gives an example of superdiversity, citing the Somali community in the UK, which includes British citizens; asylum seekers and refugees; irregular, illegal and undocumented migrants; and secondary migrants from other European states. Superdiversity thus points to new social and sociocultural constellations, that is, a changed set of conditions which requires a multidimensional perspective on multiplicity ('diversification within diversity') that goes beyond describing diversity in terms of socioeconomic status, gender, age, ethnicity, language and religion, but also incorporates immigration status, patterns of spatial distribution, migration trajectories, employment and social justice (Maly & Varis, 2016). The notion of superdiversity has also increasingly become the focus of attention in linguistic work aimed both at understanding changes in language use in extremely diverse societies (see Duarte & Gogolin, 2013) and at tracing the complex social layering of the superdiversity of a given place/space as indexed by situated language use and multilingual signage (Arnaut *et al.*, 2016). However, some scholars have raised serious concerns about the concept of superdiversity as seen from a Eurocentric perspective (for other criticism, see Budach & de Saint-Georges, 2017: 71–73; Deumert, 2014; Makoni, 2012).

Makoni (2012: 193), for example, argues that the concept

> contains a powerful sense of social romanticism, creating an illusion of equality in a highly asymmetrical world, particularly in contexts characterized by a search for homogenization… I find it disconcerting, to say the least, to have an open celebration of diversity in societies marked by violent xenophobia, such as South Africa.

Although the problematic issue of 'social romanticism' may arise within the analysis, quite a number of researchers felt the need to incorporate the notion of superdiversity, that is, the diversification of its diversity (Martiniello, 2004), into the sociolinguistic environment termed LL because it offers a more elaborate and ethnolinguistic perspective into the underlying structures of socially constructed spaces. Arnaut (2012: 1) explores the potential of 'superdiversity' as a perspective or lens for looking at diversity as discourse and as social practice, thereby replacing 'the model of orderly multiculturalism by taking into account the fluidities and complexities of diversity in the age of heightened mobility and digital communication'. Blommaert's (2013) ethnographic-historical study on texts, signs and discourses in his own neighbourhood in Antwerp (Belgium) is certainly one of the first publications addressing the sociolinguistics of superdiversity to move beyond a mere synchronic picture of diverse neighbourhoods to an intrinsically diachronic and historicising perspective, at times uncovering inequality and social injustice. Blommaert's concept of superdiversity, he insists, is characterised 'by the confluence between migration patterns (and we may add refugee patterns) and the presence of new technologies for communication and knowledge distribution, that has shaped a fundamentally new *sociolinguistic* environment' (Blommaert, 2013: 7).

From the perspective of superdiversity and the LL paradigm, there is a pressing need to also investigate residents' or passers-by's awareness of language heterogeneity in culturally diverse communities and their attitudes towards living in a multilingual city.

There are quite a number of LL studies that have qualitatively investigated the signs obtained from ethnographic fieldwork in order to examine their sociocultural, historical and political meanings and therefore to better understand how the multilingual space in cities and public places is symbolically constructed. Traditionally, attitudes towards languages or perceptions were considered essential in a multilingual context as they contribute to the maintenance or shift of languages or to the failure or success of language policy and planning (Baker, 1992: 21). These personal opinions, beliefs and ideas are important in order to understand how multilingualism and diversity are perceived within a given space. In Cenoz and Gorter's case study (2008) of two multilingual cities in the LL of the Netherlands and Spain, the authors confirm Landry and Bourhis' (1997: 27ff) claim that the functions of (minority) languages are informative and symbolic. For example, Cenoz and Gorter (2008: 79) argue that the use of Basque, a minority language, in Donostia does not only serve communicative purposes but also affective ones, and that it relates to 'the feeling of Basque as a symbol of identity' (Cenoz & Gorter, 2008: 79). Textual elements in the public space are used to construct and negotiate (minority) identities, and inhabitants develop attitudes towards the languages on display.

In their account of the 'multilingual cityscape' in the city of Donostia-San Sebastián, Aiestaran *et al.* (2010) examine expectations and attitudes of the local inhabitants in terms of preference (of languages, i.e. Spanish or Basque/Euskara) and payments, that is, how much importance raters attach to the languages on the signs. As a result, it became obvious that there is a seeming contradiction between the stated preference for the number of languages on the signs and the 'objective' measurement of the number of languages on individual signs. From the perspective of 'walkers', Trumper-Hecht (2010) analyses Jews' and Arabs' perceptions, preferences and attitudes towards the visibility of Israel's two official languages, Hebrew and Arabic, in public spaces of the 'mixed city' of Upper Nazareth (Israel). As one of the outcomes of the study, Trumper-Hecht makes reference to the notion of a *cognitive map* borrowed from cultural geography, which is invisible, subjective and personal/ interpersonal and by which members of a cultural or ethnic group 'construct a distinct representation of the space they share with another group' (Trumper-Hecht, 2010: 247). One of the few attitudinal studies focusing on LL in the USA is concerned with individual cognitive and emotional 'responses' to the LL in Memphis, Tennessee (Garvin, 2010), an urban space in transition due to heavy flows of transnational migration to the region. By means of a 'walking tour' methodology, Garvin's qualitative study investigates self-reported understandings and visual perceptions of public signage, suggesting that 'being in the body, reflecting in action, at the moment of seeing, sharpens the senses and brings to the surface thoughts and emotions that are often socially constrained or suppressed by time' (Garvin, 2010: 256).

6 The Contributions to the Volume

This collection of chapters brings together the latest achievements in the field of LL research. Part 1 of the book, 'General Issues, Methodology and Linguistic Landscapes as a Pedagogical Resource', starts with a general overview of LL studies over the past decade and suggests novel directions for future research (Chapter 1 by Elana Shohamy). Furthermore, Part 1 provides an interdisciplinary platform for a discussion of the most pertinent and urgent topics central to LL research such as methodological and technological innovations (Chapter 2 by Durk Gorter), and recently LL from a pedagogical perspective, that is, translation as symbolic action in the LL (Chapter 3 by David Malinowski).

A further area of interest (Part 2: Broadening the Field of Semiotic Landscapes: Semiotic Assemblages, Multimodality and Contemporary Urban Spaces) making space for 'the more than linguistic' and expanding the scope of LL studies (Jaworski & Thurlow, 2010) focuses on the multifaceted view on urban multimodality, that is, spatial repertoires, semiotic assemblages and olfactory ethnographies (Chapter 4 by Alastair Pennycook), space as a semiotic resource and the art of silence in contemporary consumer culture (Chapter 5 by Adam Jaworski), the whole array of communication practices (mediatization) in terms of the visible, audible and tactile resources in the multilingual cityscape (Chapter 6 by Christine Domke) and finally multilingual audio announcements in Taiwan's capital, Taipei (Chapter 7 by Ying-Hsueh Hu).

The chapters in Part 3 ('Expanding Linguistic Landscape Studies: Power Relations, Acts of Resilience and Diachronic Changes') include LL studies on power relations, acts of resilience and ideological issues pertaining to sub-Saharan African states (Chapter 8 by Karsten Legère & Tove Rosendal and Chapter 9 by Sabine Diao-Klaeger & Rosalie Zongo), an exploration of the ideological issues based on written landscapes of the Marshall Islands (Chapter 10 by Isabelle Buchstaller & Seraphim Alvanides) as well as a multimodal discourse analysis of the politically sensitive situation of the city of Vilnius, the capital of Lithuania (Chapter 11 by Irina Moore) and to visual multilingualism in the German Ruhr area (Chapter 12 by Evelyn Ziegler, Ulrich Schmitz & Haci-Halil Uslucan).

Contributions to the volume are theoretical, methodological and empirical, describing linguistic and semiotic landscapes from around the world (Africa, Asia, Europe and the Pacific), which are situated within discourses of identity, diversity, empowerment and socioeconomic transformation. Accordingly, the structure of the book is as follows:

- Part 1: General Issues, Methodology and Linguistic Landscapes as a Pedagogical Resource.
- Part 2: Broadening the Field of Semiotic Landscapes: Semiotic Assemblages, Multimodality and Contemporary Urban Spaces.
- Part 3: Expanding LL Studies: Power Relations, Acts of Resilience and Diachronic Changes.

Part 1: General Issues, Methodology and Linguistic Landscapes as a Pedagogical Resource

Elana Shohamy's opening chapter on 'Linguistic Landscape after a Decade: An overview of Themes, Debates and Future Direction' sets the scene of LL research and addresses the major issues in the field of LL over the past decade. The main focus has been on multilingualism and its representation in the public space, asking the question of how language(s) on display create social space. This focus has shifted from a quantitative approach to diverse objectives beyond the distribution of languages in a public space. In this vein, Shohamy identifies five phases that have emerged in this research field which do not necessarily follow a chronological order. The first phase describes the quantitative approach coined by Landry and Bourhis (1997), and the second phase is concerned with the extension of the LL into other fields of research such as multimodality. In the third phase, the people who create, contest and interact in the LL are at the centre of attention: the urban space is seen not only as a place of language contact but also as a home to people with diverse backgrounds and opinions. The fourth phase analyses smaller geographical units, for example neighbourhoods or institutions, because these spaces might offer a more elaborate insight into the linguistic and social diversity. The last phase entails a critical view of the LL, which is perceived as an attempt to address social justice, enable activism and engage in creating a more inclusive social space.

Taking up Shohamy's general reference to methodology in LL studies, Durk Gorter explicitly focuses on a number of methodological approaches which derive from sociolinguistics and other disciplines, and the way in which technical developments impact LL research in various ways. In Chapter 2 entitled 'Methods and Techniques for Linguistic Landscape Research: About Definitions, Core Issues and Technological Innovations', Gorter calls attention to the problem of defining the scope of LL as he sheds light on the prominently quoted definition by Landry and Bourhis (1997). Critiquing its overuse and oversimplification, he argues that current LL studies require a more recent framework which includes languages on display in public places and also attempts to analyse motives, language use, ideologies, language varieties and other aspects of the 'multilingual cityscape'. Furthermore, he elaborates on data collection in the research field of LL. First, the research area has a significant impact on the survey's results which might range from following the major public transportation routes, focusing on shopping streets or analysing particular neighbourhoods. Secondly, the 'unit of analysis' needs to be defined in the scope of a more elaborate LL research by asking the question of which 'signs' are included in the survey and which are left out. The last part of this paper also directs attention towards the impact of technical innovations in the field of LL research, for example the use of digital cameras, smartphones, virtual reality and others, which make LL research more comprehensible.

Finally in this part, the pedagogical benefit of LL studies comes to the fore, an innovative nature of this book. The LL is important not only because it provides the backdrop to our day-to-day lives, but also because it may act as a valuable language learning resource. As an experiment in thinking between research and pedagogical design, David Malinowski's narrative essay 'Learning to Translate the Linguistic Landscape' (Chapter 3) argues that translation holds particular promise, both as an approach for language learning and teaching in the LL and, more broadly, as a figure or metaphor through which LL researchers may reinterpret their work. Accordingly, Malinowski proposes an interdisciplinary translational approach to language learning, teaching and LL research. He explores the LL from a translational study perspective in order to achieve a new understanding of signs which are placed in a socially and culturally constructed context. In this vein, translation is employed to indicate gaps and/or differences within a text, as moving from one language to another might create difficulties. Furthermore, translation is considered to play a responsible role in constructing and reconstructing texts as they are translated 'word for word' or 'sense for sense'. Especially in the LL, language learners as well as researchers actively pursue the LL by producing, reproducing and transforming it. They focus on the practised, conceived and lived spaces (Lefebvre, 1991) which are shaped by the current social and political needs. Lastly, translation is seen as an act of public action and activation in order to create awareness of the intertwined processes, involving personal, political, economic and communal aspects, which are at work in social spaces.

Part 2: Broadening the Field of Semiotic Landscapes: Semiotic Assemblages, Multimodality and Contemporary Urban Spaces

The first chapter entitled 'Linguistic Landscapes and Semiotic Assemblages' by Alastair Pennycook (Chapter 4) explores the direction of current LL research, which extends its focus from a 'logocentric approach' that included the representation of language(s) and multilingualism in public places to a more extensive urban ethnography comprising aspects such as translanguaging, touch, smell, clothes, objects, graffiti, tattoos and other semiotic resources. This highly complex architecture of semiotic resources that shape the urban experience is a ground for coining the term *semiotic assemblages* to describe the multilingual, multimodal and multisensorial nature of socially construed spaces. In this context, semiotic assemblages are understood to illustrate how linguistic resources, activities and socially construed spaces are linked in order to function in a new manner; it is especially important to discern how the combination of linguistic resources at play are interwoven and intersect at a particular moment in time. Drawing on olfactory ethnographies and studies of intersectional sensescapes in shops and markets in Sydney and Tokyo, the paper looks at how the intersection of people, objects, activities and senses make up the spatial repertoire of a place.

Another attempt to direct the attention away from textual and verbal elements is made by Adam Jaworski, who analyses the commodification of silence as deployed in a semiotic landscape which reinforces organisational structures of luxury (i.e. the city of Hong Kong). In his chapter 'The Art of Silence in Upmarket Spaces of Commerce' (Chapter 5), silence does not only describe the absence of textual and auditory elements, but also a form of multimodal medium of communication in which the intention of silence fulfils a metacommunicative function. In this vein, silence is a semiotic resource whose organisational pattern underlies socially and culturally predetermined norms; in particular, it is a salient resource indicating luxury, exclusivity and 'elite' spaces. Four major motives are presented in this chapter: first, the author describes the underestimated high-end signs; secondly, silence is employed as a commodified analogy of secrecy; thirdly, silence is utilised in advertisement to evoke a sophisticated connotation; and fourthly, silence is evident in fashion and its display in shops, which offers an insight into social patterns.

Likewise from a multimodal perspective, Christine Domke focuses on the diversity of media and modes of perception in the LL which are publicly perceivable textscapes, namely textual/visual, audible and tactile elements. In her chapter 'Multimodality in the City: On the Media, Perception and Locatedness of Public Textscapes' (Chapter 6), the relationship between the choice of media and its pragmatic function is based on distinctive features, for example mediality and materiality, semiotic resource, mode of perception, material locatedness and time-boundedness. Based on these features, three categories of communicative forms in public spaces in German cities (e.g. train stations, etc.) emerge: first, non-time-bound perceivable communication forms are signs which are permanently accessible and used for different textual function; this also includes tactilely perceivable signs, for example as directional structures on pavements. Secondly, temporary communication forms may be used for various functions, for example commercials, job employment or instructions which are valid only for a particular time. This also includes publicly perceivable audible communication forms which are available and valid only for a short period of time, for example an announcement at a train station. Thirdly, hybrid communication forms include features of both permanent and temporary categories. This diversity of media and modes of perception with a focus on visible, audible and tactile communication, that is, whether a text is to be *read*, *heard* or *felt* (like Braille codes), shapes the human experience in a social space, suggesting the increasing *mediatization* in everyday life.

Based on a superdiverse area involving a number of linguistic/ethnic communities, Ying-Hsueh Hu's soundscape study explores the multitude of languages used in the public announcements on the Taipei Mass Rapid Transit System (henceforth, MRT) and investigates to what extent this constructs and creates a Taiwanese identity, including the cultural tensions linked to it. In her case study 'Multilingual Audio Announcements: Power and Identity' (Chapter 7), the various announcements in Mandarin Chinese, English, as well as the dialects of Holo and Hakka are investigated from a quantitative perspective on the informants' self-perception and identification of ethnicity, and their experiences and perceptions of these announcements to reveal underlying power dynamics and other influences, for example age or gender. Personal attitudes and opinions towards the governmental effort to implement minority languages are focused upon in this soundscape study as the informants agree on the need for a commonly shared lingua franca, such as Mandarin Chinese, and the effort to embrace the diverse and multilingual social context. Again, from a political and ideological point of view these audio announcements and signs can be viewed as a process of 'glocalisation' which promotes respect for the different ethnic groups that inhabit the island, while forging a global perspective at the same time.

Part 3: Expanding Linguistic Landscape Studies: Power Relations, Acts of Resilience and Diachronic Changes

Dissent and protest are the focus of the studies in Part 3 of the volume, where LL becomes a site of mass demonstrations or gatherings to protest against injustice and where public signs are emplaced and conceptualised as a form of political activism indexing contestation and dissent in situations of sociohistorical, economic and ideological conflict (see Rubdy & Ben Said, 2015). Several case studies in this section consider the extent to which semiotic signage reveals political tensions between the official governmental language policies (top-down) and local practices among speakers within a particular region or nation. Karsten Legère and Tove Rosendal are concerned with the spatial emplacement of text or 'ideological acts' that are part of the visible or non-visible LL as they examine the LL of three east African countries, namely Rwanda, Uganda and Tanzania. In their chapter 'Linguistic Landscapes and the African Perspective' (Chapter 8) the empowerment of the well-established national languages Swahili and Rwanda, which have official status in Tanzania and Uganda (Swahili) and Rwanda (Rwanda), is investigated from an ethnographic point of view. In addition, the outstanding role of English and French as well as the underrepresentation of African languages is explored from a diachronic perspective focusing on social order, power relations and identity negotiations in these countries' cityscapes. However, at times companies employ African languages in advertisement for commercial interests, which hints at a '*de-ethicised*' identities. Generally, however, the use of national vs. foreign languages is an ideological and symbolic act, which is emphasised in the official language policy and which acts as an expression of power relations.

An additional perspective on LL research in Africa is offered by Sabine Diao-Klaeger and Rosalie Zongo, who focus on political demonstrations in Ouagadougou, the capital of Burkina Faso (West Africa). The chapter explores the role of signage (here mainly slogans) in constructing symbolic and representational meanings during mass demonstrations, thus suggesting transitory LL as political discourse. In their case study 'Slogans as Part of Burkina Faso's Linguistic Landscape during the Insurrection in 2014' (Chapter 9), the authors investigate textual elements displayed at mass demonstrations which addressed the modification of article 37 of the Constitution, thereby heavily criticising the Compaoré regime (President of Burkina Faso from 1987–2014). Although these demonstrations are only temporarily visible, they change and influence the LL of Ouagadougou due to the fact that they are also retained in the 'cybernetic' LL, for example social networks, online magazines or newspapers. The chapter analyses the slogans used during these mass demonstrations, in particular paying attention to messages in forms of graffiti on walls, buildings or monuments, and posters, banners and T-shirts (for the semiotics of printed T-shirts, see Caldwell, 2017). These are classified into four groups according to the choice of reference, namely revolutionary references, references to current and foreign political events, the metaphorical notion of a 'disease' and the use of abbreviations as rhetorical means.

Also contributing to language policy issues, Isabelle Buchstaller and Seraphim Alvanides explore the LL of the Majuro conurbation in the Republic of the Marshall Islands (RMI) in the North Pacific whose official languages are English and the indigenous language Marshallese. In their case study 'Investigating the Bilingual Landscape of the Marshall Islands' (Chapter 10), they employ geosemiotic methods of textual signs in order to pursue a geo-spatial analysis of the distribution of languages and linguistic choices. Their analysis of more than 2000 geotagged photographs of the urban centre of the RMI (governmental/commercial buildings, advertisements, flyers, graffiti, announcements and so on) reveals that Marshallese has been marginalised in the public sphere by the dominant status and use of English, and thus denied visibility in the public domain owing to a history of language imposition by the colonial power of the USA. Although in 2015 a bill was introduced which requires all signs in the public domain to be bilingual, the data show that only a small number of signs follow the official language policy and that Marshallese textual signs are rarely present in the LL of the Majuro conurbation.

Likewise from a language policy perspective and its impact on the LL arena, Irina Moore's chapter 'Linguistic, Ethnic and Cultural Tensions in the Sociolinguistic Landscape of Vilnius: A Diachronic Analysis' (Chapter 11) is concerned with the post-Soviet LL of Vilnius, the capital of Lithuania, as observed since the nation's declaration of independence in March 1990. New language policies that were enacted in non-Russian republics thereafter led to the renewal of LL of all ex-Soviet republics with the aim of de-russification and a shift towards the titular languages through processes of language removal (of signage) and language replacement. Using a multimodal discourse analysis, Moore investigates textual signs by way of language practices (street toponymy and brand names) and a range of physical objects (from historical-cultural heritage to consumer goods) through the lens of power, ideology and social change in order to investigate how new *memory landscapes* are shaped, how ethnic tensions are visualised and inequalities detected in the LL. Ethnic tensions are visible in post-Soviet Vilnius, for example the marginalisation of the Lithuanian Polish community and Russian/Soviet tensions are evident and have an impact on the LL of Vilnius in the form of a *landscape sweep*, or in other words, a removal and replacement of remaining items of the former political power.

Finally, Evelyn Ziegler, Ulrich Schmitz and Haci-Halil Uslucan investigate 'Attitudes towards Visual Multilingualism in the Linguistic Landscape of the Ruhr Area' (Chapter 12), focusing on aspects of superdiversity (diversity within diversity) from an attitudinal and perceptional perspective. Germany's Ruhr area is a good example of a social context characterised by superdiversity. The Ruhr area is one of Germany's migrant regions historically dating back to the 19th century, which resulted in several waves of labour migration. During the last 10 years, the Ruhr area has seen an increase in poverty-driven migration from Bulgaria and Romania and a large influx of refugees due to the Syrian Civil War. The authors' research is based on a survey study exploring the attitudes and perceptions of inhabitants in the Ruhr area which includes industrial cities such as Duisburg, Essen and Dortmund. Their study comprised a corpus of 120 interviews (semi-standardised on-site interviews and multilingual telephone interviews) and more than 25,000 geocoded digital photographs. Among other issues, they were interested in finding out whether the diversity of languages also reflects the settlement pattern of ethnic groups in the area characterised by a north-south divide (north and south of the highway A 40) serving as 'the social equator' in terms of ethnicity and affluence or socioeconomic status. The somewhat less affluent, but ethnically more diverse neighbourhoods north of the highway displayed far greater visual multilingualism than could be located south of it. Not surprisingly, the interviews also revealed that in the ethnically diverse areas informants held far more positive attitudes towards visual multilingualism. For example, the most common argumentation pattern to justify a positive attitude towards visual multilingualism was in a pragmatic sense, that is, the concern with orientation and barrier-free communication of public order rules and regulations. Generally, the results of the telephone interviews indicated that informants both with and without a migrant background widely accepted multilingualism in public space and regarded it as a cultural enrichment. To conclude, the authors not only pointed out the sociolinguistic value of the study, but also its ideological and political implications regarding local integration policies and urban planning.

Concluding Remarks

The range and depth of exploration presented in these pages hold powerful implications for future collaboration in LL research. Thus, the book has broadened the scope of linguistic landscape analysis beyond the presence or absence of particular languages/dialects or visual writing in public spaces so as to include the analysis of displayed texts' multimodality, materiality and emplacement in real-world contexts (Stroud & Mpendukana, 2009). An understanding of semiotic assemblages and the use of space as a semiotic resource presents alternative ways of thinking about LL that locate the linguistic within a wider set of semiotic relations and addresses the complexity of things that come together in the vibrant, changeable exchanges of everyday urban life.

The editors and authors offer this book as an invitation to contribute to the promising avenues for future research into the many LL issues raised within the volume such as refinements of theory, an advanced methodology, multimodality, pedagogy, as well as attitudes and perceptions on the part of sign instigators and passers-by when wondering around the LL across the world.

Notes

(1) See Lou (2016: 5) who examines the meaning and etymology of the term *landscape*.
(2) According to Tuan (1977), the notions of *place* and the more abstract *space* can be differentiated as follows: what often begins as undifferentiated space becomes place as we endow it with value.
(3) Blommaert (2016) very much argues for a consideration of signs in the 'virtual' public places, that is, 'a profound and integrated engagement with the electronic knowledge-and-communication engines that are intrinsic to it and exert a systemic influence' (Blommaert, 2016: 8).
(4) Recently, a whole conference was devoted to 'Translanguaging and repertoires across signed and spoken languages', organised by the Max Planck Institute for the Study of Ethnic and Religious Diversity (Göttingen, 2016).

References

Aiestaran, J., Cenoz, J. and Gorter, D. (2010) Multilingual cityscapes: Perceptions and preferences of the inhabitants of Donostia-San Sebastián. In E. Shohamy, E. Ben-Rafael and M. Barni (eds) *Linguistic Landscape in the City* (pp. 219–234). Bristol: Multilingual Matters.

Arnaut, K. (2012) Super-diversity: Elements of an emerging perspective. *Diversities* 14 (2), 1–16.

Arnaut, K. (2016) Superdiversity: Elements of an emerging perspective. In K. Arnaut, J. Blommaert, B. Rampton and M. Spotti (eds) *Language and Superdiversity* (pp. 49–70). New York/London: Routledge.

Arnaut, K., Blommaert, J., Rampton, B. and Spotti, M. (2016) Introduction: Superdiversity and sociolinguistics. In K. Arnaut, J. Blommaert, B. Rampton and M. Spotti (eds) *Language and Superdiversity* (pp. 1–18) New York/London: Routledge.

Aronin, L. and Singleton, D. (2012) *Multilingualism* <IMPACT: Studies in Language and Society 30>. Amsterdam/Philadelphia: John Benjamins.

Backhaus, P. (2007) *Linguistic Landscapes: A Comparative Study of Urban Multilingualism in Tokyo*. Clevedon: Multilingual Matters.

Baker, C. (1992) *Attitudes and Languages*. Clevedon: Multilingual Matters.

Banda, F. and Jimaima, H. (2015) The semiotic ecology of linguistic landscapes in rural Zambia. *Journal of Sociolinguistics* 19 (5), 643–670.

Barni, M. and Bagna, C. (2010) Linguistic landscape and language vitality. In E. Shohamy, E. Ben-Rafael and M. Barni (eds) *Linguistic Landscape in the City* (pp. 3–18). Bristol: Multilingual Matters.

Barni, M. and Bagna, C. (2015) The critical turn in LL: New methodologies and new items in LL. *Linguistic Landscape. An International Journal* 1 (1/2), 6–18.

Ben-Rafael, E. and Ben-Rafael, M. (2015) Linguistic landscapes in an era of multiple globalizations. *Linguistic Landscape. An International Journal* 1 (1/2), 19–37.

Ben-Rafael, E., Shohamy, E., Amara, M. and Trumper-Hecht, N. (2006) Linguistic landscape as symbolic construction of the public space: The case of Israel. In D. Gorter (ed.) *Linguistic Landscape: A New Approach to Multilingualism. Journal of Multilingualism* 3 (1), 7–30.

Blackwood, R., Lanza, E. and Woldemariam, H. (eds) (2016) *Negotiating and Contesting Identities in Linguistic Landscapes*. London/New York: Bloomsbury.

Blommaert, J. (2013) *Ethnography, Superdiversity and Linguistic Landscapes: Chronicles of Complexity*. Bristol: Multilingual Matters.

Blommaert, J. (2016) The conservative turn in linguistic landscape studies. *Tilburg Papers in Culture Studies*. Tilburg: Tilburg University 156, 1–10.

Blommaert, J. and Maly, I. (2016) Ethnographic linguistic landscape analysis and social change: A case study. In K. Arnaut, J. Blommaert, B. Rampton and M. Spotti (eds) *Language and Superdiversity* (pp. 197–217). New York: Routledge.

Bolton, K. (2012) World Englishes and linguistic landscapes. *World Englishes* 31 (1), 30–33.

Budach, G. and de Saint-Georges, I. (2017) Superdiversity and language. In S. Canagarajah (ed.) *The Routledge Handbook of Migration and Language* (pp. 63–78). London/New York: Routledge.

Caldwell, D. (2017) Printed t-shirts in the linguistic landscape. *Linguistic Landscape* 3 (2), 122–148.

Cenoz, J. and Gorter, D. (2008) The linguistic landscape as an additional source of input in second language acquisition. *International Review of Applied Linguistics in Language Teaching* 46, 257–276.

Chern, C.-l. and Dooley, K. (2014) Learning English by walking down the street. *ELT Journal* 68 (2), 113–123.

Dagenais, D., Moore, D., Sabatier, C., Lamarre, S. and Armand, F. (2009) Linguistic landscape and language awareness. In E. Shohamy and D. Gorter (eds) *Linguistic Landscape: Expanding the Scenery* (pp. 253–269). New York: Routledge.

Deumert, A. (2014) Digital superdiversity: A commentary. *Discourse, Context & Media* 4 (5), 116–120.

Dressler, R. (2015) Signgeist: Promoting bilingualism through the linguistic landscape of school signage. *International Journal of Multilingualism* 12 (1), 128–145.

Duarte, J. and Gogolin, I. (eds) (2013) *Linguistic Superdiversity in Urban Areas: Research Approaches*. Amsterdam/Philadelphia: John Benjamins.

Franceschini, R. (2009) Genesis and development of research in multilingualism: Perspectives for future research. In L. Aronin and B. Hufeisen (eds) *The Exploration of Multilingualism: Development of Research on L3, Multilingualism and Multiple Language Acquisition* (pp. 27–61). AILA Applied Linguistics Series 6. Amsterdam: John Benjamins.

García, O. (2009) Education, multilingualism and translanguaging in the 21st century. In A. Mohanty, M. Panda, R. Phillipson and T. Skutnabb-Kangas (eds) *Multilingual Education for Social Justice: Globalising the Local* (pp. 128–145). New Delhi: Orient Blackswan.

Garvin, R. (2010) Responses to the linguistic landscape in Memphis, Tennessee: An urban space in transition. In E. Shohamy, E. Ben-Rafael and M. Barni (eds) *Linguistic Landscape in the City* (pp. 252–271). Bristol: Multilingual Matters.

Gorter, D. (2006b) Further possibilities for linguistic landscape research. In D. Gorter (ed.) *Linguistic Landscape: A New Approach to Multilingualism* (pp. 81–89). Clevedon: Multilingual Matters.

Gorter, D. (2013) Linguistic landscapes in a multilingual world. *Annual Review of Applied Linguistics* 33, 190–212.

Gorter, D. and Cenoz, J. (2015) Translanguaging and linguistic landscapes. *Linguistic Landscape. An International Journal* 1 (1/2), 54–74.

Gorter, D., Marten, H. and Van Mensel, L. (eds) (2012) *Minority Languages in the Linguistic Landscape*. Basingstoke: Palgrave Macmillan.

Hewitt-Bradshaw, I. (2014) Linguistic landscape as a language learning and literacy resource in Caribbean Creole contexts. *Caribbean Curriculum* 22, 157–173.

Huebner, T. (2006) Bangkok's linguistic landscapes: Environmental print, codemixing, and language change. In D. Gorter (ed.) *Linguistic Landscape: A New Approach to Multilingualism* (pp. 31–51). Clevedon: Multilingual Matters.

Huebner, T. (2016) Linguistic landscape: History, trajectory and pedagogy. *MANUSYA Journal of Humanities*, Special Issue (22), 1–11.

Jaworski, A. (2015) Wordcities and language objects: 'Love' sculptures and signs as shifters. *Linguistic Landscape. An International Journal* 1 (1/2), 75–94.

Jaworski, A. and Thurlow, C. (eds) (2010) *Semiotic Landscapes. Language, Image, Space*. London/New York: Continuum.

Juffermans, K. (2015) *Local Languaging, Literacy and Multilingualism in a West African society*. Bristol: Multilingual Matters.

Kallen, J.L. (2009) Tourism and representation in the Irish linguistic landscape. In E. Shohamy and D. Gorter (eds) *Linguistic Landscape. Expanding the Scenery*. New York/London: Routledge

Landry, R. and Bourhis, R. (1997) Linguistic landscape and ethnolinguistic vitality: An empirical study. *Journal of language and Social Psychology* 16 (1), 23–49.

Lefebvre, H. (1991) *The Production of Space*. Oxford: Blackwell.

Lou, J. (2016) *The Linguistic Landscape of Chinatown. A Sociolinguistic Ethnography*. Bristol: Multilingual Matters.

Makoni, S. (2012) A critique of language, languaging and supervernacular. *Muitas Vozes* 1 (2), 189–199.

Malinowski, D. (2015) Opening spaces of learning in the linguistic landscape. *Linguistic Landscape. An International Journal* 1 (1/2), 95–113.

Maly, I. (2016) Detecting social changes in times of superdiversity: An ethnographic linguistic landscape analysis of Ostend in Belgium. *Journal of Ethnic and Migration Studies* 42 (5), 707–723.

Maly, I. and Varis, P. (2016) The 21st-century hipster: On micro-populations in times of superdiversity. *European Journal of Cultural Studies* 19 (6), 637–653.

Marten, H., Van Mensel, L. and Gorter, D. (2012) Studying minority languages in the linguistic landscape. In D. Gorter, H. Marten and L. Van Mensel (eds) *Minority Languages in the Linguistic Landscape* (pp. 1–15). Basingstoke: Palgrave Macmillan.

Martín Rojo, L. (ed.) (2016) *Occupy: The Spatial Dynamics of Discourse in Global Protest Movements*. Benjamins Current Topics 83. Amsterdam/Philadelphia: John Benjamins.

Martiniello, M. (2004) The many dimensions of Belgian diversity. *Canadian Diversity/Diversité Canadienne* 3 (2), 43–46.

Mc Laughlin, F. (2015) Linguistic warscapes of northern Mali. *Linguistic Landscape. An International Journal* 1 (3), 213–242.

Mendisu, B.S., Malinowski, D. and Woldemariam, H. (2016) Absence from the linguistic landscape as de facto language policy: The case of two local languages in Southern Ethiopia. In R. Blackwood, E. Lanza and H. Woldemariam (eds) *Negotiating and Contesting Identities in Linguistic Landscapes* (pp. 117–129). London: Bloomsbury.

Otheguy, R., García, O. and Reid, W. (2015) Clarifying translanguaging and deconstructing named languages: A perspective from linguistics. *Applied Linguistics Review* 6 (3), 281–307.

Otsuji, E. and Pennycook, A. (2010) Metrolingualism: Fixity, fluidity and language in flux. *International Journal of Multilingualism* 7, 240–254.

Pavlenko, A. and Mullen, A. (2015) Why diachronicity matters in the study of linguistic landscapes. *Linguistic Landscape: An International Journal* 1 (1/2), 114–132.

Peck, A. and Stroud, C. (2015) Skinscapes. *Linguistic Landscape: An International Journal* 1 (1/2), 133–151.

Pennycook, A. (2017) Translanguaging and semiotic assemblages. *International Journal of Multilingualism* 14 (3), 269–282.

Reh, M. (2004) Multilingual writing: A reader-oriented typology – with examples from Lira Municipality (Uganda). *International Journal of the Sociology of Language* 170, 1–41.

Rubdy, R. and Ben Said, S. (eds) (2015) *Conflict, Exclusion and Dissent in the Linguistic Landscape*. Basingstoke: Palgrave Macmillan.

Scollon, R. and Scollon, S. (2003) *Discourses in Place. Language in the Material World*. London: Routledge.

Shohamy, E. (2015) LL research as expanding language and language policy. *Linguistic Landscape. An International Journal* 1 (1/2), 152–171.

Shohamy, E. and Gorter, D. (eds) (2009a) *Linguistic Landscape. Expanding the Scenery*. New York/London: Routledge.

Shohamy, E. and Gorter, D. (2009b) Introduction. In E. Shohamy and D. Gorter (eds) *Linguistic Landscape: Expanding the Scenery* (pp. 1–10). New York/London: Routledge.

Shohamy, E., Ben Rafael, E. and Barni, M. (eds) (2010) *Linguistic Landscape in the City*. Bristol: Multilingual Matters.

Stroud, C. and Mpendukana, S. (2009) Towards a material ethnography of linguistic landscape: Multilingualism, mobility and space in a South African township. *Journal of Sociolinguistics* 13 (3), 363–386.

Thurlow, C. and Jaworski, A. (2014) 'Two hundred ninety-four': Remediation and multimodal performance in tourist placemaking. *Journal of Sociolinguistics* 18 (4), 459–494.

Trumper-Hecht, N. (2010) Linguistic landscape in mixed cities in Israel from the perspective of 'Walkers': The case of Arabic. In E. Shohamy, E. Ben Rafael and M. Barni (eds) *Linguistic Landscape in the City* (pp. 235–251). Bristol: Multilingual Matters.

Tuan, Y. (1977) *Space and Place: The Perspective of Experience*. Minneapolis: University of Minnesota Press.

Vertovec, S. (2007) Super-diversity and its implications. *Ethnic and Racial Studies* 30 (6), 1024–1054.

Waksman, S. and Shohamy, E. (2010) Decorating the city of Tel Aviv-Jaffa for its centennial: Complementary narratives via linguistic landscape. In E. Shohamy, E. Ben Rafael and M. Barni (eds) *Linguistic Landscape in the City* (pp. 57–73). Bristol: Multilingual Matters.

Woldemariam, H. and Lanza, E. (2012) Religious wars in the linguistic landscape. In C. Hélot, M. Barni, R. Janssens and C. Bagna (eds) *Linguistic Landscapes, Multilingualism and Social Change: Diversité des Approaches* (pp. 169–184). Bern: Lang.

Part 1

General Issues, Methodology and Linguistic Landscapes as a Pedagogical Resource

1 Linguistic Landscape after a Decade: An Overview of Themes, Debates and Future Directions

Elana Shohamy

This chapter surveys the field of linguistic landscape (LL) from its early focus on multilingualism in public spaces. It begins with an overview of the early years of the past decade (2006–2016) and major research findings, activities and publications (annual conferences, edited books, a peer-reviewed journal and publications). It then surveys research findings and activities that have taken place over the past decade according to five (not exhaustive) themes: LL and representations; LL and multimodality; LL in cities, neighbourhoods and entities; LL and contestations in public spaces; and LL and education. The chapter ends with major conclusions, debates, new upcoming topics and prospects for the future.

1.1 Introduction: Conception of a Field

The purpose of this chapter is to provide an overview of some of the developments in the field of LL over the past decade (2006–2016). Books and papers about languages displayed in public spaces had already been published prior to the start of this decade (e.g. Spolsky & Cooper, 1991, among others). However, it was the publication of the special issue of the *Journal of Multilingualism* (2006), later published as an edited book (Gorter, 2006), that marked the initiatives taken by a group of scholars who began researching the topic of LL with the goal of documenting multilingualism in public spaces. While languages are spoken and heard, they are also displayed for functional and/or symbolic purposes. Language in public spaces had mostly been overlooked in mainstream research in applied linguistics; however, language displays in public spaces offer rich and stimulating texts that yield multiple interpretations. Examples of such language displays include texts consisting of single French words displayed in Thai orthography in Bangkok, or signs with words such as 'danger' or 'silence', written in Swedish when people in the area do not speak or read the language. These displays may deliver messages that those who reside in the areas are not welcome and by extension point to the low status of their languages. Thus, the presence of multilingualism in public spaces and the interaction of people with these languages provide rich sociolinguistic information as well as sources for learning new languages and cultures.

The growing attention afforded to LL as a research discipline originated from the increased focus on the environment and ecology in the past decade as well as advances in technologies for documentation such as mobile phones and digital cameras. Furthermore, the emergence of the internet as a vivid space with its multimodal representations of texts, sounds, colour images, music and moving objects expanded the repertoire of diverse, fluid and dynamic texts.

The concept of LL in the early years of the decade built on the research of Landry and Bourhis (1997), who provided the following definition:

> The language of public road signs, advertising billboards, street names, place names, commercial shop signs, and public signs on government buildings combine to form the LL of a given territory, region, or urban agglomeration. (Landry & Bourhis, 1997: 25)

Although Landry and Bourhis (1997) provided the fundamental definition of LL, their research mainly utilised attitudinal questionnaires to elicit information on people's views *about* LL. In contrast, the data that have been elicited in LL research in the past decade documents *actual* language displays as captured by cameras, yielding photos and more recently also videos.

The research goals of taking and interpreting LL photos were to describe and identify systematic patterns of the presence and absence of languages in public spaces and to understand the motives, pressures, ideologies, reactions and rationales for those signs. For example, in Gorter's 2006 publication mentioned above, a chapter by Cenoz and Gorter (2006) documented one street in Friesland and one street in San Sebastián in order to examine multilingual patterns of Frisian and Basque in relation to Dutch and Spanish, respectively. In the same publication, Huebner (2006) presented details of his research on hybrids of Thai and English in public spaces in Bangkok by analysing the construction of new unfamiliar words; and Ben Rafael *et al.* (2006) discussed their documentation of signs, examining the representations of Hebrew, Arabic and English in Israel in areas where Arabs and Jews reside. In these studies, the results provided information that was not hitherto available about language representations, globalisation, vitality, economics and collective identities. The studies showed that while the LL seems random and arbitrary, it is in fact systematic and can be used to identify patterns of behaviours as these are grounded in several theories.

LL research underwent major developments in the early period of 2006–2016, which further expanded the field, with LL emerging as an interdisciplinary area of study anchored in a number of disciplines. LL was anchored in disciplines such as politics, economics, semiotics, gender, sexuality, education, literature, law, applied linguistics, sociolinguistics, language policy, language teaching and learning, art, tourism, ethnic studies, immigration and urbanism. The relationship with these disciplines implied that LL research was contextualised in the perspectives of these disciplines. Regarding research methodologies, varied types of research methods and designs, data collection and data analyses were employed and these were grounded in the very disciplines just mentioned, using qualitative and quantitative case studies, ethnography, mixed methods, historical approaches, descriptions, critical discourse analysis and more.

An important question that emerged from these early studies related to whether language representations in public spaces differ significantly from those spoken and heard by individuals. The theoretical construct that emerged from Ben Rafael *et al.*'s study (2006) referred to LL as a *representation* of languages in public spaces and pointed to different patterns of behaviour rather than the language proficiency of people in the very languages they used as LL. Thus, it is often the case that store owners may put up a sign in front of their shop in a language they do not know, in order to attract clients or to demonstrate identity. This finding led Ben Rafael *et al.* (2006: 10) to refer to LL as 'symbolic construction of the public space'.

LL research over the past decade has become a very dynamic and productive field of study. This is manifested in the long list of activities that have been carried out in the field: ample publications in academic journals, eight edited books and research presentations at major conferences. In addition, an annual international conference (the last one, LL10, took place in Bern, Switzerland in May 2018 and LL11 is planned for 2019 in Bangkok, Thailand). Lastly, a new peer-reviewed journal entitled *Linguistic Landscape* was launched in 2015 and is now in its fourth volume (*Gender, Sexuality and Linguistic Landscapes*).

Over the years, a major development in the definition of LL was its expansion beyond written texts displayed in public spaces. This refers to the incorporation of additional components of text types in public spaces, grounded in theories of multimodality. These text types include displays of images, sounds, drawings, movements, visuals, graffiti, tattoos, colours, smells as well as people. In other words, LL can be defined as any display in public spaces which communicates varied types of messages.

1.2 Main Themes

In this part of the chapter, I will report on selected themes that have emerged over the last decade. The choice of themes represents my own interpretation; other researchers may select different ones. A number of themes have been identified to describe the developments in LL research over the past decade. The themes selected here are not exhaustive but nevertheless provide knowledge about the areas of LL research. The list of themes is not chronological but is instead cumulative and represents the interests of researchers in different disciplines. Further information about the themes can be found in various published books, as papers in the journal *Linguistic Landscape* and in other sources. The chapters included in the edited books had previously been presented at the annual international LL conferences or at local conferences. These edited books include *Linguistic Landscape: Expanding the Scenery* (Shohamy & Gorter, 2009); *Linguistic Landscape in the City* (Shohamy et al., 2010); *Linguistic Landscapes, Multilingualism and Social Change* (Hélot et al., 2012); *Minority Languages in the Linguistic Landscape* (Gorter et al., 2012) and *Negotiating and Contesting Identities in Linguistic Landscapes* (Blackwood et al., 2016). Additional books addressing specific LL research are published in *Semiotic Landscapes: Language, Image and Space* (Jaworski & Thurlow, 2010); *Occupy* (Martin Rojo, 2014), *Linguistic Landscapes: A Comparative Study of Urban Multilingualism in Tokyo* (Backhaus, 2007), *Linguistic Landscapes in the*

Netherlands: A Study of Multilingualism in Amsterdam and Friesland (Edelman, 2010) and *The Linguistic Landscape of Chinatown: A Sociolinguistic Ethnography* (Lou, 2016); these books may categorise LLs differently (see also Shohamy, 2012).

1.2.1 Theme 1: LL and representations

The theme that reflects the early research on LL in the first half of the decade relates to the representations of different languages in public spaces. Such research involved the collection of representative samples of LL items in public spaces, followed by quantitative statistical analyses comparing the frequency of the appearance of the languages according to a number of parameters and mostly pointing to levels of diversity. Most of the data in this category consists of signs on shops, public buildings and public institutions such as religious, governmental, municipal, cultural, educational and medical institutions, and also announcements, street names, business signs, wanted ads and so on. The sampling of the data in many of these studies differentiated between 'top-down' and 'bottom-up' signs, which refers to LL items displayed by governmental institutions and corporations (top-down) vs. those initiated by individuals on their shops (bottom-up) (Ben Rafael *et al.*, 2006).

The findings were then interpreted in terms of various theories, depending on the very discipline from which the study originated, such as sociology, language policy, linguistics, tourism and so on. For example, in Ben Rafael *et al.* (2006), the theoretical interpretations originated from language and social conflicts between Arabs and Jews. The findings were interpreted in terms of theories of globalisation related to market principles and choice of rationale with regard to English, and collective and national identities theories related to Arabic and Hebrew.

Many of the studies in this theme were published in the book *Linguistic Landscape: Expanding the Scenery* (Shohamy & Gorter, 2009), along with additional types of methods such as indexicality (Curtin, 2009) and genre analysis (Hanauer, 2009). The book also referred to theoretical approaches to LL, methodological issues, language policy issues, identity and awareness, and ways forward. The studies were carried out in various places – in cities and countries worldwide such as Taipei, Québec, Amsterdam, Oakland, Addis Ababa, Tel Aviv, the Basque Country, Ireland and Sweden.

In most of these LL studies, less attention was given to the content of the signs while more emphasis was granted to the very languages displayed and represented in public spaces and their frequencies. Criticism of these studies included the limited information that can be drawn from quantitative studies given that the results did not always yield meaningful theoretical interpretations. The sole use of quantitative methods often masks the complexities of language diversity and is viewed as 'necessary' but not 'sufficient'. Such criticism is similar to that directed at other quantitative studies which often overlook the real diversity of local and smaller languages, such as those used by immigrants and minority groups. Thus, the use of quantitative studies led to the realisation of the need to use more ethnographic studies to capture broader and deeper explanations of people's reasons and rationale for selecting a particular LL in public spaces. The types of studies found in Theme 1 continue to be conducted but they are often the first phase in a broader qualitative/ethnographic study, utilising additional tools such as interviews, observations and reflections.

1.2.2 Theme 2: LL and multimodality

In the early days of LL research in the past decade, some researchers were already showing a growing interest in an *expanded* perspective of LL (Shohamy & Waksman, 2009). This was a reflection of the fact that a focus on written languages per se does not capture the public space in valid ways as there is a need to include additional features in accordance with theories of multimodality (New London Group, 1996). In other words, LL research needs to include additional sources that play a pivotal role in communicating the meaning of public spaces as a focus on written language is insufficient. For example, many LL signs are accompanied by pictures and colourful images that complement the meaning of the written items. These images are essential for understanding the written signs in a broader context. Theories of multimodality were introduced in education through the work of Kress and van Leeuwen (2001), Kress (2003), Jewitt and Triggs (2006) and Jaworski and Thurlow (2010), who examined visuality, 'grammar of visuality' and other semiotic representations. The work of Scollon and Scollon (2003) added further understanding by introducing the notion of *nexus analysis* and expanding the definition of spaces and its components to more diverse contexts related to geography and physical spaces.

Within the field of LL there were also those who opposed the use of anything that is not strictly 'written texts in public spaces' as they did not view it as part of LL. Questions such as 'So where are the boundaries of LL?' emerged and continue to appear as a controversial topic among LL researchers. Some are rarely willing to accept the need for additional features as long as these are viewed as part of semiotics. Pennycook and Otsuji (2015), in their study on smells as LL, deliberated on this issue and proposed that smells are semiotic and not language. Others (e.g. Shohamy, 2015) argued that a broader definition of the construct of 'language' is needed as these features are linguistic since they serve as communicative devices and hence should not be separated from other language dimensions. In other words, given that LL refers to research on language in spaces and territories, the public space is a unique territory where different communicative devices are needed for more accurate interpretation of public messages.

While arguments as to the limits of LL have been taking place at every LL conference and in journal papers, the general feeling of the LL community is not to set boundaries as to the meanings and definitions of LL, at least not for now as the field is still in the process of emergence. There is a need to keep the field open and allow it to grow in various directions, options and definitions with no declared limits. Hence, research studies have expanded the LL field in many new directions, for example, LL in diaries and biographies within literatures, sexuality and bodies, smells, warscapes and so on.

1.2.3 Theme 3: LL in cities, neighbourhoods and entities

1.2.3.1 Cities

Many of the studies in the first phase focused on nations and cities, but the book *Linguistic Landscape in the City* (Shohamy *et al.*, 2010) consists of 18 chapters which focus exclusively on LL in cities from multiple perspectives. These include studies about reception centres for new immigrants in Italy, monuments in Tel Aviv, mixed towns (Arab and Jews) in Israel, Bloemfontein in South Africa, Latvia, Kyiv, Hong Kong, Memphis, Strasbourg, Valley of the Sun in Arizona, San Sebastián in the Basque and many more.

1.2.3.2 Neighbourhoods

The focus on cities also led to research on neighbourhoods, which are smaller territories. Such research can provide an accurate measure of superdiversity, which is often overlooked when examining the big unit of a city. Research on cities showed that the diversity in cities, especially big ones, flattens the diversity that exists in neighbourhoods. The focus on neighbourhoods and their language diversity, especially where ethnic groups reside, demonstrates the vitality of languages within these spaces as displayed in the LL. This relates to the book edited by Gorter *et al.* (2012) about LLs among minority groups in neighbourhoods.

In a study by Bogatto and Hélot (2010) on the Quartier Gare (railway station district) of Strasbourg, the researchers found that the commercial signage in the area reflected the multilingual composition of the neighbourhood. They also showed that the regional language (Alsatien) intermingled with the other languages displayed in the local LL. Research has also documented the emergence of new diasporic spaces within cities. For example, Ben Rafael and Ben Rafael (2010) reported on changes in local LLs in the city of Natanya, Israel, which reflect the presence of French-speaking Jews who settled in the country and who continue to define themselves as a distinct group.

The focus on the LL of neighbourhoods, especially those where immigrants and asylum seekers reside, showed that multilingualism is the norm as people display LL items that reflect the needs of people in the community and everyday practices which include interacting with the authorities. Our studies on Tel Aviv-Jaffa (Shohamy, 2017; Shohamy & Waksman, 2015) focused on a neighbourhood where refugees and asylum seekers reside. The analysis of the LL items showed that the LL responded to everyday practices such as instructions, employment, selling and buying, all written in a number of languages together with ample translanguaging, and hence reflecting everyday practices: eating, walking, talking, marrying, looking for employment and so on. None of these LL items reflected any of the ideology of Israel as to the officiality that is found in all other parts of the country. Thus, close congruence between humans and their everyday needs is reflected in the languages of the LL. Many of the signs are handwritten by the residents and in diverse and unique styles, remote from the standard language. There is ample superdiversity and multilingualism in these neighbourhoods and these are reflected in the LL, which responds to vibrant everyday practices. The definition of a 'neighbourhood' is very fluid and loose, ranging from one to several streets, different from the bureaucratic markings of municipalities; in fact, the boundaries can be identified according to the LL. One can conclude that in these neighbourhoods the LL marks the territory but the boundaries are organic and 'natural', according to the needs of the heterogeneous populations that reside there.

1.2.3.3 Entities

In addition to cities and neighbourhoods, many studies focus on specific entities such as signs in football games, wine stickers, shopping centres, refugee camps, health services, hospitals, religious institutions (Coluzzi & Kitade, 2015), schools, universities, markets (Pennycook & Otsuji, 2015) or war spaces (McLaughlin, 2015) etc.

1.2.4 Theme 4: LL and contestations in public spaces

In the early phase of LL research, there was a heavy emphasis on signs while there was not much research on people and their reactions and interactions with the LL. However, people should not be ignored as they are the agents, the mediators, of languages in public spaces. People play a special role as actors and participants in different capacities. Some people interact with space and its derivatives and mediate it; while others produce and hang signs, display posters, design advertisements and create websites. While people act, at times, as agents for institutions, they also serve as those who read, contest, critique and negotiate the public spaces, especially when it comes to users of minority languages and immigrants.

Contestation in the public space reacts to critical questions about the LL: 'Who owns the public space?' and 'Who has the right to write in the public space?' Thus, the focus here is on people's responses to the LL, via contestations, protests and various types of actions. 'Talking back to the LL' is a response where it is possible to see how people are engaged with and react to the LL, especially when it is offensive and exclusive. Such engagement is also evident when the LL sends messages which are not in agreement with the people and they feel the need to change the LL and make spaces more inclusive and just.

In the book entitled *Occupy*, Martin Rojo (2014) included seven chapters by different authors who surveyed the roles of people in contestations of public spaces, especially as part of the global protests in a number of countries worldwide demanding social justice. These chapters cover protest movements in Tahrir Square, Egypt; in Madrid; in Los Angeles' City Hall Park; the Greek protests of Syntagma Square; and the Chilean students' protests. Indeed, focusing on the types of LL they choose to employ indicates both local and global patterns in the role of people in demonstrations and highlights the usefulness of LL as a major source of activism.

Additional studies examining protests include Waksman and Shohamy (2016) on the social protests in Tel Aviv in 2011 and their impact on educational institutions. In Waksman and Shohamy (2012), we focused on contestation between the municipality imposing a homogenous identity on the city during the Tel Aviv centennial and the 'talking back to the city' that took place during the celebrations. The municipality decorated the city with new LL signs that included new designs and writings of street names in Hebrew only; patriotic poems and songs in public spaces; and images and scripts of history. However, groups of activists took to the streets and protested against the homogenous and exclusive LL. They created alternative types of LL, such as a re-mapping of the city to contest the ideological portrayal of Arabs who used to live in the city before 1948. They put graffiti on photos that were delivering what they perceived to be inaccurate and propaganda information, and displayed politically loaded signs in Arabic in very popular and wealthy areas of Tel Aviv. Other groups created exhibitions that included photos and texts of residents of Jaffa who felt marginalised. Signs that read: 'who is not included' were displayed around the city. In analysing the types of LL that were used for contestation, we realised that additional types of LL resources were employed as LL and included signs, pictures, graffiti, photos, voices, films, trips, talk-backs, oral narratives, biographies, exhibits, multiple languages, excursions and documentation of practices. The criteria for using these resources were the protesters' belief that they were more sustainable than signs that are erased by the authorities.

1.2.5 Theme 5: LL and education

A theme that has received major attention, especially at the end of the decade, is the role of the LL in various dimensions of education (Cenoz & Gorter, 2015; Malinowski, 2015). Conducting research on LL in education has highlighted the need to conceptualise, concretise and collect data on ways that students and adults become aware, begin to observe and notice the multiple layers of meanings displayed in the LL in public spaces.

A number of approaches can be identified. One is the way that a LL can serve as a means and repertoire for effective language learning/teaching and input, referring to a view that the city is like a textbook. There are courses that teach students how to utilise LLs in public spaces as an essential input for teaching and learning languages. These types of programmes are administered in a number of institutions in the US such as in the Foreign Language Department at Columbia University. A paper by Sayer (2009) demonstrates how students become engaged with the study of LL and gain knowledge about the different uses of English LLs in Mexico. Educational programmes are used to teach students how to read and interpret spaces in both first and second languages.

The LL can be viewed as a mirror of societies, and therefore can be used as a tool for learners to become aware of social, economic and political issues: equality, inclusion and exclusion, at a deep cultural level, leading to activism (Shohamy, 2017). It is argued that through the LL, one can interpret and understand deeper issues of society; thus, it is viewed as 'a tip of the iceberg' that leads to deeper cultural and social interpretations of societal issues. Thus, documenting LL in various public spaces can trigger not only language learning but also critical learning about societies by focusing on diversity, discrimination, exclusion, controversies, ideologies and justice. Students are taught to pose questions such as: which languages or people are included/excluded; who resides where and why; who participates; who does not and why? If it is 'un-just', can an LL be changed and used to transform societies, cities and neighbourhoods?

In a study by Dagenais *et al.* (2009), students in primary schools were taught to observe the LL in neighbourhoods via field trips and to develop views about the cities, especially of neighbourhoods where new immigrants and asylum seekers reside. In a study by Goldstein-Havetzki (2012), 11th-grade Arab students in Tel Aviv-Jaffa were asked to document 15 signs in their neighbourhoods after receiving training in ways of reading the space; they then analysed the signs and reached conclusions based on this analysis about their neighbourhood. In the pre-test, the students claimed that Arabic was a dominant language in Jaffa, but after their own documentation they realised that their own language, Arabic, has a very low representation in the public space, even among their own families, parents and relatives. This awareness turned them towards activism, where they demonstrated a willingness to change the neighbourhood.

The students wrote their own emotional reactions to their study, demonstrating their fear that their language is being lost. For example, in a reaction to a sign where English comes before Arabic, Huda wrote:

> And I ask myself why is English written before Arabic? Arabic is the second official language in Israel, isn't that so? And I live in a city where all inhabitants or most of them are Arabs and Arabic speakers.

Another student, reacting to a sign where Arabic is not included in the LL signs at all, wrote:

> If Hebrew and English appear on the sign, at least they should add Arabic for the Arab inhabitants so they will understand the point of respect.

A third student wrote:

> This research reminds me of a research which was conducted in the U.S.A. on black and white dolls for little children, where the black girls chose the white dolls because even in their thoughts and hearts they thought white was more beautiful than black and that this was a symbol for beauty.

The conclusion of this study pointed to the importance of making students aware of the LL as a prism of societies and as a significant source of input into a broader language repertoire, identities, knowledge and awareness. It was suggested that LL should be brought into communities and schools as effective tools for language learning, activism, equality, transformation and change. The use of various types of LL is quickly expanding and entering the classroom as a tool to connect the ecology to the classroom and the classroom to the ecology. One issue that emerges refers to the specific methods that can be implemented to use LL as an educational tool. Michalovich (2017) examined ways of teaching high school students to develop a deeper understanding of commercials in public spaces using a method of metaphors. He demonstrated how some training in analysing commercials contributes to the development of critical views of commercials and sensing the manipulation behind them. Additional studies along these lines on developing effective methods that can contribute to the teaching and learning of LL are currently being conducted by a number of researchers.

1.3 Conclusions, Debates and Future Trends

A number of concluding remarks can be made at this point regarding the themes of the previous decade. LL is viewed today as a significantly broader construct than it was a decade ago. Based on the research examined in this chapter, we can see how the mostly written texts on LL signs nowadays incorporate additional components of public spaces. Take, for example, the broad repertoire of topics included in the first issue of the journal *Linguistic Landscape* (1 (2), 2015), which focused on advances on critical methodology, globalisation, regional languages, translanguaging, word cities, education and learning, diachronicity matters in LL, skinscacpes, language policy and diasporas. Issue 1 (3) (2015) that followed addressed issues such as smells/scents as LL (Pennycook & Otsuji, 2015), a paper on warscapes (McLaughlin, 2015), a paper on the religious landscape (Coluzzi & Kitade, 2015) and a study by Kitis and Milani (2015) on performativity of the body as LL. These topics demonstrated that LL research can provide new insights in relation to whether language in public spaces offers different, new definitions of languages. The interdisciplinary nature of LL encourages new research directions along with the view of LL research as being open to many directions and innovations 'on the go'.

The field of LL is dynamic and active but also critical and responsive. The discussions at the LL conferences and in papers demonstrate the uneasiness regarding some of the topics. The major debates that emerged regarding the boundaries and scope of LL research continue to be prominent and often centre around the question: 'So, is *everything* linguistic landscape?' (my emphasis). A major issue that continues to have relevance is whether the new components of space are still language and semiotics or whether LL has gone too far beyond its 'legitimate' boundaries.

Another issue surrounds the methodologies of LL. Although there is growing interest in ethnographic methods, many studies still employ quantitative methods and there is a consensus that any method is legitimate if it addresses the research questions and goals. Another issue surrounds the ethics of taking photos, especially of people. Related to this is the extent to which using photographs from the internet bias the results and whether the internet should even be considered as providing a legitimate source of data. Almost all of the photos in LL research at this point are taken by the researchers themselves. Another issue relates to the often-made claim that LL lacks a solid theory, but given the interdisciplinary nature of LL it can be called into question whether there is a need to arrive at a single theory. Another worry has been the commercialisation and commodification of LLs via internet applications and questions about the validity of the data, as well as whether LL will turn to a profit-making industry that will hinder its criticality and developments. Views are also expressed about the role of LL researchers – whether it is to describe and research or to transform societies and to become active in creating spaces which are more just and inclusive. Not much evidence exists of LL researchers as activists who try to change spaces. At this point in time, most of the research highlights the inequalities in society; this is important as well, but will it bring about more ethical spaces?

New topics are constantly emerging, and given the limited space of this chapter were not dealt with here. One such theme relates to bodies, sexuality and skin-scapes (Milani, 2013; Peck & Stroud, 2015; Shohamy & Correa, in press) as an upcoming theme in the field, focusing on the body as a space for LL, including breast augmentations, issues of sexual identity, moving bodies in demonstrations and tattoos as LL (Peck & Stroud, 2015). Most LL research has been anchored in sociolinguistics and a very limited number of studies focus on cognition; however, the current work in cognitive science employing eye-tracking devices to follow the ways that people read languages in public spaces is a welcomed research direction. Another future direction which is often mentioned by researchers is the extent to which *noticing* LL in public spaces can enhance memory. Research in cognitive neuroscience with its current focus on the role of context in memory needs to be examined. Finally, the current work on LL and education, mentioned above, dem-onstrates the effort to incorporate LL as part of learning languages and learning how to read spaces.

The research on LL introduces new questions and answers that have not been posed before, about the validity of spaces, about LL as propaganda, about LL and sexuality and about LL as mediation. At the same time, it provides answers about social arenas such as justice and exclusion, and about ways in which people can be engaged in public spaces and attempt to critique them as well as change them to create more just and inclusive spaces. In a virtual era when people overlook spaces and focus on mobile devices, focus on the public space could introduce a new move-ment towards involvement with real people and real spaces.

One wonders, if LL in space has always been there, why has it been overlooked? It is time to bridge this gap in many directions and to continue to develop under-standing over the next decades. This will involve interpreting 'languages' in a broader sense, including learning and developing awareness of the public space and engaging in activism to make our spaces more just and inclusive.

References

Backhaus P. (2007) *Linguistic Landscapes: A Comparative Study of Urban Multilingualism in Tokyo*. Clevedon: Multilingual Matters.

Ben Rafael, E. and Ben Rafael, M. (2010) Diaspora and returning diaspora: French-Hebrew and vice-versa. In E. Shohamy, E. Ben Rafael and M. Barni (eds) *Linguistic Landscape in the City* (pp. 326–343). Bristol: Multilingual Matters.

Ben Rafael, E., Shohamy, E., Amara, M.H. and Trumper-Hecht, N. (2006) Linguistic landscape as a symbolic construction of the public space: The case of Israel. *International Journal of Multilingualism* 3 (1), 7–31.

Blackwood, R., Lanza, E. and Woldemariam, H. (eds) (2016) *Negotiating and Contesting Identities in Linguistic Landscape*. Oxford: Bloomsbury.

Bogatto, F. and Hélot, C. (2010) Linguistic landscape and language diversity in Strasbourg: The 'Quartier Gare'. In E. Shohamy, E. Ben-Rafael and M. Barni (eds) *Linguistic Landscape in the City* (pp. 275–292). Bristol: Multilingual Matters.

Cenoz, J. and Gorter, D. (2006) Linguistic landscape and minority languages. In D. Gorter (ed.) (2006) *Linguistic Landscape: A New Approach to Multilingualism* (pp. 67–80). Clevedon: Multilingual Matters.

Cenoz, J. and Gorter, D. (2015) (eds) *Multilingual Education: Between Language Learning and Translanguaging*. Cambridge: Cambridge University Press.

Coluzzi, P. and Kitade, R. (2015) The languages of places of worship in the Kuala Lumpur area: A study on the 'religious' linguistic landscape in Malaysia. *Linguistics Landscape* 1 (3), 243–267.

Curtin, M. (2009) Language on display: Indexical signs, identities and the linguistic landscape of Taipei. In E. Shohamy and D. Gorter (eds) *Linguistic Landscape: Expanding the Scenery* (pp. 219–221). London: Routledge.

Dagenais, D., Moore, D., Sabatier, C., Lamarre, P. and Armand, F. (2009) Linguistic landscape and language awareness. In E. Shohamy and D. Gorter (eds) *Linguistic Landscape: Expanding the Scenery* (pp. 253–270). London: Routledge.

Edelman, L. (2010) *Linguistic Landscapes in the Netherlands: A Study of Multilingualism in Amsterdam and Friesland*. Utrecht: LOT International Series.

Goldstein-Havetzki, R. (2012) Travel diary in Jaffa: Development of linguistic landscape awareness and attitudes among teenagers. MA thesis, Tel Aviv University.

Gorter, D. (ed.) (2006) *Linguistic Landscape: A New Approach to Multilingualism*. Clevedon: Multilingual Matters.

Gorter, D., Marten, H.F. and Van Mensel, L. (eds) (2012) *Minority Languages in the Linguistic Landscape*. London: Palgrave.

Hanauer, D. (2009) Science and the linguistic landscape: A genre analysis of representational wall space in a microbiology laboratory. In E. Shohamy and D. Gorter (eds) *Linguistic Landscape: Expanding the Scenery* (pp. 287–301). London: Routledge.

Hélot, C., Barni, M., Janssens, R. and Bagna, C. (eds) (2012) *Linguistic Landscapes, Multilingualism and Social Change*. Frankfurt am Main: Peter Lang.

Huebner, T. (2006) Bangkok's linguistic landscape: Environmental print, code-mixing and language change. In: D. Gorter (ed.) *Linguistic Landscape: A New Approach to Multilingualism* (pp. 31–51). Clevedon: Multilingual Matters.

Jaworski, A. and Thurlow, C. (eds) (2010) *Semiotic Landscapes: Language, Space, Image*. London: Continuum.

Jewitt, C. and Triggs, T. (2006) Screens and the social landscape. *Visual Communication* 5 (2), 131–140.

Kitis, E. and Milani, T. (2015) The performativity of the body: Turbulent spaces in Greece. *Linguistic Landscape* 1 (3), 268–290.

Kress, G. (2003) *Literacy in the New Media Age*. London: Routledge.

Kress, G. and van Leeuwen, T. (2001) *Multimodal Discourse*. London: Arnold.

Landry, R. and Bourhis, R. (1997) Linguistic landscape and ethnolinguistic vitality: An empirical study. *Journal of Language and Social Psychology* 16 (1), 23–49.

Lou, J.J. (2016) *The Linguistic Landscape of Chinatown: A Sociolinguistic Ethnography*. Bristol: Multilingual Matters.

Malinowski, D. (2015) Opening spaces of learning in the linguistic landscape. *Linguistic Landscape* 1 (1–2), 95–114.

Martin Rojo, L. (ed.) (2014) *Occupy: The Spatial Dynamics of Discourse in Global Protest Movements*. Amsterdam/Philadelphia: John Benjamins.

McLaughlin, F. (2015) Linguistic warscapes of northern Mali. *Linguistic Landscape* 1 (3), 213–243.

Michalovich, A. (2017) Facilitating critical interpretation of commercials via multimodal metaphor analysis in the classroom. MA thesis, Tel Aviv University.

Milani, T. (2013) Are 'queers' really 'queer'? Language, identity and same-sex desire in a South African online community. *Discourse in Society* 24 (5), 615–630.

New London Group (1996) A pedagogy of multiliteracies: Designing social futures. *Harvard Educational Review* 66 (1), 60–92.

Peck, A. and Stroud, C. (2015) Skinscapes. *Linguistic Landscape* 1 (1–2), 133–152.

Pennycook, A. and Otsuji, E. (2015) Making scents of the landscape. *Linguistic Landscape* 1 (3), 243–267.

Sayer, P. (2009) Using the linguistic landscape as a pedagogical resource. *ELT Journal* 64 (2), 143–154.

Scollon, R. and Scollon, S. (2003) *Discourses in Place: Language in the Material World*. London: Routledge.

Shohamy, E. (2012) Linguistic landscape and multilingualism. In M. Martin-Jones, A. Blackledge and A. Creese (eds) *The Routledge Handbook on Multilingualism* (pp. 538–551). London: Routledge.

Shohamy, E. (2015) LL research as expanding language and language policy. *Linguistic Landscape* 1 (2–3), 152–171.

Shohamy, E. (2017) Linguistic landscape: Interpreting and expanding language diversities. In A. de Fina, D. Ikizoglu and J. Wegner (eds) *Diversity and Super-Diversity: Sociocultural Linguistic Perspectives* (pp. 37–63). Washington: Georgetown University Press.

Shohamy, E. and Correa, D. In press. Commodification of women's breasts: Internet sites modes of delivery to local and transnational audiences. In D. Malinowski and S. Tufi (eds) *Questioning Boundaries, Opening Spaces: Reterritorializing Linguistic Landscape*. London: Bloomsbury.

Shohamy, E. and Gorter, D. (eds) (2009) *Linguistic Landscape: Expanding the Scenery*. London: Routledge.

Shohamy, E. and Waksman, S. (2009) Linguistic landscape as an ecological arena: Modalities, meanings, negotiations, education. In E. Shohamy and D. Gorter (eds) *Linguistic Landscape: Expanding the Scenery* (pp. 313–331). London: Routledge.

Shohamy, E. and Waksman, S. (2015) Dismantling and undoing the city via LL: Interpreting neighborhoods as urban spaces. Paper presented at LL6: Hope and Precarity. April 9–11, 2014. Cape Town, South Africa.

Shohamy, E., Ben Rafael, E. and Barni, M. (eds) (2010) *Linguistic Landscape in the City*. Bristol: Multilingual Matters.

Spolsky, B. and Cooper, R.L. (1991) *The Languages of Jerusalem*. Oxford: Clarendon Press.

Waksman, S. and Shohamy, E. (2012) Talking back to the Tel Aviv centennial: LL responses to top-down agendas. In C. Hélot, M. Barni, R. Janssens and C. Bagna (eds) *Linguistic Landscapes, Multilingualism and Social Change* (pp. 109–125). Frankfurt am Main: Peter Lang.

Waksman, S. and Shohamy, E. (2016) Linguistic landscape of social protests: Moving from 'open' to 'institutional' spaces. In R. Blackwood, E. Lanza and H. Woldemariam (eds) *Negotiating and Contesting Identities in Linguistic Landscape* (pp. 85–100). Oxford: Bloomsbury.

2 Methods and Techniques for Linguistic Landscape Research: About Definitions, Core Issues and Technological Innovations

Durk Gorter

This chapter discusses some issues related to the development of the study of linguistic landscapes (LL), with a focus on methods and techniques of data collection and presentation. The chapter has three parts. In the first part, two definitions of this field of study and how these definitions have been used will be discussed, followed by a brief treatment of a more up-to-date definition. The second part of the chapter deals with three issues more specific to LL studies: the research area, the unit of analysis and the use of photographs as data and as a part of publications. The third part deals with the influence of technological developments on the LL field and some of the consequences and challenges of recent innovations for conducting LL research.

2.1 Introduction

People have not always been surrounded by as many signs, advertisements, texts, images and so on, as they are today. The postcard in Figure 2.1 shows an image of a street in Landau, probably taken about 100 years ago. In this view we see hardly any signs and, at the time, there were obviously not many textual items to be read in the streets of the city. So, perhaps there was not much linguistic landscape to be studied? However, on closer inspection there is one element that stands out because it carries various posters (see Figure 2.2a on the left for an enlargement).

That piece of street furniture is an advertising column, a so-called *Litfassäule*. They were invented by Ernst Litfass as a centralised place for advertisements, notices and posters. The first 100 columns were placed in Berlin in 1855 and their counterparts, the *Colonne Morris*, were erected a little later in Paris. The overall effect of this technological innovation has been an important change in urban landscapes and they became omnipresent in several European cities during the second half of the 19th century. Even today, you can find them in many places around the world (see Figure 2.2b on the right for a picture of an advertising pillar at the same place in Landau in 2016). These cylindrical outdoor pavement structures with a

Figure 2.1 Postcard of the Ostbahnstrasse in Landau
Source: http://www.zeno.org; Contumax GmbH & Co. KG.

characteristic style are only one of the many types of signage structures that physically support and are part of the LL in our world.

The following outline of the chapter can be given. Many interesting LL studies have been published in the past decade or so, but it is not my aim to provide an overview of methodological developments of LL studies. Instead, I begin in Section 2.2 with 'snapshots' of the two most frequently cited definitions of linguistic landscape and propose replacing them with a more current definition. In Section 2.3, I focus on issues specific to LL research linked to its methods of data collection, in particular taking pictures and presenting photographic material. In Section 2.4, I will discuss technological innovations and how they may change the field of LL studies.

Figure 2.2 (a) Enlargement of the *Litfassäule* in the postcard and (b) to the right a renovated pillar at the same location about 100 years later (April 2016)

2.2 Snapshots of the Definitions of Linguistic Landscape

It is not necessary to provide an overview of the field of LL studies, because summaries are already published in, among others, Backhaus (2007: 12–63), Gorter (2013), Gorter and Cenoz (2017), Huebner (2016), Shohamy (2012) and Van Mensel *et al.* (2016) (see also Shohamy, Chapter 1). Here, I want to examine in detail the use of two definitions of *linguistic landscape* (Section 2.2.1) and thereafter examine a more recent reformulation (Section 2.2.2).

2.2.1 Two well-known definitions

There is something special about the way in which the concept of linguistic landscape has been defined by several researchers. To understand the development of the field, it may help to focus on its definition. Although earlier studies into linguistic landscapes had been conducted (e.g. Rosenbaum *et al.*, 1977 or Spolsky & Cooper, 1991; for a detailed overview, see Backhaus, 2007), Landry and Bourhis published a paper in 1997 that contained two complementary definitions of linguistic landscape. One I call the 'short' version and the other the 'list' version. The 'short definition' is the opening sentence of the abstract (and does not appear in the body of the paper): 'Linguistic landscape refers to the visibility and salience of languages on public and commercial signs in a given territory or region' (Landry & Bourhis, 1997: 23). At the end of the section called 'The Concept of Linguistic Landscape' appears the 'list definition': 'The language of public road signs, advertising billboards, street names, place names, commercial shop signs, and public signs on government buildings combine to form the linguistic landscape of a given territory, region or urban agglomeration' (Landry & Bourhis, 1997: 25). This list definition is appealing because it has common items which we associate with textual signs in public space. On closer inspection, it is like a catalogue of six different sign types and, of course, it would be easy to add other types of signs in the public space.

LL researchers frequently quote one of these two definitions to introduce their work as contributing to LL studies; according to Google Scholar and Google Books, the list definition is quoted far more often than the short version.[1]

Bruyèl-Olmedo and Juan-Garau (2009: 387) also quote the list definition and then go on to claim that 'this definition has been quoted *in most papers* committed to the study of the language(s) displayed around us' [emphasis mine]. It is easy to verify that this cannot be correct: there are indeed many publications that quote the definition, but there are far more publications on LL that do not use the quotation. Two book reviewers have also noted a frequent use of the definition and they both write about its supposed over-utilisation. First, in her review of the book edited by Shohamy and Gorter (2009b), Zabrodskaja (2010: 273) remarks: 'some notions are repeated many times (so that a reader will learn the definition of LL by heart)'. Checking the factual correctness of this statement, it turns out that in 21 chapters the 'list definition' is quoted twice in full (by Coulmas and by Huebner) and the 'short definition' is mentioned once (by Lanza & Woldemariam). Even if some kind of reference to the Landry and Bourhis (1997) paper is made in the other 13 chapters, those authors do not quote either definition. Quoting two different definitions three times in 21 chapters seems hardly enough to qualify it as 'repeated many times'.

A few years later, the same reviewer edited a book on LL studies (Laitinen & Zabrodskaja, 2015). As a curious coincidence, when Amos (2016a) reviewed that book, he refers again to overuse of the Landry and Bourhis definition: 'This includes Landry and Bourhis' seminal but over-quoted description of the LL (appearing also in Perotto's chapter and cited elsewhere ad nauseam). It is a shame that the editors apparently overlook this repetition' (Amos, 2016a: 436). Checking the full text of the book, this seems somewhat overstated, because the 'list definition' is quoted in full in two of the 11 chapters and the short definition not even once. However, perhaps the point both reviewers wanted to make is that too many authors too often make a reference to the Landry and Bourhis paper, as if it contained the origins of the study of linguistic landscape. Without a doubt, the paper by Landry and Bourhis has been quoted often and has been influential, but some authors tend to attribute the paper to having an impact on how LL studies are carried out that it evidently cannot have. For example, Laihonen (2015: 178) claims that 'The Landry and Bourhis (1997) approach to LL, i.e. cataloguing language choice in signs, can be criticised for over-simplification'. But how can this be the case when Landry and Bourhis distributed a questionnaire that includes a few questions about linguistic landscape among a sample of francophone students? Similarly, Muth (2015: 206) asserts that 'the established methodological approach in linguistic landscape analysis follows Landry and Bourhis (1997: 25)'. Again, how can this be the case if there are few, if any, LL studies that have used a data collection instrument or a factor analysis similar to Landry and Bourhis? Moreover, to suggest that there is something like *the established approach* disregards the variation in approaches among studies under the LL umbrella. It seems that the paper by Landry and Bourhis (1997) deserves re-reading as it contains some important reflections on LL, but its research method has not been followed in the LL field and both the short and the list definition, even if attractive, seem a bit dated. A more current definition seems better suited to determine the essential qualities of the LL field, as I hope to demonstrate in the next section.

2.2.2 A more current definition of linguistic landscape studies

Some years ago, the thought-provoking question was asked: 'What is LL, ... really?' (Shohamy & Gorter, 2009a: 1–2). This was followed by asking: 'Does it refer to language only or to additional things which are present around us: images, sounds, buildings, clothes or even people?' The answer was: yes, it does. But, it was also argued that the 'attention to language in the environment, words and images displayed and exposed in public spaces, that is the centre of attention in ... LL' (Shohamy & Gorter, 2009a: 1). Now, looking at this 'What is LL, ... really?' question again several years later, we might again give the same answer. Of course, the field has developed since then and its definition could be in need of reformulation. Here, I will obtain guidance from a text in *Linguistic Landscape: An International Journal* that was first published in 2015. In the 'Aims and Scopes' of the journal we can read that the 'field of Linguistic Landscape (LL) attempts to understand the motives, uses, ideologies, language varieties and contestations of multiple forms of "languages" as they are displayed in public spaces'. This provides a broad and workable definition of LL that can replace earlier definitions that may have become worn out and jaded.

The main idea can be visualised by putting '"languages" as they are displayed' at the centre of a circle representing the field. The 'languages' between quotation marks can imply debates about 'named languages' and how they are invented and constructed (Makoni & Pennycook, 2007) or that language has to be seen as a wider concept of visual, multimodal components (Shohamy, 2015). The *display* of languages is not the exclusive focus, because the field is like a dynamic and expanding circle. Even *public spaces* are no longer its exclusive research domain, as investigators have moved into semi-public or non-public contexts such as schools or cyberspace. The question can be asked whether we can (or want) to demarcate the boundaries of the field at all, because it extends in many directions, and its boundaries are continuously crossed by scholars who bring in innovative theoretical and methodological approaches. The 'languages' as they are on public display are studied through the lenses of several disciplines, including sociolinguistics and applied linguistics. The theoretical lenses of various disciplines are brought into the LL field and contribute to its development, and it can work in reverse as well when the application of LL findings influences those disciplines. An example is the plea by Shohamy (2015), who outlines the importance of LL studies to change the field of language policy studies. One finds a multitude of themes and topics in LL publications; some of them are unique and others recurrent. The LL field is diverse and heterogeneity seems to be an inherent feature.

Linguistic landscape, or LL for short, has undeniably caught on as a term to denote the field, even when other, competing labels have been proposed such as 'environmental print' (Huebner, 2006); 'the decorum of the public life' (Ben-Rafael *et al.*, 2006); or, as I suggested myself, 'multilingual cityscape' (Gorter, 2006). Because of its wider connotations, some researchers in the field prefer 'semiotic landscape' (Jaworski & Thurlow, 2010), which places it somehow within the study of semiotics. This may not be unproblematic because, for example, the urban sociologist Gottdiener (2012: 108) did not contest the term semiotic landscape, but he criticised the introduction of the book by Jaworski and Thurlow rather harshly for a 'pedestrian' and 'unscholarly' use of semiotics.

The word *landscape* has its historical roots in Dutch, as literally a 'tract of land', as well as in English as 'a painting depicting a scenery on land' (Gorter, 2006: 83). As a way to rethink the concept of landscape, Leeman and Modan (2009) propose that LL researchers should base themselves more on the use of the term in cultural geography, both as a place and a way of seeing (see also Jaworski & Thurlow, 2010: 2–4).

The second part of the word 'land-*scape*' has given rise to creative ideas, and various forms of -*scape* have been proposed as an alternative to or to be added to LL studies. An almost endless list of possibilities can be found in the LL literature. To include spoken language there is 'soundscape' (Scarvaglieri *et al.*, 2013); in education 'school-scape' (Brown, 2012); online the linguistic 'cyberscape' (Ivkovic & Lotherington, 2009); body inscriptions or tattoos form a 'skinscape' (Peck & Stroud, 2015); an olfactory ethnography leads to a 'smellscape' (Pennycook & Otsuji, 2015); a 'linguascape' for tourists (Jaworski & Thurlow, 2010); 'cityscape' as contrasted to 'ruralscape' (Muth, 2015). Some of the thinking about different types of *-scape* can be traced back to Appadurai (1990) who, in his influential paper on globalisation, proposed five scapes as dimensions of global cultural flows (ethnoscapes, mediascapes, technoscapes, ideoscapes and finanscapes). Perhaps inspiration also comes from the geographer Porteous (1990, cited in Pennycook & Otsuji, 2015), who proposed a list of scapes based on the senses (allscapes, dreamscapes, etc.). For the time being, the expression *linguistic landscape* has achieved acceptance and seems to hold against efforts at terminological refinement.

The LL field is varied, complex and rapidly developing, and there are shifts between different sets of ideas. Looking through a specific (disciplinary or theoretical) lens at a specific LL theme will be important for the researcher in question; however, each lens will limit the field of view and thus the extent of the observable world that is seen at any given moment. Thus far, I have mentioned disciplinary backgrounds, theoretical approaches and recurring themes, but not the research methods and techniques, and I want to discuss those in more detail in the next section.

2.3 Methods and Techniques of Data Collection in LL Research

Many LL studies draw on well-known existing research methods and techniques from sociolinguistics, applied linguistics or other disciplines, so there is no need here for an explanation of well-documented methods and techniques of data collection such as questionnaires, interviews, observations, ethnography or discourse analysis.

In the following three sections, I will discuss some issues related to data collection specifically for LL studies. These issues are: the research site or survey area (Section 2.3.1), the survey items or unit of analysis (Section 2.3.2) and the use of photographs as data in publications (Section 2.3.3), which is perhaps the most specific issue related to LL work.

2.3.1 Research sites

LL researchers who collect data on the display of language in public space want to go to specific geographic areas, although it could also be cyberspace (Ivkovic & Lotherington, 2009) or a combination of both (see Section 2.4). LL researchers may sometimes struggle with the boundaries of the geographic areas to investigate. Some questions are 'How to choose?' and 'What is the most relevant focal geographical area?' (Hult, 2014: 511). One solution LL researchers have found is to follow a (public) transport axis. Tulp (1978), in one of the earliest LL studies, examined the distribution of Dutch and French on advertising billboards along the most prominent tram lines crossing Brussels. Similarly, Backhaus (2007: 65–66) followed the Yamanote train line that runs in a loop through the centre of Tokyo and chose 28 areas next to each station. A relatively recent example is Lai (2013), who studied the LL in four neighbourhoods located along the south–north line of the light rail network Mass Transit Railway (MTR) in Hong Kong.

Figure 2.3 Two shopping streets in Donostia-San Sebastián (left) and Leeuwarden-Ljouwert (right)

Another solution is to focus on one or more (shopping) streets. In LL studies, using streets as a survey area has become a frequent choice. We did our own first LL study in one street (Cenoz & Gorter, 2003) based on the example of Rosenbaum *et al.* (1977), who studied signs in one street in Jerusalem. For our second study, we chose the main shopping street of Donostia-San Sebastián, in the Basque Country, Spain and we compared the signage with a similar street in Leeuwarden-Ljouwert in Friesland, the Netherlands (Cenoz & Gorter, 2006) (see Figure 2.3). The two streets became a kind of *pars pro toto* for the LL of the city, or even the whole region.

Blackwood and Tufi (2015) consistently selected a 50-metre stretch of a main street to study the LL of a series of cities along the Mediterranean coast in France and Italy. Shopping malls have also featured as survey areas in several studies (e.g. Coluzzi, 2017; Trumper-Hecht, 2009). However, Pietikäinen *et al.* (2011) carried out their LL research in villages in the north of Norway, Sweden, Finland and Russia, and observed that the layout is rather different from cities. They wanted to 'rethink the "main street" starting point typical of much previous LL research' (Pietikäinen *et al.*, 2011: 284) and selected 20 sites that were central for language activities. The case of Laitinen (2014) is a rather exceptional example because he cycled 630 kilometres on the road between Helsinki and Oulu in Finland to study English on signs. Hult (2014) used the radial highways passing through different neighbourhoods of San Antonio, Texas to capture the LL on video from a car travelling at about 65 mph (±105 km/h).[2]

These examples show that research sites can also be thought of as larger areas than streets. Huebner (2006: 32) already hints at the importance of a neighbourhood as a survey area when he observes in Bangkok 'separate and identifiable neighbourhoods, each with its own linguistic culture'. Papen (2012) focused her LL study of gentrification on the area in Berlin known as Helmholtzkiez, where *Kiez* is a northern German word for 'neighbourhood'. Blommaert (2013) carried out his ethnographic LL fieldwork in Antwerp (Belgium) in the neighbourhood where he lives. He provided an account of social change told by in-depth reading of multilingual signage throughout this neighbourhood of Berchem. A number of LL researchers have studied Chinatowns as special neighbourhoods in big cities; examples are the studies in Washington DC (Leeman & Modan, 2009; Lou, 2007, 2016), Liverpool (Amos, 2016b) and in different cities in Belgium and the Netherlands (Wang & Van der Velde, 2015).

In a later LL study in Donostia-San Sebastián, we observed differences between neighbourhoods in the use of Basque (Gorter *et al.*, 2012). In a recent paper, we have suggested that the neighbourhood as LL survey area is an appropriate and suitable level of analysis. We argue that the LL gives a neighbourhood a certain identity and 'the ambiance of a neighbourhood can be experienced and seen as a unity, even if geographic, social or language borders are not clearly demarcated' (Gorter & Cenoz, 2015: 69). Also, Shohamy (2015: 165) examined the LL of two neighbourhoods as smaller units than the city of Tel Aviv Jaffa, and emphasised that '"neighborhood identities" [are] making up a meaningful territorial space and special connection with its people'.

However, it is not always clear how LL researchers chose their survey areas. Blackwood (2015: 41) is convinced that the choice of survey area remains problematic. He argues that 'it is challenging to the point of being unfeasible to survey an entire city or town', although he hints at possible future technological changes that might make it possible and perhaps he was thinking about 'big data' or Google Street View. Blackwood may be right that the survey area remains an important issue, but it would help if LL researchers started to report more precisely how they chose their survey areas and which decisions they took. For example, Backhaus (2007) described his procedures in great detail and the arbitrary decisions he had to make. Sometimes part of the problem can be solved by describing the exact location or by including a map as research practice in cases where it is useful. One way is to insert the GPS coordinates of longitude and latitude and another solution is to use a short URL from Google Street View. In our paper on translanguaging and linguistic landscapes (Gorter & Cenoz, 2015), we inserted a link (http://goo.gl/maps/Oppec) to give readers the opportunity to go to the exact location in front of the bookshop in Donostia-San Sebastián (in 2012) that we are describing. Google Street View is a tool that can offer interesting new ways to conduct LL studies. As Puzey (2015: 398) points out: 'Google street view enables users to scout the LL of distant or less accessible areas viewing panoramic images along routes around the world'. Of course, this only applies to the places where it is available and excludes, for example, parts of Germany where Google Street View was stopped for privacy reasons. For his review of the book edited by Blackwood *et al.* (2016), Troyer (2016: 92) uses Google Maps and Street View to visit all the research sites in the book because the editors state in their preface that 'the reader is invited to journey across Europe, North America, Asia and Africa' (Troyer, 2016: xxiii). Troyer even goes as far as to recommend that all future LL work include GPS coordinates.

2.3.2 Signage and survey items

LL researchers take as a point of departure the investigation of the 'multiple forms of "languages" as they are displayed'. In many LL studies this implies looking at 'signs', in particular the signs that have written text on them. Backhaus (2007: 4–9; 61) has already reflected on the nature of 'signs' and the 'language on signs', and he considers what constitutes a 'unit of analysis'. Investigating signage in one way or the other implies some sort of a selection process. It is possible to do research on only one particular type of sign, for example, place names (Puzey, 2012) or the LOVE sculptures (Jaworski, 2015). On the other hand, researchers may try to collect a representative cross-section of one or more geographic areas; the example of Blackwood and Tufi (2015) in several Mediterranean cities was mentioned above.

An attempt to classify or codify the textual signs usually leads to adopting a definition of the 'unit of analysis'. According to Blackwood (2015: 41), '*many of those* undertaking quantitative research ... adopt the definition proposed by Backhaus (2007: 66) "any piece of text within a spatially definable frame"'. In a more recent publication (with co-authors), he goes one step further and states, 'researchers have *largely settled on* Backhaus's designation' (Van Mensel *et al.*, 2016: 439 [my emphasis]). As an alternative, these authors also refer to our work, a publication in which we decided on another unit of analysis after considering some difficulties and arbitrary decisions in terms of 'the larger whole of the establishment as the unit of analysis' (Cenoz & Gorter, 2006: 71). We reasoned that some texts are placed by the same company and thus form an assemblage that belongs together. It seems that researchers still struggle with these issues (e.g. Hepford, 2015; Neves, 2016). It may be true that the 'solution' of the unit as a 'text within a ... frame' has been chosen more frequently, but several LL researchers, among those Vandenbroucke, opt for 'the establishment (i.e. façade of a shop or house) and not the individual sign' (Vandenbroucke, 2015: 6). A problem with 'text within a ... frame' is repetition, because, for example, a shop may have its name repeated numerous times on its front. In quantifying all those occurrences, just one or two shops can skew results in one direction. Another problem may be that it leads to large numbers of signs. Laitinen (2014), for example, used Backhaus's definition of a sign as a guideline, but he collected such an enormous amount of material containing English (on his long trip; see Section 2.3.1) that he decided to present only 'selected observations and impressions' (Laitinen, 2014: 60).

Another issue related to the unit of analysis is whether signs are fixed or not. Backhaus (2007: 67) only considered signs fixed on a carrier, whereas I had already asked, 'are texts on moving objects such as buses or cars to be included?' (Gorter, 2006: 3) (although for convenience sake we left them out of our sample). Other LL researchers, such as Sebba (2010), have argued for the inclusion of non-fixed mobile signs such as newspapers, T-shirts, banknotes or bus tickets. The advice was followed, for example, by Dunlevy (2012: 4) and Moriarty (2014: 468; 2015: 203), who both decided to include non-stationary signs. However, none of those authors mention the ever-changing texts included on digital screens of video displays, which today make up a substantial part of urban landscapes (see Section 2.4). We also pointed out that when defining the 'unit of analysis' one can move from the smallest individual sign to the level of an establishment, and, following Ben-Rafael *et al.* (2006: 8), to the LL as a larger unit, a *Gestalt*. There, we proposed taking an even wider perspective and suggested 'an approach in which the unit of analysis becomes "a landscape" as it can be seen in a single view' (Marten *et al.*, 2012: 5). This is somehow what we tried to apply in our publication on translanguaging and linguistic landscapes (Gorter & Cenoz, 2015).

2.3.3 Photographs as LL data

One of the distinguishing traits of LL studies is the use of photographic material to analyse signage. Taking photographs of signs as part of the data collection process has become a research technique that is characteristic of many LL studies, and LL publications often include photographs. I want to briefly discuss three elements related to the use of photographs: (1) the LL researcher as photographer; (2) the LL photo as data or 'LL genre'; and (3) the author and the readers of an academic text featuring pictures.

In Jerusalem, Spolsky and Cooper (1991) included the linguistic landscape in a larger sociolinguistic research project. The opening sentence of the book reads like an introduction to a linguistic landscape study: 'Anyone walking the Old City through the Jaffa Gate is immediately struck by the multiliteracy proclaimed by the signs' (Spolsky & Cooper, 1991: 1; see Figure 2.4).

Spolsky describes in uncomplicated words how he carried out his data collection: 'My curiosity piqued by these signs, I set off with my camera to record as many as I could' (Spolsky & Cooper, 1991: 8). He recorded over 100 signs on analogue film rolls. In a long table, he presents a full list of all photographs, including the languages

Figure 2.4 Multiliteracy in signs at Jaffa Gate in Jerusalem (detail)

on each sign and the material of the signs. That last piece of information shows that he already understood the importance of the materiality of the signs (cf. Aronin & Ó Laoire, 2012; Cook, 2015).

The photographer – as far as this fact is reported – is usually the researcher, unless the help of an assistant or student is mentioned. The following question then arises: are LL researchers sufficiently skilled as photographers? Puzey (2015: 398) comments that the cameras on mobile phones today are 'the key piece of equipment', so that 'capturing of large amounts of LL materials can be a relatively straightforward matter'. LL photographs are not an artistic, but a technical form of photography, although there is of course a difference between a 'snapshot' and a 'professional photograph'. What I see published in LL studies, which is thus *after* some selection has taken place, can many times be characterised as amateurish snapshot photography. It is hard to understand why more effort does not go into presenting better quality photographs. Perhaps this is also the reason why Nash (2016: 383) was critical when he quoted me saying: 'taking photos of the LL requires hardly any effort and poses no particular difficulties (Gorter, 2012: 9)', and he argued, 'Gorter overlooks the required skill and astuteness demanded of an LL fieldworker'. Still, I agree with Puzey and remain convinced that taking a picture does not require a lot of training, especially not when it is a photo of a fixed sign, and fixed signs are still predominant in the genre of LL photographs. Of course, LL researchers have to use common sense and accept some simple advice about the way they shoot: 'take your time', 'frame the sign', 'focus', 'pay attention to the light' and 'check the picture immediately afterwards'. Such simple rules of thumb do not ask for sophisticated skills and if needed, software is increasingly capable of making corrections afterwards. Technological advancements also make it less of an issue because digital cameras, also those included on mobile phones, can take pictures with a high resolution. Although of course, afterwards the editing of photographs brings up issues of what is permissible: some cropping or colour adjustment may be acceptable or even recommended, but not, of course, photoshopping of signs so that they appear completely new. Nash (2016) does have a point though, because the published pictures of LL researchers could be improved considerably from a technical reproduction point of view. For example, photographs of signs on shop windows with a reflection of the LL photographer/author can be avoided. Researchers also have to consider issues such as the context of the signage (how much of the surrounding area do you include?) or the angle at which you take the photograph (is the sign in the centre of the photo or not?). Kallen *et al.* (2016) also discuss some of these issues.

Pictures collected during fieldwork are primarily used as data for interpretation and analysis. Usually, authors report how many signs they have photographed or how many pictures they have taken. They may also report on how they coded or interpreted what can be seen in the image, in particular characteristics of textual elements. There are some methodological issues of how to analyse photographs of signs related to 'language', text, colour, material, placement, surroundings and so on. But in a general sense, photographs are like any other data source and sufficient details about procedures should be reported in the same way as using observations, interviews or questionnaires as data.

Most pictures in LL work can be recognised as belonging to a kind of 'LL genre' because they depict a shop window, a poster, a street sign and so on. Pictures of such types of signage are the most frequent. Those signs usually have just one word or a few words on them, but typically less than 10, although exceptionally longer texts are presented. Considerations of legibility can be important for data presentation: How much do you see? Can the points of interest on the object (often a sign) be seen well? Can the language items be read? Is there a clear centre of interest? In general, I find LL as a genre of photography in LL publications aesthetically boring, but then probably those photographs of signs should not be looked at as a genre for its aesthetic qualities, but rather as a form of technical photography, as there is for other fields such as architecture or biology.

The 'quality' of an image is a rather subjective element, but in our case 'image quality' refers more specifically to how free the image is from defects such as blur, low readability and so on. From what appears in published work, it seems that some LL authors could still improve on these aspects of image quality. Regularly one finds images in LL publications that are blurred, with words half missing or with linguistic elements that are too small to read. For a reader it is unpleasant when the text states, 'In the picture we see an example of', but in the published photo it is impossible to figure it out. Solutions in such cases can be to take the picture again, compose the picture better, or, in other cases, crop the image. Another solution can be to provide a transcript of a text that cannot be read. We did this with a shop window in four languages (Gorter & Cenoz, 2015; see the Google Street View link above). Transcripts are rather uncommon, although translations of signs in other languages than English are sometimes provided.

LL researchers are often confronted with the issue of how to compose a paper or chapter that is going to consist of mainly text and a few selected pictures. The relationship between the text and a figure can be complex. A photo of a sign can be an example of (raw) data, it can have the function of supporting an argument, but it can also be an illustration or even mere decoration. Sometimes photographs are intended to illustrate a point in the text, but a clear link is missing.

Another reason can be that some publishers do not publish the photographs well or a publisher poses certain limitations which become a barrier for LL authors, such as a restriction on the number of pictures, the maximum size of each image or the placement on the page (only top or bottom). Obviously, within the norms set by the publisher and probably guided by an editor, a selection process takes place where an LL author has to make choices. Sometimes authors report that they could not include a sign 'due to space constraints' (e.g. Rubdy, 2015: 295).

The following question can be asked: what is the author's intent in publishing this photo and not another? How is a figure used to convey a meaning or a message? How is it related to the content of the publication? Authors usually do not report why certain photographs were selected for inclusion. Sometimes one comes across a remark about the importance of colour for LL photography, but until recently most figures of signs we published in black and white and colour reproduction was an exception. Technological and price developments will help to make it easier to reproduce colour in future publications.

What an author writes and selects to present as figures is not the only issue, but also how the reader interprets the text. We know that texts can be read in different ways and that not all viewers see the same image content therefore, in the LL literature it is important to consider in what way the readers construct their own interpretations. Of fundamental importance is the issue of what is there to see when a reader looks at the picture in the publication? How does a reader look at the image? How can it be read? After reading many LL publications, it seems to me that the inclusion of a few pictures sometimes seems more like an afterthought than a key part of publishing an LL study. The pictures used in LL studies as illustrations sometimes seem like the Cinderella of research instead of its most important data. Of course, some very good LL publications have been published without including pictures.

In conclusion, I would like to advocate that LL researchers take their images more seriously. LL researchers have to give careful attention to their images as data and also as part of their publications. They have to give it some thought, even when photographing signs with a modern mobile phone can be relatively straightforward. They have to consider the conditions in which their images are produced and the effects images can have. If researchers want to develop the LL field further, it is not only about theories, themes, locations or methods, but also about improvement of the technical standards of one of their basic materials, the photographic data as presented in LL publications. After all, as the saying goes, 'one picture is worth a thousand words'.

2.4 Technological Innovations and LL Studies

In this section, I will discuss some technological innovations that can have an influence on data collection in LL studies.

In the 1980s, when Spolsky took his pictures of signs in Jerusalem, he used a camera with analogue film of 36 images per roll (Spolsky & Cooper, 1991). At the time, it was relatively expensive and cumbersome to develop, print and then analyse the photographs. Some years later, in 2002, when we carried out our first LL investigation in Donostia-San Sebastián, we used a small digital camera and we could take an almost limitless number of pictures to cover all the signs (Cenoz & Gorter, 2003). After the transfer of the files to a desktop computer, they could be coded and analysed on screen. At the time, for us it was obvious that 'Recent developments in digital camera technology make the study of the linguistic landscape possible at a relatively low cost' (Gorter, 2006: 83). Moving from analogue film to digital recording was an important technological change and one can even observe that the transition from analogue to digital cameras coincides more or less with the explosive growth of the field of LL studies. The introduction of mobile phones, around 2003, that include an onboard camera, and the rapid adoption of smartphones after 2007, has further facilitated LL fieldwork. Today, people take pictures with their smartphones all the time and the LL fieldworker does not stand out of the crowd as much as 10 or even five years ago.

Over a similar time span, digital screens have become common in the urban landscape. Digital signage is rapidly increasing in outdoor environments, especially since flat-panel LCD displays became affordable as an effective way to communicate and share content with target audiences. For example, the number of large digital billboards doubled in the US between 2012 and 2016 (Dundas, 2016). Screens of all types and sizes have rapidly appeared in about every location, such as shops, bars, public transport and so on. (A collection of early studies was brought together in the special issue on 'Screens and the social landscape' by Jewitt & Triggs, 2006.) To date, most LL studies have focused on static signs, but those digital screens intermingle with fixed signage and are a challenge for studies of 'language' in public space.

Another innovation is QR codes, a type of bar code that can be added to almost any publicly displayed sign or any other object, such as flyers, business cards or even coins. A smartphone camera can scan the image of the QR code to gain access to further information, for example, a website or a video. Although, recent developments in recognition software based on artificial intelligence soon may make the QR codes superfluous. Also, website URLs have become omnipresent in the LL and shops increasingly encourage customers to go online while they are shopping. One study found in November 2015 that about 50% of US adults compare prices on a mobile device while in a store (IAB, 2015).

Smartphones have spread even faster than digital outdoor advertising and information panels. Numerous people hold the personal screen of a mobile device in their hands at almost every point, which brings them an incessant stream of messages, texts, still images and videos. Digital screens can be observed everywhere and all those screens contain continuously changing 'language'. The distinction between offline and online worlds is blurring and both are part of the 'linguistic landscape' that its users are immersed in. Androutsopoulos (2014) discusses two new areas of sociolinguistic research and he separates data collection methods in computer-mediated communication from LLs, but these research areas may become increasingly intermingled.

The following quotation concisely expresses developments about computer technology since the 1950s: 'First they were in big rooms, then they sat on desktops, then they sat on our laps, and now they're in our palms. Next they'll be on our faces' (Carlson, 2012). The author discusses computerised glasses, in particular Google Glass, where a microcomputer at the rim of the glass projects an image, superimposed on the surroundings, into the eye of its user to display additional information. The project failed miserably; not for technological reasons, but because it lacked social acceptance. It was seen as an elitist expensive gadget and there were concerns about privacy because the glasses could unobtrusively take pictures or record video. Once persons wearing the special glasses started to be made fun of as 'Glasshole', the experiment soon terminated. The choice of a catchy insulting word shows the power of language, but most likely it will not mean the end of similar wearable devices.

Another evolution has taken place with VR or virtual reality, an existing technology that since 2015 received a boost through the powerful computing possibilities available in smartphones. By wearing a VR headset, users are immersed in a three-dimensional artificial world. A simple cardboard viewer with a smartphone is enough to get the basic experience. A major disadvantage is that users are blocked out from their immediate surroundings. Thus far, its success is mainly limited to gaming and training in specialised technical skills. The *li.lab* research group in Innsbruck, Austria is exploring possibilities of LL data collection via a type of 'spherical photography' in 360° degrees of signage in urban landscapes (Unterthiner *et al.*, 2016).

The most important technological development to influence or to disrupt linguistic landscape studies could be AR or augmented reality. With AR, the physical real world becomes supplemented with a computer-generated overlay of reality. An early example, launched in late 2010, is Word Lens, which is an augmented reality app for smartphones that recognises printed texts on signs in Spanish and English and translates them instantaneously. In 2015, Word Lens was integrated into the Google Translate app, and it now works with dozens of languages. Another example that has been around for some years are digital advertisements projected onto the sideboards of sports games. In the Spanish football league, advertisements are regionalised when Real Madrid plays Barcelona. Fans see different advertisements on different TV stations and those ads can also be in different languages. This has been taken one step further by using different languages for the same digital advertisement at a major airport, where the language depends on the majority language at the destination of a departure gate (JCDecaux, 2013). These are still indirect and passive examples, where a choice is made according to the expected dominant language of the audience.

Passers-by or potential clients can also more directly interact and become engaged with their digital surroundings and thus they themselves can influence and change the linguistic landscapes of their surroundings. For example, at Times Square in New York in July 2015, it was possible to send a tweet with your own name to a dedicated hashtag and in response some trivia about that name was projected onto a huge digital billboard, of which the sender would receive a photo on their device (Johnson, 2015). During the summer of 2016, augmented reality became a worldwide phenomenon through the game Pokémon Go. Basically, it is an app that projects images of virtual creatures onto a smartphone screen as if they were in the same location. Similar apps exist already that can add tourist information by pointing the phone at a well-known tourist site. Advertising companies want people to directly engage with their commercial messages displayed in public spaces, so that they use their phone to buy the product, share their messages on social media and so on. Their aim is to analyse human behaviour in public spaces such as shopping malls and tourist sites to offer real-time, personalised advertising (Dundas, 2016).

The inventor of the advertising pillar, Ernst Litfass, wanted to concentrate official announcements and commercial messages in one recognisable place to go against what he saw as a disturbing littering of posters and notices on the city walls of Berlin. Could he have imagined that one and a half centuries later the digital interactive pillars would become integrated into an urban linguistic landscape overloaded with omnipresent messages? In a high-tech world, the advertising pillar (*Litfasssäule*), mentioned in the Introduction (Section 2.1), becomes a multilingual messaging structure that interacts with its passers-by. People engage with the linguistic landscape and linguistic landscapes react and change continually.

Already in the 1990s it became clear that 'the internet changes everything' (J. Neil Weintraut, cited in Cortese, 1995). In Section 2.3, we pointed to some possibilities for LL research with, for example, Google Street View, such as a virtual visit to all the places in a study. In this section, we outlined recent technological developments that led to digital signage and the screens of smartphones being everywhere in public space. Through smartphones and other tools, the virtual, the augmented and the real may merge into one. It will be interesting to see how LL researchers are going to deal with such new challenges of customisation, mobility and fluidity.

Of course, LL studies will move forward and researchers are going to widen their 'field of view'. It implies coming up with creative, innovative ideas and expanding current approaches. At the same time, in order to develop the LL field and to make it stronger, the 'depth of field', the part that you see sharply, also needs to be reinforced. LL studies that aim to develop further methods and theories have to be based on an adequate knowledge of former studies and the history of the field. Studies need to be published in ways that make it possible for future researchers to understand the details of such research. Progress in LL work, as in any specialised field, can be achieved by constantly improving one's interpretations and conclusions, taking into account the ideas and observations of others. This requires that we look critically behind us at previous work and keep paying attention to '"languages" as they are displayed in public space' to improve future work.

Acknowledgements

This work was supported by the MINECO/FEDER under Grant EDU2015-63967-R and the Basque Government under Grant DREAM IT-714-13; UFI 11/54. I would like to thank the reviewers for critical and constructive comments that have improved the text.

Notes

(1) Google Scholar finds the list definition 252 times and Google Books 140 times, but with substantial overlap. The short definition, in contrast, has only 36 instances and in Google Books 41 results; but there is again overlap (December 2016).
(2) A rather curious example is a YouTube video of 'A look at the linguistic landscape of Mexico-city' which stretches north–south for 60 km; see https://www.youtube.com/watch?v=pjwhD5Udclk.

References

Amos, H.W. (2016a) Book review: Dimensions of sociolinguistic landscapes in Europe: Materials and methodological solutions, edited by M. Laitinen and A. Zabrodskaja. *Journal of Multilingual and Multicultural Development* 37 (4), 435–437.
Amos, H.W. (2016b) Chinatown by numbers: Defining an ethnic space by empirical linguistic landscape. *Linguistic Landscape* 2 (2), 127–156.
Androutsopoulos, J. (2014) Computer-mediated communication and linguistic landscapes. In J. Holmes and K. Hazen (eds) *Research Methods in Sociolinguistics: A Practical Guide* (pp. 74–90). Oxford: Wiley Blackwell.

Appadurai, A. (1990) Disjuncture and difference in the global cultural economy. *Theory, Culture & Society* 1, 295–310.

Aronin, L. and Ó Laoire, M. (2012) The material culture of multilingualism. In D. Gorter, H.F. Marten and L. Van Mensel (eds) *Minority Languages in the Linguistic Landscape* (pp. 299–318). London: Palgrave Macmillan.

Backhaus, P. (2007) *Linguistic Landscapes: A Comparative Study of Urban Multilingualism in Tokyo*. Clevedon: Multilingual Matters.

Ben-Rafael, E., Shohamy, E., Amara, M.H. and Trumper-Hecht, N. (2006) The symbolic construction of public space: The case of Israel. *International Journal of Multilingualism* 3 (1), 7–28.

Blackwood, R. (2015) LL explorations and methodological challenges: Analysing France's regional languages. *Linguistic Landscape: An International Journal* 1 (1/2), 38–53.

Blackwood, R. and Tufi, S. (2015) *The Linguistic Landscape of the Mediterranean: French and Italian Coastal Cities*. Basingstoke: Palgrave Macmillan.

Blackwood, R., Lanza, E. and Woldemariam, H. (eds) (2016) *Negotiating and Contesting Identities in Linguistic Landscapes*. London: Bloomsbury Publishing.

Blommaert, J. (2013) *Ethnography, Superdiversity and Linguistic Landscapes: Chronicles of Complexity*. Bristol: Multilingual Matters.

Brown, K.D. (2012) The linguistic landscape of educational spaces: Language revitalization and schools in Southeastern Estonia. In D. Gorter, H.F. Marten and L. Van Mensel (eds) *Minority Languages in the Linguistic Landscape* (pp. 281–298). Basingstoke: Palgrave Macmillan.

Bruyèl-Olmedo, A. and Juan-Garau, M. (2009) English as a lingua franca in the linguistic landscape of the multilingual resort of S'Arenal in Mallorca. *International Journal of Multilingualism* 6 (4), 386–411.

Carlson, N. (2012) The end of the Smartphone era is coming. *Business Insider*, 22 November 2012. See www.businessinsider.com/the-end-of-the-smartphone-era-is-coming-2012-11 (accessed 1 December 2016).

Cenoz, J. and Gorter, D. (2003) The linguistic landscape of Erregezainen/Escolta Real. Paper presented at the Third Conference on Third Language Acquisition and Trilingualism, September 2003, Tralee, Ireland.

Cenoz, J. and Gorter, D. (2006) Linguistic landscape and minority languages. In D. Gorter (ed.) *Linguistic Landscape: A New Approach to Multilingualism* (pp. 67–80). Clevedon: Multilingual Matters.

Coluzzi, P. (2017) Italian in the linguistic landscape of Kuala Lumpur (Malaysia). *International Journal of Multilingualism* 14 (2), 109–123.

Cook, V. (2015) Meaning and material in the language of the street. *Social Semiotics* 25 (1), 81–109.

Cortese, A. (1995) The software revolution – part 1. *Business Week*, 4 December 1995. See https://www.bloomberg.com/news/articles/1995-12-03/the-software-revolution-part-1.

Dundas, B. (2016) Digital signage on the fast track. *Signs of the Times*, 4 October 2016. See www.signweb.com/content/digital-signage-fast-track (accessed 1 December 2016).

Dunlevy, D.A. (2012) Linguistic policy and linguistic choice: A study of the Galician linguistic landscape. In C. Hélot, M. Barni, R. Janssens and C. Bagna (eds) *Linguistic Landscape, Multilingualism and Social Change* (pp. 53–68). Frankfurt: Peter Lang.

Gorter, D. (2006) Further possibilities for linguistic landscape research. In D. Gorter (ed.) *Linguistic Landscape: A New Approach to Multilingualism* (pp. 81–89). Clevedon: Multilingual Matters.

Gorter, D. (2012) Foreword. Signposts in the linguistic landscape. In C. Hélot, M. Barni, R. Janssens and C. Bagna (eds) *Linguistic Landscapes, Multilingualism and Social Change* (pp. 9–12). Frankfurt am Main: Peter Lang.

Gorter, D. (2013) Linguistic landscapes in a multilingual world. *Annual Review of Applied Linguistics* 33, 190–212.

Gorter, D. and Cenoz, J. (2015) Translanguaging and linguistic landscapes. *Linguistic Landscape* 1 (1), 54–74.

Gorter, D. and Cenoz, J. (2017). Linguistic landscape and multilingualism. In J. Cenoz, D. Gorter and S. May (eds) *Language Awareness and Multilingualism* (pp. 1–13). Cham: Springer International Publishing.

Gorter, D., Aiestaran, J. and Cenoz, J. (2012) The revitalization of Basque and the linguistic landscape of Donostia-San Sebastián. In D. Gorter, H.F. Marten and L. Van Mensel (eds) *Minority Languages in the Linguistic Landscape* (pp. 148–163). Basingstoke: Palgrave Macmillan.

Gottdiener, M. (2012) Review of Adam Jaworski and Crispin Thurlow (eds): Semiotic landscapes: Language, image, space. *Applied Linguistics* 33 (1), 107–111.

Hepford, E.A. (2015) Language for profit: Spanish–English bilingualism in Lowe's home improvement. *International Journal of Bilingual Education and Bilingualism* (August), 1–15.

Huebner, T. (2006) Bangkok's linguistic landscapes: Environmental print, codemixing, and language change. In D. Gorter (ed.) *Linguistic Landscape: A New Approach to Multilingualism* (pp. 31–51). Clevedon: Multilingual Matters.

Huebner, T. (2016) Linguistic landscape: History, trajectory and pedagogy. *Manusya* (22), 1–11.

Hult, F.M. (2014) Drive-thru linguistic landscaping: Constructing a linguistically dominant place in a bilingual space. *International Journal of Bilingualism* 18 (5), 507–523.

IAB (2015) IAB Digital shopping report. See www.iab.com/wpcontent/uploads/2015/11/IAB-Digital-Shopping-Report1.pdf.

Ivkovic, D. and Lotherington, H. (2009) Multilingualism in cyberspace: Conceptualising the virtual linguistic landscape. *International Journal of Multilingualism* 6 (1), 17–36.

Jaworski, A. (2015) Word cities and language objects 'Love' sculptures and signs as shifters. *Linguistic Landscape: An International Journal* 2 (1999), 75–94.

Jaworski, A. and Thurlow, C. (eds) (2010) *Semiotic Landscapes: Language, Image, Space*. London: Continuum.

JCDecaux (2013) Under the magnifying glass: The benefits of display digital advertising (Part II), 18 July 2013. See www.jcdecaux-oneworld.com/2013/07/under-the-magnifying-glass-the-benefits-of-display-digital-advertising-part-ii/ (accessed 1 December 2017).

Jewitt, C. and Triggs, T. (2006) Screens and the social landscape – Editorial. *Visual Communication* 5 (2), 131–140.

Johnson, L. (2015). Send a tweet to Coke's digital billboard, and it'll tell you fun facts about your name. *AdWeek*. See www.adweek.com/digital/send-tweet-cokes-digital-billboard-and-itll-tell-you-fun-facts-about-your-name-165780/.

Kallen, J., Dunlevy, D. and Balaeva, O. (2016) Contextualising units in the linguistic landscape: How should data be framed? Paper presented at the Linguistic Landscape Workshop, May 7–9, 2015, Berkeley, University of California.

Lai, M. (2013) The linguistic landscape of Hong Kong after the change of sovereignty. *International Journal of Multilingualism* 10 (3), 37–41.

Laihonen, P. (2015) Linguistic landscapes of a minoritized regional majority: Language ideologies among Hungarians in South-West Slovakia. In M. Laitinen and A. Zabrodskaja (eds) *Dimensions of Sociolinguistic Landscapes in Europe* (pp. 171–198). Frankfurt am Main: Peter Lang.

Laitinen, M. (2014) 630 kilometers by bicycle: Observations of English in urban and rural Finland. *International Journal of the Sociology of Language* 2014 (228), 55–77.

Laitinen, M. and Zabrodskaja, A. (2015) *Dimensions of Sociolinguistic Landscapes in Europe*. Frankfurt am Main: Peter Lang.

Landry, R. and Bourhis, R.Y. (1997) Linguistic landscape and ethnolinguistic vitality: An empirical study. *Journal of Language and Social Psychology* 16 (1), 23–49.

Leeman, J. and Modan, G. (2009) Commodified language in Chinatown: A contextualized approach to linguistic landscape. *Journal of Sociolinguistics* 13 (3), 332–362.

Lou, J. (2007) Revitalizing Chinatown into a heterotopia: A geosemiotic analysis of shop signs in Washington, D.C.'s Chinatown. *Space and Culture* 10 (2), 170–194.

Lou, J. (2016) *The Linguistic Landscape of Chinatown: A Sociolinguistic Ethnography*. Bristol: Multilingual Matters.

Makoni, S. and Pennycook, A. (2007) Disinventing and reconstituting languages. In S. Makoni and A. Pennycook (eds) *Disinventing and Reconstituting Languages* (pp. 1–41). Clevedon: Multilingual Matters.

Marten, H.F., Van Mensel, L. and Gorter, D. (2012) Studying minority languages in the linguistic landscape. In D. Gorter, H.F. Marten and L. Van Mensel (eds) *Minority Languages in the Linguistic Landscape* (pp. 1–18). Basingstoke: Palgrave Macmillan.

Moriarty, M. (2014) Contesting language ideologies in the linguistic landscape of an Irish tourist town. *International Journal of Bilingualism* 18 (5), 464–477.

Moriarty, M. (2015) Indexing authenticity: The linguistic landscape of an Irish tourist town. *International Journal of the Sociology of Language* (232), 195–214.

Muth, S. (2015) 'Ruralscapes' in post-Soviet Transnistria: Ideology and language use on the fringes of a contested space. In M. Laitinen and A. Zabrodskaja (eds) *Dimensions of Sociolinguistic Landscapes in Europe: Materials and Methodological Solutions* (pp. 199–231). Frankfurt am Main: Peter Lang.

Nash, J. (2016) Is linguistic landscape necessary? *Landscape Research* 41 (3), 380–384.

Neves, A.C. (2016) Linguistic landscape of Macau: A quantitative analysis. In L. Sciriha (ed.) *International Perspectives on Bilingualism* (pp. 43–62). Newcastle upon Tyne: Cambridge Scholars Publishing.

Papen, U. (2012) Commercial discourses, gentrification and citizens' protest: The linguistic landscape of Prenzlauer Berg, Berlin. *Journal of Sociolinguistics* 16 (1), 56–80.

Peck, A. and Stroud, C. (2015) Skinscapes. *Linguistic Landscape* 1 (1–2), 133–151.

Pennycook, A. and Otsuji, E. (2015) Making scents of the landscape. *Linguistic Landscape* 1 (3), 191–212.

Pietikäinen, S., Lane, P., Salo, H. and Laihiala-Kankainen, S. (2011) Frozen actions in the arctic linguistic landscape: A nexus analysis of language processes in visual space. *International Journal of Multilingualism* 8 (4), 277–298.

Puzey, G. (2012) New research directions in toponomastics and linguistic landscapes. *Onoma* 46, 211–226.

Puzey, G. (2015) Linguistic landscapes. In C. Hough (ed.) *The Oxford Handbook of Names and Naming* (pp. 395–411). Oxford: Oxford University Press.

Rosenbaum, Y., Nadel, E., Cooper, R.L. and Fishman, J.A. (1977) English on Keren Kayemet Street. In J.A Fishman, R.L. Cooper and A.W. Conrad (eds) *The Spread of English: The Sociology of English as an Additional Language* (pp. 179–196). Rowley: Newbury House.

Rubdy, R. (2015) A multimodal analysis of the graffiti commemorating the 26/11 Mumbai terror attacks: Constructing self-understandings of a senseless violence. In R. Rubdy and S. Ben Said (eds) *Conflict, Exclusion and Dissent in the Linguistic Landscape* (pp. 280–303). Basingstoke: Palgrave Macmillan.

Scarvaglieri, C., Redder, A., Pappenhagen, R. and Brehmer, B. (2013) Capturing diversity: Linguistic land- and soundscaping. In J. Duarte and I. Gogolin (eds) *Linguistic Superdiversity in Urban Areas: Research Approaches* (pp. 45–74). Amsterdam: John Benjamins.

Sebba, M. (2010) Discourses in transit. In A. Jaworski and C. Thurlow (eds) *Semiotic Landscapes: Language, Image, Space* (pp. 59–76). London: Continuum.

Shohamy, E. (2012) Linguistic landscapes and multilingualism. In M. Martin-Jones, A. Blackledge and A. Creese (eds) *The Routledge Handbook of Multilingualism* (pp. 538–551). London: Routledge.

Shohamy, E. (2015) LL research as expanding language and language policy. *Linguistic Landscape: An International Journal* 1 (1/2), 152–171.

Shohamy, E. and Gorter, D. (2009a) Introduction. In E. Shohamy and D. Gorter (eds) *Linguistic Landscape: Expanding the Scenery* (pp. 1–10). New York: Routledge.

Shohamy, E. and Gorter, D. (eds) (2009b) *Linguistic Landscape: Expanding the Scenery*. New York: Routledge.

Spolsky, B. and Cooper, R.L. (1991) *The Languages of Jerusalem*. Oxford: Clarendon.

Troyer, R. (2016) Book Review: Robert Blackwood, Elizabeth Lanza and Hirut Woldemariam (eds) Negotiating and Contesting Identities in Linguistic Landscapes. *Manusya* (22), 88–93.

Trumper-Hecht, N. (2009) Constructing national identity in mixed cities in Israel: Arabic on signs in the public space of upper Nazareth. In E. Shohamy and D. Gorter (eds) *Linguistic Landscape: Expanding the Scenery* (pp. 238–252). London: Routledge.

Tulp, S.M. (1978) Reklame en tweetaligheid: Een onderzoek naar de geographische verspreiding van franstalige en nederlandstalige affiches in Brussel. [Commercials and bilingualism: A study into the geographic distribution of French and Dutch advertisements in Brussels]. *Taal en Sociale Integratie* 1, 261–288.

Unterthiner, D., Baur, S. and Topf, A. (2016) Shifting perspectives on linguistic landscapes. Rethinking linguistic landscape data collection: Implications for multilingual learning and multilingual language. Poster presentation at Donostia Young Researchers Symposium on Multilingualism (DISM2016), 2–4 March 2016, University of the Basque Country, Donostia-San Sebastian, Basque Country, Spain.

Van Mensel, L., Vandenbroucke, M. and Blackwood, R. (2016) Linguistic landscapes. In O. García, N. Flores and M. Spotti (eds) *Oxford Handbook of Language and Society* (pp. 423–449). Oxford: Oxford University Press.

Vandenbroucke, M. (2015) Language visibility, functionality and meaning across various TimeSpace scales in Brussels' multilingual landscapes. *Journal of Multilingual and Multicultural Development* 36 (2), 163–181.

Wang, X. and Van de Velde, H. (2015) Constructing identities through multilingualism and multiscriptualism: The linguistic landscape in Dutch and Belgian Chinatowns. *Journal of Chinese Overseas* 11 (2), 119–145.

Zabrodskaja, A. (2010) Book Review: Elana Shohamy and Durk Gorter (eds), 2009b. Linguistic landscape: Expanding the scenery. *In: International Journal of Bilingualism* 14 (2), 271–274.

3 Learning to Translate the Linguistic Landscape

David Malinowski

As an experiment in thinking between research and pedagogical design, this narrative essay argues that translation holds particular promise, both as an approach for language learning and teaching in the linguistic landscape and, more broadly, as a figure or metaphor through which linguistic landscape researchers may reinterpret their work. In the essay, three salient aspects of translation are developed: as revelatory of gaps or 'faultlines' of meaning in texts, as response to the social and political demands of time and place and as a form of public action. The relevance of a translational approach to linguistic landscape research is argued through the figure and real-world examples of second language and literacy learning, in which the active disposition, exploratory operations and still-incomplete knowledge of the language learner offer new possibilities to the subject position of the linguistic landscape researcher.

3.1 Introduction

Since its ascendance a decade ago, the field of linguistic landscape (LL) has depended upon the objectivist logic of the photographic image, offering the 'visibility and salience' (Landry & Bourhis, 1997) of languages on signs as evidence of social heterogeneity and political change. Only relatively recently, with an increasing concern for the human practices and physical processes through which discourses in place may just as easily remain unseen as seen, have critical and ethnographically-inclined researchers endeavoured to privilege other means of knowing (e.g. Blommaert, 2013; Stroud & Mpendukana, 2010; Waksman & Shohamy, 2015). Still, in name and in practice, LL remains bound to that which is visible, in certain places and at certain times, always made salient through ideologically valenced 'ways of seeing' (Jaworski & Thurlow, 2010) and their modes of expression.

If representational practices and their claims on real-world truth remain a definitional problem for the field, then one valuable mode of inquiry might be to subject both (representational practices and the truths they tell) to exposure, critique, and constructive forms of testing and challenge. This narrative essay proposes *translation* as a rubric for understanding the knowledge work already being done, and available to be done, by practitioners in the field of LL. Translation, as a palette of mobile practices of translingual inscription, has of course been recognized in the LL literature as a technique by which bi- or multilingual signage presents itself in the urban scene with duplicate, parallel, overlapping or fragmentary content (e.g. Backhaus, 2007; Koskinen, 2012; Reh, 2004). However, this chapter borrows from a body of literature in translation studies embodying a more critical, postmodern approach in order to draw lessons from translation as *process* rather than *product*. As one might study urban social dynamics through observation of ongoing interaction and exchange on the street corner, focusing attention upon the negotiations and choices through which knowledge in the field of LL – and of the linguistic landscape as site of research – helps to centre attention on the 'difference and friction' and 'tension and conflict' attendant to all languaging practices in heterogeneous geographies (Simon, 2012; cf. Pennycook & Otsuji, 2015). In a series of writing experiments on translation as revelatory of gaps or 'faultlines' of meaning in texts (Miller, 1992), as responsibility and response to social and political demands (Robinson, 1997), and as a form of public action and activation (Venuti, 1995), this chapter invites self-reflexive inquiry on the part of LL researchers on the methodological choices and representational practices of the field as a collective whole.

As a practical mode of developing more translational practice in LL research – and as an end unto itself, with its own long developmental trajectory and goals – this chapter argues for a pedagogical approach. Assertions about the suitability of translational approaches to LL research are illustrated through the example of second language (L2) and literacy learning, where efforts to understand the LL as a learning resource have been underway for years already (e.g. Cenoz & Gorter, 2008; Dagenais *et al.*, 2009; Rowland, 2012; Sayer, 2009). After illustrating areas of potential traffic between LL research methods and L2 pedagogy, the chapter narrates an experimental project currently underway between language students and faculty at the author's university, the university language centre, and the local city government to envision a more diverse urban environment through translation of the city's LL, thus highlighting the potential of LL translation as public action.

3.2 Linguistic Landscape as 'Translational Space'

In introducing her small-scale photographic analysis of translation activity in the Tampere suburb of Hervanta, Koskinen (2012: 79) remarks that 'since translation is often the process through which any documentation comes to take on a new linguistic form, translatedness is an issue closely related to linguistic landscape research.' Indeed, whether named as such or not, studies of the bilingual or multilingual linguistic landscape, by the very nature of their objects of analysis, have investigated in detail the enabling conditions and traits of translated texts in public spaces. Spolsky and Cooper's three rules for determining what language(s) should appear on signs from an authorial perspective ([1] Write in a language you know; [2] Prefer to write in the language or languages that intended readers are assumed to read; [3] Prefer to write signs in your own language or in a language with which you want to be identified; cf. Spolsky & Cooper, 1991: 74–94) may be interpreted as an early recipe for translation in signage. In a complementary sense, Reh's (2004) 'reader-oriented typology' of translation types in bilingual signage (duplicating–fragmentary–overlapping–complementary) has had lasting influence in the field (cf. Backhaus, 2007; Gorter, 2013).

Koskinen (2012) suggests that the field of translation studies (TS) itself can lend valuable tools to the analysis of LL data. In approaching the written discourse on public signage, she suggests that TS gives strategies for identifying 'overt and covert translations, non-translation, foreignising or domestication strategies, and pragmatic adaptations such as explicitation and implication, additions and omission, simplification, and so on' (Koskinen, 2012: 80). Indeed, Robinson's history of 'centrifugal' moments in 1980s and 1990s translation theory (Robinson, 1997) offers lineages for each of these conceptual pairings, while underlining the human element of the act of translating itself: translating is not just a textual/literary process between source and target, but an ethical and cultural one that draws upon the person of the translator, pushing them to find a third, separate space beyond the assumed binarisms of the field. As he writes, 'What can we do about these phantoms that continue to dominate our debates? How can we poke fun at them, parody them, say NOT! to them, thumb our noses (and whatever's in front of our noses) at them – and begin, gradually, to work past them?' (Robinson, 1997: 131).

It is this orthogonal relationship – the emergence of the translator in relation to, and even as a product of, the effort to translate between texts – that is of interest to this chapter's purpose of furthering the pedagogical potential of linguistic landscape through translation. As Cronin and Simon (2014) note, this potential can be seen in the material logic of language contact in (most often) urban space. Drawing upon Pratt's (1992) notion of the *contact zone*, they remark that the 'border logics' of disparate groups coming into contact in closed spaces are expressed through language; the mutual understandings (or lack thereof), conflicts, and negotiated coexistences among people make language visible as a primary instrument of identity and difference, and it is the translator who occupies a unique place as cultural mediator (Cronin & Simon, 2014: 122). Of this role, Simon (2012: 6) writes:

> The translator emerges as a full participant in the stories of modernity that are enacted across urban space – modernity understood as an awareness of the plurality of codes, a thinking with and through translation, a continual testing of the limits of expression. Translators are flâneurs of a special sort, adding language as another layer of dissonance to the clash of histories and narratives on offer in the streets and passageways.

As the remainder of this chapter argues, the figure of the translator – and the task of translation – can profitably be read in at least three ways as they pertain to knowledge creation in and of the linguistic landscape (summarised in Table 3.1). At the meta-level, practitioners in the interdisciplinary field of LL may be able to engage in self-reflection and critique by confronting 'translations' of the field into neighbouring or mirroring fields, such as landscape studies. At the meso-level, focusing on strategies of translation in light of the social and political responsibilities of the vocation gives impetus to consider how LL research methodology and the methods of language pedagogy might mutually inform one another. And, at a more local level, a focus on the 'visibility' of the translator (Venuti, 1995) in their word-by-word navigation between two often incommensurate worlds of discourse urges us to consider translation as a form of public action and, potentially, as an activation of the public.

Table 3.1 Orientations and textual instigations from translation studies

Translation studies orientation/goal	Instigating text	Response/application
1. Translation as revealing 'faultlines'	Miller (1992), 'Translation as the double production of texts'	Cross-disciplinary meta-reflection: Nash (2016), 'Is linguistic landscape necessary?'
2. Translation as responsibility and response	Robinson (1997), 'What is translation?'	Pedagogical design: Transferring LL research methods to L2 pedagogy
3. Translation as public action and activation	Venuti (1995), 'The translator's invisibility'	Classroom application: 'Translate New Haven' civic/L2 educational project

3.3 Translation as Revealing Faultlines in the Primary Text

In the edited collection, *Text and Context: Cross-disciplinary Perspectives on Language Study* (Kramsch & McConnell-Ginet, 1992), the American literary critic Joseph Hillis Miller explores the word *Bild* in Goethe's *Die Wahlverwandtschaften*, a text that performs the difficulties of translation even as it is, in an abstract sense, about those difficulties. As Miller (1992) analyses a number of existing translations of this text, he remarks that one thing the translator discovers through what cannot be translated is 'the way any text in any language, both the "original" and the transla-tion, are idiomatic, timebound, marked by their places in history' (Miller, 1992: 125). As he argues, translators are confronted with the inevitability of loss of situated meaning but what they can gain is twofold:

> Translation produces two texts. As translators move from word to word and from sentence to sentence through the text they produce bit by bit replicas of the original in a different language. At the same time [...] an original text is also produced. A different translation produces a different original, by emphasizing different faultlines in the original, that is, by traducing the original in one way rather than another. The original is led out into the open where the translator is obliged to see hitherto hidden features. [...] To encounter them is to encounter what is, strictly speaking, untrans-latable in the original. (Miller, 1992: 124)

In this sense, a productive understanding of the nature of knowledge production and representation in linguistic landscape research may be invited by asking how it has been 'translated' (or how it could be) across disciplines, and then taking note of the disciplinary and methodological 'faultlines' within the field of LL studies that come to the surface in the process of such an inquiry. This is a form of reflexivity at the transdisciplinary level, an invitation and responsibility for LL researchers 'to exam-ine our own positionings, our own investments "in the game," so to speak – that is, how and why we come to subscribe to and appropriate certain ways of thinking, doing, and being, and how and why we become attached to certain positionings' (Byrd Clark, 2016: 11). In the LL literature, a call for such reflexive awareness and critique may be read in Spolsky's (2009) 'Prolegomena to a sociolinguistic theory of public signage', in which he asks of this 'awkwardly but attractively labelled' new area of study, 'Whatever we call it, is linguistic landscape a phenomenon calling for a theory, or simply a collection of somewhat disparate methodologies for studying the nature of public written signs?' (Spolsky, 2009: 25). The entire project of Jaworski and Thurlow's (2010) influential *Semiotic Landscapes* may be seen as another translational effort, as it critiqued the narrowness of a field that appeared (and often still appears) to identify itself with the appearance of isolable linguistic codes despite the richly multimodal semiotic fabric of the signed environment.

In light of the continued alignment of the preponderance of LL research with the theories and methods of language study (broadly speaking), one might find productive faultline-revealing insights to LL studies from spatially-oriented vantage points of disciplines such as cultural geography and landscape studies. This is precisely the opportunity presented by Nash's (2016) short critique, 'Is linguistic landscape necessary' – taken up here not for its thoroughness, but primarily from its disciplinary situatedness and assumed audience in the pages of the journal *Landscape Research*. In his six-page essay, Nash uses readings of Blommaert (2013) and Hélot *et al.* (2012) to give two basic critiques: first, that LL does not substantially advance the study of *landscape* per se, and second, that what passes for most LL research amounts basically to old sociolinguistic wine in new bottles. As he writes, 'The methodological and theoretical thrust of LL can be posed as a logical extension of any detailed consideration of elements of analysis necessitated under what can be considered traditional sociolinguistics' (Nash, 2016: 381).

He finds some exception in the first of two pieces he briefly reviews, Blommaert's *Ethnography, Superdiversity and Linguistic Landscapes: Chronicles of Complexity* (2013). This he reads as a positioning in 'classic and modern sociolinguistic research' that shows that 'modern scholarship must involve and concern new and dynamic interpretations of cultural and linguistic complexity and diversity as measured by, among other things, analysis of the LL' (Blommaert, 2013: 382). The benefit of Blommaert's work, according to Nash, is primarily in the way that a historically aware and textually ethnographic approach implicates the landscape as a changing, agential force more than synchronic analyses that would see it as mere backdrop for language. Nash praises Blommaert's work for what it offers to sociolinguistics, while still remarking that 'With a lack of an explicit foregrounding of the relevance of LL to landscape, it is unlikely hardcore landscape scholars will be satisfied' (Nash, 2016: 383). A similar charge is levelled upon the Hélot *et al.* (2012) volume, where he disappointedly remarks, again, that the frame of linguistic landscape is applied to 'already well established and directed' (Nash, 2016: 383) areas of sociolinguistic research and not to phenomena or effects of landscape.

From within the disciplinary foci of LL studies as it has come to be known in sociolinguistics and language policy and planning circles (to name a few), such critiques may appear trifling or even irrelevant: as popular glosses of the very term 'linguistic landscape' make abundantly clear, *language* (multilingualism, code-mixing, pragmatics and so on) is the focal object of analysis and is contextualised by the landscape – and not the other way around. And yet, critique's such as Nash's, or even Spolsky's, Jaworski and Thurlow's, Pennycook and Otsuji's (2015) – who argue in *Metrolingualism: Language and the City* that language use is inextricable from place-embedded 'spatial repertoires' – may be seen in Miller's (1992) sense as 'traducing the original in one way rather than another' (p. 124), bringing to the fore the 'faultline' of landscape in linguistic landscape studies. Such a translation might profitably leave scholars of LL with questions such as the following (while other translations would of course yield others):

- What is the responsibility of linguistic landscape research to *landscape*? To its modes, and practices of representation and interpretation? To avenues of inquiry informed or inflected by the concerns of landscape studies, geography, urban planning, architecture, visual studies or other fields?
- More locally, what are the affordances, limitations, and ideologies of the visual mode – and the medium of the digital image – for the representation and interpretation of data and phenomena of interest?
- At the meta-level (after having gone through translation exercises such as these), what is to be gained from 'translating' the concerns, frameworks, methods, and practices of one field to another?

3.4 Translation as Responsibility and Response

In his historical review of translation theory, Robinson (1997) notes that translation has gone from a concern simply with texts and whether, as St. Jerome said in the 4th century CE, one should translate 'word-for-word' or 'sense-for-sense', to the recognition of a more complex ecology of languages, people and sociocultural contexts of reception and production. Although there continue to be dedicated literalists (such as Walter Benjamin) who argue that the responsibility of the translator is 'just to the text', questions of where, how and by whom a translated text will be received have cast increasing light on the sociocultural situatedness of translation as discursive action. As Hermans (2009: 95) remarked in light of the growing relevance of cultural studies in the 1980s, 'translation, enmeshed as it is in social and ideological structures, cannot be thought of as a transparent, neutral or innocent philological activity.'

In an effort to 'traduce the original [text/field of linguistic landscape] one way' (Miller, 1992: 124) while translating across disciplines, I have experimented with applying methodological orientations from LL research to second language (L2) pedagogy (Malinowski, 2015, 2016). In the paragraphs that follow, I review the import of this effort as a translation of sorts not only from 'source text' (LL studies) to 'target text' (L2 teaching and learning), but in the reverse direction as well, considering (as in my reading of Nash, 2016 above) how linguistic landscape research might be pushed in productive directions by adopting the stance of language learners and teachers.

In fact, a significant and growing body of literature on language learning in and with the linguistic landscape has already begun to bridge this gap. Studies include those that see the LL as an additional source of input for second language acquisition with contextualised, authentic texts (Cenoz & Gorter, 2008; Sayer, 2009), to those that highlight the potential of the LL to foster students' critical sociopolitical awareness (Rowland, 2012; Shohamy & Waksman, 2009), to those that adopt a multiliteracies approach to see youth rewriting their collective and individual identities in place (Burwell & Lenters, 2015; Dagenais *et al.*, 2009). While some learning projects treat the urban landscape of signs more or less as a convenient backdrop of authentic and contextualised materials, others seek to actively incorporate thematic and theoretical concerns of LL research, instances of the kind of traffic in meaning across disciplines argued for in this chapter. As Burwell and Lenters (2015: 5) argue, 'integrating linguistic landscape research with multiliteracies pedagogy creates opportunities for students to learn about – and through – multimodality, multilingualism, production and critique.'

In my own work spanning LL research, L2 teaching and language teacher training and, many years before, as a language learner myself, the face-to-face confrontation with the visible and audible languages of the public sphere has been first and foremost an *educational* one. The LL presents a wealth of often hidden and sometimes irreconcilable differences in intent and meaning that must be actively queried and negotiated if they are to be understood in relation to one another; as well, the interpretation of voices in dialogue through the landscape in a particular place and time requires not just a nuanced reading on the part of a supposedly neutral observer, but may be said to demand participation by virtue of (at very least) the viewer's embodied and emplaced subjectivity.

A growing demand in the field of L2 teaching and learning to make good on these generalisations is clear: since 1996, the American Council on the Teaching of Foreign Languages in the USA has identified as one of its five National Standards a 'Communities' Standard, by which 'students [should] use the language both within and beyond the school setting' (ACTFL, 2006: 4). Meanwhile, language and literacy instructors following a pedagogy of multiliteracies (New London Group, 1996) have for decades wrestled with how to incorporate spatial and visual design elements into their synthetic, critical and creative approaches that see linguistic meaning as only one facet of the multimodal whole of human semiosis.

In the view taken in this chapter, the 'translation' of LL methods to the site of L2 learning offers a powerful opportunity to fulfil this mandate. In particular, the so-called qualitative turn in LL studies (Blackwood, 2015; Milani, 2013) has foregrounded processes of textual interpretation and on-site, interpersonal communication (interviews, walking tours and so on) that are well adapted to scenarios of applied language learning. As a tangible illustration of this borrowing of research methods for the purposes of language pedagogy, I have drawn from the work of Nira Trumper-Hecht (2010), who asserted the need for a multilayered spatial approach to understanding discourse in the LL that would not overlook local inhabitants' (or, as she put it, 'walkers'') readings of place (see Malinowski, 2016: 105–106). What resulted was a map of teaching and activity strategies that sought to ground L2 learners' understandings of discourse in place (cf. Scollon & Scollon, 2003) in three distinct, yet overlapping, kinds of spatial knowledge: 'perceived space', 'conceived space' and 'lived space' (cf. Lefebvre, 1991; Trumper-Hecht, 2010). Visualised as a three-bladed wind turbine to evoke both the division of a two-dimensional space into three equal parts and the electric power/L2 knowledge-generating action of the rotating blades, this map appears as Figure 3.1.

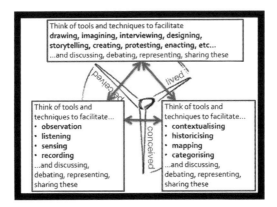

Figure 3.1 Illustration of L2 learning ideas in three separate spaces of knowledge (perceived, conceived, lived) based on Trumper-Hecht's (2010) adaptation of concepts from Lefebvre (1991)

In Trumper-Hecht's estimation (2010), LL research up to the time of her chapter had privileged official, governmental or other top-down knowledge about language use in signs ('conceived spaces'), as well as the plainly visible and audible 'perceived spaces' to the eye and ear of the LL researcher. What it had largely overlooked, however, was the 'lived spaces' of local inhabitants – the understandings of the significance of the appearance of Arabic, Hebrew or English on this sign or that, for instance, in ways that might well diverge from the top-down (conceived) or research-er's (perceived) interpretations. Only by taking all three into account together, she asserted, could a more accurate and *ethical* understanding of the LL be reached.

This is the premise of the translation of methods to L2 learning in the LL as well: while language students could read textbook histories of a place, for instance, and then observe, listen and otherwise document the LL of a given place with their own senses and recording devices for applied 'fieldwork' ('perceived space' activities), they would *also* need to attend to the sensory, artistic and interpretive meanings of others through such techniques as collaborative storytelling, artistic creation and interview-ing ('lived space' activities; see Figure 3.1) – all potentially rich language learning activities in their own right.

As in Trumper-Hecht's study and in other qualitatively oriented LL studies of the past several years (Blommaert, 2013; Curtin, 2014; Lou, 2016; Stroud & Mpendukana, 2010; Waksman & Shohamy, 2015), this assemblage, or juxtaposition, of methods in the service of a single inquiry is designed to answer new sorts of questions. As is illustrated in Figure 3.2, language teaching tools and techniques belonging to each space call for learners to engage linguistically and subjectively with the people and places of the LL in qualitatively different ways: when identifying demographic boundaries in one's neighbourhood or city, for example, one may not have to visit a neighbourhood or talk to its residents in order to read maps, census data or news articles mentioning government-recognised boundaries. Students on a walking tour taking photos and written notes, looking up unknown words in signs and document-ing their observations may check with peers to verify the accuracy of their findings.

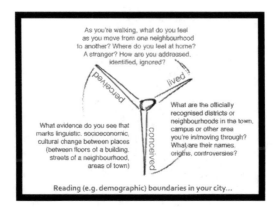

Figure 3.2 Sample language learning activity (reading boundaries in one's city) with guiding questions for each of the three knowledge spaces translated from Trumper-Hecht (2010)

Yet 'lived space' prompts such as this, asking students to attune themselves to their subjective responses to the place – and to those of its workers, residents, and 'walkers' – prompt them to use language in creative and potentially idiosyncratic ways that may open up new avenues of knowledge and expression in language classrooms, even as they may prove challenging to assess or test with standardised instruments.

Determining the effectiveness and particular applications of this particular translation from LL research to L2 pedagogy – and its aptness for the discursive communities in which it finds itself – is of course quite different from conducting the exercise of translation itself. The proposed framework would certainly have to be re-evaluated and re-tempered to suit the specific demands of each setting; indeed, in terms of learning outcomes, such a model might well prove to be indistinguishable from other frameworks. Yet these are concerns for another time and place. Here, the *process* of this translation is designed to focus attention beyond the source and target 'texts' (LL methods and L2 teaching, respectively) to the nature of their relationality – how the kinds of world-knowing called for by Trumper-Hecht (2010) and language educators setting out to 'teach the languages of the city' may speak to each other and give researchers and teachers pause to reflect upon their tasks. In such a calculation, one persistent 'faultline' to emerge from processes of translation must be the dispositions, commitments and actions of translators themselves in (and as) the landscape. In particular, drawing parallels between the (wondering, struggling, mistaken, correcting, reflecting, growing) person of the language learner and the often-invisible LL researcher may be helpful, as both do not simply read 'what's there' but actively produce, reproduce and transform the LL through their own representational practices.

3.5 Translation as Public Action and Activation

'Visibility' and 'invisibility' are the terms used by the American scholar in TS, Lawrence Venuti (1995), in his book *The Translator's Invisibility*, to describe the place of the translator in the translated text. The overwhelming pressure in the US translation market and professional practice, according to Venuti, is to 'domesticate' foreign texts, to make them read 'fluently' in translation, without 'linguistic or stylistic peculiarities' (p. 20) and reflecting the dominant sociodiscursive conventions of the target reader. In opposition to this expectation that the foreignness of the text and the translator her/himself should disappear, Venuti argues for an ethical and cultural imperative to *foreignise*: to engage in dialogue and dialogical self-transformation by not submitting to normative modes of expression and linguistic life, and to oppose normative economic and political pressures. As he writes, 'A translated text should be the site where a different culture emerges, where a reader gets a glimpse of a cultural other' (Venuti, 1995: 306).

Venuti regards the languaging activity of translation as moving in (at least) two directions at once. First, it seeks to foreignise or defamiliarise translations in the face of normative social, economic and political pressures, in light of the contention that translation is itself a site of discursive struggle and even conflict between vastly unequal powers. At the same time, Venuti asserts that the translator's resistance to normativity through tactics of 'foreignisation' works by making his or her own subjectivity part of the text, by exposing the site of struggle, that is, the mechanics of the text – the choice to insert a 'non-fluent' grammatical construction, use 'unconventional' punctuation, typographic or stylistic conventions and so on – and that this is a process of subjectivation, of social and linguistic becoming that is enacted by taking a stance.

In LL research, we see great curiosity and analytical focus on what could be termed the translational 'disfluencies' of signage in public spaces – languages that appear to be out of place where they are posted, or missing where they should be; bilingual signs in which messages in one language diverge from or even contradict those of the other; word choice or spelling that seems to some observers to be mistaken. As Koskinen (2012: 74) asserts, careful attention to such 'translational effects' in publicly visible signage helps to illuminate 'issues of authorship, audiences, and community and their connections with "elsewhere"'. The contention of the previous section of this chapter is that such 'disfluencies' can and should be approached from a pedagogical standpoint not only as valuable sources of information about differences between language and worldview, but as rich learning opportunities unto themselves. In fact, in the field of L2 teaching and learning, translation is regaining attention precisely for this reason, as it 'illuminates the nature of language per se as well as pointing to specific contrasts between the students' L1 [native language] and the target L2' (Godwin-Jones, 2015: 14). Increasingly, it is seen as a vital activity with numerous approaches and uncertain outcomes, as Cook (2010: xix) writes

> Translation, of its nature, spills over into a host of neighbouring activities and uses of language. This is not surprising. Translation is a living, moving activity, not a dead one to be pinned down in a museum. It is this dynamism which can make it so interesting and so stimulating, not only to linguists and translators, but to teachers and students too.

As an experiment in LL translation as pedagogy, I have recently begun a collaboration with a small group of language teachers and community stakeholders in the small north-eastern US city where my institution is located. Provisionally titled 'Translate New Haven,' the project seeks to create public resources to visualise a linguistic cityscape that reflects some of the 60 or more languages actually spoken in the city, while serving as a canvas for language students to develop translingual, transcultural competences (MLA, 2007) for positioning themselves with respect to these languages as community languages.

At the classroom level, teams of students are told that they are commissioned by the city government to enrich the town's multilingual identity and visible identity through translation of existing English signage, and creation of new Spanish, Italian, Arabic and other signs. Students must take into account the demographics, community histories and local identities in the area, while debating the linguistic, demographic and cultural significance of various translations for the specific places where they wish to install new signs. At all stages, maximal participation is designed with and solicited from community members; in addition to small face-to-face focus group meetings, this involves public posting of translation options and proposals for public comments and voting in an online forum. Final translations are to be prepared for submission to the city and produced as actual material signs (as of the writing of this chapter, city offices have expressed interest in prototyping, producing and installing a limited number of bilingual signs). All signs and translation options are also included for public display in a virtual map exhibit.

One hoped for outcome of LL translations through this project is the instigation of public discussion about the significance of a visibly multilingual (or noticeably monolingual) cityscape, and the larger issue of the role of languages in public life. Indeed, seeing one's city in a different language may well be an extreme example of the *foreignising* effect that Venuti advocates for in translated texts (see Figure 3.3).

However, just as the simplicity of the two-word proper (business) name translation depicted in Figure 3.3 conceals the several-person, multistage trial-and-error process that produced it, the deeper intent of the Translate New Haven project is to expose, develop, and reflect upon translation as a multitude of processes laden with deep personal, political, and communal significance. One of the first trainings that student participants in the project undergo is the documentation and analysis of the multilingual LL as it currently exists in their city; a schematic representation of a sample text and discussion prompts appears as Figure 3.4.

Of course, students tasked with translating 'No Loitering' from English to Spanish might be tempted to turn to dictionaries or online translation tools. The most common of these, Google Translate (queried in November, 2016), gives 'Sin Merodear' as the translation, however. What are students to make of the difference between the dictionary translation and the translation as it exists in front of them on the street? How should they, and other emerging speakers of Spanish, feel that, in English, the sign prohibits an activity ('loitering'), while in Spanish it prohibits a class of people ('vagabundos')? These are but a few of the questions that may have few ready answers but that, it is hoped, the very asking of which may contribute to learners' *visibility* as translators and self-reflexive development as language users. A full report on outcomes and future potential for learning-through-translation in the LL to act in public consciousness and space is forthcoming after the project runs its course in Spring, 2017.

Figure 3.3 Citizen's Bank on Church Street, New Haven, Connecticut, rendered in Chinese as '市民銀行' with a left-right slider tool allowing the viewer to seamlessly show the scene in English and/or Chinese

Figure 3.4 'Police Take Notice' sign near automated teller machine at a bank in New Haven, Connecticut

3.6 Conclusion

As an experiment in thinking between research and pedagogical design, this study argues that translation holds particular promise, both as an approach for language learning and teaching in the LL and, more broadly, as a figure or metaphor through which LL researchers-as-practitioners understand and position ourselves, and our own work, in the field. In this sense, translation is seen not as an 'endpoint' or one-way traversal as a target-language text is produced from an original, but as an '*andpoint*', eliciting new interpretations of the original text and new understandings of sign readers, sign writers and the world they inhabit. As such, the chapter makes the case that representations of the LL cannot be avoided – nor should they. Rather, by more intentional engagement in active processes of deconstruction, comparison, debate, imagination and – crucially – purposive re-making of signs, the contingency and along-the-way-ness of representations may come to the fore, allowing linguistic landscapers to better contextualise our data and mobilise our analyses.

References

ACTFL (American Council on the Teaching of Foreign Languages) (2006) Standards for foreign language learning: Preparing for the 21st Century: Executive Summary. Hastings-on-Hudson: ACTFL (American Council on the Teaching of Foreign Languages).

Backhaus, P. (2007) *Linguistic Landscapes: A Comparative Study of Urban Multilingualism in Tokyo.* Clevedon: Multilingual Matters.

Blackwood, R. (2015) LL explorations and methodological challenges: Analysing France's regional languages. *Linguistic Landscape* 1, 38–53.

Blommaert, J. (2013) *Ethnography, Superdiversity and Linguistic Landscapes: Chronicles of Complexity.* Bristol: Multilingual Matters.

Burwell, C. and Lenters, K. (2015) Word on the street: Investigating linguistic landscapes with urban Canadian youth. *Pedagogies: An International Journal* 10, 201–221.

Byrd Clark, J.S. (2016) Introduction to the special issue. *L2 Journal* 8, 3–19.

Cenoz, J. and Gorter, D. (2008) The linguistic landscape as an additional source of input in second language acquisition. *International Review of Applied Linguistics in Language Teaching* 46, 267–287.

Cook, G. (2010) *Translation in Language Teaching: An Argument for Reassessment.* Oxford: Oxford University Press.

Cronin, M. and Simon, S. (2014) Introduction: The city as translation zone. *Translation Studies* 7, 119–132.

Curtin, M.L. (2014) Mapping cosmopolitanisms in Taipei: Toward a theorisation of cosmopolitanism in linguistic landscape research. *International Journal of the Sociology of Language*, 153–177.

Dagenais, D., Moore, D., Sabatier, C., Lamarre, P. and Armand, F. (2009) Linguistic landscape and language awareness. In E. Shohamy and D. Gorter (eds) *Linguistic Landscape: Expanding the Scenery* (pp. 253–269). New York: Routledge.

Godwin-Jones, R. (2015) Emerging technologies: Contributing, creating, curating: Digital literacies for language learners. *Language Learning & Technology* 19, 8–20.

Gorter, D. (2013) Linguistic landscapes in a multilingual world. *Annual Review of Applied Linguistics* 33, 190–212.

Hélot, C., Barni, M., Janssens, R. and Bagna, C. (eds) (2012) *Linguistic Landscapes, Multilingualism and Social Change.* Frankfurt am Main: Peter Lang.

Hermans, T. (2009) Translation, ethics, politics. In J. Munday (ed.) *The Routledge Companion to Translation Studies* (pp. 93–105). London: Routledge.

Jaworski, A. and Thurlow, C. (eds) (2010) *Semiotic Landscapes: Language, Image, Space.* London: Continuum.

Koskinen, K. (2012) Linguistic landscape as a translational space: The case of Hervanta, Tampere. In J. Vuolteenaho, L. Ameel, A. Newby and M. Scott (eds) *Language, Space and Power: Urban Entanglements* (pp. 73–92). Helsinki: Helsinki Collegium for Advanced Studies.

Kramsch, C. and McConnell-Ginet (1992) *Text and Context: Cross-disciplinary Perspectives on Language Study.* Boston: Houghton Mifflin.

Landry, R. and Bourhis, R.Y. (1997) Linguistic landscape and ethnolinguistic vitality. *Journal of Language and Social Psychology* 16, 23–49.

Lefebvre, H. (1991) *The Production of Space*. Oxford: Blackwell.

Lou, J.J. (2016) *The Linguistic Landscape of Chinatown: A Sociolinguistic Ethnography*. Bristol: Multilingual Matters.

Malinowski, D. (2015) Opening spaces of learning in the linguistic landscape. *Linguistic Landscape: An International Journal* 1, 95–113.

Malinowski, D. (2016) Localizing the transdisciplinary in practice: A teaching account of a prototype undergraduate seminar on linguistic landscape. *L2 Journal* 8, 100–117.

Milani, T.M. (2013) Whither linguistic landscapes? The sexed facets of ordinary signs. *Tilburg Papers in Culture Studies* 53, 1–34.

Miller, J.H. (1992) Translation as the double production of texts. In C. Kramsch and S. McConnell-Ginet (eds) *Text and Context: Cross-Disciplinary Perspectives on Language Study* (pp. 124–134). Lexington: DC Heath & Co.

MLA (Modern Language Association; Ad Hoc Committee on Foreign Languages) (2007) *Foreign Languages and Higher Education: New Structures for a Changed World*. New York: Modern Language Association.

Nash, J. (2016) Is linguistic landscape necessary? *Landscape Research* 41, 380–384.

New London Group (1996) A pedagogy of multiliteracies: Designing social futures. *Harvard Educational Review* 66 (1), 60–92.

Pennycook, A. and Otsuji, E. (2015) *Metrolingualism: Language in the City*. New York: Routledge.

Pratt, M.L. (1992) *Imperial Eyes: Travel Writing and Transculturation*. London: Routledge.

Reh, M. (2004) Multilingual writing: A reader-oriented typology – with examples from Lira municipality (Uganda). *International Journal of the Sociology of Language* 170, 1–41.

Robinson, D. (1997) *What is Translation? Centrifugal Theories, Critical Interventions*. Kent: Kent State University Press.

Rowland, L. (2012) The pedagogical benefits of a linguistic landscape project in Japan. *International Journal of Bilingual Education and Bilingualism* 16, 494–505.

Sayer, P. (2009) Using the linguistic landscape as a pedagogical resource. *ELT Journal* 64, 143–154.

Scollon, R. and Scollon, S. (2003) *Discourses in Place: Language in the Material World*. London: Routledge.

Shohamy, E. and Waksman, S. (2009) Linguistic landscape as an ecological arena: Modalities, meanings, negotiations, education. In E. Shohamy and D. Gorter (eds) *Linguistic Landscape: Expanding the Scenery* (pp. 313–330). New York: Routledge.

Simon, S. (2012) *Cities in Translation: Intersections of Language and Memory. New Perspectives in Translation Studies*. New York: Routledge.

Spolsky, B. (2009) Prolegomena to a sociolinguistic theory of public signage. In E. Shohamy and D. Gorter (eds) *Linguistic Landscape: Expanding the Scenery* (pp. 25–39). New York: Routledge.

Spolsky, B. and Cooper, R.L. (1991) *The Languages of Jerusalem*. Oxford: Oxford University.

Stroud, C. and Mpendukana, S. (2010) Multilingual signage: A multimodal approach to discourses of consumption in a South African township. *Social Semiotics* 20, 469–493.

Trumper-Hecht, N. (2010) Linguistic landscape in mixed cities in Israel from the perspective of 'walkers': The case of Arabic. In E. Shohamy, E. Ben-Rafael and M. Barni (eds) *Linguistic Landscape in the City* (pp. 235–251). Bristol: Multilingual Matters.

Venuti, L. (1995) *The Invisibility of the Translator: A History of Translation*. London: Routledge.

Waksman, S. and Shohamy, E. (2015) Linguistic landscape of social protests: Moving from 'open' to 'institutional' spaces. In R. Blackwood, E. Lanza and H. Woldemariam (eds) *Negotiating and Contesting Identities in Linguistic Landscapes* (pp. 85–98). New York: Bloomsbury.

Part 2

Broadening the Field of Semiotic Landscapes: Semiotic Assemblages, Multimodality and Contemporary Urban Spaces

4 Linguistic Landscapes and Semiotic Assemblages

Alastair Pennycook

Once studies of linguistic landscapes start to open up to a broad set of semiotic possibilities, the issue of how much can be included and how different elements fit together poses a number of theoretical and empirical questions. This chapter explores the implications of studies of the linguistic landscape that move beyond the logocentric approaches of early work to engage instead with space, place, bodies, languages and senses. Not only do we need to add multisensorial relations to multilingual and multimodal analysis, but we also need to be able to account for the ways languages, people, objects and places come together in temporary, ad hoc assemblages. Developing the ideas of *spatial repertoires* and *semiotic assemblages*, and looking at data from a Bangladeshi corner shop, this chapter suggests that we cannot merely add more semiotic items to our linguistic landscape inventories, but need instead to seek out a way of grasping the relationships among different ways of meaning.

4.1 Introduction

Research in linguistic landscapes faces two obvious questions: the status of the term *linguistic* and the scope of the term *landscape*. Once the field has started to open up to a broad set of semiotic possibilities, the question of what is encompassed by the idea of a linguistic landscape, and how the different elements of a landscape may fit together, raise a number of questions that need exploration, if not resolution. In general, studies of the linguistic landscape focus on 'the presence, representation, meanings and interpretation of languages displayed in public places' (Shohamy & Ben Rafael, 2015: 1). As the field has developed, however, it has moved beyond the logocentric focus of early work that took text, signs and language identification as central to the research. While much linguistic landscape research still aims to quantify the representation of languages in public space, for some a 'critical turn' in linguistic landscape studies has shed new light on contexts of multilingualism by going beyond quantitative overviews of signs in the landscape to account in qualitative terms for the ways in which signs are read and interpreted (Barni & Bagna, 2015).

Recent work has also sought to take on board implications from the idea of *translanguaging* by questioning a focus on enumerable and separable languages in favour of an understanding that, on the one hand 'communication transcends individual languages' – that is to say we use repertoires of linguistic resources without necessary recourse to the notions of languages – and on the other hand, 'communication transcends words and involves diverse semiotic resources and ecological affordances' (Canagarajah, 2013: 6) – that is to say we draw on a wide set of possible resources to achieve communication. Gorter and Cenoz (2015: 63) have sought to incorporate translingual implications into their work, arguing for 'a holistic view that goes beyond the analysis of individual signs as monolingual or multilingual' that can make it 'possible to propose that the linguistic landscape itself is a multilingual and multimodal repertoire, which is used as a communication tool to appeal to passers-by' (Gorter & Cenoz, 2015: 71).

Other work has pushed this further by moving towards greater contextual (ethnographic) and historical understandings of texts in the landscape; who put them there, how they are interpreted, and what role they play in relation to space, migration and mobility (Blommaert, 2013). Questions of mobility – not only of those who put up or read signs but also of the signs themselves – have further pushed the boundaries of what constitutes a landscape. Work on graffiti, for example, has pointed to the importance of its location either near or on forms of transport (Pennycook, 2009) so that studies of graffiti on trains as they move through underground networks suggest that semiosis 'is inseparable from mobility' (Karlander, 2018: 41). Other studies of graffiti have also pointed to the importance of the relation between offline and online environments (Blommaert, 2016b; Pennycook, 2010a), thus further complicating what counts as 'linguistic' ('writing' from a graffiti point of view includes all sorts of image and text) and 'landscape' (from a moving train to an online forum). Another site of mobility is the body, of particular interest in relation to tattoos, which make central 'the body (the material stuff of identity and affect) as a corporeal linguistic landscape, or skinscape, a collection of *inscriptions in place*' (Peck & Stroud, 2015: 134). Hiramoto's (2015: 120) study of Japanese tattoos in Hawaii likewise draws attention not only to the ways these 'inked identities' draw on local identifications of Japaneseness, but also to the ways in which their movement through the social space has important semiotic ramifications. This focus on the body, furthermore, starts to challenge another given of linguistic landscape research, the 'public space,' since bodies are mobile, move in and out of public and private spaces, and can display or reveal their inked semiotics. The focus on the body 'through spaces, its discursive and material (inter)actions with other texts and material artefacts' suggests the need 'to investigate the material and discursive processes through which individuals and groups contest the very contours of what counts as public' (Kitis & Milani, 2015: 269).

The relations between bodies, semiotics and landscapes is also unsettled by studies of sensescapes (Pennycook & Otsuji, 2015b), suggesting that smell needs to be incorporated into our understanding of semiotic landscapes. Smell does a lot of important semiotic work, particularly in its interpellative and associational capacities: It evokes memories, people, activities and places. These may also have linguistic correlates – people, language and places are closely intertwined – but the mobility of such resources suggests the need for caution here. Of greater interest are the complexity of relations among the diversity of language and everyday activities (buying, eating, fishing, growing, selling and cooking) and the larger linguistic and sensory-scapes within geopolitical, economic and historical settings. Smells are an important part of how we make sense of our surroundings; how we interpret, associate and invoke relations of culture and taste, as well as assumptions about gender, class, background and development.

From a focus on signs in public spaces, where both were taken to be fairly obvious 'givens' (despite debates about the unit of analysis, for many studies what constituted a sign and the public space were seen as easily identifiable entities), and a focus on languages, where these were assumed to be clear and enumerable entities, new directions in linguistic landscape research have suggested that none of these can be taken for granted. From Shohamy's (2015) point of view, these developments in linguistic landscape studies greatly expand what is understood under the umbrella of the 'linguistic', including 'images, photos, sounds (soundscapes), movements, music, smells (smellscapes), graffiti, clothes, food, buildings, history, as well as people who are immersed and absorbed in spaces by interacting with LL in different ways' (Shohamy, 2015: 153–154). Yet these rapid developments not only raise concerns about more traditional approaches to linguistic landscapes (quantifying the presence of languages in public space), but also pose questions about the relations among different kinds of semiotic resources: how do we start to account for the relations among linguistic resources (things we might identify as words or different scripts, for example), clothes, objects, bodies, buildings, touch, smells and so on?

In this chapter, I want to explore the implications of these studies of the linguistic landscape that move beyond the logocentric approaches of early work – engaging instead with space, place, bodies, languages, and senses – since they pose important questions for this emerging field: how should we understand the role of language (as text or discourse) in relation to this broader semiotic field (or do we consider all this to be language)? How can we develop an understanding of the relationship between different types of semiosis (signs, architecture and touch, for example)? How do we conceive of the intersectional relationships among, say, gender, bodies, tattoos and place? Developing the idea of spatial repertoires and assemblages, and looking at data from a Bangladeshi corner shop, this chapter suggests that we cannot merely add more semiotic items to our linguistic landscape inventories, but need instead to seek out a way of grasping the relationships among different ways of meaning.

4.2 Distributed Language, Spatial Repertoires and Assemblages

The idea of distributed language helps open up the discussion here, since it challenges the idea of languages as internalised systems or individual competence, and argues instead for an understanding of language as embodied, embedded and distributed across people, places and time. This focus emerged, in Cowley's (2012) account, by linking integrational linguistics (Harris, 1998, 2009) with distributed cognition (Hutchins, 1995). From this perspective, 'far from being a synchronic "system", language is a mode of organization that functions by linking people with each other, external resources and cultural traditions' (Cowley, 2012: 2). The central goal of integrational linguistics has been to reject the *segregational* view of language, by which it is assumed that communication is a process of choosing among a prede-termined set of options from a linguistic system that operates independently from other communicative modes. Integrational linguistics embraces the *radical indeter-minacy* of the sign by which communication is a set of open-ended opportunities (Harris, 1996). The notion of distributed cognition goes beyond the idea of extended mind (Clark, 2008) by operating not only on a spatial scale larger than the individ-ual, but by expanding such insights beyond the cognitive affordances in immediate time and space towards broader cognitive ecosystems.

Integrational linguists have been arguing for something akin to a distributed view of language for some time, placing communication (broadly understood) at the core and suggesting languages are not necessarily central to this process. Linguistics, Harris (1990: 45) pointed out long ago, 'does not need to postulate the existence of languages as part of its theoretical apparatus.' This urges us to rethink what is at stake when we look at language since it is unclear whether 'the concept of "a lan-guage", as defined by orthodox modern linguistics, corresponds to any determinate or determinable object of analysis at all, whether social or individual, whether insti-tutional or psychological' (Harris, 1990: 45). Distributed cognition, meanwhile, is not a kind of cognition, moving out from an assumed centre (as arguably is the case with the idea of extended mind), but rather the condition of all cognition: 'Distributed cognition begins with the assumption that all instances of cognition can be seen as emerging from distributed processes' (Hutchins, 2014: 36).

The point here is not merely that language serves communicative purposes, that it happens in social spaces, but rather that language cannot be reduced to a notion of system, is bound up with real time activity, and plays a role in socially moulded cognitive and linguistic niches rather than individual cognition (Steffensen, 2012). The focus on language as system located in the mind in the body of single organisms masks the 'interdependency of voices, gestures and artefacts' (Cowley, 2012: 2), over-looks the centrality of activity and practice and 'excludes real time dynamics' (Cowley, 2012: 3). Like Scollon and Scollon's (2004: 89) notion of a *nexus of prac-tice*, as a 'semiotic ecosystem,' where 'historical trajectories of people, places, dis-course, ideas, and objects come together' (Scollon & Scollon, 2004: 159), the focus here is on how we can account for the accumulation of all these factors in any one moment. The shift away from a Cartesian view of a mind engaged in symbol process-ing involves an understanding that humans are metabolic before they are symbolic, that cognition is on the one hand embodied, embedded and enacted (it is far more than representational activity in the mind) and on the other hand extended, distrib-uted and situated (it involves the world outside the head) (Steffensen, 2012).

Thinking from this point of view becomes spatial: the conception of thought being locked away in a mind (in there) that is separate from a world (out there) (Latour, 1999) is challenged by framing language and cognition as distributed. We came to similar conclusions in a series of studies exploring the notion of repertoire (Dovchin *et al.*, 2015; Pennycook, 2018; Pennycook & Otsuji, 2014a, 2014b, 2015a; Sultana *et al.*, 2015). It became clear that to imagine that repertoires are somehow an internalised individual competence (Wardaugh, 1986) or can be found in a com-munity *reservoir* (Bernstein, 2000), is to overlook the dynamics of objects, places and linguistic resources. From this point of view, rather than being individual, biographical or something that people possess, repertoires are better considered as an emergent property deriving from the interactions between people, artefacts and space. Kell's (2015: 442) discussion of how 'things make people happen,' suggests that 'objects, in and of themselves, have consequences'. This is to take more seriously the idea that 'technological and natural materialities' might themselves be understood as 'actors alongside and within us' as 'vitalities, trajectories, and powers irreducible to the meanings, intentions, or symbolic values humans invest in them' (Bennett, 2010b: 47). Repertoires are the product of social spaces as semiotic resources, objects and space interact.

This notion of spatial repertoires pushes language outside the head, not merely as a social resource but also as a spatial and artefactual one. The implications for thinking about linguistic landscapes are evident, since this perspective renders the landscape not merely as a context in which we interact, but rather as part of an interactive whole that includes people, objects and space through a focus on 'how the composite ecology of human and nonhuman interactions in public space works on sociality and political orientation' (Amin, 2015: 239). From this point of view, there is a strong focus on both *practices* those repeated social and material acts that have gained sufficient stability over time to reproduce themselves – and on 'the vast spillage of *things*' which are given equal weight to other actors and become 'part of hybrid assemblages: concretions, settings and flows' (Thrift, 2007: 9). From this perspective 'the human is not approached as an autonomous agent, but is located within an extensive system of relations' (Ferrando, 2013: 32). Thrift (2007: 8) talks of a '*material schematism* in which the world is made up of all kinds of things brought in to relation with one another by many and various spaces through a continuous and largely involuntary process of encounter.'

Bennett (2010a: 6) is likewise interested in *thingpower*: 'the curious ability of inanimate things to animate, to act, to produce effects dramatic and subtle', and the ways these things come together in *assemblages*, a notion she develops from the work of Deleuze and Guattari (1987: 88), who focus on an 'assemblage of bodies, of actions and passions, an intermingling of bodies reacting to one another' as well as a 'collective assemblage of enunciation, of acts and statements of incorporeal transformations attributed to bodies' (Deleuze & Guattari, 1987: 88). Assemblages can be understood as 'ad hoc groupings of diverse elements, of vibrant materials of all sorts,' as 'living, throbbing confederations' (Bennett, 2010a: 23). Assemblages are 'temporary arrangements of many kinds of monads, actants, molecules, and other dynamic "dividuals" in an endless, non-hierarchical array of shifting associations of varying degrees of durability' (Appadurai, 2015: 221).

We need to understand 'the effects of relational interactions and assemblages, in various kinds of more than human networks entangled with one another, that may be messy and incoherent, spread across time and space' (Fenwick & Edwards, 2011: 712). With their 'uneven topographies' (Bennett, 2010a: 24) assemblages are not centrally governed by one material or event: 'The effects generated by an assemblage are, rather, emergent properties, emergent in that their ability to make something happen (a newly inflected materialism, a blackout, a hurricane, a war on terror) is distinct from the sum of the vital force of each materiality considered alone' (Bennett, 2010a: 24). Assemblages describe the way things are brought together and function in new ways, and provide a way of thinking about *distributive* agency' (Bennett, 2010a: 21), which can enable us to envisage how agency, cognition and language can all be understood as distributed beyond any supposed human centre.

4.3 Shop Assemblages

In order to show how notions of distribution, spatial repertoire and assemblage can help us regroup amid the dizzying array of semiotic possibilities presented by an expanded notion of linguistic landscapes, let us turn now to a particular example. The following excerpt (see also Otsuji & Pennycook, 2017) takes place around a freezer at the intersection between different people, food and artefacts, during our ethnographic observation at the Bangladeshi owned corner shop in Sydney.[1]

We were following a female customer of Bangladeshi background (FCB) who was shopping in Lakemba, a diverse suburb in southwest Sydney (only 32% of people living in the suburb were born in Australia) that is often identified as 'Lebanese', an identification that derives not only from its fairly substantial Lebanese population, but also from its prominent mosque and a sense of Lebanese being the default Arabic community in Sydney (18% of people living in Lakemba speak Arabic). Only around 5% of the Lebanese population in the suburb were born overseas – it is a place of longer term Lebanese settlement, which also contributed to this stronger sense of identification – with far more recent arrivals coming from Bangladesh (13%), Pakistan, Vietnam and India (each about 4%), China, Indonesia and Greece (around 3% each), followed by a range of other people from Fiji, Egypt, Burma, the Philippines, Iraq and so on. English is spoken as a first language by about 14% of the population, trailing Arabic (18%) and Bengali (16%), and followed by Urdu (7%), Greek and Vietnamese (5%), Indonesian (4%) and Cantonese (3.4%) (Lakemba, 2016).

As we have suggested elsewhere (Pennycook & Otsuji, 2015a), we do not put much store in such figures as a way of understanding urban multilingualism (metrolingualism), but they nonetheless give us one way of seeing how at any one point, an assemblage of people and things in this suburb will involve a diversity of linguistic, cultural and artefactual resources. Along the street running parallel to the station (shops typically gather round these busy suburban stations) is a shop sign announcing 'HUT BAZAR: fruits & mixed business – Bangladesh, India, Pakistani, Island, Lebanese, African & Asian grocery'. With varied local economies and businesses ranging from travel agents, internet cafés, fishmongers, butchers (halal), jewellery shops, spice shops and corner grocery shops, people, products, artefacts and languages are organised along various trajectories, the mosque and Islamic practices (halal food, prayer times, Arabic) being one salient combination. There are obviously more complex sets of linguistic, regional and migratory affiliations at play across the neighbourhood than simply understanding the area as being a Lebanese precinct.

In the example below, the shop owner (SO) is helping FCB to choose Rui fish (a Bangla term for a fresh water fish resembling carp) when the following interaction occurs between a customer (CU1) who had just entered the shop (followed by another customer, CU2, soon after) and the shop owner. After walking around checking products (he looked both lost and excited), CU1 turned around and spoke to the SO who was extracting Rui fish from the bottom of the freezer for FCB (who does not speak, but is spoken to, in this extract):

Excerpt 1: (SO: Shop owner; CU1 Customer; CU2 Customer)
English: plain, Bangla: *Italic*, Arabic: **bold**

1. SO: *Aa. ....shokto hoie gese* (the fish is stuck. Hard) [to FCB] [trying to dig out the fish packet from the freezer; considerable noise from the struggle with these packets of frozen fish].

Another customer enters

2. CU2: **Assalamualaikum** [greeting SO].
3. SO: **Alaikumassalam** [to the customer].
4. CU1: *Usse Usse*, Have you got *usse*? Like, what is it for English? What is it called?
5. SO: This one vegetable?
6. CU1: Yea, it's a sort of vegetables.
7. SO: *Usta?*
8. CU1: *Usta Usta.*
9. SO: Yea yea this one have.
10. CU1: *Amnar ase?* (do you have?)
11. SO: oh, Bangladeshi *vai* (Bangladeshi Bro)?
12. CU1: Aaa?
13. SO: ha.
14. CU1: You are from Bangladesh?
15. SO: yea.
16. CU1: oh... *Amake usta den* (can you give me some usta) [to shop assistant]

It is apparently CU1's first visit to the shop (and perhaps Lakemba) and he is evidently not familiar with the layout and products of the shop or with the area more generally (note the customary greeting – **Assalamualaikum**; **alaikumassalam** between CU2, a more regular customer, and the shop owner in lines 2 and 3). Perhaps because he was deeply immersed in checking the variety of South Asian products around the shop, CU1 did not appear to have recognised that SO and FCB were discussing Rui fish in Bangla, or that the products on display suggested the shop was owned by someone of Bangladeshi background. In line 4, when he asks for bitter melons, CU1 speaks in English and struggles to find an appropriate term for what he wants, even struggling too, it seems, for the word in Bangla: '*Usse Usse*'. This *usse usse* appears to be a version of *uche*, the colloquial variety of the term *usta*, a small variety of bitter melon. But SO quickly works out what is being asked for (the customer gestures with his hands), and asks if he is looking for '*Usta*' in line 7, affirmed by CU1 '*Usta, Usta*'. At this moment, as he notices that SO knows the term '*usta*' and that he does not therefore need to find an English equivalent, CU1 finally appears to register that SO speaks Bangla, and asks in Bangla if the shop has *usta* (*Amnar ase?*).

Moving beyond these observations about the various linguistic moves the participants make, how do we start to make sense of this interaction in terms of semiotic assemblages? The scope here is much broader than in traditional studies of linguistic landscapes, where the focus on languages and signs displayed in public places (Shohamy & Ben Rafael, 2015) would encourage an emphasis on what is perceived as the public space of the street, rather than the interior of the shop, and on the signs displaying identifiable languages (Bangla, English) outwards towards this public domain rather than the circulation of mobile linguistic and other semiotic resources within the shop. Here, by contrast, we have moved inside the shop and focused predominantly on spoken language (though the written language on goods and signs in the shops matters too) and all that surrounds it. Of importance to the analysis here are not only the linguistic resources available – the conversation in Bangla over the freezer centring around the frozen fish, the **Assalamualaikum** greeting, the confusion over the term for small bitter melon, the negotiation of code between English and Bangla – but also the conditions of possibility that enable this conversation: the material artefacts, the spatial layout, the people moving about.

Semiotic assemblages refer to the ways in which linguistic resources, everyday tasks and social space are intertwined. The various combinations of linguistic resources are of course an important part of the action here: the conversation over the freezer in Bangla as they try to prise the fish from the bottom: *shokto hoie gese* (the fish is stuck); the standard greetings among many Muslims: **Assalamualaikum**; **alaikumassalam**; the absence of such a greeting from the new customer and his mixture of Bangla terms and English (in many ways a default language for Sydney and among different communities, but not necessarily in a suburb such as Lakemba): *Usse Usse*, Have you got *usse*?; the negotiation between different forms of the term in Bangla so that they settle on one: *Usta? Usta Usta*; the continued attempt to establish whether English or Bangla might be their preferred code: Bangladeshi *vai?*; and the final move towards a satisfactory transaction in terms of identity, language and the buying and selling of bitter melon: *Amake usta den* (can you give me some *usta*).

These linguistic resources matter, but it is the way in which they are intertwined with the rest of the action, the dynamic relations between semiotic resources, activities, artefacts and space, which are of equal interest. Playing an equal part in this interaction are also the frozen Rui fish, whose obstinate refusal to be lifted easily from the freezer is drawing the attention of the shopkeeper and the female customer. These fish are also part of a much larger circuit of fish production and consumption: Indeed, as Sen (2016) notes, the fondness for riverine fish from the Ganga and Brahmaputra deltas unites people from the region across nationalities, ethnicities and religions. Such fish serve as *boundary objects* through their 'ability to mediate across geographies, environments, culinary traditions, and histories' (Sen, 2016: 71).

It is therefore very common to find various types of freshwater fish, either dried or frozen, and exported from Bangladesh or Myanmar, in Bangladeshi-run stores (in Sydney, Tokyo, Chicago or London).

The large freezers that contain these and other frozen products often take up a prominent place in the store (the freezer in this shop is in the middle) and thus become a significant factor in the organisation of space and interaction. In a context where frozen fish are an important item for customers, the freezer and the conversations around it, and the sounds of the fish being pulled out, and the attention of the female customer and the shop owner, become essential parts of the action that also affect how the new customer interacts with the store itself. Where dried fish are more prevalent, the sensory landscape of the shop changes – along with South Asian spices, dried fish give shops a very particular smellscape – and had this shop specialised more in dried rather than frozen fish, the linguistic choices of the new customer might also have changed.

Understanding the urban smellscape (Pennycook & Otsuji, 2015b) can be crucial for appreciating the role of different people, foods, restaurants and shops in any suburban mixture. While the linguistic landscape may interpellate us through its multilingual signage (Kramsch, 2014), it is also important to consider how spaces are sensorily organised in relation to broader social, linguistic and cultural practices. In the same way that we do not treat place as a flat surface or backdrop, we do not conceive smell as a background, wafting among other activities, but understand it as a resource for emplacement. Smells call to us, summoning associations with people, places, times and activities. Such associations are not simply between smell and object, or smell and place, or smell in the present and the past. Nor are they simply part of an individual life trajectory. Rather, smells open up a different terrain of semiosis, one that associates meaning with objects, people, affect and places in a different way.

Important, too, are the bitter melon (they were in boxes outside the shop, which the new customer did not see on his way in). Like the fish, these are also an important part of Bangladeshi cuisine, though their trajectory to shops such as this is a very different one. These vegetables (*kugua* [苦瓜] in Chinese; *korola*, *usta* or *uche* in Bangla, depending on both variety of melon and language) are used in a variety of different types of Asian cuisine and are generally grown in the market gardens that surround Sydney, which have their own complex cultural histories (Pennycook & Otsuji, 2015a). Eighty percent of market gardeners in the Sydney Basin are from non-English speaking backgrounds (James, 2008), including Chinese, Lebanese, Italian, Maltese, Vietnamese and Cambodian. These market gardens link along language, culture and culinary trading lines to markets, shops and restaurants. As local economies and tastes change, so too do these networks, so that bitter melons grown by Cantonese-speaking market gardeners may be sold both to the Chinese markets, shops and restaurants and to the Bangladeshi shop and restaurant owners.

An interaction over bitter melons in a Bangladeshi shop in Lakemba, therefore, also needs to be understood in relation to the market gardens of Sydney (Otsuji & Pennycook, 2017), and then, for example, to the history of Chinese migration to Australia, the changing economic roles of different generations of Chinese, the significance of different food items for different communities, the linguistic resources of different interactants as they negotiate products and prices, the history of interactions between these particular people, and their understandings of their own locatedness in terms of soil, vegetables and language. The appearance of these bitter melons in a Bangladeshi run store in a particular suburb of Sydney further suggests a need to understand not only the social, historical and economic conditions of their cultivation, but also their place within a trade network across Sydney and position within a local food economy in a different suburb. All these things and the meanings attached to them come together in the relations between artefacts (such as bitter melons), places (such as market gardens or fruit and vegetable shops) and people (such as buyers, sellers, cooks or producers). It is through the locatedness of these intersections that we can understand the shifting moments and assemblages of the city.

All of this accumulates at this moment in this shop: different people of different backgrounds assemble at particular moments. Bangladeshi shops attract people of Bangladeshi background, and the repeated experience of shopping in Bangladeshi grocery stores – an experience that involves sound, smell, touch, proprioception and vision – creates 'spatial memories and habitual practices that produce new forms of communal experiences for immigrants' (Sen, 2016: 71). But these shops also entice others of South Asian background or people looking for halal products, Asian spices, or, as another example from our data show, a customer of Fijian background looking for fish. These customers and shop owners come with particular sets of linguistic resources that may include English and Bangla, but also Hindi, Arabic and others.[2] The ways in which these linguistic resources are deployed depends very much on who is present, how the interaction unfolds and what activities they are engaged in (selling, asking, explaining, digging out frozen fish). Of significance, too, is the layout of the shop, with its shelves and fridges focusing attention in particular directions. The products themselves have their own trajectories, from imported frozen fish, to locally packed imported spices and regionally grown vegetables. At any moment a particular assemblage of people, linguistic resources, products and spatial organisation comes together to produce a particular set of interactions.

4.4 Conclusion: Assembling Semiotics

An understanding of *semiotic assemblages* presents an alternative way of thinking about linguistic landscapes that locates the linguistic within a wider set of semiotic relations and addresses the complexity of things that come together in the vibrant, changeable exchanges of everyday urban life. Asking the question 'Where is language?' – a question that may make little sense to the mainstream of language studies – Finnegan (2015) suggests that the 'cognitive language centred model of the nature and destiny of humanity' with its focus on language in the mind misses so much that matters, including not only many other cultural modes such as music, dance and drama, but also 'the gestural, pictorial, sculptural, sonic, tactile, bodily, affective and artefactual dimensions of human life' (Finnegan, 2015: 18). Linguistic landscape research potentially offers us an important way forward here, suggesting that multilingual and multimodal repertoires are in the landscape rather than the mind. Also useful here is a focus on translingual practices, which, as Canagarajah (2013) reminds us, emphasises both the use of repertoires of linguistic resources without necessary recourse to the notions of languages (that is to say we might still identify a resource as 'Tamil' without invoking the larger picture of Tamil as a discrete and bounded entity) and the use of a broad repertoire of semiotic resources to achieve communication. This expands the semiotic terrain (beyond language more narrowly construed) in relation to material surrounds and space, with an increased focus on place, objects and semiotics. It also draws attention to the importance of understanding language as a local practice (Pennycook, 2010b), emphasising place and sedimented action. To arrive at a better understanding of semiotic assemblages, it is important to move beyond the commonplace focus on multilingualism and multimodality to bring in the multisensorial nature of our worlds, the vibrancy of objects and the ways these come together in particular and momentary constellations. This is important not just to accomplish better and more complete urban ethnographies, but also to redress an historical imbalance that has placed language and cognition in the head, while relegating the body and the senses to the physical. Recent shifts to encompass an understanding of the body, senses and material artefacts have brought much greater attention to 'touches, sights, smells, movements, material artefacts' and 'shared experiences, dynamic interactions and bodily engagements' to go beyond the narrow story of cognition and language in the head (Finnegan, 2015: 19).

Although sociolinguistics has been better than its logocentric linguistic cousin in acknowledging various roles for the body – studies of non-verbal communication, for example – it has often been conceived as 'secondary to language rather than as the sine qua non of language' (Bucholz & Hall, 2016: 174). In their call for 'an embodied sociocultural linguistics' (Bucholz & Hall, 2016: 174) Bucholz and Hall argue not only for making more salient bodily aspects of communication commonly acknowledged but often peripheralised, such as voice ('the embodied heart of spoken language' (Bucholz & Hall, 2016: 178)) or style (where clothing, posture and attitude may do a lot of the work of enregisterment), but also for understanding how the body is discursively constructed, and how recent thinking has sought to understand how the body is 'imbricated in complex arrangements that include nonhuman as well as human participants, whether animals, epidemics, objects, or technologies' (Bucholz & Hall, 2016: 186). To understand language, cognition and agency as distributed allows us to see how they are produced in material webs of human and non-human assemblages. Looking at language in these terms helps us see that meaning – as *radically indeterminate* signs – emerges from interaction. Rather than considering linguistic repertoires as internalised individual competence or as the property of an imagined community, the notion of a semiotic assemblage expands the semiotic inventory and relocates repertoires in the dynamic relations among objects, places and linguistic resources, an emergent property deriving from the interactions between people, artefacts and space. This adds vast complexity to what was once in linguistic landscape research a more manageable semiotic inventory. Rather than looking at written signs in the public sphere, we now have bodies, buildings, tattoos, sounds, smells, objects, space and much more.

The notion of *assemblages* allows for an understanding of how different trajectories of people, semiotic resources and objects meet at particular moments and places. To this understanding of the vibrancy of matter, the importance of things (bitter melon, Rui fish) and the significance of place as the geographical context for the mediation of physical, social and economic processes, we can then reintroduce our interest in the key ingredient of linguistic resources. Significant for the vitality of many assemblages is the role of language as mediation since 'materiality and mediation are best treated as mutual conditions of possibility and as effects of each other' (Appadurai, 2015: 233). The interest here is not so much in the identification of an assemblage (to give a name to a particular assemblage), but in an understanding of the momentary material and semiotic resources that intersect at a given place and time. Akin to Li Wei's (2011: 1224) *moment analysis*, which shifts the focus away from the search for regularity and patterns and looks instead at 'spontaneous, impromptu, and momentary actions and performances', the focus here is not so much on establishing patterns of linguistic use, but on understanding *practices in place*, those sedimented or momentary language practices in particular places at particular times.

One might argue that this focus on 'moments of action rather than on abstractable structures such as cultures and languages' (Scollon & Scollon, 2007: 620), on 'spontaneous, impromptu, and momentary actions and performances' (Li Wei, 2011: 1224) and on 'temporary arrangements... of varying degrees of durability' (Appadurai, 2015: 221), suggests the downside of an attempt to deal with complexity: it is impossible to look at such a broad array of semiotic happenings over time so we are left only with quick snapshots of the here and now. One might also argue that this focus away from regularity and patterns is an abrogation of a researcher's responsibility to supply a set of more generalisable principles and to say more than just 'look at this!'. Yet assemblages deal with far more than a superficial here and now, bringing in the history and mobility of people and objects, the vibrancy of material, the conditions of possibility of spatial repertoires. Once we come to realise that the chimerical assumptions of stability and system embedded in normative sociolinguistics were imagined rather than real, and that the onus on sociolinguistic work has to be on diverse understandings of complexity (Blommaert, 2016a), then it becomes clear that if we want to get at sociolinguistic realities, we need to focus on ad hoc, temporary and diverse assemblages rather than on imagined forms of regularity.

Notes

(1) The data are from a larger linguistic ethnographic project with Emi Otsuji looking at corner shops and markets in Sydney and Tokyo.
(2) A question that often emerges (and indeed was raised by a reviewer of this chapter) is whether there is a contradiction between this naming of languages and the translinguistic framework the chapter draws on. The point is not to deny that certain linguistic resources are identifiable as, say, Bangla – surely it would be foolish to do so – while also noting that naming **Assalamualaikum**, for example, simply as 'Arabic' may be problematic. Rather it is the way these resources are framed (as resources available as part of spatial repertoires) that matters.

References

Amin, A. (2015) Animated space. *Public Culture* 27 (2), 239–258.

Appadurai, A. (2015) Mediants, materiality, normativity. *Public Culture* 27 (2), 221–237.

Barni, M. and Bagna, C. (2015) The critical turn in LL: New methodologies and new items in LL. *Linguistic Landscape* 1 (1/2), 6–18.

Bernstein, B. (2000) *Pedagogy, Symbolic Control and Identity: Theory, Research, Critique.* London: Taylor & Francis.

Bennett, J. (2010a) *Vibrant Matter: A Political Ecology of Things.* Durham: Duke University Press.

Bennett, J. (2010b) A vitalist stopover on the way to a new materialism. In D. Coole and S. Frost (eds) *New Materialisms: Ontology, Agency and Politics* (pp. 47–69). Durham: Duke University Press.

Blommaert, J. (2013) *Ethnography, Superdiversity and Linguistic Landscapes: Chronicles of Complexity.* Bristol: Multilingual Matters.

Blommaert, J. (2016a) From mobility to complexity in sociolinguistic theory and method. In N. Coupland (ed.) *Sociolinguistics: Theoretical Debates* (pp. 242–259). Cambridge: Cambridge University Press.

Blommaert, J. (2016b) 'Meeting of styles' and the online infrastructures of graffiti. *Applied Linguistics Review* 7 (2), 99–115.

Bucholz, M. and Hall, K. (2016) Embodied sociolinguistics. In N. Coupland (ed.) *Sociolinguistics: Theoretical Debates* (pp. 173–197). Cambridge: Cambridge University Press.

Canagarajah, S. (2013) *Translingual Practice: Global Englishes and Cosmopolitan Relations.* New York: Routledge.

Clark, A. (2008) *Supersizing the Mind: Embodiment, Action, and Cognitive Extension.* Oxford: Oxford University Press.

Cowley, S. (2012) Distributed language. In S. Cowley (ed.) *Distributed Language* (pp. 1–14). Amsterdam: John Benjamins.

Deleuze, G. and Guattari, F. (1987) *A Thousand Plateaus: Capitalism and Schizophrenia* (trans. B. Massumi). Minneapolis: University of Minnesota Press.

Dovchin, S., Sultana, S. and Pennycook, A. (2015) Relocalizing the translingual practices of young adults in Mongolia and Bangladesh. *Translation and Translanguaging in Multilingual Contexts* 1 (1), 4–26.

Fenwick, T. and Edwards, R. (2011) Considering materiality in educational policy: Messy objects and multiple reals. *Educational Theory* 61 (6), 709–726.

Ferrando, F. (2013) Posthumanism, transhumanism, antihumanism, metahumanism, and new materialisms: Differences and relations. *Existenz* 8 (2), 26–32.

Finnegan, R. (2015) *Where is Language? An Anthropologist's Questions on Language, Literature and Performance.* London: Bloomsbury.

Gorter, D. and Cenoz, J. (2015) Translanguaging and linguistic landscapes. *Linguistic Landscape* 1 (1/2), 54–74.

Harris, R. (1990) On redefining linguistics. In H. Davis and T. Taylor (eds) *Redefining Linguistics* (pp. 18–52). London: Routledge.

Harris, R. (1996) *Signs, Language and Communication.* London: Routledge.

Harris, R. (1998) *Introduction to Integrational Linguistics.* Oxford: Pergamon.

Harris, R. (2009) *After Epistemology.* Gamlingay: Authors Online.

Hiramoto, M. (2015) Inked nostalgia: Displaying identity through tattoos as Hawaii local practice. *Journal of Multilingual and Multicultural Development* 36 (2), 107–123.

Hutchins, E. (1995) *Cognition in the Wild.* Cambridge: MIT Press.

Hutchins, E. (2014) The cultural ecosystem of human cognition. *Philosophical Psychology* 27 (1), 34–49.

James, S. (2008) Market gardens and McMansions: Contesting the concept of 'growth' on Sydney's peri-urban fringe. Online Proceedings of 'Sustaining Culture' Annual Conference of the Cultural Studies Association of Australia (CSAA), UniSA, Adelaide, 6–8 December 2007. See https://www.researchgate.net/publication/271625694_Market_Lingos_and_Metrolingua_Francas

Karlander, D. (2018) Backjumps: Writing, watching, erasing train graffiti. *Social Semiotics* 1, 41–59.

Kell, C. (2015) Making people happen: Materiality and movement in meaning-making trajectories. *Social Semiotics* 25 (4), 423–445.

Kitis, E.D. and Milani, T. (2015) The perfomativity of the body: Turbulent spaces in Greece. *Linguistic Landscape* 1 (3), 268–290.

Kramsch, C. (2014) A researcher's auto-socioanalysis: Making space for the personal. In B. Spolsky, O. Inbar-Lourie and M. Tannenbaum (eds) *Challenges for Language Education and Policy: Making Space for People* (pp. 235–244). New York: Routledge.

Lakemba (2016) Local Stats. See http://lakemba.localstats.com.au/demographics/nsw/sydney/canterbury-bankstown/lakemba (accessed 22 July 2016).

Latour, B. (1999) *Pandora's Hope: Essays on the Reality of Science Studies.* Cambridge: Harvard University Press.

Li Wei (2011) Moment analysis and translanguaging space: Discursive construction of identities by multilingual Chinese youth in Britain. *Journal of Pragmatics* 43, 1222–1235.

Otsuji, E. and Pennycook, A. (2017) Sydney's intersecting worlds of languages and things. In P. Heinrich and D. Smakman (eds) *Urban Sociolinguistics: The City as a Linguistic Process and Experience* (pp. 204–219). New York: Routledge.

Peck, A. and Stroud, C. (2015) Skinscapes. *Linguistic Landscape* 1 (1/2), 133–151.

Pennycook, A. (2009) Linguistic landscapes and the transgressive semiotics of graffiti. In E. Shohamy and D. Gorter (eds) *Linguistic Landscape: Expanding the Scenery* (pp. 302–312). Abingdon: Routledge.

Pennycook, A. (2010a) Spatial narrations: Graffscapes and city souls. In A. Jaworski and C. Thurlow (eds) *Semiotic Landscapes: Language, Image, Space* (pp. 137–150). London: Continuum.

Pennycook, A. (2010b) *Language as a Local Practice.* London: Routledge.

Pennycook, A. (2018) *Posthumanist Applied Linguistics.* London: Routledge.

Pennycook, A. and Otsuji, E. (2014a) Metrolingual multitasking and spatial repertoires: 'Pizza mo two minutes coming'. *Journal of Sociolinguistics* 18 (2), 161–184.

Pennycook, A. and Otsuji, E. (2014b) Market lingos and metrolingua francas. *International Multilingual Research Journal* 8 (4), 255–270.

Pennycook A. and Otsuji, E. (2015a) *Metrolingualism: Language in the City.* London: Routledge.

Pennycook, A. and Otsuji, E. (2015b) Making scents of the landscape. *Linguistic Landscape* 1 (3) 191–212.

Scollon, R. and Scollon, S.W. (2004) *Nexus Analysis: Discourse and the Emerging Internet.* London: Routledge.

Scollon, R. and Scollon, S.W. (2007) Nexus analysis: Refocusing ethnography on action. *Journal of Sociolinguistics* 11 (5), 608–662.

Sen, A. (2016) Food, place, and memory: Bangladeshi fish stores on Devon Avenue, Chicago. *Food and Foodways* 24 (1–2), 67–88.

Shohamy, E. (2015) LL research as expanding language and language policy. *Linguistic Landscape* 1 (1/2), 152–171.

Shohamy, A. and Ben Rafael, E. (2015) Introduction: Linguistic landscape. A new journal. *Linguistic Landscape* 1(1/2), 1–5.

Steffensen, S.V. (2012) Beyond mind: An extended ecology of languaging. In S. Cowley (ed.) *Distributed Language* (pp. 185–210). Amsterdam: John Benjamins.

Sultana, S., Dovchin, S. and Pennycook, A. (2015) Transglossic language practices of young adults in Bangladesh and Mongolia. *International Journal of Multilingualism* 12 (1), 93–108.

Thrift, N. (2007) *Non-Representational Theory: Space | Politics | Affect.* London: Routledge.

Wardaugh, R. (1986) *An Introduction to Sociolinguistics.* Oxford: Wiley.

5 The Art of Silence in Upmarket Spaces of Commerce

Adam Jaworski

Silence is considered as a semiotic resource used to style commercial spaces and their target customers as 'elite'. Four broad categories of silence in the contemporary semiotic landscape of commerce include: the understated design of upmarket signage; 'secrecy' as a marketing trope; silence as a branding resource; and silence as a styling element of fashion models. The chapter identifies the sources and parallels of these uses and representations of visual silence in art.

5.1 Introduction: Semiotic Landscape

This chapter explores the manifestations and thematisation of 'silence' in the commercial semiotic landscape. Following Coupland (2010: 77), the concept of 'semiotic landscape', like its near synonym, 'linguistic landscape', is understood as 'a metaphorical concept, extrapolated from the concept of natural landscape'. Nikolas Coupland (2010: 78) cites Barbara Adam's (1998) observation that visible features of landscape in the natural world are often shaped by invisible or hidden forces, human or non-human, such as

> lopsided, canted over trees showing the influence over time of a prevailing wind direction and intensity. A landscape provides, she says, 'a record of reality-generating activity'; the visible phenomena making up a landscape have 'invisible constitutive activities inescapably embedded within them'. (Adams, 1998: 54)

However, even 'natural landscape' involves an ideological transformation of land (space) into scenery as a way of seeing and of 'consumption' of place (Urry, 2005). Thus, semiotic landscape is the staging of space through the mediational means, or technologies of communication (Jones, 2016), such as writing, speech, sounds, images, bodies, artefacts, architecture, scents and textures. In this sense, the term 'semiotic landscape' is intended to capture the multimodal and multisensory means of signification in the environment and our 'ways of seeing' it (Jaworski & Thurlow, 2010).

While most studies of linguistic and semiotic landscapes have focused on different aspects of multilingual and multimodal displays and their underlying ideologies, relatively little attention has been paid to the uses and displays of specifically non-verbal communication, which is, obviously, signified multimodally. With regard to silence, Thurlow and Jaworski (2010) have considered the relative absence of signage in the representations of high-end tourism spaces in advertising, alongside metalinguistic comments on 'silence' and 'quietude' as indexes of luxury. Other authors have considered silence as a metaphor for the erasure of marginalised voices from different locations, for example, through the removal of (undesirable) graffiti (Hanauer, 2004), the relative absence of minority languages in the linguistic landscape of an increasingly multilingual nation (Macalister, 2010), or the 'forgetting' of controversial past events through the renaming of streets and the removal of statues in times of transition from one political regime to another (Guilat & Espinosa-Ramírez, 2016).

Generally, non-verbal communication has only recently come to the attention of scholars working in the area of linguistic landscape studies under the new term of 'corporeal sociolinguistics' (Kitis & Milani, 2015; Milani, 2015; Peck & Stroud, 2015). However, the relationship between bodies and the built environment has for some time been an ongoing concern in sociology (e.g. Sennett, 1994) and interactional sociolinguistics (e.g. Streeck et al., 2011). Another term, 'embodied sociolinguistics' (Bucholtz & Hall, 2016) captures a rich tradition of different aspects of bodily communication, including the emplacement of social actors in the built and natural environment, for example, tourists in their travel destinations (Jaworski & Thurlow, 2011, 2014; Thurlow & Jaworski, 2011, 2014, 2015).

In this chapter, I build on my earlier work with Crispin Thurlow on silence in luxury tourism landscapes (Thurlow & Jaworski, 2010). Although luxury is not the only trope that can be linked to commodification of silence, the ideology of luxury, and hence class privilege, underpins most uses and metadiscursive displays of silence in commercial spaces, such as retail and gastronomy sites, and in the housing market. In particular, I am interested in demonstrating the connections between some of the characteristics of silence deployed in semiotic landscapes and their origins in art. Naturally, as will be noted below, art itself is frequently invoked as a resource for the production of distinction.

The format of this chapter is part textual, part visual essay. The latter element takes the form of a collage of images arranged thematically to correspond to the analytic sections of the chapter. The somewhat repetitive nature of the collage aims to illustrate the fact that as a marketing tool the idea of silence is quite widespread, takes some regular forms and has identifiable historical precedents.

The organisation of the chapter is as follows. In Section 5.2, I discuss the way silence is conceptualised here. Section 5.3 deals with the semiotic mechanisms of transforming language into a 'luxury' commodity. In Section 5.4, I present an overview of a few selected examples of semiotic landscape studies across economically stratified areas, including the use of silence in 'elite' spaces. In Section 5.5, I present and analyse some new data organised into four themes: the understated design of upmarket signage (Section 5.5.1), 'secrecy' as a marketing trope (Section 5.5.2), silence as a branding resource (Section 5.5.3), and silence as a styling element found in fashion models in photographic displays and in shop window dummies (Section 5.5.4). In conclusion, I emphasise the role of silence in creating a sense of distinction.

5.2 Silence

My use of the concept of 'silence' is understood broadly, not simply as absence of words or sound, but as a multimodal, mediational means mobilising a wide range of 'verbal and textual tools' (Jones & Norris, 2005: 9). The mediational tools conveying acoustic silence may include pauses, interruptions and ellipsis, but they are better characterised as an open-ended pool of resources that blur (but not necessarily obliterate) the figure-ground distinction of the auditory or visual channel. In this respect I draw on Duez's definition of silence as 'any interval of the oscillographic trace where the amplitude is indistinguishable from that of background noise' (Duez, 1982: 13).

When silence is assumed to have communicative intention and produces contextual effects, it may become communicatively *relevant* (Jaworski, 1993; Sperber & Wilson, 1986). In terms of Halliday's (1978) tripartite taxonomy of communicative metafunctions of language and other semiotic systems, such silences can be *ideational* (communicating something about the world), *interpersonal* (communicating something about our relationships with others) and *textual* (creating coherence of texts and signalling their interpretive frames). In other words, silence can manifest notable absences or omissions, secrets, acts of censorship, restraint and understatement, even if we can only guess or speculate on the denotational content of such omissions, secrets or what exactly is being censored (ideational metafunction). Silence can express a wide range of emotions and subject positions, such as calmness, anxiety, embarrassment, anger and so on, or provide a space for reflection and 'subject formation – privacy, interiority, sexuality' (Buchloh, 2000 [1998]: 274) (interpersonal metafunction). Finally, silence can be used as a keying device (Goffman, 1974), for example when a pause signals that the following word is rare or unusual, what Chafe (1985: 80) calls 'low in codability' (textual metafunction).

Apart from silence realised through different mediational tools, I also consider the thematisation of silence through metadiscursive comments and display, as well as metaphorical and metonymic references, which may be verbal or visual, or both, as is the case with writing. In other words, silence understood primarily as an 'acoustic fact' can be *transducted* (e.g. Kress, 2010) into non-acoustic or non-vocal modalities, such as written representation and visual imagery. As I have demonstrated elsewhere (Jaworski, 2016a, 2016b), the transduction of silence as an acoustic fact into visual modalities in art – such as monochrome painting, understated geometric design, the display of the word 'silence' or an image of sealed mouths – allows silence to be noticed or made visible beyond its prototypical, often elusive and fleeting auditory presence. For example, Joseph Beuys' *Das Schweigen* (*The Silence*) (1973) is a sculpture consisting of five 35mm reels of Ingmar Bergman's feature film *Tystnaden* (*The Silence*) (1963), varnished and galvanised in copper and zinc. Here, Bergman's transposition of silence as an acoustic or anecdotal fact into a psychological drama featuring prolonged pauses, understatements, allusions and innuendo is further recontextualised and transformed into a silent or 'silenced' object. In this case, Beuys' transposition of silence from one semiotic mode to another becomes a powerful concretisation and an 'emblem of the eponymous film and subject, as well as of a leaden time in Germany, when Cold War tensions, internal terrorism, and the horror of the Nazi past gripped the country' (Kamps, 2012: 71). I will allude to some aspects of transductions of silence in art in my data analysis to follow.

5.3 Commodification of Language and Silence as Luxury Register

Commodification of language has emerged as one of the key topics in contemporary sociolinguistics. Fairclough (1992: 207) defines commodification as a shift in the organisation of social domains whereby institutions that have not traditionally been concerned with the production of commodities in the narrow sense come to be associated with commodity production, distribution and consumption. Heller (2010) outlines the following conditions in late capitalism that have led to the increasing role of language in economic processes, both as communicative labour (the work process) and as a cultural artefact (the work product):

> (a) capitalist expansion or globalization, requiring the management of communication … across linguistic difference; (b) computerization of the work process, requiring new kinds of language and literacy skills among workers; (c) the growth of the service sector, in largely communication based form; and (d) responses to the saturation of markets in the form of the development of niche markets … and of the use of symbolic, often linguistic, resources to add value to standardized products. (Heller, 2010: 102)

It is the last two of these conditions that are particularly relevant to this study, as I will aim to demonstrate how the contemporary, commercial landscape has incorporated silence as one of its marketing tools. On the one hand, silence will be shown to create symbolic added value for goods and services, and on the other, it will be shown to be part of the expected conduct of some people working in the fashion industry, specifically fashion models.

Drawing on Appadurai (1986), Pietikäinen *et al.* (2016: 108) argue that new economic conditions have created increased opportunities for small, or peripheral, languages to be positioned as commodities that 'can cast a semiotically rich aura of "luxury" upon otherwise mundane products'. Such 'minority' languages used to be of little value outside of the intimate contexts of family and community. They were associated with backwardness and lack of economic opportunities, requiring their speakers to rely on learning large, 'national' languages (such as English for the speakers of Irish, or French for the speakers of Corsican) to ensure access to well-paid jobs, say, in the public sector controlled and regulated by the nation state. With the development of the tourist industry in many minority or peripheral regions, local languages have become valuable resources for the authentication of these 'remote' places as tourist destinations, as well as locally sourced commodities, whether durable (souvenirs) or fleeting experiences (interactions) (see also Heller *et al.*, 2014).

Appadurai (1986: 38) considers luxury goods as *incarnated* signs, or goods 'whose principal use is *rhetorical* and *social*'. Rather than distinguish them as a special class of things, he considers luxury goods, by analogy to language, as a specific 'register' of goods for social consumption. For Appadurai, some or all of the following attributes may characterise the signs of this commodity register:

> (1) restriction, either by price or by law, to elites; (2) complexity of acquisition, which may or may not be a function of real 'scarcity'; (3) semiotic virtuosity, that is, the capacity to signal fairly complex social messages (as do pepper in cuisine, silk in dress, jewels in adornment, and relics in worship); (4) specialized knowledge as a prerequisite for their 'appropriate' consumption, that is, regulation by fashion; and (5) a high degree of linkage of their consumption to body, person, and personality. (Appadurai, 1986: 38)

Thus, the conditions for the reassessment of small languages, together with consumers' knowledge of their value as authentic signifiers of people, places and products, have made them available for consumption in the 'experience economy' (Pine & Gilmore, 1999), whereby products and their consumption (including the point of purchase) are construed as positive aesthetic and emotional sensations. Pietikäinen *et al*. (2016) discuss, for example, the linguistic branding of Cwtch Restaurant in the Welsh coastal city of St Davids. The restaurant's name is derived from the 'untranslatable', polysemous Welsh word 'cwtch', which, as a verb, means 'cuddle', 'settle down' or 'get cosy'; and, as a noun, can refer to a 'cuddle', a 'hug', or 'a small place and quiet place'. Apart from its metaculturally salient name (with its complex, uniquely 'Welsh' meaning), the restaurant's menu makes liberal use of Welsh for the names of dishes, local produce and the ingredients' places of origin. The restaurant taps into the middle-class proclivity of its target clientele for the consumption of authenticated, culturally unique and localised and locally sourced, hence 'scarce', products (e.g. food) and experiences (e.g. heritage). Owing to its symbolic and semantic complexities, the name exploits 'semiotic virtuosity'. The Welsh names of local produce and their places of origin in the menu appeal to 'knowing' consumers, who can demonstrate specialised linguistic knowledge as 'a prerequisite for their "appropriate" consumption' of the food (see Appadurai, 1986: 5).

Of course, large languages, especially those associated with elite, powerful European nations, have been used for the marketing of mundane commodities as luxuries for much longer. For example, Barthes (1977) demonstrates how, in an advertisement for pasta in a French magazine, the Italian brand name, 'Panzani', reinforced by the colour scheme of the photograph (yellow/white, green, red), signifies *Italianicity* in a way that it would not to an Italian reader. Additionally, the photograph showing packets of pasta, Parmesan cheese and a tin of tomato concentrate (all branded by Panzani), together with a fresh tomato, mushroom and onions spilling out from a half-open string bag connote a leisurely, individualistic lifestyle; the freshness and wholesomeness associated with the image of an Italian holiday; and daily shopping at a local market, as opposed to a hasty lifestyle relying on preserved or refrigerated food. Finally, the artful composition of the photograph brings associations (to the 'knowing' reader) of still life painting, hence 'high' art, sophistication and good taste.

Later studies of multilingual marketing and advertising have explored the links between specific language codes and elite ethno-national stereotypes associated with them. For example, a number of authors have demonstrated how French (outside of predominantly French-speaking contexts) is used to add symbolic value to advertised products and businesses, invoking a sense of elegance, sophistication, beauty and fine cuisine (e.g. Haarman, 1989; Kelly-Holmes, 2005; Martin, 2007; Serwe *et al.*, 2013). English can be positively linked with Americanness (Kelly-Holmes, 2010), or, as a dominant international language, it may be exploited for its connotations of cosmopolitanism, modernity, transnational mobility, power and success (e.g. Cheshire & Moser, 1994; Haarman, 1989; Piller, 2003). Piller (2001) argues that advertisers in Germany set up bilingualism in English and German as the 'natural', highest form of linguistic currency for successful middle-class Germans, hence the most valuable form of linguistic capital (Bourdieu, 1991).

5.4 Semiotic Landscape in Economically Stratified Areas

A growing body of work has investigated variation in the linguistic and semiotic landscapes across economically stratified urban areas. Drawing on Bourdieu (1984), Stroud and Mpendukana (2009) demonstrate how in the Western Cape township of Khayelitsha, signage varies between 'sites of luxury' and 'sites of necessity'. While the former use linguistic and visual forms with esoteric and evocative meanings that index national, regional and global scale levels (e.g. 'standard' and other, pan-African varieties of English), the latter tend to be anchored locally, providing essential information about the nature of local businesses, goods and services on offer.

Trinch and Snajdr (2017) discuss the linguistic landscape of Brooklyn pre- and post-gentrification in terms of *Old School Vernacular* and *Distinction-making Signs*. Old School Vernacular signage is 'busy', with the main sign often accompanied by ancillary signs, large typefaces, information about business owners and products or services, repetition, non-standard written English forms, use of non-Roman scripts or transliteration in Roman script, complementary symbols or pictures, and sincere references to religion, ethnicity, national origin, race and class. The latter characteristic is indicative of the traditional, diverse populations residing side-by-side in Brooklyn. Distinction-making signs in newly gentrified areas target well-educated and affluent residents, while alienating traditional residents and non-middle-class clients by adopting globally homogenised marketing strategies: single words or short phrases, polysemic or cryptic names of businesses (e.g. restaurants), often with historical and literary references, reduced font-size, all lower case letters, and languages other than English that index sophistication and worldliness.

Vandenbroucke's (2016) study of the use of English in the linguistic landscapes of Amsterdam and Brussels focuses on economically stratified commercial shopping streets: the 'downscale', 'midscale' and 'upscale'. Hence, the author reports different degrees of the presence and semiotic manifestations of the use of English across three 'linguistic markets'. For example, in the downscale, multi-ethnic, predominantly French-speaking streets in Brussels, defined as a 'site of necessity' (Stroud & Mpendukana, 2009), the widely present English-language shop names appear to be emblematic, hence aspirational of, prestige. In the Brussels upscale street, dominated by affluent, English-speaking expats, a 'site of luxury', English on signage includes emblematic uses, but the striking feature is its widespread instrumental or referential use (e.g. job adverts), indicative of the area's dominant demographic. The midscale shopping streets, both in Amsterdam and Brussels, dominated by international chains of mid-range fashion stores and fast food restaurants, attract more heterogeneous cross-sections of the cities' demographics. English-language signs are both emblematic and referential, but the former, like the businesses they index, appear to be more uniform, homogenised and 'chain-like', ensuring familiarity or continuity for the target clientele, wherever they decide to shop or eat (also Park & Wee, 2012). Naturally, it is important to emphasise that in Vandenbroucke's and the other studies overviewed briefly in this section, English is not a uniform resource (Vandenbroucke uses the term 'polymorphic'), nor does it operate in isolation from the other languages, visual and spatial resources typical of their localities and/or of 'higher' scale levels.

These studies, then, point to the fact that semiotic landscapes are arranged unequally by indexing and accommodating economically and socially stratified populations in different locations. Privilege, or lack of it, is communicated by the deployment of signage that indexes these hierarchies and implicitly arranges access and movement through space.

My work with Crispin Thurlow on elite status and the social semiotics of luxury as a classed discourse (e.g. Jaworski & Thurlow, 2009; Thurlow & Jaworski, 2012, 2017a), has followed the idea of *elite* as a discursive accomplishment – a social process rather than some essentially fixed, personal attribute. We are interested in the way that elite subjectivities and feelings are structured and enacted by what Rampton (2003: 68) calls 'processes of symbolic differentiation' and through stylised performances of class identity. Accordingly, we consider the conscious enactment and explicit representation of elitism in terms of identificational adjustments and interpersonal alignments. For us, elitism entails a person's orienting – or being oriented – to some ideological position and/or its discursive representations in order to claim exclusivity and/or superiority on the grounds of knowledge, authenticity, taste, erudition, experience, insight, access to resources, wealth, group membership or any other quality which warrants the individual to take a higher moral, aesthetic, intellectual, material, etc. ground against 'the masses' or some specific social grouping defined on the grounds of wealth, lifestyle, ethnicity, profession or language use (see papers in Thurlow & Jaworski, 2017b). In Thurlow and Jaworski (2010), for example, we examine how these elite identities are discursively accomplished through the semiotic resource of silence.

Our data set at the time was drawn from print media advertisements for high-end tourism. What we found across our examples was a strong preference of advertisers to represent luxury holiday spaces as silent. Apart from the genre-defining *absence of signage* on buildings and other architectural locations, and the representation of indoor and outdoor spaces as devoid of people (especially in long shots), we noted six key, somewhat overlapping strategies:

(1) *Lexicalisation and metaphorisation*: Advertisers make explicit metalinguistic appeals to 'silence' and 'peace', or they use metaphoric references to mythologically non-linguistic or otherwise tranquil, other-worldly places drawing heavily

on quasi-religious referents, for example, 'paradise', 'heaven', 'sanctuary', 'halo' or 'dream', and subtle, normally imperceptible sounds, such as the 'soothing and calming sound of the sea' and 'the faint sound of your beating heart'.

(2) *Non-interactive represented participants*: Relative absence of people; when people are depicted, they are typically shown not to interact verbally with each other.

(3) *Disengaged viewing participants (i.e. readers)*: Readers are positioned voyeuristically as silent onlookers with their gaze missing the gaze of the represented actors (Kress & Van Leeuwen's 1996 'offer images').

(4) *Inactivity, stillness and 'empty' spaces*: Omnipresence of uncluttered, polished, shiny surfaces, such as lobbies, undisturbed water in swimming pools or in the sea, uncrowded beaches, rows of unoccupied deck chairs and so on (see below, Hutton's 2011 'text-poor' spaces).

(5) *The silence of nature*: Representations of vast, 'primeval', spaces seemingly untouched by anyone, and only waiting to be tamed, to be occupied by the elite traveller.

(6) *Multimodal design*: A visual 'texturing' (or transduction) of silence through typography, for example, the use of small, 'discrete', often undulating, italicised lettering, used occasionally for a single, isolated word (e.g. 'speechless'), which connotatively corresponds to the paralinguistic expression of soft volume and 'whispering' signage; large swathes of a single colour; predominance of white clothes and accessories (e.g. towels), except the primarily red swimsuits of the women, arguably connoting 'passion'.

In the represented world of absolute leisure for the absolutely wealthy, absolute silence exists. Although the two dominant resources commodified in the advertisements are relatively limited – silence and space – they appear to work very effectively in the construction, or accomplishment, of elite status and sense of privilege for the target audience, and as aspirational ones for everyone else.

The reality of physical urban spaces is messier, less clear-cut, and a matter of degree, rather than of sharp, binary distinctions. Yet, analytically, it is possible to make a distinction between relatively 'silent' and relatively 'noisy' commercial areas. For example, Hutton (2011) discusses the textscape of Hong Kong, drawing a distinction between 'text-rich' and 'text-poor' areas. The former are locally scaled or *vernacular* spaces (see Stroud & Mpendukana, 2009; Trinch & Snajdr, 2017; Vandenbroucke, 2016) 'buzzing' with semiotic activity 'in which the nonstandard is spoken, or which are framed by the vernacular, or which impart the affect of the vernacular' (Hutton, 2011: 166). The latter are 'text poor' or 'text minimal' globally scaled spaces of the atriums of high end shopping malls, lobbies of five-star hotels, and expensive apartment blocks with their spaces of 'reflective, metallic, smooth and cool modernity' (Hutton, 2011: 166).

Jaworski and Yeung's (2010) Hong Kong study of residential, displayed signage (names of buildings and housing estates, i.e. the housing market) in several upscale, midscale and downscale areas reveals that silence is mostly present at the opposite extremes of the linguistic market: the downscale and the upscale. However, it takes two distinct forms and functions. In the busiest, mixed use (residential and commercial) areas, the functional, relatively small and simple signage, typically in Chinese, placed directly over the entrances to buildings, is often obstructed from view by the large and dense commercial signage, as well as traffic. Names of buildings can effectively be seen only when one stands in the doorway to the building. In the upscale residential areas, most of the buildings (apartment compounds, townhouses or villas) have expensively designed and produced, large, highly ornamental signs, typically in Chinese and another European language, or monolingual in a European language. However, many of the most exclusive buildings are simply hidden from view from public roads, being located at the ends of private driveways. Neither the buildings nor the signage can be seen by the public. The location of the buildings is only hinted at by 'bare' street numbers or collective, municipal street signposts. Thus, in downscale, text-rich areas, signage (of one type) is silenced by its busy environment, while in upscale areas, signage (of another kind) is voluntarily withdrawn from view by some of the most privileged residents in the city. The invisibility of signage in each case signifies opposing endpoints of the economic scale.

5.5 Silence in the Commercial Semiotic Landscape

In this section, I consider some data examples, all presented in Figure 5.1 (images 1–100), which aim to illustrate different ways in which silence is present or implied in the design or content of signage, inscriptions, product labels, billboards and shop window displays. The images constituting my data sample have been drawn from various locations and were collected between 2011 and 2016 in Aalborg, Auckland, Bandar Seri Begawan, Bern, Dresden, Hong Kong, London, Penang, Poznań and Tokyo, although many of these texts, or very similar ones, can be found across many other cities. Silence appears to be part of the global register of the relatively high-end, text poor or otherwise aspirational commercial semiotic landscape.

5.5.1 Understated signage

In visual art, one of the most understated forms is the monochrome, and it has typically been interpreted as a visual metaphor or representation of silence (e.g. Hafif, 1997; Jaworski, 1993, 1997). While contemporary gentrifying signage tends to be playful, often based on word-play and intertextual allusions, relatively cheerful, trendy and colourful (Papen, 2012; Trinch & Snajdr, 2017), traditional high-end signage, associated with well-established or aspiring luxury brands, tends to be more serious, understated and monochrome. There is certainly much variation in all areas of signage, but a cursory look at a selection of default signage in one of the most expensive shopping malls in Hong Kong in 2011 (Figure 5.1, images 1–48) suggests the dominance of 'stylish' black and white design, with brand names shaped into recognisable company logos. While the shops and restaurants in gentrifying areas are typically one-off, small-scale businesses, which need to 'stand out' among their competitors, well-established high-end stores are international chains with greater brand recognition, which probably allows them to rely on more discreet design.

Figure 5.1 'Silence' in the upmarket semiotic landscape

Figure 5.1 'Silence' in the upmarket semiotic landscape (*Continued*)

Figure 5.1 'Silence' in the upmarket semiotic landscape (*Continued*)

Figure 5.1   'Silence' in the upmarket semiotic landscape (*Continued*)

Figure 5.1 'Silence' in the upmarket semiotic landscape (*Continued*)

White lettering on black background (or some variety of dark, e.g. different shades of purple, Figure 5.1, images 41–44) may increase legibility; it also connotes a smart and sophisticated appearance.

Some features shared with the gentrifying typography include the sporadic use of all lower case letters (Figure 5.1, images 1, 5, 6, 8, 12 and 21), unusual combinations of lower and upper case letters (Figure 5.1, images 9, 10 and 17), the predominance of English and other elite languages (most notably French) and the use of made up words (e.g. Figure 5.1, image 24). However, the signs' typefaces tend to be quite static (or still), with the occasional styling of a more cursive, or italicised script, occasionally also mixed with print-like typography (Figure 5.1, images 1, 4, 16, 32, 33 and 41). In the case of Figure 5.1, image 41, the choice of italics is probably connected with the dynamism of sport, and in Figure 5.1, images 32 and 33, the cursive 'b' is part of a signature-like logo of the label 'agnès b'.

Even designer stores for children are indexed with sober black and white designs (Figure 5.1, images 31 and 32), not the colourful and 'dancing' typography, or non-standard orthography found on the signs of many toy and children's clothes stores (e.g. 'TOYS 'Я' US'). Colours other than white and black (or some other dark, subdued background) are found in but a few examples, such as in the Swiss flag in Figure 5.1, image 5, or in the green 'A' in Figure 5.1, image 18. Some of the signs employ non-standard uses of punctuation marks (Figure 5.1, images 2, 8, 24 and 30); diacritics (Figure 5.1, image 46); playful tittles over the letter 'i', such as the tip of the monkey's tail (Figure 5.1, image 11); colour coordination, as with the yellow words 'BAKERY CAFÉ' (Figure 5.1, image 12) and non-standard orthography (Figure 5.1, image 2). All of these features are typical of what I have called elsewhere 'globalese', a middle brow consumer register tending towards 'playful and humorous semiotics … appealing to the mass consumer, in contrast to the aloof and dead-serious semiotics of top end marketing' (Jaworski, 2015: 233). Other things being equal, the more upscale the signage appears to be, the more minimalist design prevails.

Intertextual links to art are made in a specific reference to the name of a German art school (Figure 5.1, image 45) and in a more generic fashion (Figure 5.1, images 44 and 46). Unsurprisingly, shopping malls are often called 'galleries'. Another indirect reference to art is detectable in the choice of neon in Figure 5.1, image 34, a widely used material in contemporary art since the 1960s. According to Frank Popper (2009), while the original associations of neon light in places such as Las Vegas and Tokyo bring to mind 'the energy and vitality of modern life, its presence in works conceived by artists operates rather as an antidote to hectic agitation and invites quiet contemplation and meditation'. With lower-end business seemingly replacing their neon signage with cheaper LED lighting (as appears to be the case in Hong Kong, for example), neon is now predominantly associated with expensive art objects, high-end company signage and luxury in-store displays.

The minimal graphic detail of the individual signs makes each appear relatively 'hushed' and corresponds to the production of silent spaces, especially by the ultra high-end brands, inside their shops. This is certainly one of the ways in which these companies create a sense of scarcity for their products. By ensuring that their shop floors are not too crowded, and perhaps to discourage 'mere' window shoppers from coming inside, they regulate the flow of clients by admitting only a limited number of shoppers at any one time. Thus, it is not uncommon (at least in Hong Kong) to see people queuing to enter some of the most 'exclusive' shops, – in 2007, one such establishment displaying a printed sign in the window next to the door 'guarded' by a porter:

> In order to serve you better, we must restrict the number of customers into the store during peak hour. We ask for your patience to wait a few minutes until a member of our staff becomes available. Thank you.

Admittedly, this is an infrequent restriction, but it is indicative of the orientation of these companies to the elimination of 'noise' from their image. Visually, this can be manifested in the design of window displays, with only a few items on view or further allusions to understated contemporary art. For example, the window display in Figure 5.1, image 49 (photographed in Poznań in 2013), possibly in a nod to Kazimir Malevich's painting *White on White* (1918), displays the name/logo of the company in raised, white lettering on a white background (suggestive of a minimal 'amplitude' between the figure and ground), next to a Mark Rothko-esque red, monochrome print (see also discussion of Figure 5.1, image 51, below).

My two final examples illustrating a difference in the styling of economically stratified spaces are two 'welcome' signs at Auckland Airport (photographed in 2013). One is located in the general (economy) check-in area (Figure 5.1, image 50), the other one at the entrance to the Air New Zealand premium (business/first class) check-in area (Figure 5.1, image 51). On both signs, branded by Air New Zealand, the word 'welcome' is written in blue, lower case, cursive script. It stands out from the other, multilingual greetings all written in white, randomly appearing in either roman or italic script, in a mixture of upper and lower case letters. However, as the background of the economy sign is transparent, its white text is more legible than that on the white background of the sign in the upscale area. The premium sign welcomes its customers with the volume visually turned down. Besides, despite obvious similarities, the economy check-in area sign is smaller in a larger but potentially more crowded space, and the premium sign is larger in a smaller, more exclusive, less crowded space. Finally, the differential design of the two signs is indicated by the contrast in the number and selection of languages on each sign. Table 5.1 compares the greetings in the two signs with the approximation of the typography of each of the greetings.

Apart from the English word 'welcome', the economy sign contains additional greetings in English ('hey', 'Hi'), Australian English ('gidday'), Maori ('KIA ORA'), Mandarin ('NǏ HǍO'), Fijian ('bula'), German ('guten tag'), French ('bonjour'), Japanese ('ようこそ') and Samoan ('talofa'). The premium sign has English ('hello'), Maori ('KIA ORA'), Mandarin ('NǏ HǍO'), Japanese ('ようこそ', 'KONICHIWA'), German ('guten tag') and French ('bonjour'). By taking the idea of audience design (Bell, 1984) to its extreme, one could argue that Air New Zealand assumes a preference for non-localised greetings from its Australian premium customers (preference for the standard and higher scale English forms in sites of luxury, Stroud & Mpendukana, 2009), that premium customers from Japan are happy with a greeting

Table 5.1 Tabulation of greetings in the 'welcome' signs at Auckland Airport (Figure 5.1, images 50 and 51)

'Welcome' sign in the general check-in area of Auckland airport (image 50)		'Welcome' sign in the premium check-in area of Auckland airport (image 51)	
English	Welcome	English	Welcome
English (and possibly other languages)	hey	–	–
Maori	KIA ORA	Maori	KIA ORA
Australian English	gidday	–	–
English	Hi	English	hello
Mandarin Chinese	NĬ HǍO	Mandarin Chinese	NĬ HǍO
Fijian	bula	–	–
French	bonjour	French	bonjour
German	guten tag	German	guten tag
Japanese	ようこそ	Japanese	ようこそ
Samoan	talofa	–	–
–	–	Japanese	KONICHIWA

either in the hiragana or roman script (which echoes Piller's 2001 discussion of the German–English ideal for the German elite), that elite Fijians and Samoans are also equally happy with English (or Maori), and that there is no 'hey'-saying riff raff attempting premium check-in. As we have shown elsewhere, 'centred', hence privileged, spaces at airports tend to be characterised by displays of relatively limited (emblematic) signage, while in symbolically 'peripheral' spaces there is far more linguistic diversity to be found, less aestheticised and more referential (Jaworski & Thurlow, 2013). Overall, following Appadurai (1986), the understated design in the signage discussed in this section appears to be indexing spaces restricted, either by price or by law (as in the case of segregated check-in areas), to elites.

5.5.2 Trade secrets

Exclusivity, hence preferential treatment and a sense of distinction, can be invoked by creating an aura of restriction in access to privileged information and complexity of product acquisition, which requires sharing a secret (Appadurai, 1986). Figure 5.1, images 52–63 illustrate a common trope of the 'best kept secret' used in all kinds of marketing discourse. The examples fall into two clear categories. One, an image of a model with her index finger on her lips in the probably universal 'shushing' gesture as part of advertisements for different products and services (Figures 52–58). The other takes the form of a textual reference to the idea of secrecy. This may be included in the name of the business, for example, 'TOP SECRET & FRIENDS' (Figure 5.1, image 59), 'Sushi Secrets' (Figure 5.1, image 60); 'The Secrets of Thai Cuisine' (Figure 5.1, image 61), or as a promotional tag line of the KFC restaurant's 'Secret recipe' (Figure 5.1, image 62), or the Polish, two-part 'Art of Sushi...............Nie mów nikomu [Don't tell anyone]' (Figure 5.1, images 63a and 63b), where the 15 dots appear as metonym of textual elision.

Naturally, the idea of keeping marketed goods and services secret is antithetical to the businesses' need to attract as many customers as possible. These visual and textual appeals to confidentiality are purely symbolic, rather playful, and illustrate Fairclough's (1989: 62) notion of *synthetic personalisation* to characterise the way that, for example, advertisers and politicians often use language to give the impression of 'treating each of the people "handled" *en masse* as an individual'. Implying that some customers are invited to be 'in the know' about certain products while keeping everyone else 'out' may be an example of democratising a sense of distinction by allowing mass consumers to emulate elite lifestyles (see Thurlow & Jaworski, 2017a).

5.5.3 Branding with 'silence'

Bourdieu (1984) cites examples of silence being associated with nature, calm, comfortable living, bourgeois apartments uncluttered by cheap trinkets and souvenirs, meditative spaces linked to connoisseurship (libraries and museums) and other markers of distinction. When it is not oppressive, silence is considered sophisticated, exuding an aura of mystery. Poets and artists, especially those inspired by Zen, find silence a perfect antidote to the unreliability of other, 'corrupt' means of communication, such as speaking and writing (Hutton, 2016; Jaworski, 1993). This poetic potential of silence is exploited in businesses using overt references to silence as part of their branding or in the names of their products.

Images 64 and 65 in Figure 5.1 depict two nearly identical inscriptions at the Hong Kong fashion store 'initial'. The text under the logo reads as follows: 'THE UNUSUAL EXPERIENCE Step into the silence of time. It has truly been an extraordinary experience. It touches your soul with five senses'. The one-word, vague, all lower case name/logo of the shop is indicative of the gentrification semiotics (Trinch & Snajdr, 2017) in sites of luxury (Stroud & Mpendukana, 2009). The target clientele can be considered young, cool, hip and middle class, seemingly predisposed to the consumption of luxury goods and luxury registers (Appadurai, 1986). The monolingual English text in the context of Hong Kong is clearly indicative of the shop as a site of luxury. Additionally, its poetic tone and esoteric meaning – as evidenced, for instance, in the rather cryptic 'silence of time' – create conditions of restricted appreciation of the wording and its 'message'. The 'virtuosity' of the inscription may lie more in its visual and material characteristics, with two different versions appearing throughout the different branches of the store. In Figure 5.1, image 64, the text is presented as a framed picture with a (fake) dedicated lamp to illuminate it like a 'proper' work of art. In Figure 5.1, image 65, the reference to art invokes associations with contemporary, conceptual text-based pieces, whereby letterset text is applied directly onto a white gallery wall. Additionally, the violin bow invokes the virtuosity and sophistication of classical music. References to the 'extraordinariness' of the 'experience', its sensuality ('five senses') and spirituality (the 'soul') join consumption with the 'body, person, and personality' (Appadurai, 1986: 3).

Two other examples of mundane, mass produced, standardised products with the word 'silence' used as an embellishment or brand name appear in Figure 5.1, images 66 and 67. The former is a baseball cap featuring the capitalised word 'SILENCE' worn by a young man in Bandar Seri Begawan in 2015. The fact that he is wearing it back-to-front may suggest that he is a cool, somewhat rebellious dude. The typeface of the word 'silence' is artfully designed with a horizontal line splitting the letters in two. The line creates an empty space, metonymically referring to silence and adding multimodal complexity to the word through its visual design. A recent installation 'NOTHING', by the artist Tsang Kin-Wah at the M+ Pavilion at the West Kowloon Cultural District in Hong Kong, used a similar void line across its title (West Kowloon Cultural District Authority, 2016)

'Silence' is an ambiguously French/English word used as a name for one of the products of the Swiss 'luxury' mineral water company Valser (owned by Coca Cola Switzerland). The name appeals to the sense of quietude, well-being and purity found in nature – tropes often used in the marketing of bottled water and luxury leisure spaces (Thurlow & Jaworski, 2010). This particular bottle was photographed in a restaurant. Its connotations as a luxury product are reinforced by the silver framing of the label and a glass, rather than plastic, bottle. When sold in supermarkets, the same product is available in six packs of arguably more down-market plastic bottles.

5.5.4 Embodied silence: Distance and affect

Shopping malls have been referred to as 'cathedrals of consumption' as they have become 'the monuments of a new faith, the consumer religion, which has largely replaced the old' (Kowinski, 1985: 218). They offer the 'centeredness traditionally provided by religious temples, and they are constructed to have a similar balance, symmetry, and order' (Ritzer, 2008: 8). There are obvious architectural parallels. Both types of structures tend to be monumental in size, with awe-inspiring, soaring naves/atria, built with expensive materials, often filled with art and music. Important decorative elements of cathedrals are free-standing statues in niches and on rooflines, as in the Dresden Hofkirche (Figure 5.1, image 68). Shopping malls are obviously filled with mannequins lining shop windows along the street-like, indoor passages, as in the Dresden Altmarkt-Galerie (Figure 5.1, images 69 and 70). The analogy between statues of saints and fashion dummies may be somewhat far-fetched; however, a close look at some of the formal features of the representation of the human figure in Mannerist painting, sculpture and photographic images of models, and poses of the dummies reveals some striking similarities.

According to Shearman (1967), Mannerism, or the 'stylish style', originated in Italy in the High Renaissance in the first half of the 16th century and continued in the Baroque art of the 17th century. The style placed more emphasis on the virtuosity of the artist and the expressive power of the work rather than its content or subject. It was praised for its artifice intent on representing ideal behaviour, poise, refinement, courtly grace, effortless accomplishment and sophistication. It marked a departure from an earlier convention of the 15th century in which the human figure was represented as inanimate, in an icon-like style. An early example of the Mannerist style can be seen in parts of Michelangelo's Sistine Ceilings (1508–1512). For example, his *ignudi* (Figure 5.1, image 71), wingless, male angels, draw attention to the beauty of the work of art as never before through emphasis on such qualities as grace, elegance and poise. The figures show 'an air of refined detachment and ... a formula for twisting the wrist and holding the fingers in an apparently easy and elegant tension' (Shearman, 1967: 53). Likewise, as observed by Shearman (1976: 185), in Parmigianino's *Madonna dal Collo Lungo* (1543–1545) (Figure 5.1, image 73), the central character's gestures and facial expression are full of affectation, however, rather than emotional grace it was stiff and studied.

A characteristic form of Mannerism was *figura serpentiana*, that is the representation of figures often in a spiral pose. This is related to *contrapposto*, or counterpose, originally used in antique sculpture and revived in the Renaissance by Italian artists. It represents the human body 'arranged asymmetrically, so that the turn of the head opposed that of the hips, one leg was weight-bearing and straight while the other was free and flexed, and so on – all asymmetries being reconciled in a final balance [...] Movements are completed, not arrested; and thus, they seem neither to reflect a past action nor to anticipate a new one' (Shearman, 1967: 83), as in Giambologna's bronze sculpture *Astronomy* (early 1570s) (Figure 5.1, image 75).

A number of parallels can be seen in the poses and facial expressions of contemporary models and dummies. For reasons of space, only a few selected examples can be cited here. First, Michelangelo's *ignudo* in Figure 5.1, image 71 can be juxtaposed against Rafael Nadal's pose in his advertisement for Armani underwear (Figure 5.1, image 72). Parmigianino's *Madonna dal Collo Lungo* (Figure 5.1, image 73), Giambologna's *Astronomy* (Figure 5.1, image 75) and Bronzino's *The Allegory of Venus and Cupid* (c. 1545) (Figure 5.1, image 77) appear to provide uncanny templates for the models in the advertisements for La Perla (Figure 5.1, image 74), 3D Gold Jewellery (Figure 5.1, image 76) and Le Saunda (Figure 5.1, image 78), respectively.

As has been mentioned above, Mannerism represents human figures as balanced, detached and still. All of these characteristics can be treated as visually equivalent to the silence of withdrawal, contemplation or a lack of engagement with the viewer. The poses are reminiscent of Goffman's (1979) 'licensed withdrawal', that is to say, the models' (usually women) 'dissociated self-communication', typically represented by averted gaze, covered face, finger-to-finger or finger-to-mouth gestures, and self-touching. Similar qualities, with the resulting aura of aloofness and detachment, can be seen in statuesque representations of models in Figure 5.1, images 94–96.

But there is another story to tell about silence in the fashion industry. In her account of the early history of fashion modelling in Europe and America, Evans (2013) describes how by the end of the 19th century, couture houses introduced a key marketing strategy of modelling their designs with female models known as mannequins, or living mannequins (*le mannequin vivant*), whose prototypes were dressmakers' and tailors' dummies. (Male modelling was introduced on a smaller scale in

1915.) Mannequins were trained to carry themselves elegantly and walk gracefully, make dignified gestures and strike dramatic poses. They adopted exotic (i.e. 'distant') stage names such as Corisande, Gamela and Hebe. These were young women of working-class origins posing and parading for middle- and upper-class men and women. They proclaimed a new kind of glamour but at the cost of creating a concealed and strictly policed social divide. In order not to betray their origin, the mannequins never spoke. They smiled infrequently, and when they did, their smiles were not considered genuine. 'At the heart of the mannequin performance was a staged performance of impassivity in all its forms. The mannequin was inaccessible, disdainful and indifferent [...] The pose of indifference, boredom or disdain was a synecdoche of the entire mannequin performance' (Evans, 2013: 243). Contemporary press reports of fashion shows commented on the mannequins' 'bored expression', 'cold nonchalance', 'disillusioned haughtiness', 'fascination of unapproachability' and so on.

The tightly managed stage shows synchronised all movements, depriving them of their individuality. Whether in the salon, at the department store or modelling outdoors at public events (such as racecourses), the mannequins were mute, never engaging in direct social exchange with the clients. One account of a modelling event in a Paris fashion house in 1913 reports that clients treated mannequins with total indifference and never looked at their faces, rendering them 'culturally transparent and socially non-existent' (Evans, 2013: 174) – not so much objectifying as erasing the mannequin's individuality. With time, some of the mannequins acquired a degree of social prestige, celebrity status and material security, but the social and communication barriers between them and their clients were never fully removed.

This may be a far cry from the world of glamour, celebrity status and wealth accorded to at least some of the top 'supermodels' in the contemporary era; however, the aura of standoffishness, aloofness and distance characterising the early fashion shows persists. The facial expressions, gestures and movements of the models employed by top designers in their shows and advertisements, with their gaze focused in the middle distance, often looking 'past' the audience or viewer, pouted or slightly parted lips (typically signifying 'sexiness'), highly stylised gestures and synchronised movements render them as alluring and beautiful yet inaccessible and distant, their individuality indiscernible in favour of creating the image of perfect modelling types.

It is possible to see the echoes of the aloof Mannerist stylised poses and the subservient detachment of the late 19th and early 20th century live mannequins in the static, studiously graceful and de-individualised fashion photographs and dummy figures dominating contemporary shopping malls (Figure 5.1, images 69, 70 and 99). The dummies often have their eyes closed as if sleeping or otherwise absent from the scene (Figure 5.1, image 79). They are often faceless and may appear menacing (Figure 5.1, images 80–82) or headless (Figure 5.1, images 83 and 84), which also made them objects of fascination for Surrealist painters, who saw them as blurring the boundaries between 'animate and inanimate, human and machine, male and female, the sexualized and the sexless' (Wood, 2007: 10).

In the photographs in shop window displays and on advertising billboards, contemporary models frequently look bored, standoffish or withdrawn (Figure 5.1, images 85–93), just as their predecessors over a hundred years ago. When their gaze is directed at the viewer it is piercing and scrutinising rather than inviting. Being cool and chic requires adopting an equally aloof stance, even when the target customers are children (or children's parents), and when a faint smile appears it suggests irony rather than friendliness (Figure 5.1, images 97, 98 and 100). In this regard, present day modelling continues what Simmel identified as early as 1903 as 'a trend of the blasé attitude that modern urban life engendered' (Evans, 2013: 244). For Simmel (1971 [1903]),

> that reserve was a typically urban mental attitude and [he] noted the 'specifically metropolitan extravagances of self-distanciation, of caprice, of fastidiousness, the meaning of which is no longer to be found in the content of such activity itself but rather in its being a form of 'being different' – of making oneself noticeable' … and it is in this way that fashion comes to be central to metropolitan life. The mannequin simply professionalised this cultivation of affectlessness. In this respect, her perfor-mance pre-empted the postmodern concept of the waning of affect by many decades, for the modern mannequin was 'affectless' from the outset, even in the nineteenth century when her resemblance to the inanimate doll and automaton first troubled her observers. (Evans, 2013: 244)

Of course, Simmel's 'affectlessness' is a manifestation of specific affective positions, as described above. The distant, silent demeanour of the living mannequins was not only an index of their generally inferior social status and their defence mechanism against the aloofness of their upper class clients. The female models were as much the object of the male gaze of the clients' husbands, the 'modern man', the *flâneur* who emerged as a lone and silent spectator of urban life, himself to be seen but not spoken to, free to pursue the image of the world beyond the rigidity of his family life. Silence became a signifier of highly gendered and classed relations that 'superim-posed public and private imagery [making] it possible to be both visible to others and isolated from them' (Sennett, 1974: 217).

5.6 Conclusion

The aim of this chapter has been to contribute to the growing literature on how contemporary places of consumption are unevenly economically structured by dif-ferential linguistic and other semiotic resources. My focus here has been on the use and display of 'silence'. Bourdieu obviously made a similar point several decades ago, linking silence to a sense of distinction both in terms of taste and its display.

> Where the petit bourgeois or nouveau riche 'overdoes it', betraying his own insecu-rity, bourgeois discretion signals its presence by a sort of ostentatious discretion, sobriety and understatement, a refusal of everything which is 'showy', 'flashy' and pretentious, and which devalues itself by the very intention of distinction. (Bourdieu, 1984: 249)

The thematisation and displays of silence in the semiotic landscape continue to rein-force the uneven organisation of commercial spaces into sites of necessity and sites of luxury across the globe. I hope to have demonstrated that displayed silence, alongside other semiotic resources, appears to style businesses, products and, by implication, their target customers as savvy, sophisticated and somehow superior or elite, in the sense borrowed from Appadurai (1986). For this reason, understated aesthetic design, more or less 'knowing' references to art, pretending to keep one's products and services as secrets, and creating an aura of standoffishness and distance, are not mere formal choices but highly charged ideological stances.

Commercial urban spaces are dense and diverse. The distribution and display of language codes, images, objects, architectural detail, bodies and other semiotic resources regulate and legitimate ownership and access to space, as well as the interactional order of implied and target participants. In specific contexts of use, semiotic resources display orientations to *orders of indexicality*, that is socially and culturally patterned 'norms' of control, authority and evaluation associated with these resources in their microenvironments, settings and networks (Silverstein, 2003). Silence is just one such, potentially overlooked, resource which is frequently deployed by designers, advertisers and marketers to style their spaces of business and to position target customers as 'elite'. The use of silence in these contexts is subtly related to regimes of power/knowledge in that responses to some of the formal features of design draw on historically, culturally and aesthetically salient tropes imbued with social meaning and authority.

Acknowledgements

I am most grateful to Johan Järlehed and Martin Pütz for their very useful comments on the penultimate draft of this chapter. All errors are my own.

Notes

Unless otherwise stated, all images in Figure 5.1 are my own. Additional sources are as follows:

Image 71: http://www.slideshare.net/sotos1/michelangelo-capella-sistina.

Image 73: https://commons.wikimedia.org/wiki/File:Parmigianino_Madonna_dal_ collo_lungo_-_ Google_Art_Project.jpg.

Image 75: Giambologna's Astronomy, used by kind permission from Collection of Mr. and Mrs. J. Tomilson Hill; image © The Frick Collection.

Image 77: Bronzino's *The Allegory with Venus and Cupid* (*c*. 1545) Photo © The National Gallery, London.

All visual extracts/quotes are reproduced solely for the purposes of scholarly comment and critique. The research for this chapter was supported by an HKSAR Government Funded Research Project (GRF) 2016–2019 titled 'Word as image: The sociolinguistics of art' (RGC ref. no. 17600415).

References

Adam, B. (1998) *Timescapes of Modernity: The Environment and Invisible Hazards*. London: Routledge.

Appadurai, A. (1986) Introduction: Commodities and the politics of value. In A. Appadurai (ed.) *The Social Life of Things: Commodities in Cultural Perspective* (pp. 3–63). Cambridge: Cambridge University Press.

Barthes, R. (1977) *Image, Music, Text*. London: Fontana.

Bell, A. (1984) Language style as audience design. *Language in Society* 13, 145–204.

Bourdieu, P. (1984) *Distinction: A Social Critique of the Judgement of Taste*. Cambridge, MA: Harvard University Press.

Bourdieu, P. (1991) *Language & Symbolic Power*. Cambridge: Polity.

Buchloh, B.H.D. (2000) Plenty of nothing: From Yves Klein's *Le vide* to Arman's *Le plein*. In B.H.D. Buchloh (ed.) *Neo-Avantgarde and Culture Industry: Essays on European and American Art from 1955 to 1975* (pp. 257–284). Cambridge, MA: MIT Press (original work published 1988).

Bucholtz, M. and Hall, K. (2016) Embodied sociolinguistics. In C. Coupland (ed.) *Sociolinguistics: Theoretical Debates* (pp. 173–197). Cambridge: Cambridge University Press.

Chafe, W. (1985) Some reasons for hesitating. In D. Tannen and M. Saville-Troike (eds) *Perspectives on Silence* (pp. 77–89). Norwood, MA: Ablex.

Cheshire, J. and Moser, L.-M. (1994) English as a cultural symbol: The case of advertisements in French-speaking Switzerland. *Journal of Multilingual and Multicultural Development* 15, 451–469.

Coupland, N. (2010) Welsh linguistic landscapes 'from above' and 'from below.' In A. Jaworski and C. Thurlow (eds) *Semiotic Landscapes: Text, Image, Space* (pp. 77–101). London: Continuum.

Duez, D. (1982) Silent and non-silent pauses in three speech styles. *Language and Speech* 25, 11–28.

Evans, C. (2013) *The Mechanical Smile: Modernism and the First Fashion Shows in France and America, 1900–1929*. New Haven, CT: Yale University Press.

Fairclough, N. (1989) *Language and Power*. London: Longman.

Fairclough, N. (1992) *Discourse and Social Change*. Cambridge: Polity Press.

Goffman, E. (1974) *Frame Analysis: An Essay on the Organization of Experience*. New York: Harper and Row.

Goffman, E. (1979) *Gender Advertisements*. London: Macmillan.

Guilat, Y. and Espinosa-Ramírez, A.B. (2016) The historical memory law and its role in redesigning semiotic cityscapes in Spain: A case study from Granada. *Linguistic Landscape* 2 (3), 247–274.

Haarman, H. (1989) *Symbolic Values of Foreign Language Use: From the Japanese Case to a General Sociolinguistic Perspective*. Berlin: Mouton de Gruyter.

Hafif, M. (1997) Silence in painting: Let me count the ways. In A. Jaworski (ed.) *Silence: Interdisciplinary Perspectives* (pp. 339–349). Berlin: Mouton de Gruyter.

Halliday, M.A.K. (1978) *Language as Social Semiotic: The Social Interpretation of Language and Meaning*. London: Arnold.

Hanauer, D.I. (2004) Silence, voice and erasure: Psychological embodiment in graffiti at the site of Prime Minister Rabin's assassination. *The Arts in Psychotherapy* 31 (1), 29–35.

Heller, M. (2010) The commodification of language. *Annual Review of Anthropology* 39, 101–114.

Heller, M., Duchêne, A. and Pujolar, J. (2014) Linguistic commodification in tourism. *Journal of Sociolinguistics* 18 (4), 539–566.

Hutton, C.M. (2011) Vernacular spaces and 'non-places': Dynamics of the Hong Kong linguistic landscape. In M. Messling, D. Läpple and J. Trabant (eds) *Stadt und Urbanität* (pp. 162–184). Berlin: Kadmos Verlag.

Hutton, C. (2016) (Westernized) Zen Buddhism and integrationism: Non-solutions to non-problems? Paper presented at the Symposium Language, Mind & Society: Semiological Perspectives, School of English, University of Hong Kong, 2–3 December 2016.

Jaworski, A. (1993) *The Power of Silence: Social and Pragmatic Perspectives*. Newbury Park, CA: Sage Publications.

Jaworski, A. (1997) 'White and white': Metacommunicative and metaphorical silences. In A. Jaworski (ed.) *Silence: Interdisciplinary Perspectives* (pp. 381–401). Berlin: Mouton de Gruyter.

Jaworski, A. (2015) Globalese: A new visual-linguistic register. *Social Semiotics* 25 (2), 217–235.

Jaworski, A. (2016a) Visual silence and non-normative sexualities: Art, transduction and performance. *Gender and Language* 10 (3), 433–454.

Jaworski, A. (2016b) Silence and creativity: Re-mediation, transduction and performance. In R.H. Jones (ed.) *The Routledge Handbook of Language and Creativity* (pp. 322–335). London: Routledge.

Jaworski, A. and Thurlow, C. (2009) Taking an elitist stance: Ideology and the discursive production of social distinction. In A. Jaffe (ed.) *Stance: Sociolinguistic Perspectives* (pp. 195–226). New York: Oxford University Press.

Jaworski, A. and Thurlow, C. (2010) Introducing semiotic landscapes. In A. Jaworski and C. Thurlow (eds) *Semiotic Landscapes: Language, Image, Space* (pp. 1–40). London: Continuum.

Jaworski, A. and Thurlow, C. (2011) Tracing place, locating self: Embodiment and remediation in/of tourist spaces. *Visual Communication* 10 (3), 249–366.

Jaworski, A. and Thurlow, C. (2013) The (de-)centering spaces of airports: Framing mobility and multilingualism. In S. Pietikäinen and H. Kelly-Holmes (eds) *Peripheral Multilingualism* (pp. 154–198). New York: Oxford University Press.

Jaworski, A. and Thurlow, C. (2014) Gesture and movement in tourist spaces. In C. Jewitt (ed.) *The Routledge Handbook of Multimodal Analysis* (pp. 365–374). London: Routledge.

Jaworski, A. and Yeung, S. (2010) Life in the garden of Eden: The naming and imagery of residential Hong Kong. In E. Shohamy, E. Ben-Rafael and M. Barni (eds) *Linguistic Landscape in the City* (pp. 153–181). Bristol: Multilingual Matters.

Jones, R.H. (2016) *Spoken Discourse*. London: Bloomsbury.

Jones, R.H. and Norris, S. (2005) Introducing mediational means/cultural tools. In S. Norris and R.H. Jones (eds) *Discourse in Action: Introducing Mediated Discourse Analysis* (pp. 49–51). London: Routledge.

Kamps, T. (2012) (...) In T. Kamps and S. Seid (eds) *Silence* (pp. 63–81). Houston: Menil Foundation and Berkeley: UC Berkeley Art Museum and Pacific Film Archive.

Kelly-Holmes, H. (2005) *Advertising as Multilingual Communication*. Basingstoke: Palgrave Macmillan.

Kelly-Holmes, H. (2010) Languages and global marketing. In N. Coupland (ed.) *The Handbook of Language and Globalization* (pp. 475–492). Oxford: Wiley-Blackwell.

Kitis, E.D. and Milani, T.M.M. (2015) The performative body. *Linguistic Landscape* 1 (3), 268–290.

Kowinski, W.S. (1985) *The Malling of America: An Inside Look at the Great Consumer Paradise*. New York: William and Morrow.

Kress, G. (2010) *Multimodality: A Social Semiotic Approach to Contemporary Communication*. London: Routledge.

Kress, G. and van Leeuwen, T. (1996) *Reading Images: The Grammar of Visual Design*. London: Routledge.

Macalister, J. (2010) Emerging voices or linguistic silence? Examining a New Zealand linguistic landscape. *Multilingua* 29 (1), 55–75.

Martin, E. (2007) 'Frenglish' for sale: Multilingual discourses for addressing today's global consumer. *World Englishes* 26 (2), 170–188.

Milani, T.M. (2015) Sexual cityzenship: Discourses, spaces and bodies at Joburg Pride 2012. *Journal of Language and Politics* 14 (3), 431–454.

Papen, U. (2012) Commercial discourses, gentrification and citizens' protest: The linguistic landscape of Prenzlauer Berg, Berlin. *Journal of Sociolinguistics* 16 (1), 56–80.

Park, J. and Wee, L. (2012) *Markets of English*. New York: Routledge.

Peck, A. and Stroud, C. (2015) Skinscapes. *Linguistic Landscape: An International Journal* 1 (1–2), 133–151.

Pietikäinen, S., Kelly-Holmes, H., Jaffe, A. and Coupland, N. (2016) *Sociolinguistics from the Periphery: Small Languages in New Circumstances*. Cambridge: Cambridge University Press.

Piller, I. (2001) Identity constructions in multilingual advertising. *Language in Society* 30, 153–186.

Piller, I. (2003) Advertising as a site of language contact. *Annual Review of Applied Linguistics* 23, 170–183.

Pine, J. and Gilmore, J. (1999) *The Experience Economy: Work Is Theatre & Every Business a Stage*. Cambridge: Harvard Business Review Press.

Popper, F. (2009) *Neon*. Grove Art Online. Oxford: Oxford University Press.

Rampton, B. (2003) Hegemony, social class and stylization. *Pragmatics* 13 (1), 49–83.

Ritzer, G. (2008) *Enchanting a Disenchanted World: Revolutionizing the Means of Consumption*. Thousand Oaks: Pine Forge Press.

Sennett, R. (1974) *The Fall of Public Man*. London: Penguin.

Sennett, R. (1994) *Flesh and Stone: The Body and the City in Western Civilization*. London: Faber and Faber.

Serwe, S.K., Ong, K.K.W. and Ghesquière, J.F. (2013) 'Bon Appétit, Lion City': The use of French naming in Singapore. *English Today* 29 (3), 19–25.

Shearman, J. (1967) *Mannerism*. London: Penguin Books.

Silverstein, M. (2003) Indexical order and the dialectics of sociolinguistic life. *Language and Communication* 23, 193–229.

Simmel, G. (1971) *Georg Simmel on Individuality and Social Forms*. Chicago: University of Chicago Press (original work published 1903).

Sperber, D. and Wilson, D. (1986) *Relevance: Communication and Cognition*. Oxford: Blackwell.

Streeck, J., Goodwin, C. and LeBaron, C. (eds) (2011) *Embodied Interaction: Language and Body in the Material World*. Cambridge: Cambridge University Press.

Stroud, C. and Mpendukana, S. (2009) Towards a material ethnography of linguistic landscape: Multilingualism, mobility and space in a South African township. *Journal of Sociolinguistics* 13 (3), 363–386.

Thurlow, C. and Jaworski, A. (2010) Silence is golden: The 'anti-communicational' linguascaping of super-elite mobility. In A. Jaworski and C. Thurlow (eds) *Semiotic Landscapes: Text, Image, Space* (pp. 187–218). London: Continuum.

Thurlow, C. and Jaworski, A. (2011) Banal globalization? Embodied actions and mediated practices in tourists' online photo-sharing. In C. Thurlow and K. Mroczek (eds) *Digital Discourse: Language in the New Media* (pp. 220–250). New York: Oxford University Press.

Thurlow, C. and Jaworski, A. (2012) Elite mobilities: The semiotic landscapes of luxury and privilege. *Social Semiotics* 22 (4), 487–516.

Thurlow, C. and Jaworski, A. (2014) 'Two hundred ninety-four': Remediation and multimodal performance in tourist placemaking. *Journal of Sociolinguistics* 18 (4), 459–494.

Thurlow, C. and Jaworski, A. (2015) On top of the world: Tourists' spectacular self-locations as multimodal travel writing. In J. Kuehn and P. Smethurst (eds) *New Directions in Travel Writing Studies* (pp. 35–53). Basingstoke: Palgrave Macmillan.

Thurlow, C. and Jaworski, A. (2017a) The discursive production and maintenance of class privilege: Permeable geographies, slippery rhetorics. *Discourse & Society* 28 (5), 535–558.

Thurlow, C. and Jaworski, A. (eds) (2017b) Elite discourse: The rhetorics of status, privilege and power. *Special Issue of Social Semiotics* 27 (3), 243–381.

Trinch, S. and Snajdr, E. (2017) What the signs say: Gentrification and the disappearance of capitalism without distinction in Brooklyn. *Journal of Sociolinguistics* 21 (1), 64–89.

Urry, J. (2005) The 'consuming' place. In A. Jaworski and A. Pritchard (eds) *Discourse, Communication and Tourism* (pp. 19–27). Clevedon: Channel View Publications.

Vandenbroucke, M. (2016) Socio-economic stratification of English in globalized landscapes: A market-oriented perspective. *Journal of Sociolinguistics* 20 (1), 86–108.

West Kowloon Cultural District Authority (2016) See http://www.westkowloon.hk/en/nothing.

Wood, G. (2007) *The Surreal Body: Fetish and Fashion*. London: V&A Publications.

6 Multimodality in the City: On the Media, Perception and Locatedness of Public Textscapes

Christine Domke

In linguistic landscapes, a lot of research has recently focused on analysing a city's public texts in a broader sense, including both different semiotic resources and the communicative construction of space/place. However, one aspect has been largely ignored so far: a city's semiotic landscape is not only *visible*, but also *audible* and perceptible in a *tactile* manner. Focusing on this, my contribution aims at bridging this gap between a city's diversity of public communications and the possible modes of perception. Therefore, I want to elaborate on whether a text is to be *read*, *heard* or *felt* (like Braille codes), including a focus on the interplay between modes of perception and addressee orientation. Finally, I will discuss the increasing media differentiation of public texts as a part of and as an example of the increasing 'mediatization' (Krotz & Hepp, 2012) of everyday life.

6.1 Introduction: On the Need for Media-orientated Perspectives on Public Textscapes

Linguistic landscape studies have shown that walking through a city leads to at least one finding from an everyday life perspective: the streets and buildings, corners and walls we may walk along or see are inseparable from the many signs, stickers, notices and posters being attached to these places (see Figure 6.1). It is clear that even a person just walking to the bus stop or through a main station in a city may read a sign, commercial or notice even if they did not intend to do so. By focusing on these publicly perceivable texts, linguistic analysis is able to highlight the immense symbolic and local functions of this textual landscape, or rather, *textscape* (see below), and to examine the variety of language(s) (Shohamy *et al.*, 2010) and discourses (e.g. Kallen, 2010; Scollon & Scollon, 2003) present.

With reference to more recent studies in the broad field of linguistic landscapes, an expanded perspective is needed. The (first) studies of linguistic landscapes, the scope of which was famously defined by Landry and Bourhis (1997: 25), led to mostly quantitative insights into multilingual societies and 'the presence and dominance of one language over others' (Jaworski & Thurlow, 2010b: 10; e.g. Backhaus, 2007). However, more recent studies reflect a broader understanding of public texts,

Figure 6.1 Mariahilfer Street, Vienna

redefining the scope of linguistic landscapes as *semiotic* landscapes (see Jaworski & Thurlow, 2010a, 2010b: 2). This involves not only different semiotic resources, but also the meaning-making that occurs through the text's *locatedness* (see Domke, 2015, 2017) and therefore the social and communicative construction of space and place (see e.g. Ben-Rafael *et al.*, 2010: xiv). To date, different resources such as printed or handwritten writings have been examined as well as local naming of shops and their typography in different quarters (see e.g. Dray, 2010; Papen, 2012). Graffiti and different materialities and locations (such as floors, windows, stairs, traffic lights and walls) are also an established part of the semiotic analysis, which includes the question of what type of social discourse may be generated by the use of these resources. Accordingly, the different resources are interpreted as indicating different discourses, such as commercial, political, regulatory and transgressive discourses (cf. Domke, 2014, 2015; Kallen, 2010; Scollon & Scollon, 2003; Warnke, 2011). In general, it is increasingly being considered important to examine this form of public communication to address a current crucial question: 'How does the social construction of space/place take place?' (see Busse & Warnke, 2014: 2ff.; see also Jaworski & Thurlow, 2010b: 5ff.)

In spite of such a broad perspective, one aspect of public communication has been largely ignored in most of the studies mentioned so far: a city's semiotic landscape is not only *visible*, but also *audible* and perceptible in a *tactile* manner. Publicly perceivable communication forms (see below) include billboards, stickers, announcements, display panels, guidance systems, public signs, notices, QR-codes and physical barriers (see Figure 6.1) – and therefore involve different media, materialities and *modes* of perception.

However, this diversity regarding the media used and the modes of perception has been mostly overlooked while concentrating on *visually* perceivable texts. Accordingly, the scope of linguistic landscape research still often seems to be literally limited to what is readable, following Landry and Bourhis' famous definition of linguistic landscapes as: 'The language of public road signs, advertising billboards, street names, place names, commercial shop signs, and public signs on government buildings' (Landry & Bourhis, 1997: 25). This definition lists only *visibly* perceivable texts in public places, comparable to studies analysing which languages and what signs, stickers or notices we may *see* in public. As mentioned above, Jaworski and Thurlow (2010a) aim at expanding this perspective by including different semiotic resources such as images and architecture. Nevertheless, their broad understanding of semiotic landscape research seems to indicate yet another kind of restriction:

> We have chosen not to call this book 'Linguistic Landscapes' [...] because in this collection we are keen to emphasize the way *written* discourse interacts with other discursive modalities. [...] We thus take semiotic landscape to mean, in the most general sense, any (public) space with *visible* inscription made through deliberate human intervention and meaning making. (Jaworski & Thurlow, 2010b: 2, my emphasis)

However, besides visible texts there are other forms that generate public space by means of communication (see below, Domke, 2014). The focus of semiotic landscape studies on mainly *visual* communication has also been discussed by Pappenhagen *et al.* (2013) and Scarvaglieri *et al.* (2013), who suggest a 'Linguistic Soundscaping' approach (Pappenhagen *et al.* 2013: 132ff.), which aims at analysing the discursive use of language(s) in public spaces. Based on findings like these, the interplay between written *and* spoken language varieties in public places moves increasingly into focus, avoiding the limitation of only examining visible perceivable texts. Pennycook and Otsuji's (2015) analysis of *smellscapes* clearly shows the possibility and relevance of expanding the analytic perspective. Based on an olfactory ethnography of Sydney, they discuss the relation between smells and space/place, underlining both the methodological need and daily use of realising, or rather perceiving, very different semiotic resources in the everyday life construction of social space.

Accordingly, one aspect should be emphasised: different modes of perception and likewise the differentiation of the media being used cannot yet be considered as a common analytic focus in the field; their inclusion as a *natural* part of the analysis of any recent (public) communication is still very rare. With regard to different forms of verbal language use and the use of semiotic resources in public, which may be perceivable audibly, visually or even in a tactile manner (and olfactorily, see above), it seems to be rather important to consider linguistic landscapes as *semiotic textscapes*, which include not only different semiotic resources such as images and buildings (see Jaworski & Thurlow, 2010a; Scollon & Scollon, 2003; Shohamy & Gorter, 2010), but also all possible modes of perception. Furthermore, an expanded perspective like this allows linguistic landscape research to be combined with the broader discussion on multimodality (see Jewitt, 2011), which is considered a characteristic feature of all texts (see e.g. Van Leeuwen, 2005) and a basic part of a mediatized everyday life. At the same time, media and communication studies could benefit from semiotic textscapes as an important field of multimodal texts with a broad range of semiotic resources, including different materialities, places and pragmatic functions.

This is where the present contribution comes in. My aim is to outline the functional use of visible, audible and/or tactile communication as an important feature of the public textscape in general, with the discussion being structured according to the following steps. First of all (see Section 6.2), I want to elaborate on the media used for public texts (analogue or digital, permanent or temporarily perceivable), the possible modes of perception and the functional differentiation of this *place-bound communication* (see also Domke, 2014, 2015). While using the media-linguistic concept of *communication forms* (see below), the contribution argues for a media-orientated analysis of the public textscape, which is an important part of the public construction of social space. Secondly (see Section 6.3), the contribution briefly discusses – with reference to public prohibitions and direction signs – the interplay between a text's function, different kinds of perception (visual, audible and tactile) and the text's material 'locatedness'. Thirdly (see Section 6.4), this media-linguistic differentiation of public texts will be finally discussed as a part of the increasing 'mediatization' (Krotz, 2007) of everyday life.

6.2 Public Textscapes and their Media: From Empirical Data to Pragmatic Functions

A media-orientated analysis of publicly perceivable texts coexists with empirical data which offers the possibility to both document and interpret a city's textscape. At this point, photographs become important as a never entirely objective (see Meier, 2012), but particularly detailed device of documentation. In addition to the well-established linguistic methodology of audio-recording, photographs make it possible to elaborate and reconstruct structural patterns of public communication and to analyse the interplay between the media used and pragmatic functions.

The examples I am going to discuss belong to a corpus (see also Domke, 2014) of about 3000 pictures and recordings mostly from cities, railway stations and airports in large German cities (such as Berlin, Hamburg, Leipzig and Freiburg), but also from other European cities such as Paris and Vienna. The texts captured in the pictures and recordings are part of the *publicly perceivable communication*, which excludes private conversation at this moment; the analysis of the empirical data based on pragmatic and media-linguistic considerations leads to different main groups of public texts and recurring patterns being established, which will be outlined later in this section. Thereby, the analysis follows the basic assumption that this *place-bound textscape* (see Domke, 2014, 2015) is potentially perceivable by everybody on location, underlining its definition as *public* communication and *publicly perceivable*.

In this sense, the public textscape serves as a permanently available possibility for any walker to create their own 'reading' of a specific place: de Certeau defines space as a practiced place and focuses on 'users reappropriating the space' (de Certeau, 1988: xiv) through their individual routes and social activities in the city. Accordingly, public texts serve as communicative offers for the people walking by, potentially ascribing to a place specific features such as being public, regulated or touristy. In the terms of Jäger, one could say that signs, announcements or notices make a place 'readable' (e.g. Jäger, 2010) as a specific social space, for example, as historically relevant or a pedestrian zone.

To be able to form groups of public texts and investigate the interplay between media, perception and function, it is important to analyse both the variety of media being used and the pragmatic use of the texts that are publicly perceivable. The media-linguistic concept of *communication forms* (see Domke, 2017) makes it possible to differentiate between a text's media and text's function (see also Holly, 2011): it implies and encompasses a basic differentiation between the structural and media-based frames of any text (the very communication *form* such as a sign or poster, see below) and the specific pragmatic use (or rather text type) for which a communication form may be used (such as prohibition or direction signs, poster advertising, wanted poster or election poster). In this concept, *medium* is considered a constructed device usable for different communication forms; accordingly, communication forms emerge from media use and reflect the medium's specific mediality. The medium *paper*, for example, may be used in public places for the communication form 'notice' or 'tear-off', often used for text types such as searching for lost belongings or offering side jobs. To identify communication forms, distinctive features such as the following are useful (cf. Domke, 2014, 2015, 2017):

- the *mediality/materiality* (such as analogue or digital, printed, fixed, moveable, embodied, technical and so on);
- the *semiotic resources* available (such as language, images, sounds);
- the mode of perception (such as visible, audible or tactile);
- the possible number of *participants* (such as one-to-one, one-to-many and so on);
- the material locatedness (place-bound, non-place-bound, see below);
- the time-boundedness (such as temporary, permanently perceivable).

The concept of communication forms offers the possibility to elaborate on the interplay between media choice and pragmatic function and therefore to highlight contemporary communicative practices in a broad sense. Following the basic understanding that communication forms are to be considered *frames of contingency* (see Domke, 2017) from which the person who wants to communicate has to choose for their communicative purpose, the question of which communication forms we find in public places becomes important. The analysis makes it possible to form three major groups with some subcategories, which will be detailed in the following sections.

6.2.1 Permanent order: Non-time-bound perceivable communication forms

First of all, there are the group of *permanently visible communication forms*. The group includes signs, fixed positioners and boards. Semiotic landscape research conducted to date has mostly focused on these forms, which correlates with their omnipresence in public places (see Figure 6.1). What signs, information columns and fixed boards have in common is, of course, their mode of perception and their mediality: the weather-resistant material of the permanent inscription and the fixed placement allow a non-time-bound reception.

Figure 6.2 Town Hall Square, Freiburg

In Figure 6.2, you may notice a sign with a historicised place name (Rathausplatz/ town hall square), an information sign for public toilets, a prohibition sign for cars in a certain weight range and – located below – a sign (in blue) which informs the fire service about the next option for water supply. This may be considered as a typical visual public textscape as it has been examined in many studies so far. The communication form 'sign' is clearly used for different textual functions such as communicating prohibitions, information or directions. This demonstrates the usefulness of the differentiation between communication forms and their pragmatic use discussed above; the signs presented in Figures 6.1 and 6.2 also underline what Kallen has emphasised:

> What gives the landscape its discursive, and even at times chaotic, appearance, is that these systems are not hierarchically nested within each other. Some are parasitic on others [...], and some [...] involve little conscious planning and considerable spatial independence. (Kallen, 2010: 42)

With reference to the media-related considerations discussed above, the question arises as to whether (and how) this heterogeneity correlates with the communication forms and media used. This has to be taken into account when focusing on the group of permanently perceivable texts in public places. Because of their material and fixed placement on walls or pole signs as well as fixed positioners or monuments, they are *permanently perceivable*. This makes them utilisable for information of non-time-bound validity such as directions or public institutions, a place's history or terms of use. One could say that the function of these permanent texts lies in arranging a place's basic (and obviously permanent) character as public or culturally relevant. In comparison to time-bound communication forms such as display panels or notices (see below), this group of communication forms is used to make a specific place readable as a *steady* space, referring by means of signs or monuments to permanent existing institutions, structures, orders and (assumed) historical facts. With graffiti – a permanent communication form that is in most cases unwanted by the building's owner (see Pennycook, 2010) – it is exactly this permanent quality that makes expensive removal necessary. Also, the intense debates on replacements of historical monuments or street signs reflect the relevance of communication forms ascribing *permanently* specific features to places, quarters and streets (cf. e.g. Abousnnouga & Machin, 2010).

However, what is permanently perceivable is *not always just visible*. This has not been a major focus in semiotic landscape research to date although it demonstrates in particular the multimodality of public textscapes. This leads to the group of *tactilely perceivable* texts. Communication forms such as guidance systems on pavements (see Figure 6.3) are used to give direction information such as 'walk this way'. When they contain different stripes and dots (see the framed zone in front of the entrance in Figure 6.3), they indicate 'here, a change of direction is possible', which reflects their textuality as defined and encoded communication (see Domke, 2014: 289ff.). These guidance systems are permanently perceivable by sense of touch unless they become 'unreadable' due to snowfall or luggage. They make it possible for visually-impaired people to follow the coded paving with their white cane and to orientate themselves in the city or stations. Because of the cane's regular sound on this surface, some guidance systems can be considered *multimodally* perceivable, combining tactile and audible information (see below).

Alongside this, more tactilely perceivable communication forms exist. Tactile tablets in front of public institutions, famous buildings or inside railway stations are fixed by robust media-material and serve different pragmatic uses. In Braille they contain, for example, tactilely perceivable cultural information concerning a place's history as well as floor or direction plans (see Figure 6.4). Their materiality indicates permanently valid information, as with the signs and monuments mentioned above. Also, these texts may be perceived only by one person at a time.

6.2.2 Only valid for a certain time: Time-bound communication forms

The fixed and robust media-material of the place-bound communication forms discussed so far indicates permanence and steady validation of a given text's contents. But there are other place-bound communication forms used to indicate and generate public space. At this point, what may be seen or heard or is tactilely perceivable only *temporarily* comes into focus. Time-bound content is realised by using

Figure 6.3 Entrance to main station, Erfurt

Figure 6.4 Gelsenkirchen main station

Figure 6.5 Leipzig, Karl-Liebknecht-Street

communication forms such as notices, display panels, mobile positioners or semiotic barriers (such as warning tapes at sites). They are based on more flexible media-material and are used for time-bound infrastructural matters such as digital arrival boards or for public information such as a prohibition notice.

They reflect the variety of media and functions of the public textscape and accordingly they offer or rather attach more differentiation to their places. For example, by referring to the many different notices in public we are able to distinguish job offers, event promotions or requests for lost belongings. Obviously, they make their location 'readable', in the sense of Jäger (2010), as a social space to be used not only by institutions but also by individuals. This individualisation of communication *and* space realised by means of quite simple media-material also applies to mobile positioners in front of restaurants or shops. They also make it possible to use typography in creative ways and to attract the attention of people walking by. The example in Figure 6.5 ('Today fresh clothes') demonstrates this by using the knowledge about typical texts on mobile positioners such as 'Today: cheese cake!' while transferring its typical use for promoting food to promote 'fresh' and obviously not industrial-made clothes from the 'Unikaterie'.

Mobile positioners are used for commercials, job offers and instructions for parking places, which reflects the many textual functions this communication form may be used for. Mobile positioners, together with notices and posters, belong to the group of only temporarily perceivable communication forms. These forms can be considered as well-established possibilities for private, commercial, political and regulatory discourses to communicate temporary requests, events or variations in time schedules (see Domke, 2014: 235ff.). Digital display panels also reveal time-bound information but are – because of their cost, maintenance and specific materiality – not used for so many different discourses. It is possible to discover an increasing number of digital display panels in, for example, railway or tram stations, broadcasting news or commercials and in front of a museum to inform people about the tickets still available. They enable information to be provided which is updated frequently and is visible for a specific time. In contrast and in addition to permanently visible texts available in analogue media (such as printed time schedules), their main function can be considered as offering news (such as on a train delay). Digital displays are permanently fixed by means of their media-material such as screens or big boards and are perceivable by several people at the same time.

The group of temporarily perceivable texts can be completed by referring to *publicly perceivable audible communication forms*. Audible communication in public places mainly includes announcements and is used for both verbal information (human/computer-generated) about arrivals, departures and cancellations of trains and non-verbal information by means of coded acoustic signals. In contrast to visible texts in front of or inside of buildings, announcements may be described as 'omnipresent' (Raffaseder, 2010: 19f.) owing to the fact that we are not able to unfocus from or ignore what is publicly announced by public announcement systems: a public announcement such as a train cancellation, for example, can be heard by every person on location. Therefore, audible communication is shaping public spaces more directly, sustainably and inescapably, which explains its restricted use mainly for traffic issues and for other events only on occasion.

However, an increasing use of audible communication forms must be mentioned, to which the features of omnipresence just mentioned do not apply. At bus stations or in elevators we may discover little buttons at waist level which can be pressed; *then* an announcement about a building's floors, possible directions or the bus schedule can be heard. Obviously, the same textual functions (site maps and timetables) are realised by means of different (visible and audible) communication forms used to address different groups of walkers or visitors. This underlines the interesting interplay between communication forms and pragmatic use and the public textscape's *multimodal differentiation*.

6.2.3 Combining modes and/or media: Hybrid communication forms

Finishing this overview of public communication forms, there is still to mention the increasingly found group of *hybrid place-bound communication forms*, which combine modes of perception or media resources and differ in the distinctive feature of 'time-boundedness/non-time-boundedness'. *Place-bound communication forms* as discussed so far are visible, audible and tactually perceivable in their place. They offer a broad range of possibilities to ascribe different features to a place, including time-bound and non-time-bound texts. These forms are used by institutions, groups and individuals, creating what emerges as the public textscape we may perceive in our everyday lives and/or examine owing to our analytic interests. Besides their particular function to inform, navigate or promote, they indicate different discourses and therefore social spaces. In the sense of de Certeau (1988), social spaces in the city are also the result of walkers re-appropriating places using, for example, texts in their individual route. With reference to that, the importance of place-bound communication in shaping social space seems to be evident. Besides the forms mentioned above, this also applies to more complex, or rather, hybrid, forms combining modes of perception and media. Three examples will be used to briefly illustrate the variety of these complex and (partly) increasingly used communication forms.

The first example focuses on temporary public communication forms based on attendees such as demonstrations or outdoor or public screenings of sporting events. As someone walking through a city, you may hear and/or see a political group marching, clapping, singing and holding banners, and therefore shaping public places as social and political places while forming 'interaction spaces' (cf. McIlvenny *et al.*, 2009). This combination of modes of perception also applies to signs such as yellow buttons at traffic lights. In Germany, there is often an audible sound indicating the traffic lights' position. When the button is pressed, it starts vibrating when the audible signal is getting faster, indicating 'walk'. Obviously, this hybrid form offers both an audible and tactile sign for visually-impaired people.

The last example combines analogue and digital media. With QR-codes printed on posters, for example, their producers try to attract the attention of local attendees; scanning the QR-codes with a smartphone makes it possible to load a website with articles or audio files promoting restaurants, events or books (see Figure 6.6, promoting a book from the author Thomas Brussig). This form of intertextuality connects visible place-bound posters with non-place-bound websites and texts or audio files – and is one example of the new relevance of smartphones for and in public spaces.

Figure 6.6 Floor of the main station, Leipzig

6.3 On the Interplay between Communication Form and Pragmatic Use

The overview given so far reflects the range of communication forms that have emerged for public communication and the differentiation with reference to modes of perception and pragmatic purposes. To highlight the differentiated interplay between communication forms and pragmatic use, I will now focus briefly on two specific text types: prohibitions and direction devices.

Prohibitions and warnings, as well as direction devices in cities are put up by official institutions as well as shop owners and private owners as 'principles', in the terms of Goffman (1981). While prohibitions in a broader sense also include warnings, instructions and requests (cf. Domke, 2015), they are meant to regulate, for example, access to buildings and places and the use of market squares and playgrounds. Direction devices offer orientation while reflecting at the same time what is considered as an important destination and institution. Obviously both text types fulfil an important pragmatic function, ascribing special features to places and generating by means of communication the way we are supposed to behave at a place or how to get to a place.

Prohibitions are realised by very different communication forms such as signs, stickers, notices and guidance systems. This variety of media being used for the same pragmatic function indicates differences with reference to their period of validity. In Figure 6.7, for example, we see stickers at the entrance of the German Railways

Figure 6.7 Main station, Braunschweig

counter in Braunschweig, which prohibit bicycling (twice) and smoking, while a sticker also draws people's attention towards walking-impaired people.

The stickers are attached to the door and can thus be considered as the counter's 'house rules'. They are used in public places not only for transgressive discourse as Scollon and Scollon (2003: 188f.) have suggested, but also for commercial, political and regulatory discourse. The stickers, as well as signs on a platform (for example, warning against walking towards the platform's edge), share their brevity and are often realised without verbal elements. This compactness makes it possible for the reader/walker to perceive the texts while they are in motion. The weatherproof materiality and the fixation of stickers and signs go along with both the texts' permanent visibility and permanent validity. This correlates with tactilely perceivable prohibitions. The guidance systems mentioned above are also used on platforms, making it possible for visually-impaired people to follow the coded paving consisting of stripes and dots with their white cane. On the platform, these stripes and dots inform people about the possible route, also including a warning to stay on the stripe and not to cross it to go towards the platform edge. They are – theoretically – permanently tactilely perceivable and of permanent validity but in practice, as mentioned above, they are often made ineffective by snowfall and luggage.

However, it has to be emphasised that not all visible prohibitions are perceivable in another mode of perception. The multiple smoking bans we may see on stickers or signs when walking through a station, airport or shopping mall are not perceivable by visually-impaired people. Sometimes we hear prohibitions like these periodically over public announcement (PA) systems, such as 'this is a non-smoking area', but that does not apply to every place or every prohibition. It has to be mentioned that this realisation of *one* pragmatic function with *different* communication forms serves its memorising and different addressees – while the lack of differentiation may exclude some local attendees.

Some prohibitions are only acoustically perceivable owing to their significance and their time-bound content. While announcements at railway stations are in general used for time-bound purposes such as arrivals (see Section 6.2.2), standard warnings at platforms are heard when trains are approaching, such as 'Caution! The train is arriving'. While permanent prohibitions are realised by written language and permanent material such as signs or guidance system announcements over the PA system are most relevant in unexpected situations of danger. For example, when a person gets too close to the rail tracks, there may be an immediate announcement such as 'Step back!'.

This leads to the last group of prohibition signage, which combines modes of perception in a specific way: *semiotic* and *physical barriers* (cf. Schmauks, 2002: 16ff.). It is possible to find semiotic barriers of permanent validity, for example, designated smoking areas on the floor. In contrast, physical barriers are often used for time-bound prohibitions, for example, in the case of construction sites. In Figure 6.8, a physical barrier prevents walkers from entering that specific spot of the platform in Munich and the red warning fence serves as a semiotic barrier. Visually-impaired walkers may not be able to perceive the semiotic barrier; however, the physical part of the signage forms a perceivable barrier at that moment.

Figure 6.8 Main station, Munich

With reference to direction devices, it seems obvious that their usually expectable validation explains the usual realisation by means of permanent, visible communication forms such as signs, information columns, fixed positioners or in a broader sense for orientation by means of guidance systems (see above). While focusing on media differentiation it must be mentioned that a direction's permanent validity is also increasingly realised by means of audible communication forms. In Berlin main station, for example, one may find buttons on small columns in front of elevators. When pressed, they offer detailed information about the user's position and the present floor and its structure.

6.4 The Public Textscape as a Part of the Mediatized Everyday Life

Even if I have just highlighted some examples (such as prohibition signs and stickers, announcements, guidance systems, physical barriers, QR-codes and commercials), it seems quite clear that walking through a city or station reveals public texts with different modes of perception and different pragmatic purposes. There is an increasing amount of differentiation with reference to communication forms and their pragmatic use. Sometimes the differentiation can be explained by the different capabilities of the assumed recipients (see Section 6.3) and equality laws; sometimes the choice for making information readable and hearable relies on the information's relevance (see Section 6.2.2) and/or the consideration of individual routes; sometimes just one mode of perception is perceivable despite these obvious needs.

However, we do find order in this variety. What is permanently visible or tactile indicates non-time-bound validity (see Section 6.2.1). When digital media as well as more flexible materiality is used, we are expecting more time-bound content (see Section 6.2.2f.). These increasing possibilities and differentiation of modes reflect different pragmatic functions as well as the relevance of different media for the emergence of boards, signs, stickers, notices, digital display panels, QR-codes and announcements. It seems to be also evident that focusing on communication forms and therefore the media being used makes it possible to investigate the interplay between *form* and *function*. Accordingly, it brings into focus the fact that different communication forms are used to realise the same text type such as prohibitions (see Section 6.3) by means of signs, stickers or barriers, which differ obviously with reference to their validity and visibility. Furthermore, the usefulness of one communication form (such as signs, see Section 2.1) for many different pragmatic purposes seems to be obvious.

A media-orientated analysis of public textscapes helps to examine functional differentiation such as this. The relevance of analogue and digital media and visible, audible and tactile communication for public communication becomes apparent, as well as their importance for the social construction of space. In the terms of de Certeau, places *become* social spaces (de Certeau, 1988: 218) and this obviously requires different communication forms based on current media. Thus, public textscapes can be considered as an important but at the same time overlooked part of the 'mediatization' of everyday life. Krotz's term *mediatization* (e.g. Krotz, 2007; Krotz & Hepp, 2012) refers to the increasing existence and use of different media in our everyday lives and the cultural impact of these changes. The special characteristics of place-bound communication as an important part of the 'mediatization' of everyday life now come into focus. Public communication offers guidance for a place's attendees'. But public communication uses the presence of the attendees at specific places also for their own purposes. Commercials at bus stations may be seen by someone who is waiting or walking by (see also Figure 6.5 and Figure 6.6) and political demonstrations are taking place where they can be seen and heard by many.

This functionality of place-bound communication also emerges when public space is connected to virtual spaces: QR-codes on posters are linked to websites. This place-bound/non-place-bound intertextuality underlines the relevance of smartphones in the construction of social space. Also, the increasing interplay between place-bound texts and their online, and therefore non-place-bound, distribution comes into focus. For example, at present we may see big posters in different German cities with the text 'refugees welcome', making cities *readable* as non-xenophobic. These posters are addressing more non-place-bound viewers when posted on Facebook or Twitter, reflecting what Jenkins (2006) calls a 'convergence culture'. This reflects the existing media and the range of emerged multimodal communication forms from which we may choose at present and which are the basis for the concrete textscape shaping the social space of our everyday lives.

References

Abousnnouga, G. and Machin, D. (2010) War monuments and the changing discourse of nation and soldiery. In A. Jaworski and C. Thurlow (eds) *Semiotic Landscapes: Language, Image, Space* (pp. 219–240). London: Continuum.

Backhaus, P. (2007) *Linguistic Landscapes: A Comparative Study of Urban Multilingualism in Tokyo.* Clevedon: Multilingual Matters.

Ben-Rafael, E., Shohamy, E. and Barni, M. (2010) Introduction: An approach to an 'ordered disorder'. In E. Shohamy, E. Ben-Rafael and M. Barni (eds) *Linguistic Landscape in the City* (pp. xi–xxviii). Bristol: Multilingual Matters.

Busse, B. and Warnke, I.H. (2014) Ortsherstellung als sprachliche Praxis – sprachliche Praxis als Ortsherstellung. In I.H. Warnke and B. Busse (eds) *Place-making in urbanen Diskursen* (pp. 1–10). Berlin/Boston: De Gruyter.

de Certeau, M. (1988) *Kunst des Handelns*. Berlin: Merve.

Domke, C. (2014) *Die Betextung des öffentlichen Raumes: Eine Studie zur Spezifik von Meso-Kommunikation am Beispiel von Bahnhöfen, Innenstädten und Flughäfen*. Heidelberg: Winter.

Domke, C. (2015) Prohibition signage in public places: On the functional organization of different media, communication forms and text types. *10plus1. Living Linguistics. Media Linguistics*. See http://10plus1journal.com/Issue1/05_WEB_GRA_Domke/Main.swf (accessed 29 April 2017).

Domke, C. (2017) Communication forms and locatedness: From theoretical needs to methodological possibilities. In A. Brock and P. Schildhauer (eds) *Communication Forms and Communicative Practices: New Perspectives on Communication Forms, Affordances and What Users Make of Them* (pp. 67–86). Frankfurt: Peter Lang.

Dray, S. (2010) Ideological struggles on signage in Jamaica. In A. Jaworski and C. Thurlow (eds) *Semiotic Landscapes: Language, Image, Space* (pp. 102–122). London: Continuum.

Goffman, E. (1981) *Forms of Talk*. Oxford: Blackwell Publishers.

Holly, W. (2011) Medien, Kommunikationsformen, Textsortenfamilien. In S. Habscheid (ed.) *Textsorten, Handlungsmuster, Oberflächen: Linguistische Typologien der Kommunikation* (pp. 144–163). Berlin: De Gruyter.

Jäger, L. (2010) Intermedialität – Intramedialität – Transkriptivität. Überlegungen zu einigen Prinzipien der kulturellen Semiosis. In A. Deppermann and A. Linke (eds) *Sprache intermedial: Stimme und Schrift, Bild und Ton* (pp. 301 – 323). Berlin/New York: De Gruyter.

Jaworski, A. and Thurlow, C. (eds) (2010a) *Semiotic Landscapes: Language, Image, Space*. London: Continuum.

Jaworski, A. and Thurlow, C. (2010b) Introducing semiotic landscapes. In A. Jaworski and C. Thurlow (eds) *Semiotic Landscapes: Language, Image, Space* (pp. 1–40). London: Continuum.

Jenkins, H. (2006) *Convergence Culture: Where Old and New Media Collide*. New York: New York University Press.

Jewitt, C. (ed.) (2011) *The Routledge Handbook of Multimodal Analysis*. London: Routledge.

Kallen, J.L. (2010) Changing landscapes: Language, space and policy in the Dublin linguistic landscape. In A. Jaworski and C. Thurlow (eds) *Semiotic Landscapes: Language, Image, Space* (pp. 41–58). London: Continuum.

Krotz, F. (2007) *Mediatisierung: Fallstudien zum Wandel von Kommunikation*. Wiesbaden: VS Verlag.

Krotz, F. and Hepp, A. (eds) (2012) Mediatisierte Welten: Forschungsfelder und Beschreibung sansätze – Zur Einleitung. In *Mediatisierte Welten: Forschungsfelder und Beschreibungsansätze* (pp. 7–23). Wiesbaden: VS Verlag.

Landry, R. and Bourhis, R.Y. (1997) Linguistic landscape and ethnolinguistic vitality: An empirical study. *Journal of Language and Social Psychology* 16 (1), 23–49.

McIlvenny, P., Broth, M. and Haddington, P. (2009) Communicating place, space and mobility. *Journal of Pragmatics* 41 (10), 1879–2136.

Meier, S. (2012) Die Simulation von Fotografie: Konzeptuelle Überlegungen zum Zusammenhang von Materialität und digitaler Bildlichkeit. In M. Finke and M.A. Halawa (eds) *Materialität und Bildlichkeit: Visuelle Artefakte zwischen Aisthesis und Semiosis* (pp. 126–142). Berlin: Kadmos.

Papen, U. (2012) Commercial discourses, gentrification and citizens' protest: The linguistic landscape of Prenzlauer Berg, Berlin. *Journal of Sociolinguistics* 16 (1), 56–81.

Pappenhagen, R., Redder, A. and Scarvaglieri, C. (2013) Hamburgs mehrsprachige Praxis im öffentlichen Raum – sichtbar und hörbar. In A. Redder, J. Pauli, R. Kießling, K. Bührig, B. Brehmer, I. Breckner and J. Androutsopoulos (eds) *Mehrsprachige Kommunikation in der Stadt: Das Beispiel Hamburg* (pp. 127–160). Münster: Waxmann.

Pennycook, A. (2010) Spatial narrations: Graffscapes and city souls In A. Jaworski and C. Thurlow (eds) *Semiotic Landscapes. Language, Image, Space* (pp. 137–150). London: Continuum.

Pennycook, A. and Otsuji, E. (2015) Making scents of the landscape. *Linguistic Landscape* 1 (3), 191–212.

Raffaseder, H. (2010) *Audiodesign: Akustische Kommunikation, akustische Signale und Systeme, psychoakustische Grundlagen, Klangsynthese, Audioediting und Effektbearbeitung, Sounddesign, Bild-Ton-Beziehungen.* München: Hanser.

Scarvaglieri, C., Redder, A., Pappenhagen, R. and Brehmer, B. (2013) Capturing diversity: Linguistic land- and soundscaping. In J. Duarte and I. Gogolin (eds) *Linguistics Superdiversity in Urban Areas* (pp. 45–74). Amsterdam: Benjamins.

Schmauks, D. (2002) *Orientierung im Raum: Zeichen für die Fortbewegung.* Tübingen: Stauffenburg.

Scollon, R. and Scollon, S. (2003) *Discourses in Place: Language in the Material World.* London: Routledge.

Shohamy, E. and Gorter, D. (eds) (2010) *Linguistic Landscape: Expanding the Scenery.* New York: Routledge.

Shohamy, E., Ben-Rafael, E. and Barni, M. (eds) (2010) *Linguistic Landscape in the City.* Bristol: Multilingual Matters.

Van Leeuwen, T. (2005) *Introducing Social Semiotics.* New York: Routledge.

Warnke, I.H. (2011) Die Stadt als Kommunikationsraum und linguistische Landschaft. In W. Hofmann (ed.) *Die Stadt als Erfahrungsraum der Politik: Beiträge zur kulturellen Konstruktion urbaner Politik* (pp. 343–363). Münster: LIT.

7 Multilingual Audio Announcements: Power and Identity

Ying-Hsueh Hu

This research project examined the process and tension of constructing a Taiwanese identity, drawing on the theoretical framework of linguistic landscape (LL) and soundscape studies. LL studies analyse languages on signs in the public space to reveal the power dynamics of the people residing in the same spaces, while soundscape studies focus on the sounds in a particular environment and how they are perceived by individuals or groups in that sound space. This research project investigated the perception and evaluation of the multilingual public audio announcements on the Taipei Mass Rapid Transit System (MRT), where announcements are played in Mandarin Chinese, Holo, Hakka and English. The first three languages are the major languages spoken in Taipei, Taiwan. Interviews were conducted with people of diverse ethnic background ($N = 100$). Preliminary results mirror the power dynamic/struggle of the three linguistic groups over the past 60 years.

7.1 Introduction

As Blommaert and Maly (2014) aptly observe, a new branch of sociolinguistics called linguistic landscape studies (LL) has emerged over the past few decades. It explores how people's experiences of place make a difference, particularly in a bilingual or multilingual environment. To shed light on these experiences, LL studies investigate the interaction between people and written signs that include 'billboards, road and safety signs, shop signs, graffiti and all sorts of other inscriptions in the public space, both professionally produced and grassroots' (Blommaert & Maly, 2014: 2). According to Landry and Bourhis (1997), the language(s) that appear on these signs can influence and shape people's perception of the 'ethnolinguistic vitality' (Landry & Bourhis, 1997: 35) of the population who inhabit the space under investigation. In short, the languages on the signs are the 'symbolic construction of a public space' (Ben-Rafael *et al.*, 2006: 7), which not only reveal social meaning (Scollon & Scollon, 2003) but also embed issues of self-representation and power (Backhaus, 2006). More specifically, as Blommaert and Maly (2014: 3) argue, 'public space is also an instrument of power, discipline and regulation: it organizes the social dynamics deployed in that space'.

In addition to visual signs, the sounds people experience in public space are similarly filled with a myriad of social and power dynamics. The study of sound was first proposed by Schafer (1994), who urges us to rethink the evaluation of 'noise' and its effects on quality of life. Today, soundscape studies have expanded into various disciplines ranging from architecture, psychology, sociology and anthropology to physics. Cross-cultural differences have also been studied and compared. Furthermore, Brooks *et al.* (2014) point out that recent soundscape research has concentrated on urban settings. *The Cheung Chau Bun Festival: A Hong Kong Soundscape Study* (Mora, 2009), the *Soundscape of Open Urban Spaces in Hong Kong* (Lin & Lam, 2010) and Cheung and Cobussen's studies (2016) of the urban soundscapes of Bangkok and Hong Kong are some cases in point that explore cultural, social and political meanings through the sounds captured by these researchers with audio and video devices.

While the above-mentioned studies captured several sound sources, other studies have concentrated on one source: talks or vocal communication in specific physical environments. Jaworski *et al.* (2003) investigated the presentation of languages other than English on British TV shows about travel. They found that English was often portrayed favourably as a global language. Local languages of the places the reporters visited, conversely, were 'reduced to… exoticized linguascapes' (Jaworski *et al.*, 2003: 5). Kitapci *et al.* (2013), on the other hand, examined speech intelligibility in multilingual spaces and concluded that not only noise but also social and cultural factors contributed to speech intelligibility.

Despite these well-executed soundscape studies, very few studies have examined specifically the ideologies embedded in the languages we hear in urban multilingual environments. This chapter thus focuses on public audio announcements on public transport in Taipei, the capital city of Taiwan, adopting an ethnographic approach through interviews with the different linguistic groups who reside in this space. As there is only one written script (Chinese characters) for Holo, Hakka and Mandarin Chinese, the three major languages spoken in Taiwan (Chiung, 2001; Huang, 1993), it is impossible to study written signs to yield an accurate picture of a changing LL and the power dynamic in Taiwan.

An ethnographic research methodology was employed in order to gain a deeper understanding of the way in which such multilingual audio announcements capture Taiwan's changing LL and how they have affected various ethnic groups, including those with an international background. Interviews were conducted with people from various ethnic groups living in or visiting Taipei. Their perception/evaluation and responses to the multilingual audio announcements were elicited and analysed to gain insight into the shift in power among various ethnic groups, as well as the process and tension of constructing a Taiwanese identity. More specifically, this study addresses the following research questions: (1) Does ethnicity affect the perception and evaluation of the multilingual announcements? (2) How do participants' perception and evaluation reflect the power dynamic of the various ethnic/linguistic groups in Taiwan?

7.2 Background of the Study

7.2.1 Linguistic landscape, power and identity

Studying the languages we see or hear in the public space can yield a good picture of not only the synchronic but also the diachronic development of the power shift among various ethnic groups. Moreover, insight can be gained into linguistic changes and the spread of diversity in the community or society under study. For instance, Blommaert (2013) investigated the inner-city area of Oud-Berchern in Antwerp, Belgium, while Blommaert and Maly (2014) studied the neighbourhood of Rabot, Ghent, Belgium. Both studies illustrate the influence of migration, the shift in the power dynamic, and the practice of multiculturalism and multilingualism by the people residing in these neighbourhoods. In a more monolingual city such as Tokyo (Backhaus, 2007: 145), power dynamics may be displayed differently. Backhaus (2006, 2007) studied code preference on signs in Tokyo and concluded that official signs, which are still predominantly in Japanese, are designed mainly to express and reinforce existing power relations, whereas unofficial signs that make use of foreign languages communicate solidarity with things non-Japanese.

Languages on both official and unofficial signs also reflect the language ideology and language policy a community has been subjected to. By analysing the bilingual signs and public display of Welsh in various communities in Wales, Coupland (2012) identified several frames of different language ideologies that have been practised in Wales in the past few decades. These ideologies, including seeing Welsh as non-autonomous, parallel to English and exotic, often co-exist and even at times compete with one another.

Ideology and language policy are interlinked with identity. Identity can be boosted or undermined by the presence or absence of a language in public space and especially on official signs. Trumper-Hecht (2009) discussed this issue in her analysis of Arabic on signs in the public space in Upper Nazareth, a Jewish-dominated settlement in Israel with a small Arab population (13%). The majority of public signage in this area is principally in Hebrew. Although there is a government policy to add Arabic to public signs, the majority of the Jewish population refuses to comply so as to maintain their political and cultural hegemony. The Arab population consists of mostly middle-class, well-trained professionals. They also tend to be fluent bilinguals in both Arabic and Hebrew; therefore, seeing Arabic on public signs would be an important gesture of respect and acknowledgement of their Israeli citizenship. In this case, public language display can construct or deconstruct national identity.

Curtin (2007) also examined the non-Chinese public signage and official signage with Chinese Romanisations in Taipei, exploring identity issues in Taiwan. She suggests that many of the non-Chinese signs aim to demonstrate Taipei's desire to portray itself as a cosmopolitan city, tolerant of multiculturalism and multilingualism. Similarly, signs of Romanised scripts used in transliterating Chinese, she argues, are also ideologically based and are representations of Taiwanese identities. Her focus in this research is to understand the local–regional–global identity continuum embedded in the LL in Taipei. She explored the Taiwanese–Chinese identity continuum in a later study (Curtin, 2009) by comparing the two Romanisation systems, *hanyu pinyin* and *tongyong pinyin*, used in Taiwan in public space. The former was developed in China after the Communist takeover, while the latter was devised in Taiwan in 1998.

Curtin argues that the promotion of *hanyu pinying* shows a cosy relationship with China and support for reunification (2014: 169). She asserts that this may threaten the construction of a Taiwanese national identity. To her, *hanyu pinyin* is not the only threat to such an identity construction. The spread of English and treating English as a lingua franca, she points out, decreases the opportunity to promote other languages of Taiwan, such as aboriginal languages, Holo and Hakka. These languages, she contends, are notably absent in Taipei's LL. However, to recognise the presence of Holo and Hakka, one needs to turn to the linguistic soundscape of Taipei for fruitful research, especially on its Mass Rapid Transit System (MRT).

Whoever steps onto the Taipei MRT would be either amused or annoyed by the multilingual public audio announcements of each approaching station and other key information given in the order of Mandarin Chinese, Holo, Hakka and English (this order has been recently updated to place English second, pushing Hakka to the last position). On some buses in Taipei, the announcements are depicted and rendered in Mandarin Chinese and English only. To the untrained ear of many international visitors, Holo is perhaps more recognisable than Hakka as the former is more widely spoken in Taipei and other parts of the island than the latter.

These audio announcements and signs are arguably in line with the government's language policy of promoting respect for the different ethnic groups that inhabit the island, while at the same time forging a global perspective (Wu, 2009). This policy is also meant to maintain language diversity, with a focus on Holo and Hakka; it is further maintained and promoted by respective language classes in public schools and language certificate tests organised by governmental agencies. The importance of maintaining Holo and Hakka, in particular, is a process of 'Taiwanisation', asserting Taiwan's unique heritage and identity (Wu, 2009). The promotion of English, similarly, is to indicate that Taiwan is a part of an international community that encourages the building of transnational institutions (Curtin, 2014: 156) and engages in the global economy (Wu, 2009: 106). In recent years, there has been a sizeable number of new migrant workers coming from abroad, notably from the Philippines and Indonesia. Street signs and public announcements in English arguably help migrants navigate their way in a new environment, and also to feel included. However, some academics, government think tanks and members of the general public consider such a portrayal of diversity as superficial. These announcements only serve certain political purposes (Online United Daily News, 2016). In order to understand these contradictory views, the following sections provide some background to the language policies and ideologies that have evolved in Taiwan over the past six decades.

7.2.2 Language and identity issues in Taiwan

According to a Taiwan government website, the population in Taiwan as of 2012 grew to 23.32 million. Based on the demographic information given therein, there are two main groups of people in Taiwan: Han people and a number of indigenous peoples of various Austronesian tribes. Among Han people, there are Holo (also known as Hokkien or Minnan), Hakka and Mainlanders, the immigrants that arrived in Taiwan from 1945 to 1949. Among the indigenous people, there are 14 recognised groups currently registered with the government.

Huang's study (1993) on the make-up of the various ethnic groups in Taiwan has been extensively cited, and estimated the population of 'four major ethnic groups' as follows: Holo = 73.3%, Hakka = 12%, Mainlander = 13% and indigenous people = 1.7%. In a more recent publication on this issue (Hsieh, 2012), these numbers have been modified with indigenous people accounting for 2% and Han people for 98%, of which Mainlanders account for 14%, Holo 70% and Hakka 15%. Government data for the year 2008 indicates that Holo is spoken by around 73% of the population, while Hakka is spoken by roughly 10% of the population. As for Mandarin Chinese, it has been the lingua franca and de facto official language of Taiwan since 1945 (Klöter, 2004). People born after this period and those with a minimum of six years' primary education all speak Mandarin Chinese. Some but not all of the Mainlanders who came over to Taiwan after 1945 already spoke Mandarin Chinese as its implementation as a lingua franca and official language in China had started much earlier. Currently, Mandarin Chinese, Holo and Hakka are the three major languages spoken in Taiwan. There are at least 13 different indigenous languages spoken by Austronesian aboriginals (Taiwan Government Information Office, 2008).

After decades of intermarriages, it has become increasingly difficult to use bloodline for the determination of ethnicity. Most of the categories of ethnicity rely on self-identification, as the Hakka Basic Law that was implemented in 2010 resorted to doing so to identify Hakka people (Tomoyoshi, 2012). Furthermore, Taiwan's household registration system for Han people has so far put greater emphasis on a patriarchal lineage rather than a matriarchal one; therefore, if one's mother is of Mainlander background and one's father is of Holo, whether this person identifies himself or herself as Holo or Mainlander is still a highly controversial issue (He, 2009).

The self-identification issue has become even more controversial in recent years as tension between Taiwan and China has intensified. As explained by Shih (2006), a former consultant to the Hakka Affairs Council, ethnic identification is in strong tandem with political party identification (Green Party vs. Blue Party),[1] collective identity (Chinese vs. Taiwanese) and nationality identification (Taiwan as a province of China vs. a sovereign state). One way of affirming one's identification is certainly through spoken language (Cho, 2000; Fishman, 1991). The reason language has become a contentious issue in modern Taiwan is tied up with its history and language policy after the Second World War, which will be discussed in the next section.

7.2.3 Language policy in Taiwan

Before 1945, Taiwan had been ruled by Japan for 50 years, the language policy of which will not be discussed here. After Japan lost the Second World War,

Taiwan was taken over by the ruling party of China at the time, the Kuomintang, otherwise known as the Chinese Nationalist Party (KMT, or the Blue Party). In the period between 1945 and 1970, the KMT promoted Mandarin Chinese as the official language. Other languages, including Japanese, indigenous languages as well as Holo and Hakka spoken on the island, were discouraged and even forbidden in public arenas. Such a policy reached its zenith in the years between 1970 and 1987.

Under such a policy, Holo and Hakka were considered 'dialects' by the KMT, who believed in a one-language policy in the process of nation building. Unifying and standardising languages was instrumental in European nation building in the 19th century (Geeraerts, 2003: 48). The KMT adopted this belief when it overthrew China's last imperial dynasty and established the first republic in Chinese history in 1921. Mandarin Chinese, a lingua franca spoken in the Beijing area, was standardised to become a national language as part of the KMT's nation-building efforts. After the KMT lost the civil war to the Communist Party and retreated to Taiwan in 1949, it continued this language policy there. As a result, much resentment was planted in the minds of 'dialect speakers', particularly Holo speakers who accounted, and still account for, the majority of the population in Taiwan. They believed that their language and identity were being suppressed and sought to redress this issue when the Martial law was lifted in 1987 and a process of democratisation began. Nonetheless, between 1987 and 2000, the language policy was still along the lines of affirming a single Chinese identity via the promotion of Mandarin Chinese. When the opposition party, the Democratic Progressive Party (DPP, or the Green Party) came to power in 2000, the language policy underwent a major shift, pushing for minority rights and language rights (Shih & Zhang, 2003). Under this policy, a multicultural and multilingual society was valued and promoted.

According to Geeraerts (2003) and Berthele (2001, 2008), the language policy and standardisation debates can be best illustrated by two cultural models: the *rationalist* and the *romantic* model. In the romantic model, language is conceptualised as an expression of one's unique identity and emphasises language equality; thus, it is of utmost importance to maintain minority languages and identities. On the other hand, in the rationalist model language is conceptualised as a tool to unify a nation, whereby dialects or regional variations are considered as barriers to unity. Arguably, the KMT adopted the rationalist view, while the DPP attempted to implement the romantic view of language policy. Under this policy, Holo and Hakka are not dialects but languages, adhering to DeFrancis' definition of unintelligibility (1990), as noted by Chiung (2001).

When the DPP came to power in 2000, it passed legislation addressing language rights on public transport, enforcing a rule for audio announcements to include languages other than Mandarin Chinese. In 2003, the Ministry of Education proposed a Language Equal Rights Bill, recommending all languages spoken on the island to be given the status of national languages. However, owing to some practical and political issues, the bill that was finally passed still maintained the status of Mandarin Chinese as the de facto national language. Nonetheless, the shift towards a truly multilingual society was already taking shape.

7.2.4 Linguistic soundscape on public transport

The legislation in 2000 regarding the audio announcements on public transport guarantees that all languages spoken on the island are treated equally. On the Taipei Mass Rapid Transit System (MRT), Taiwan High Speed Rail and Taiwan Railways, station/stop names and selective key information are announced in four languages: Mandarin Chinese, Holo, Hakka and English. Indigenous languages are selectively broadcast based on the routes operated by Taiwan High Speed Rail and Taiwan Railways. Buses in Taipei and New Taipei cities also use these four languages for the name of each stop. English was selected as a result of globalisation and internationalisation, for the convenience of foreign visitors, as explained on the MRT official website.[2] Furthermore, with the recent increase of foreign spouses and migrant workers, English might be of some help to them until their proficiency in Mandarin Chinese becomes more adequate.

However, when browsing on the internet, especially a popular blog[3] used by many netizens in Taiwan to discuss various issues, it becomes immediately clear that the multilingual audio announcements on the MRT have not always been positively embraced. The most common complaint has been the noise and a perception that when the distance between two stops is short, such multilingual announcements become a distraction rather than a reliable source of information. Several comments posted on the blog mentioned political motivation, claiming that the government simply wanted to appear to be fair and to respect all ethnic groups. They called the multilingual announcements a cosmetic gesture and called for reduction in length and noise by eliminating some languages. As for what languages should go, interestingly, it is usually a debate between Holo and Hakka, with the latter attracting more controversy than the former. Unfortunately, from an ethnographic point of view, these blogs could not provide a comprehensive picture of the people behind these opinions. In this light, the survey/interviews conducted in this preliminary study aim to provide a more comprehensive picture of who thinks what and why.

7.3 Methodology

In order to gain access to speakers from various speech communities in Taiwan of a diverse background in terms of age, educational level and ethnicity, a snowball sampling technique was deployed. Apart from the researcher, several of her students from the university where she works, as well as acquaintances and friends from yoga and badminton classes, were requested to interview their family members or friends and acquaintances (e.g. from a chess club) for data collection. There are of course limitations with this technique as people are constrained to interviewing people from their own connections. At this preliminary stage, survey results from 100 participants were collected and analysed.

Participants were required to answer questions on their gender, age, educational level, place of residence, first languages, and most spoken languages at work and home. They were also asked if they had taken any public transport prior to the interview. Ethnicity, as discussed earlier, was defined by self-perception and identification. Hence, the terms employed in the survey for ethnicity and languages follow conventions shared by the majority of the speakers in the speech communities in Taiwan rather than any linguistic or political principle (see Appendix). For example, the term 外省人 (which can be literally translated as 'a person from outer province'), referring to the Mainlanders who came with the KMT after 1949 from Mainland China, may be frowned upon by some people in Taiwan as the locals see Taiwan as an independent state rather than a province of China. Nonetheless, this term is still commonly used in daily life to refer to such an origin. Similarly, the terms 台灣人 ('Taiwanese', the people) and 台語 ('Taiwanese', the language), in fact, refer to Holo, the people and the language.

The second part of the survey/interview addresses participants' experience and perception/evaluation of the multilingual announcements on the MRT. They were subsequently asked to provide explanations. Participants were also asked to comment on the reason(s) why there are such announcements. Two follow-up questions were added about the order of the announcements and the number of languages used (e.g. should there be more or less than the existing four and what should be added/eliminated).

Their statements were written down either by the participants themselves or by the interviewers on a survey sheet (see Appendix). The verbatim responses were in turn categorised and coded by the researcher and a trained assistant for quantitative analyses. Regarding participants' experience and perception, the coding of positive, negative and neutral categories was applied. Statements such as 'I can learn how to say different station names in these languages', 'I will never forget what station to get off' or 'It shows respect to other ethnic groups' were coded as positive. Comments such as 'Too long', 'Too noisy' or 'It's political' were categorised as negative. Comments such as 'No particular feeling' or 'I think it's OK' were considered neutral. Their reasoning for *why* there is such a multilingual announcement was given at least five codes: (1) an indication of a multicultural society; (2) internationalisation; (3) practicality (e.g. for older people who cannot understand Mandarin Chinese); (4) political motivation (e.g. appeasing certain ethnic groups or to gain their votes in key elections); and (5) population size and others (e.g. based on the size of each ethnic group, noisy and got used to it).

These statements were in turn correlated with participants' personal backgrounds via Pearson's chi-squared test (χ^2) (SPSS version 10.5 for Windows), exploring whether some of their personal backgrounds are related to their perception and reasoning of the announcements. In this case, *gender*, *ethnicity*, *age* and *educational level* were the independent variables while *perception* and *reasoning* were the dependent variables. However, Pearson's chi-squared test in itself was only able to capture whether or not variables were reliably related to each other, but was not sufficient in explaining the extent and nature of the relationship. To arrive at a more detailed interpretation, the qualitative data elicited from interviews were also taken into consideration.

7.4 Results

Tables 7.1 to 7.4 present the descriptive statistics for participants' perceptions by *gender*, *ethnicity*, *age* and *educational level*. There was nearly an equal number of men

Table 7.1 Number of participants in each perception category by *gender*

Gender/perception	Positive	Negative	Neutral	Total
Male	26	10	12	48
Female	17	15	20	52

Table 7.2 Number of participants in each perception category by *ethnicity*

Ethnicity/perception	Positive	Negative	Neutral	Total
Holo	10	6	9	25
Hakka	7	6	10	23
Mainlander (2nd/3rd)	7	10	3	20
China	2	1	3	6
International	17	2	7	26

Note: 2nd/3rd = second and third generation; China = students or residents from People's Republic of China; International = international students or residents.

Table 7.3 Number of participants in each perception category by *age*

Age/perception	Positive	Negative	Neutral	Total
18–29	26	5	14	45
30–39	7	3	3	13
40–49	3	6	3	12
50–59	2	10	4	21
60 and above	5	1	3	9

Table 7.4 Number of participants in each perception category by *educational level*

Education/perception	Positive	Negative	Neutral	Total
Elementary	3	0	1	4
High school	1	1	0	2
College	24	14	25	63
Postgraduate	15	10	6	31

and women in the study ($N = 100$, $F = 52$, $M = 48$); in terms of the three other independent variables, there were more young people than older people (45 in the 18–29 age group, 30 in the 50 and above age group), but more of an equal number of the major ethnic groups in Taiwan (Holo = 25, Hakka = 23, second and third generation Mainlander = 20), with an additional 26 participants of international background and six participants from China. Unfortunately, none of Taiwan's indigenous people participated in this study. There were also far more people educated at college level than other educational levels in this cohort (94 out of 100) and nearly half of them were between the ages of 18 and 29 ($N = 45$). These totals basically reflect the bias set by the social networks of the researcher herself, who teaches at a higher education institute in Northern Taiwan. Predictably, as a result of the snowball sampling technique through students' social networks, there were more participants of Holo background since Holo speakers make up the majority of the population in Taiwan. This also explains why there were no participants of indigenous background in this study.

Table 7.1 indicates that male participants held a more positive view towards the announcements than the female participants. Table 7.2 shows that most international residents held positive views, followed by Holo speakers. Table 7.3 suggests that participants under 29 years thought positively of the announcements, whereas most participants between 50 and 59 years held negative views. Finally, Table 7.4 points to an even distribution of different views among the college-educated participants who made up the majority. In order to establish whether these findings arose by chance, a Pearson's chi-squared contingency test was employed. The test examines sets of categorical data (or variables) to evaluate how likely it is that any observed difference between the sets arose by chance. In other words, it tests the null hypothesis that the variables are independent, so when test results do not support this model (i.e. if the p-value is less than a given significance level α), the null hypothesis can be proven incorrect, suggesting a dependent relationship does exist between observed variables.

The test was applied in this study to determine if each of the independent variables such as *gender*, *ethnicity*, *age* and *educational level* was related to *perception/ evaluation* and was set at a 0.05 significance level (a 0.01 level indicates a higher significance). A high significance was found in *age* ($\chi^2 = 22.12$, $df = 8$, $p < 0.01$), followed by *ethnicity* ($\chi^2 = 16.35$, $df = 8$, $p < 0.05$), but not in *education* ($\chi^2 = 7.29$, $df = 6$, $p > 0.05$) nor *gender* ($\chi^2 = 4.73$, $df = 2$, $p > 0.05$). In short, statistical analysis indicates that the participants' evaluation of the audio announcements (positive, neutral or negative) was dependent on their age and ethnicity. Their educational level and gender were independent from their evaluation.

A further partitioning chi-squared contingency test using *gender* as the partition variable was applied to understand in which gender the participants' perception was independent from their ethnicity age, and education. It showed that among male participants, the perceptions of the audio announcements were more significantly related to their *age* ($\chi^2 = 21.77$, $df = 8$, $p < 0.05$) and *ethnicity* ($\chi^2 = 18.03$, $df = 6$, $p < 0.05$), but not *educational level*. Among female participants, these variables were independent from their perception/evaluation. In short, the educational level, age and ethnicity of the female participants did not affect their perception/evaluation of the announcements.

Tables 7.5 to 7.8 present the descriptive statistics of participants' *reasoning* for the multilingual audio announcements (i.e. why such announcements were necessary) according to their *gender*, *ethnicity*, *age* and *educational level*. Apparently, 'multiculturalism' was the most frequent reason mentioned by the participants. Table 7.5 shows that more male participants associated 'multiculturalism' with the announcements than female participants, whose reasoning tended to be either pragmatic ('in proportion to population size') or negative ('noisy'). Table 7.6 suggests that

Table 7.5 Number of participants in each reasoning category by *gender*

Gender/reasoning	M	I	Pr	Po	Others	Total
Male	18	7	8	6	9	48
Female	12	10	10	4	16	52

Note: M = multiculturalism; I = internationalisation; Pr = practicality; Po = political motivation; Others = e.g. noisy, indifferent and proportion to population size.

Table 7.6 Number of participants in each reasoning category by *ethnicity*

Ethnicity/reasoning	M	I	Pr	Po	Others	Total
Holo	5	5	6	3	6	25
Hakka	2	5	5	3	8	23
Mainlander (2nd/3rd)	5	4	2	4	5	20
China	1	3	2	0	0	6
International	17	0	3	0	6	26

Note: 2nd/3rd = second and third generation; China = students or residents from People's Republic of China; International = international students or residents. M = multiculturalism; I = internationalisation; Pr = practicality; Po = political motivation; Others = e.g. noisy, indifferent and proportion to population size.

Table 7.7 Number of participants in each reasoning category by *age*

Age/reasoning	M	I	Pr	Po	Others	Total
18–29	20	3	9	0	13	45
30–39	5	4	2	1	1	13
40–49	4	4	1	1	2	12
50–59	1	4	4	7	5	21
60 and above	0	2	2	1	4	9

Note: M = multiculturalism; I = internationalisation; Pr = practicality; Po = political motivation; Others = e.g. noisy, indifferent and proportion to population size.

Table 7.8 Number of participants in each reasoning category by *educational level*

Education/reasoning	M	I	Pr	Po	Others	Total
Elementary	0	0	1	0	3	4
High school	0	0	1	1	0	2
College	21	11	9	3	19	63
Postgraduate	9	6	7	6	3	31

Note: M = multiculturalism; I = internationalisation; Pr = practicality; Po = political motivation; Others = e.g. noisy, indifferent, and proportion to population size.

the reasoning of 'multiculturalism' was derived mostly from the participants of international background, followed by those of Holo background. Table 7.7 indicates that young participants (aged 18–29) believed that 'multiculturalism' was behind the motivation for the announcements, while older participants (aged 50–59) thought that political purposes such as appeasement and winning votes were the motivation. Finally, Table 7.8 shows that the view of 'multiculturalism' was mostly shared by college-level participants.

A Pearson's chi-squared contingency test was performed at a $p < 0.05$ significance level. A high level of significance was uncovered in *ethnicity* ($\chi^2 = 35.21$, $df = 16$, $p < 0.01$), *age* ($\chi^2 = 37.45$, $df = 16$, $p < 0.01$) and to a lesser degree in *education* ($\chi^2 = 21.38$, $df = 12$, $p < 0.05$), but not in *gender* ($\chi^2 = 4.15$, $df = 4$, $p > 0.05$). A further partitioning chi-squared contingency test using *gender* as the partition variable was applied to illustrate the relationship between male and female participants' perception and their *ethnicity*, *age* and *educational level*. It shows that the *reasoning* of the male participants was more significantly dependent on their background in the category of *age* ($\chi^2 = 33.56$, $df = 16$, $p < 0.01$), *ethnicity* ($\chi^2 = 21.83$, $df = 12$, $p < 0.05$), and *education* ($\chi^2 = 15.65$, $df = 8$, $p < 0.05$). With female participants, a significant dependency was found in *educational level* ($\chi^2 = 28.16$, $df = 12$, $p < 0.01$), but not in *ethnicity* or *age*.

As mentioned above, nearly half of the participants were aged 18–29. In order to yield a more detailed picture of this age group, further analysis was performed with another partitioning chi-squared contingency test, adopting *age* as the partition variable. The grouping for this analysis divided the participants into two age groups, with participants aged 18–29 and 30–39 in group 1 ($N = 58$), while those aged 40 and over were in group 2 ($N = 42$).

Results regarding reaction to the multilingual audio announcements indicate that *gender* and *reasoning* were dependent of each other in group 1 ($\chi^2 = 10.99$, $df = 2$, $p < 0.01$). There were 28 males and 30 females in group 1, and 20 males and 22 females in group 2. From the previous results of the positive correlation between age and reaction among male participants, young, male participants presumably showed some consistent preference towards the announcements. Another significant correlation was found in the younger age group (group 1) between *reasoning* and *ethnicity* ($\chi^2 = 27.57$, $df = 16$, $p < 0.05$). It is important to note that all the international participants ($N = 26$) were in the younger age group, or group 1, alongside 15 Holo speakers, six Hakka speakers and six visitors from China. In the older group, or group 2, we find mostly Hakka speakers ($N = 18$), followed by 2nd and 3rd generation Mainlanders ($N = 14$) and Holo speakers ($N = 10$). No significance could be established between any variables in this group.

7.5 Discussion

7.5.1 Variables affecting perception and evaluation

The analyses of participants' perceptions suggest that they were dependent on ethnicity and age, and this dependency was significant among male participants.

In other words, one's ethnicity can somewhat predict one's experience with the multilingual audio announcements, particularly among men. Holo participants as well as international students and residents living in Taipei had a positive experience, while the 2nd and 3rd generation Mainlanders as well as the visiting students and residents from China experienced the announcements more negatively or neutrally. The experience of Hakka participants seemed to be less positive as well.

Statistical analyses show that reasoning was dependent on ethnicity, age and to a lesser degree educational level. These relationships were more observable among male participants. Furthermore, within the younger age group (18–39), reasoning was dependent on gender and ethnicity.

A closer inspection of the reasons provided by various ethnic groups shows that most international students/residents had a positive experience, such as regarding it as a sign of 'multiculturalism'. This reasoning is quite different from the rest of the participants. To them, the announcements were positive signs of Taiwan's emphasis on diversity. This may be due to the background of these international participants. Many of them come from multilingual countries (e.g. European and South American countries); they seemed to appreciate the announcements from a multicultural perspective. It could also be the case that as foreigners they were not able to comprehend the ethnic tension that locals experience. For most people in Taiwan, as expressed on the internet (e.g. see note 3) and in this study, demonstrating multiculturalism through multilingual announcements in public places is not a sincere gesture, and resolving ethnic tension requires a great deal more effort. Furthermore, only very few of the Hakka participants mentioned multiculturalism as a positive reason for their experience in their statements, even though having the announcements in Hakka is a sign of inclusion and respect for this minority language.

This perception might well be explained by age. As most of the Hakka speakers interviewed in the study were somewhat older people (40 and above), their experience of Taiwan is different from that of the younger generations. They may still view Holo people as the dominant group in society (Shih, 2006). Even though no significant correlations could be identified in the older age group in the further partition contingency test, we could still observe that older participants tended to have a more negative perception of the multilingual audio announcements. Younger participants also tended to see these announcements as a progressive sign of multiculturalism evolving in Taiwan. With education, which is very likely tied to the age of the participants in the study, participants with an educational level of higher education also reported a more positive experience of multiculturalism. Closer examination reveals that they are mostly current students who are studying various undergraduate and postgraduate courses at the university where the researcher works. They are generally between 18 and 39 years old.

Numerous sociolinguistic studies (e.g. Labov, 1972; Trudgill, 1972, 1974) have shown gender to be an important independent variable affecting linguistic variables and language attitudes. Therefore, gender was separated for further analysis in this study to establish whether the relationship among other variables was more significant in one gender than the other. It was found that most of the significant relationships were uncovered among male participants. This arguably suggests that young, college-level, male participants of Holo background experienced the multilingual audio announcements significantly more positively for reasons of multiculturalism and internationalisation than was the case for female participants.

The overall data indicate that people of Holo background feel positive about such an audio arrangement in that on the one hand, they see the necessity of having Mandarin Chinese since it is the de facto official language in Taiwan and nearly every Taiwanese can understand and speak it, while on the other hand, they see inclusion of Holo and Hakka in the announcements as indicating respect to local people and cultures. This is in contrast to earlier eras when only Mandarin Chinese was allowed to be spoken in public places. This view reflects the romantic model of language policy that was discussed above (Berthele, 2001, 2008; Geeraerts, 2003); and it appears to be closely related to age and educational level in our cohort. In short, the younger and more educated people are, the more they adopt a romantic view of language.

The perception of English in the study is extremely positive, recognising it as a sign of internationalisation. Not only do international people living in or visiting Taipei find hearing English very helpful, the local people also believe that it is important to have English as there are increasingly more tourists visiting Taiwan. English is the first compulsory foreign language in school starting from elementary school. People see it as a necessity for successful business and a prosperous economy. Not surprisingly, when it comes to English as a global language, Taiwanese people adopt a very rationalist view, not worrying about its influences over local identities and cultures.

7.5.2 Power dynamic

Interestingly, when participants were asked what language(s) should be dropped if it was possible to do so, they all selected Hakka. This opinion was even expressed by one Hakka participant who said that the variety of Hakka (there are mainly two varieties of Hakka spoken in Taiwan) on the Taipei MRT was not really spoken by all Hakka people, and thus there was no point of it being played in important public places. Other Hakka participants mostly gave reasons associated with the relatively small number of Hakka people in Taiwan, and the fact that nearly every Hakka person understands either Mandarin Chinese or Holo. Even though they were pleased with the inclusion of Hakka, they remained realistic about the importance of this language in Taiwan. That said, a couple of older Hakka participants maintained that the importance of including Hakka on the MRT is for the cultivation of social harmony, healing old wounds resulting from earlier divides between Holo speakers and Hakka speakers, as well as the previous one-language policy implemented by the KMT party.

For some people the presence of Hakka on the MRT as a symbol of respect, inclusion and diversity is merely tokenism. From this study and discussion boards on various online blogs, one argument for Hakka's exclusion that often emerged is about fairness; namely, if Hakka is included out of respect for minority languages, then indigenous languages should also be included in the announcements on the MRT. Hence, according to this argument, the presence of Hakka in the announcements is only a means for the politicians to win votes as there are still more Hakka voters than all the indigenous tribes combined. These views reflect an imbalance of population, which can be in turn translated into an imbalance in language power.

7.5.3 Implications for the linguistic landscape

Curtin's studies (2009, 2014) on Taipei's signage could not identify the presence of Holo and Hakka in today's LL in Taipei. This may have resulted from her methodology. This study in turn demonstrates that linguistic soundscape investigation can complement LL in areas where written signage is impossible to find. In short, when a language is 'invisible' in the public space it does not necessarily mean it has no presence in the speech community. It is crucial to explore all possible avenues provided by the nature of the languages that are under investigation. In the case of Chinese, as most Han Chinese varieties share the same script, to 'hear' them is perhaps more important than to 'see' them.

7.6 Conclusion

Despite the small scale and preliminary nature of the study, some insights have emerged regarding language, power and the identity of the people who take public transport regularly in Taipei and Taiwan. These multilingual announcements allow us to observe how various people interact with one another and think about themselves and other peoples. Such announcements constantly remind us of the historical and linguistic changes in Taiwan and help us contemplate the future of Taiwan economically, culturally and politically.

It can be concluded that the majority of people in Taiwan agree that it is necessary to have a lingua franca, such as Mandarin Chinese. Nonetheless, there are reservations in the consolidation of Mandarin Chinese as the only official language. They are also aware of and embrace an increasingly diverse and multilingual society, even though such enthusiasm is not equally shared by all ethnic groups in Taiwan, depending on their population size and political sway in society. Furthermore, with the current pro-independence DPP in power, the identity of people in Taiwan is still evolving. It is of great interest to observe whether the MRT broadcast system will evolve accordingly.

In this small study, it is apparent that the sampling of data is not balanced. The conclusions that have been drawn here are therefore by no means conclusive. In the following stage of the study, it is imperative to expand the scope of the research to include more participants of different ages, education levels and above all ethnicities, particularly those of indigenous people, migrant workers and new immigrants to corroborate the findings presented here.

Notes

(1) There are two major political parties in Taiwan: the Chinese Nationalist Party (KMT) and the Democratic Progressive Party (DPP). These parties are also identified by their party flags. KMT's flag is blue, and that of the DPP is green; therefore, KMT is also known as the Blue Party, while DPP is known as the Green Party.
(2) See: http://www.metro.taipei/.
(3) See: http://www.ppt.cc.

References

Backhaus, P. (2006) Multilingualism in Tokyo: A look into the linguistic landscape. *International Journal of Multilingualism* 3 (1), 52–66.

Backhaus, P. (2007) *Linguistic Landscapes: A Comparative Study of Urban Multilingualism in Tokyo.* Clevedon: Multilingual Matters.

Ben-Rafael, E., Shohamy, E., Amara, M.H. and Trumper-Hecht, N. (2006) Linguistic landscape as symbolic construction of the public space: The case of Israel. In D. Gorter (ed.) *Linguistic Landscape: A New Approach to Multilingualism* (pp. 7–30). Clevedon: Multilingual Matters.

Berthele, R. (2001) *A Tool, a Bond, or a Territory: Language Ideologies in the US and Switzerland.* LAUD Series: General and Theoretical Papers 533, 1–26. Universität-Gesamthochschule Essen: LAUD.

Berthele, R. (2008) A nation is a territory with one culture and one language: The role of metaphorical folk models in language policy debates. In G. Kristiansen and R. Dirven (eds) *Cognitive Scoiolinguistics: Language Variation, Cultural Models, Social Systems* (pp. 301–331). Berlin/New York: Mouton de Gruyter.

Blommaert, J. (2013) *Ethnography, Superdiversity and Linguistic Landscapes: Chronicles of Complexity.* Bristol: Multilingual Matters.

Blommaert, J. and Maly, I. (2014) Ethnographic linguistic landscape analysis and social change: A case study (pp. 1–20). Working Papers in Urban Language and Literacies 133. London: The Center for Language, Discourse and Communication, King's College London.

Brooks, B.M., Schulte-Fortkamp, B., Voigt, K.S. and Case, A.U. (2014) Exploring our sonic environment through soundscape research and theory. *Acoustic Today* Winter 2014, 30–40.

Cheung, K.-H. and Cobussen, M. (2016) What do the urban soundscapes of a city represent? Case studies in Bangkok and Hong Kong. *Journal of Sonic Studies* Issue 12 online. See http://sonicstudies.org/jss12

Coupland, N. (2012) Bilingualism on display: The framing of Welsh and English in Welsh public spaces. *Language in Society* 41, 1–27.

Cho, G. (2000) The role of the heritage language in social interactions and relationships: Reflections from a language minority group. *Bilingual Research Journal* 24, 369–384.

Chiung, W.-V.T. (2001) Language and ethnic identity in Taiwan. Paper presented at the 7th North American Taiwan Studies Conference, 23–25 June, University of Washington, Seattle.

Curtin, M. (2007) Language ideologies on display: Local, regional, and (trans)national identities in Taipei's linguistic landscape. PhD thesis, University of New Mexico.

Curtin, M. (2009) Language on display: Indexical signs, identities and the linguistic landscape of Taipei. In E. Shohamy and D. Gorter (eds) *Linguistic Landscape: Expanding the Scenery* (pp. 221–237). New York/London: Routledge.

Curtin, M. (2014) Mapping cosmopolitanisms in Taipei: Toward a theorization of cosmopolitanism in linguistic landscape research. *International Journal of the Sociology of Language* 208, 153–177.

DeFrancis, J. (1990) *The Chinese Language: Fact and Fantasy* (Taiwan edition). Taipei: Crane.

Fishman, J.A. (1991) *Reversing Language Shift.* Clevedon: Multilingual Matters.

Geeraerts, D. (2003) Cultural models of linguistic standardization. In R. Dirven and M. Pütz (eds) *Cognitive Models in Language and Thought: Ideology, Metaphors and Meanings* (pp. 25–68). Berlin/New York: Mouton de Gruyter.

He, W.S. (2009) Language and ethnic identity: A case of the mother tongue for the Mainlanders in Taiwan. *Language and Linguistics* 10 (2), 375–349.

Hsieh, M.-H. (2012) *From Invisible to Visible: Stories of Taiwanese Hakka Heritage Teachers.* Taipei: Xlibris Corporation. See http://www.Xlibris.com (accessed 12 February 2016).

Huang, S.-F. (1993) *Language, Society, and Ethnic Identity.* Taipei: Crane.

Jaworski, A., Thurlow, C., Lawson, S. and Ylänne-McEwen, V. (2003) The uses and representations of local language in tourist destinations: A view from British TV holiday programmes. *Language Awareness* 12 (1), 5–29.

Kitapci, K., Galbrun, L., O'Rourke, B. and Turner, G.H. (2013) Speech intelligibility in multilingual spaces. *Paper presented at 42nd International Congress and Exposition on Noise Control Engineering*, Innsbruck, Austria.

Klöter, H. (2004) Language policy in the KMT and DPP eras. *China Perspectives* 54, 56–63.

Labov, W. (1972) *Sociolinguistic Patterns.* Philadelphia: University of Pennsylvania Press.

Landry, R. and Bourhis, R.Y. (1997) Linguistic landscape and ethnolinguistic vitality: An empirical study. *Journal of Language and Social Psychology* 16 (1), 23–49.

Lin, H. and Lam, K.-C. (2010) Soundscape of urban open spaces in Hong Kong. *Asian Geographer* 27 (1–2), 29–42.

Mora, M. (2009) *The Cheung Chau Bun Festival: A Hong Kong Soundscape Study.* See http://www.soh.hku.hk/hksounds/SoundScape/Introduction.html (accessed 3 March 2017).

Online United Daily News (2016) Discussion of MRT multilingual announcements: Zhang Jing Sen jabs at the political correction of legislation, 8 October. See http://news.housefun.com.tw/news/article/192291144157.html (accessed 3 October 2017).

Schafer, M. (1994) *The Soundscape: Our Sonic Environment and the Tuning of the World.* Rochester: Destiny Books.

Scollon, R. and Scollon, S. (2003) *Discourses in Place: Language in the Material World.* London: Routledge.

Shih, Z.F. (2006) *Ethnic Politics and Policies in Taiwan.* Taipei: Han Lu Publish.

Shih, Z.F. and Zhang, X.Q. (2003) *Language Policy and its Formation: Language Equity Law.* Taipei: Qian Wei Publishing.

Taiwan Government Information Office (2008) *Taiwan Yearbook 2008.* Taipei: Government Information Office.

Taiwan Government Homepage. See http://www.taiwan.gov.tw/ct.asp?xItem=126579&CtNode=3698&mp=999 (accessed 29 February 2016).

Tomoyoshi, T. (2012) Symbolic ethnicity among the Taiwanese Hakka: An analysis of the Hakka Basic Law. *Taiwan International Studies Quarterly* 8 (2), 173–190.

Trudgill, P. (1972) Sex, covert prestige and linguistic change in the urban British English in Norwich. *Language in Society* 1, 179–195.

Trudgill, P. (1974) *The Social Differentiation of English in Norwich.* Cambridge: Cambridge University Press.

Trumper-Hecht, N. (2009) Constructing national identity in mixed cities in Israel: Arabic on signs in the public space of Upper Nazareth. In E. Shohamy and D. Gorter (eds) *Linguistic Landscape: Expanding the Scenery* (pp. 238–252). New York/London: Routledge.

Wu, M.-H. (2009) Language planning and policy in Taiwan: Past, present and future. *Working Papers in Educational Linguistics* 24 (2), 99–118.

Appendix

Questionnaire: English version

Part One: Personal Information (Please circle the item that most closely fits your personal information)

(1) Gender: Male Female
(2) Age: 18–29 30–39 40–49 50–59 60 and above

(3)   Residence:
Southern Taiwan Central Taiwan Northern Taiwan Eastern Taiwan Other _____

(4)   Educational Attainment:
Junior High School Senior High School College Masters and above

(5)   Ethnicity:
Holo Hakka 2nd and 3rd generation Mainlanders Aboriginals new immigrants international visitors/students/residents

(6)   Language(s) spoken (more than one item is possible):
Holo Hakka Mandarin Chinese indigenous languages English

(7)   Language(s) often spoken at work and home (more than one item is possible):
Holo Hakka Mandarin Chinese indigenous languages English

(8)   Have you ever been on Taipei's MRT or other public transport systems?
Yes No

Part Two: Please answer the following open-ended questions based on your personal experience and opinion.

(9)   There are four languages in the public announcements on Taipei and Kaohsiung public transport system (Mandarin, Holo, Hakka, English). What are your thoughts about this and please give reasons for your opinion.

(10) Why do you think these four languages as mentioned in the previous question were chosen (e.g. multiculturalism, respect, political motivation, or others)?

(11) What is the ideal order of these four languages and why? Currently it is Mandarin Chinese, English, Holo, Hakka in Taipei, but Mandarin Chinese, Holo, Hakka, English in Kaohsiung.

(12) Do you think there are too many or too few languages broadcast on public transport systems? If too many, what language(s) should be dropped and if too few, what language(s) should be added (e.g. indigenous languages, Japanese, Korean, or others)?

Part 3

Expanding Linguistic Landscape Studies: Power Relations, Acts of Resilience and Diachronic Changes

8 Linguistic Landscapes and the African Perspective

Karsten Legère and Tove Rosendal

This chapter focuses on sub-Saharan Africa and examines the linguistic landscape (LL) in three countries, that is, Tanzania, Uganda and Rwanda, which represent typical linguistic patterns found in this region. In multilingual Tanzania, the national language Swahili (spoken as a first or second language by the overwhelming majority of Tanzanians) enjoys a prominent status in the country's LL. In linguistically heterogeneous Uganda, the official language English is widely used in public in the capital and its cityscape, while to a certain extent at the regional level Ugandan languages can be traced in LL documents and elsewhere. Although Rwanda has a single national language, which is the mother tongue of almost 100% of the population, the country promotes official multilingualism (the languages are Rwanda, French, English and Swahili); this is also represented in LL examples in this chapter.

8.1 Introduction

This paper addresses semiotic practices in urban neighbourhoods as documented in the linguistic landscapes (LL) of sub-Saharan Africa. The LLs in this subcontinent are not well studied, in particular with reference to African languages.[1] In this respect, it is sufficient to note here that the situation in the countries south of the Sahara and in other parts of the Global South is distinctive; for example, there was a pre-independence period under foreign domination. Thus, while in the recent past the influx of immigrants, especially of non-European origin, has played a prominent role in reshaping urban areas, the complexity of what has happened and still continues to happen in Africa and elsewhere in the Global South is striking. Cities and urban agglomerations in this part of the world and especially in sub-Saharan Africa are exposed, on the one hand, to a massive migration process from within the country. For many years, an exodus of rural (poor, mainly young) people originating from all corners of a given country and from almost all ethnic communities has been observed. These migrants are an important factor that has contributed, and still contributes, to the impressive urbanisation rates in the Global South.[2] On the other hand, the political instability in a number of sub-Saharan countries (e.g. South Sudan, Democratic Republic of Congo, Ethiopia, Somalia, earlier Rwanda or Burundi and more) forces people to seek shelter in neighbouring countries and elsewhere. The largest number of refugees, from crisis areas with political and ethnic conflict in sub-Saharan Africa, can be found in cities and towns. According to UNHCR (2016), in this region a total of 4.1 million people are refugees.

Moreover, economic constraints and unemployment stimulate people from, for example, Nigeria and other African states to leave home in search of greener pastures in South Africa and overseas, especially Europe, where they join the large contingent of immigrants.

Most sub-Saharan African countries have been multi-ethnic, and hence multilingual, from before colonial times. This multi-ethnicity is impressive in countries such as Nigeria, Cameroon, Tanzania or Uganda where approximately 520, 280, 150 or 60 ethnic communities, respectively, have been listed.[3] The same is typical for the linguistic superdiversity seen not only in urban areas, but also in a number of rural areas. Thus, in Tanzania, for example, glossonyms of national languages which belong to all four African language phyla (i.e. Niger-Congo, Nilo-Saharan, Afroasiatic as well as Khoisan) are recorded. In addition, even in the few countries that are almost ethnically homogeneous, the pre-independence period has left its linguistic traces with regard to the imposition of a non-African official language. Accordingly, in sub-Saharan Africa country-specific ecologies have been shaped in the colonial (or quasi-colonial such as a mandate/trusteeship administration) past. In this regard, in independent Rwanda, Burundi, Lesotho, Swaziland or Somalia, the continuous maintenance of and official focus on non-African languages (English, French, Portuguese, Spanish, Italian) and Arabic (mainly for religious reasons) has diversified the linguistic situation, especially in urban areas. The heterogeneous character of sub-Saharan Africa, with conflicting policies and a multitude of situations, is in particular reflected in multifaceted LLs in urban areas. Accordingly, it is necessary to thoroughly analyse LLs against the background of specific aspects peculiar to this region using an ethnographic approach.

Much of the existing limited sub-Saharan LL documentation has been quantitative and synchronic. Given the top-down practice of decision making and implementation, it is, especially in urban areas, mainly a reflection of the official language policy. But, as stated in Pennycook (2010: 127), 'language is a social activity and acts at a meso-political level between the larger social worlds and the local linguistic instantiations'. These social practices can only be studied locally but are part of a wider perspective. The same is, of course, also true for the African situation, where Western and other ideologies had (and still have) a far-reaching impact on language status and use. Hence, against the sub-Saharan background the spatial placement of text or other visual meaningful symbols and pictures are part of ideological acts, even when not visible in the LL. The orders of indexicality (social, political, economic and cultural value attribution) are seen in this connection. Thus, each sign in the LL is related to a larger discourse.

Written signs in Africa are mainly an urban phenomenon, with only very limited manifestations visible in rural environments. This geographically unequal visibility of languages in sub-Saharan Africa is closely linked to language policy and to power. Literacy and visible literacy practices are the products of 'culturally modelled and socially patterned ways in which languages are used' (Juffermans, 2015: 2). In fact, the symbolic construction of public space is both the result of language policy formulated and implemented before and after independence as well as of grassroots initiatives. Thus, as argued above, political factors are a major stimulus for shaping urban neighbourhoods through top-down processes imposing official non-African languages, but also for empowering and upgrading African languages that were marginalised and kept at a low profile. Simultaneous grassroots literacy development (e.g. community response to or reflecting language policies as well as language choice determined by local institutions or individuals such as shopkeepers) may be found.

From the aforementioned perspective, this chapter attempts to illustrate both top-down processes and African/national language empowerment in some sub-Saharan nation states. It also investigates local practices as suggested by Pennycook (2010), local resources and conditions for language practices – all from a Global South perspective. This perspective is needed, as much focus in LL research and documentation today is given to cityscapes and neighbourhoods in urban Western contexts. As Blommaert (2005: 20) argues: 'in the age of globalisation, it is worth looking at material from the peripheries of the world system'. Taking into account Blommaert's contention, LL studies focusing on African neighbourhoods are much needed to capture an appropriate picture of what is occurring in this part of the Global South.

Even if the concept of globalisation is a product of the 1970s, some of its constituents are familiar in the context of sub-Saharan Africa. In the period of foreign rule before independence, the then administration recruited, for instance, labour from India to build the railway in the then British East Africa (Kenya). Or, to quote another example, subordinate civil servants came from outside East Africa, again mainly from India. In addition, there is a long tradition of Indian or, in West Africa, Lebanese business dating from pre-independence times.

In the present time that Blommaert has in mind, a rather prominent Chinese presence is observed in the region, which is focused on in this chapter. Thus, Chinese investors and a significant percentage of the estimated 1 million Chinese workers in sub-Saharan Africa (Neumann, 2016: 33) are based in East Africa. In the past, Africa has entered specific domains of the global market as an oil producer, for other natural resources as well as manufactured products. As part of the globalised world, and through technological progress and new technical achievements, the region has opened up as a market for exports mainly from Asia, Europe and the US.

In addition to the factors sketched initially, the superdiversity of urban areas in sub-Saharan Africa (Vertovec, 2006, 2007) is also shaped by global processes, which in Europe and elsewhere in the North have resulted in what are now called global cities. With reference to London as a global city, criteria that are quoted include 'easy exchange of people, capital, jobs, businesses and languages' (Lyall, 2017: 3) and, of course, multi-ethnicity (representing 270 nationalities). It seems that, in view of the facts and arguments presented above, a couple of African cities are also global or are at least on their way to this status. Given that the focus of this chapter is on the role of language politics and policy and grassroots initiatives, globalisation can only briefly be dealt with here.

In the following sections, the background of LLs documented in Tanzania, Rwanda and Uganda will be discussed, supported by examples illustrating both the top-down and bottom-up approaches. These examples will first present formal, official domains, followed by examples and illustrations of signage that show bottom-up initiatives, with a focus on the use of African languages. Some global aspects will be briefly discussed before the concluding remarks.

8.2 Language Politics and Policy Shaping the Linguistic Landscape

In introducing this section, we present two recent news items that show the relevance of language politics and policy in the Global South. On 16 February 2016, *News 24* reported from Somalia: 'The Somali capital Mogadishu has ordered entrepreneurs to remove English-language signboards so as to protect the Somali language'. On 26 March 2016, under the headline 'China wants cities and developments, to drop "foreign, strange" names', *US Today Weekly* reported upon an intervention by the Chinese Civil Affairs Minister. This official condemned the spread of non-Chinese toponyms and more in the LL, which function to 'damage "national dignity"' in the People's Republic of China (Gardner, 2016: 3A).

Both press sources deal with the interference of authorities in the LL. They reflect the strong influence of the English language in business and markets. This phenomenon is observed worldwide and is prevalent in the Global South. The official response by central, provincial or local authorities to the global role of English, not only in the business sector quoted above, is in accordance with the grassroots situation where the majority of people mainly speak a language other than English or French. Thus, this kind of top-down interference is a step towards stopping the uncontrolled influx and use of originally foreign languages in domains where national languages are well equipped to be used instead. This is for the benefit of those that otherwise cannot be addressed owing to a lack of linguistic knowledge.

Of course, there is also the far-reaching top-down approach that aims at expanding the competence and use of non-African languages such as English, French or Portuguese, which can be observed in sub-Saharan states. In so doing, social cohesion, as discussed in Legère and Rosendal (2015), is clearly affected, as just a small part of the African population is addressed. Examples of top-down approaches are given below, where the chapter presents a summary of some cornerstones of language policy and politics with reference to the LL in three east African nation states.

8.2.1 Tanzania

In the east African country of Tanzania,[4] a foreign language (i.e. German in early colonial years, English since 1918 and Arabic in Zanzibar) was at the top of a language hierarchy. In various domains, partly official and formal, (ki-)Swahili (currently spoken by approx. 95% of the adult mainland population, 100% in Zanzibar) has been number two in this hierarchy, while all other languages and linguistic varieties, that is, 126 languages listed by *Ethnologue* (Lewis *et al.*, 2016) and 150 by the 2009 *Atlasi ya Lugha za Tanzania* (Languages of Tanzania Project (LoT), 2009) are, if at all, prominent in informal domains.

From independence, and in particular after the 1964 Tanganyika/Zanzibar Union, which gave birth to the United Republic of Tanzania (URT, *Jamhuri ya Muungano wa Tanzania*), the political leadership was highly committed to upgrading the position of Swahili in the young nation state. In this respect, it was planned for this language to acquire the same status as English, which was stipulated by the pre-independence British administration, in order for the United Republic to have two official languages. As a consequence, the 1967 proclaimed *Ujamaa* policy (a pro-socialist, egalitarian approach to national development) gave special attention to the linguistic competence of the common Tanzanian for whom English did not play any particular role. As stated above, English competence in Tanzania was and still is low. In fact, Swahili has been prominent whenever people in Tanzania are addressed and a dialogue is expected. The use of Swahili is the rule in many domains, including the Tanzanian cityscape. In the countryside the Swahili option (if any) has always been the unmarked choice.

Language politics has been in support of the role of Swahili as the Tanzanian national language (*Lugha ya Taifa*). Following independence, the country's political leaders such as the late President Nyerere and then Vice President Kawawa were at the forefront of empowering this language. Its far-reaching role in consolidating national cohesion is the stimulating factor for enhancing the image of this language in Tanzania and beyond. The Tanzanian language policy, which took this situation into account towards the end of the 1960s and early 1970s, translated status and corpus matters into concrete measures. In relation to the former, the status of Swahili as the co-official language of Tanzania with the same footing as English (or as replacing this language) was emphasised and became a reality. Substantial corpus development for official and formal domains (e.g. administration, National Assembly, parastatal institutions, education) took place under the auspices of the 1967 established National Swahili Council/*Baraza la Taifa la Kiswahili*. In this respect the Swahili written Staff Circular 1 of 1974 (Tanzania, Ofisi ya Rais, 1974) stipulates for Tanzania Mainland the comprehensive use of Swahili for

- all ministerial correspondence;
- all communication in offices;
- *all office names (Ministries, Departments including the regional level*[5](emphasis by authors); and
- all forms[6].

Additionally, in the newspaper article 'August is deadline for Swahili' (Legère, 1975: 346, quoting *Daily News*, 20 July 1974: 4), more steps to enhance the position of Swahili were announced and immediately implemented:

> From August 1, all correspondence, forms and sign posts in all parastatal and public organizations must be in Swahili.

It is clear that these 1974 language policy directives[7] had both a direct and indirect impact on the country's LL.

At that time, corpus development (i.e. coining a large number of domain-oriented Swahili terms) by BAKITA (*Baraza la Kiswahili la Taifa*) had already taken place.

Accordingly, the official groundwork for the Swahili empowerment in 1974 having been done, the subsequent changes in the LL of Dar es Salaam city were very impressive. As a logical consequence of the policy orientation, in the then Tanzanian capital, ministries and parastatal institutions (e.g. the University of Dar es Salaam, see below) added Swahili to office names or replaced English with Swahili names.

Language politics and policy shaping the LL, and especially the linguistic cityscape, incorporated the political and ideological climate streamlined by Nyerere and the Tanganyika African National Union (TANU) leadership. There was a key breakthrough in consolidating the position of Swahili in official and formal domains, shaping Tanzania's LL by sidelining English in official as well as various formal domains and further stimulating the spontaneous use of the national language in non-formal domains.

As an example of the LL changes that took place in 1974, reference is made here to the parastatal University of Dar es Salaam (UDSM) where Swahili terms replaced English office and academic names. Below are some standardised terms that illustrate this change (> indicates the switch from English to Swahili names encountered, for example, on office doors; for a detailed account, see Brauner [1975]):

(Vice)Chancellor('s Office) > (*Ofisi ya Makamu wa*) *Mkuu wa Chuo*, Chief Academic (Administrative) Officer > *Afisa Mkuu wa Taaluma* (*Utawala*), Bursar > *Msarifu*, Librarian > *Mkutubi*, Faculty of Arts and Social Sciences (FASS) > *Kitivo cha Fani na Sayansi za Jamii*, Department of Foreign Languages and Linguistics (FLL) > *Idara ya Lugha za Kigeni na Isimu*, Department of Biology (Zoology) > *Idara ya Elimu-Mimea* (*Elimu-Wanyama*), Institute of Kiswahili Research (Development Studies) > *Taasisi ya Taaluma ya Kiswahili/TATAKI* (*Mitaala ya Maendeleo*), Estates Department > *Idara ya Miliki*, and many more.

The empowerment of Swahili in the Tanzanian LL in general and at an academic institution like the UDSM has mostly been ignored and has been rarely documented to date.[8] Accordingly, from an LL perspective it is high time to take note of the extraordinary commitment by Tanzanian authorities in response to people's dissatisfaction with the post-independence policy of maintaining and using a foreign language such as English. In so doing, the overwhelming majority of Tanzanians who appreciated the role of Swahili as their supra-ethnic medium of communication[9] were discriminated against, feeling like strangers in their own country. Thus, the Tanzanian top-down approach just described was in the interest of a large part of the country's citizens. It countered the generally negative role mostly associated with a government imposing or pursuing a policy against people's will. The latter approach is discussed below with regard to two other east African countries.

8.2.2 Uganda

Uganda, with its 30 to 63 languages or dialects from four language families (Rosendal, 2011: 82–88) and colonial past (stipulating English as the language of administration), constitutes a typical example of multilingual Africa. While English was re-appointed as the country's official language at independence in 1962,

Ugandan languages have no official status. The status of English was confirmed in the 1995 Constitution of the Republic of Uganda, Chapter 2, which states the following:

6.   (1) The official language of Uganda is English.

(2) Subject to clause (1) of this article, any other language may be used as a medium of instruction in schools or other educational institutions or for legislative, administrative or judicial purposes as may be prescribed by law.

In the Preamble of the Constitution, it is also declared in Part XXIV (Cultural Objectives) that the state shall:

(ii) encourage the development, preservation and enrichment of all Ugandan languages; [...]

(iv) encourage the development of a national language or languages [...].

Although the role of Ugandan languages is highlighted in the Constitution, their function has not officially been promoted. Despite the addition of Swahili as the co-official language through an amendment in 2005 (Uganda, 2006) and the recent re-introduction of some Ugandan languages as the medium of instruction during the very first years of education, in Uganda the dominance of English as the official language is unchallenged. English is also the medium of instruction throughout the educational system. It is therefore not surprising that the LL of Uganda is characterised by the use of English on signs, being the language of literacy through education. English functions as a language of wider distribution (LWD) in Uganda. However, the Ugandan language (lu-)Ganda, which is the first language of 16.3% of the population, is the most popular LWD. Ganda is not only employed in the central region and adjacent district but is also the LWD in the far northwest and east, rather than English. The latter language was estimated to be the second language of some 20% of the population, according to Ladefoged *et al.* (1972: 25). Even if there are no recent statistics about the distribution of English, it is clear that English is a prominent LWD in the superdiverse capital Kampala, while other Ugandan languages (major area languages) exercise the function of LWDs in regional towns. Important regional area languages are, for instance, used by the state newspaper's Sunday issue, *The Sunday Vision*, which has four sister newspapers in Ugandan languages, namely the daily *Bukedde* (literally 'Daybreak'), published in Ganda; the weekly *Orumuri* ('Daybreak'), in Nyankore and Chiga; *Rupiny* ('Daybreak'), in Lwo; and *Etop* ('Big morning star') in Teso. As English is mainly learnt through the educational system, only the well-educated elite has a good command of the language, while the majority of Ugandans do not master English or have a rudimentary knowledge, especially in writing the language. When the masses are addressed, both the state and private institutions frequently use Ugandan languages, especially in oral communication.

Despite lacking any official recognition, Ugandan languages are to a certain extent visible in the LL of Uganda. For example, in the central region (in smaller streets in the outskirts of the Kampala area and in Jinja), the regional language

Ganda is often found along with English. Further, in the west of Uganda the major area languages Tooro and Nyankore are prominent as media of communication. In the north, Acholi is used both on billboards and shop signs, often in combination with English. Swahili, despite its co-official status, plays a marginal role in the LL of Ugandan towns, while the aforementioned regional languages are used for wider communication when the need arises.

8.2.3 Rwanda

In contrast to the multilingual situation found in Tanzania and Uganda, Rwanda has a national and (co-)official language, (kinya-)Rwanda, which is understood by 99.4% of Rwandans (Rwanda, 2005). However, even in Rwanda politics have shaped the official language policy (including educational policy), and is reflected in the ecology of its LL.

Upon Rwanda's independence in 1962, Article 5 of the 1962 Constitution of the Rwandan Republic stated that the national language was Rwanda, and that the official languages were Rwanda and French (Nyirindekwe, 1999: 14). The same statement was repeated in the constitutions of 1978 (Article 4) and 1991 (Article 4): '*Le kinyarwanda est la langue nationale, les langues officielles sont le kinyarwanda et le français*' (Nyirindekwe, 1999: 15).

Although having no historical, pre-independence ties, English was added as official language in 2003, taking into account the political changes after the 1994 genocide. The imposition of English as the third official language was further reinforced by a decision in 2008 to make English the medium of instruction at all levels of education (Rwanda, 2008). The Cabinet issued the following instructions (section 11 of the Cabinet decisions):

> As a part of enhancing Rwanda's role within the East African Community in particular, and at international level in general, Cabinet requested:
>
> – The Minister of Education to put in place an intensive programme for using English in all public and Government sponsored primary and secondary schools and higher learning institutions;
>
> – The Minister of Public Service and Labour to put in place a programme to help Government employees at all levels learn English, starting with Top Ranking Officials.

As a result of both the history of foreign rule and recent political decisions, and despite its basically homogeneous linguistic situation with the national language reaching everyone, Rwanda has French and English as two additional co-official languages. Furthermore, Swahili was added as an official language as recently as February 2017, to consolidate cooperation within the East African Community.

The 2002 census reported that only 3.9% of the population speak French, 1.9% speak English and 3% speak Swahili as a second language (Rwanda, 2005: 38). The figures were slightly higher in urban areas: 12.2% for both French and Swahili, 6% for English.

8.3 Facets of the Linguistic Landscape

In the following section, several visual examples of signs found in the LLs of Tanzania, Uganda and Rwanda are presented. Tanzania and Uganda are chosen as they are typical multilingual African countries. By contrast, Rwanda is an example of a state where an African language is known by everyone, but for some 20 years has promoted a trilingual (and at present a quadrilingual) language policy. The signs and billboards in these countries illustrate how language policy and politics still influence the use of languages in shaping the LL on the African continent. Signs may thus function as a sensitive indicator of social change (Blommaert & Maly, 2014).

Each sign or billboard will be contextualised, that is, the environment where the sign was found is described. In addition, the function of the languages used will be discussed. Further, multimodality and intended receivers will be addressed, when appropriate.

8.3.1 Official empowerment of the national languages of Swahili and Rwanda

Given the official status of both Swahili (in Tanzania, Rwanda and Uganda) and Rwanda (in Rwanda), it is clear that there should be a broad use of the respective national languages. It seems logical to expect supportive photographic documentation, especially in Rwanda and Tanzania, which have a long (Rwanda) and more recent (Tanzania) tradition of using the national languages in naming the State House, ministries, and regional and city authorities at official buildings. But this has not occurred, mainly owing to security reasons. In fact, taking photographs of official buildings is risky and, in the case of police stations and other sensitive spots, even forbidden. Less problematic in public is photographic documentation of office names, official advertisements, announcements and more.

As a result of the authors' extensive exposure to the east African LL, there are a multitude of visual observations that, for example, document the prominent role of Swahili in Tanzania after 1974 or in Rwanda in the legislature (parliament), executive (government and administration) as well as the judiciary (law courts and law enforcing institutions). In the former case, some recent examples from Dar es Salaam city will be presented below to demonstrate this role. In Rwanda, at present official language use is rather complex and does not strike a balance that demonstrates the equality of all three official languages. As presented below, it is evident that in this respect the national language Rwanda is less privileged.

In Uganda, Swahili as the co-official language since 2005 could not be traced in the official linguistic cityscape. While English is the prominent language, Swahili plays a relatively minor role.

As for Tanzania, especially for Dar es Salaam and Zanzibar, the majority of central and major city institutions as well as office names are, as a rule, displayed in both official languages. The closer the offices are to the population in the street, the more Swahili is used. However, suffice it to note here and also in section 8.3.3 below, individual decisions to give a preference to English have also been seen at the municipal level. Figure 8.1 shows some cityscape examples in Swahili.

(a)   (b)

Figure 8.1 Official text (in front of the Ministry of Home Affairs): (a) Wizara ya Mambo ya Ndani/ Ministry of Home Affairs, Dar es Salaam, Tanzania; (b) Wizara ya Mambo ya Ndani/Ministry of Home Affairs, Idara ya Uhamiaji/Immigration Office/Uhamiaji Makao Makuu/Immigration Headquarter

The billboard in Figure 8.1a is displayed outside the Ministry of Home Affairs on Ohio Street, Dar es Salaam, Ilala. It is interesting due to the character of its message that goes beyond the mere identification of the nearby government office. Under the Swahili headline *Dhamira*, which is used as the equivalent of English 'vision' or 'leit-motif', the importance of holding a national identification certificate is presented.[10]

Another document, which has been issued by the Tanzanian Government and found in DSM's cityscape in July 2016 at Ardhi University, Kinondoni, deals with the prescriptive Tanzanian costume culture. In this respect, after lengthy discussion in parliament and other official circles, various popular pieces of clothing have been rejected. The latter, which are presented in the poster in Figure 8.2, are classified by Tanzanian traditionalists as being atypical and a symbol of decadency.

A very popular way of enriching the Tanzanian LL is by using SUV spare tyre covers, both for the text and the design. Thus, on the occasion of political events or anniversaries, this mobile form of displaying a political message contributes fittingly to the country's permanent focus on a nation-building concept. The cover shown in Figure 8.3 was designed to commemorate the 50th anniversary of what is now the Tanzania mainland (ex-Tanganyika) in 2011. It references a short message in Swahili, which is translated as follows:

Miaka Hamsini ya Uhuru Tanzania Bara
'Fifty years of Tanzania Mainland's Independence 1961–2011'
Tumethubutu, tumeweza
Tunazidi kusonga mbele
'We have dared, we have managed,
we will go further'

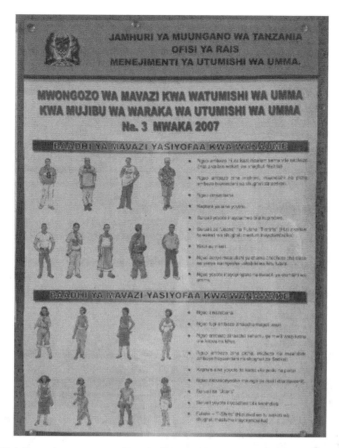

Figure 8.2 Official text (government directive): 'United Republic of Tanzania President's Office, Management of National Employment', In main caption: 'Directive regarding a costume culture for civil servants according to Staff Circular; No. 3, 2007'. Authors' comment: What follows are drawings of non-Tanzanian dresses such as for men, blue jeans (eight more fashion styles are also rejected) or for women, mini-skirts (plus seven more items are rejected). Reasons for disqualifying these dress modes are listed on the right-hand side of the poster

On the occasion of the 2015 election campaign in Dar es Salaam (October), the following spare wheel cover was spotted. Its message reads: *CHAGUA MAGUFULI* 'Vote for Magufuli'.[11]

Similarly, government projects are depicted as spare wheel covers, such that is presented in Figure 8.4b belonging to a parastatal company car, where MKURABITA stands for 'People's empowerment in participating in the market economy' (the original Swahili text is written in white on the green part of the cover).

The announcements in Figure 8.5 were issued by local authorities. In Figure 8.5a (from Ohio Street, Dar es Salaam, Ilala), the handwritten text by the Ilala municipality urges people to keep the area clean. Any deposits of waste are an offence, resulting in legal action with the culprit being punished. The text in Figure 8.5b (seen on 22 July 2016) was painted on a wall in the downtown Morogoro Street. Its message

Figure 8.3 Official text (50 years of independence)

(a)   (b)

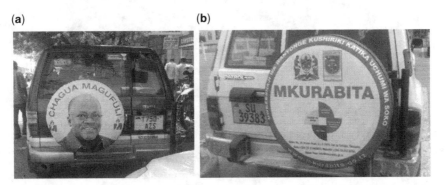

Figure 8.4 Official texts: (a) presidential elections and (b) project description

(a)   (b)

Figure 8.5 Official texts (local authorities)

Figure 8.6 Official text (local authorities): 'Ilala Municipality Council, Primary School, Tabata, P.O. Box 24149 DSM, Our promise (–) Education has no end'

in Swahili is 'It is not allowed to start or maintain business in this area as ordered by Local Government'.

Local authorities are responsible for primary schools. This responsibility is displayed in Figure 8.6, which was originally taken by Charles Bwenge in 2005 (and published in Bwenge, 2013: 185).

These figures represent only a small portion of LL examples that demonstrate the widespread use of Swahili in official domains, including even government and parastatal cars. The constraints of documentation have been previously identified in this chapter. Furthermore, as is frequently the case, in post-independence years and especially now in the era of globalisation, English is occasionally preferred, while Swahili seems to be neglected (as exemplified by the official Tanzanian websites being in English; it is only recently that Swahili versions have also been made available). In summary, despite its ups and downs, the position of Swahili in Tanzania as the co-official language has been consolidated in the urban LL.

As for Rwanda, this national language has clearly been sidelined in the official landscape after the genocide, a situation that will be addressed in Section 8.3.2 below.

8.3.2 Top-down approach regarding English and French in official domains

The use of the three official languages, namely English, French and Rwanda, in Rwanda on signs in official buildings and institutions vary. It was earlier found (Rosendal, 2011) that the sequencing or order of languages in official domains is not uniform. Signs at the Ministry of Education were, for instance, in Rwanda, English and French (in this specific order). The signs giving directions in the parliament were written in French followed by English. Likewise, signs of names, including titles, were both in French and English, with French in first position. The visitor's badges in parliament were exclusively in French as were the signs on office doors. The electronic sign, which shows the vote count in parliament, however, was in English.

Old official signs, such as street signs placed by the municipality, were mostly in Rwanda and French or French and Rwanda. The trend was that English was introduced on new signs and official announcements in public. In Uganda, the situation is similar – all signs on and in official buildings, as well as street names and on official buildings and institutions reflect the high status of English.

Given the focus of this chapter, less attention is paid here to the position of English and French in official public domains. It is sufficient to note the important role of English in all three countries. In Rwanda, French, similar to Rwanda, loses ground against English, which for the current president and his cabinet is the preferred choice. This fact is also evident in the urban LL in Rwanda and elsewhere.

8.3.3 The official language policy impact in formal domains

It goes without saying that the official status of English in all three countries and French (for Rwanda) has an effect on other domains beyond the official ones, such as education, especially universities, mobile phone companies and banks (all identified as formal domains). This language use will be considered as given and, therefore, will only be briefly addressed in this section. Emphasis will be placed on the use of east African languages instead to demonstrate that the best choice for effectively addressing national, regional and local issues is the use of these languages.

Big commercial entities, such as insurance companies, banks and multinational telecom/mobile phone companies, use African languages as the popular urban language on huge billboards in key urban locations, outside shops and in radio commercials. It is vital for business to be as inclusive as possible. These commercial companies employ African languages for strategic advertising purposes (Seargeant, 2009) and as a communicative resource to reach the masses. In these cases, the use of African languages rather than English indexes a modern identity. Figures 8.7 and 8.8 further support this contention, with the selected examples displaying mobile phone advertisement texts.

Figure 8.7 shows a huge billboard in the outskirts of the Rwandan capital of Kigali, where the national language, Rwanda, is used by MTN to voice its message, *Vuga mu masegonda...* 'speak in seconds', *wishyure ku isegonda...* 'pay per second'. A similar billboard (Figure 8.8) in Swahili (one of many documented mobile phone sources) praises *NOKIA DABO DABO* 'Nokia Double Double' with its *Laini mbili + miziki* 'two lines (i.e. networks) + music' (i.e. all kinds of music, *miziki* class 4, plural of class 3 *muziki*) promising *miziki bila kikomo* 'all kinds of never-ending music'. In addition, the two billboards in Figure 8.9 from Uganda, written in the area languages Rutooro (Fort Portal sign) and Lusoga (the Jinja sign), also capture the customer-oriented messages of big companies (MTN and the Ugandan National Insurance Corporation).

In each case, the main reason for the language choice is economic value attribution so that the linguistic competence of a wide range of potential customers is taken into account. Accordingly, in Tanzania, most mobile phone billboards are in Swahili, while in Rwanda the languages are often mixed, using both Rwanda and either French or English.

Figure 8.7 Advertisements (mobile phones): Billboard outside Kigali, Rwanda

Figure 8.8 Advertisement (mobile phones): Billboard, advertising a Nokia phone that takes two different SIM cards in Ubungo, Dar es Salaam, Tanzania

(b)

(a)

Figure 8.9 Texts in Ugandan languages: (a) Telephone company advertisement in Fort Portal, Western Uganda, and (b) insurance company advertisement in Jinja, Eastern Uganda

It is obvious that had the billboard messages been written in English or French, far fewer people would have been reached.[12] The case in Uganda is particularly interesting, where a move away from the official language of English is noted, especially regarding billboards in the western and northern regions, where the major area languages of Nyankore and Acholi are frequently used, often in combination with English.

As pointed out above, the implementation of the Tanzanian language policy was particularly successful at the parastatal UDSM, where in 1974 and thereafter the LL radically changed within a short period of time (see above for further details). The result was that English was replaced by Swahili on billboards and other signs. Up to the 1980s, the LL on the UDSM campus was dominated by Swahili. Thereafter, a lack of commitment to the cause of Swahili, fading out of the *Ujamaa* policy and subsequent liberalisation as well as other factors contributed to the return of English at UDSM. Generally, for the last two decades, offices and new buildings have been once again named or renamed in English. Figure 8.10 demonstrates this situation.

Figure 8.10a identifies the College of Arts & Social Sciences (CASS) that some years ago replaced the Faculty of Arts & Social Sciences (FASS).[13] By comparison, in Figure 8.10b there is a simple wooden plank that is a piece of historical documentary evidence dating back to 1974. This could still be found at the rear entrance of the (then FASS) office block in March 2017.

As probably a token of the sought after international flair city authorities want to spread (while simultaneously pursuing downtown 'modernisation' by destroying the historically grown cityscape), English has become more and more dominant. This change is particularly evident in the large number of the then nationalised residential buildings, which were managed by *Shirika la Nyumba la Taifa*, that is, the 'National Housing Corporation'. In the *Ujamaa* period the ownership was, therefore, identified by a logo in Swahili. This name has now been replaced by an English

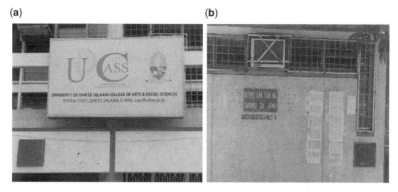

Figure 8.10 English and Swahili texts, University of Dar es Salaam: (a) The 2012 (and later until 2015) way of identifying CASS at UDSM and (b) left over from the 1974 empowerment of Swahili at UDSM – identifying a FASS building

logo. However, the street signs along this and other downtown streets are bilingual (on one side of the street the name is given in Swahili, the other is in English e.g. *Barabara la Morogoro* shortened as *Br. la Morogoro* and Morogoro Road).

The document shown in Figure 8.11b is self-explanatory and is an expression of the elitist climate that exists among some Tanzanians.

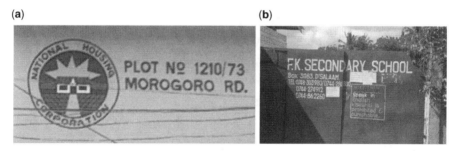

Figure 8.11 English texts in formal domains: (a) National Housing Corporation, Morogoro Street, Dar es Salaam and (b) Private F.K. Secondary School; right door – warning to speak, English, Kiswahili is prohibited and punishable[14]

In the same way, Dar es Salaam's LL no longer displays Swahili terms such as *Shirika la Umeme la Tanzania* or *RTD* (*Redio Tanzania Dar es Salaam*), which now reads again as TANESCO (Tanzania Electricity Supply Co.) and TBC (Tanzania Broadcasting Co.), respectively.

In Uganda, African languages are used by Non-Governmental Organisations (NGOs) and a variety of institutions to reach the average Ugandan in addition to the educated elite. The billboard in Figure 8.12, found at the Mbarara-Kabale Highway in western Uganda, is a good illustration. The monolingual sign in Nyankore requests people to undergo HIV/AIDS testing.

Despite the impact of the official language policy on how languages are used in the LL, there is a visible trend that big and international companies and

Figure 8.12 Formal text – Ugandan regional language: billboard at the Mbarara-Kabale Highway in western Uganda – AIDS protection

organisations target people in African languages, which reach a huge target group beyond the educated elite.

8.4 Grassroots Contributions to Shaping the Cityscape

Signs (both shop signs and billboards) in Rwanda are most often monolingual in either French or English. This pattern is more common than monolingual texts in the national and official language of Rwanda. In a study by Rosendal (2011), some 40% of the shop signs were found to be monolingual in French, 23% monolingual in English and only 7.4% in Rwanda. In Uganda, especially in the capital Kampala, but also in eight major towns in all four regions of Uganda, the official language of English dominates on placards of all kinds (see Table 8.1). The statistics are based on a full inventory of all shop signs in the main streets in these towns. In total, 2026 signs found in 43 streets were analysed. Table 8.1 displays some of the text patterns previously discussed.

Table 8.1 Shop signs in eight major Ugandan towns

Region	Town (area language)	English (%)	English > area lang. (%)	Area lang. > e (%)	Area lang. (%)	Other languages (%)	Total (%)	Total (no. of signs)
Eastern	Busia (Saamia)	97.6	0.0	0.0	0.0	2.4	100	126
Eastern	Mbale (Masaaba)	98.1	0.6	0.0	0.0	1.3	100	318
Eastern	Jinja (Soga)	96.2	1.0	2.1	0.3	0.4	100	290
Northern	Gulu (Acholi)	74.6	13.5	10.3	0.8	0.8	100	378
Western	Hoima (Nyoro)	90.9	8.6	0.5	0.0	0.0	100	187
Western	Fort Portal (Tooro)	93.5	4.5	0.8	0.8	0.4	100	244
Western	Mbarara (Nyankore)	89.5	3.8	5.2	0.9	0.6	100	345
Central	Entebbe (Ganda)	95.6	2.9	1.5	0.0	0.0	100	138

$N = 2026$

In the capital, Kampala, which is a very diverse city due to attracting people from different parts of Uganda and other countries, almost all signs are monolingual in English, as opposed to the situation in the major regional towns. Because English here is also frequently used in oral communication, the use of English for shop signs and advertisements follows logically. English is the unmarked choice.

Signs such as the example in Figure 8.13 from Makerere Hill Road, Kampala, which also includes some Ganda terms, are less frequent, but are visible especially in smaller streets. As can be seen, the Ganda term for hospital, *eddwaliro*, is added to the English text.

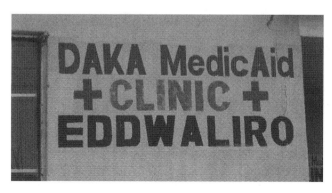

Figure 8.13 Bilingual text: sign in Makerere Hill Road, Kampala, Uganda

The use of African languages on signs in Uganda shows both differences and similarities compared to signage in Rwanda. Rwanda's official and national language, Rwanda, is found more frequently on shop signs than are African languages in Uganda. However, as Rwanda is a language known and spoken by every citizen, it is surprising to find this language used in only an average of 16.4% of the 952 shop signs investigated in the three main towns of Kigali, Butare and Gisenyi (Rosendal, 2011). As in Uganda, this African language was more frequent outside the capital, Kigali. Only slightly more than 7% of the shop signs in the capital used Rwanda. Most shop signs were monolingual in French and in English. One-third of the signs were multilingual. The bi- or multilingual signs were most frequently written in all three official languages. It was further noted that the meaning expressed in the different languages on these shop signs only partially overlapped (Rosendal, 2009).

To illustrate this point, Figure 8.14, a photograph of a shop in *Avenue du Commerce* in Kigali is given. It presents text in all three official languages. The sign heading illustrates this trilingual practice where all three official languages co-exist: 'Vous y trouverez, *Muzahasanga*', 'you will find here', We sell'. This is a combination of instrumental and symbolic constructions, with additional information given through illustrative images. The language use is not faithfully representative of the linguistic repertoire typical in Kigali. The use of French and English indicates the social position and aspirations of people who identify themselves with particular power-related languages and power relations (Ben-Rafael *et al.*, 2006). Androutsopoulos (2007) calls this use of English and French 'emblematic' or 'minimal', a usage which only requires a minimum of receptive or productive language competence.

Similar illustrations using painted images are also frequently found in Uganda, as is displayed in Figure 8.15 on a sign in Perse Road in Hoima (Western Region). In order to advertise an eye clinic, the handmade business sign shows an eye as well as glasses. Additional information to attract local customers from the lower market end is the Nyoro term for clinic *irrwaro* (in parentheses). The use of English here has both symbolic and utilitarian functions. Even if English is the

Figure 8.14 Trilingual text: shop sign, *Avenue du Commerce* in Kigali, Rwanda

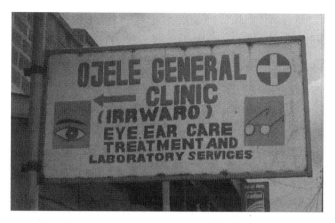

Figure 8.15 English text plus Ugandan regional language (one word): Perse Road in Hoima town, Uganda

official language, learnt through the educational system, the emblematic or minimal use of English is typical of regional towns in Uganda, where educational levels are low.

African urban shop signs and billboards often feature the above described painted illustrations. In this respect, the function of these illustrations in Africa is mostly pragmatic. They inform and attract both literate and illiterate customers as well as those whose competence in the imposed non-African language is limited. The multimodal (Kress & van Leeuwen, 1996; Scollon & Scollon, 2003) content of the handmade signs is often very informative, indicating the exact nature of the services and goods offered. A significant portion of the African customers cannot read the text on the sign, either because they are illiterate or because the sign is written in a language which only a few of the national population know. Figure 8.15 is an example of 'signage of necessity' (Stroud & Mpendukana, 2009) under marginal literary competence.

Another point of interest is that a substantial number of shops in African neighbourhoods do not have any signs at all. In some regional towns in Uganda, it was found that only about half of the shops in the main streets studied displayed a sign (Rosendal, 2011). The grassroots approach to LL described above is a further manifestation of the sociopolitical conditions and linguistic experience in sub-Saharan Africa.

Quantitative studies of language use on signs and billboards clearly demonstrate that as the result of official language policies, non-African languages are dominant in the LLs of Rwanda and Uganda. These signs show the grassroots need for communication in languages that are understood by everyone.

8.5 Global Aspects

Prior to independence, Rwanda and Tanzania (as UN Trusteeship countries) and Uganda (as a British colony) were, to a certain extent, already exposed to early forms of globalisation. During the pre-independence period, these countries and other dependent territories were important markets for foreign products such as manufactured commodities and other imports. These products were advertised in the public space, as reflected in the LL. In addition, the influx of labour as well as the presence of business people, mainly from India or the Middle East, resulted in Indian and Arabic building names (both residential and religious) and shop signs. The latter can still be found in the neighbourhoods of mosques.

From a contemporary global perspective, the situation has become more complex. In Rwanda, the political leadership built up stronger ties to English-speaking countries. This is evident in the LL, where, in addition to national institutions, foreign companies and business people started advertising brand names and offering services in English as well as establishing offices that bear English names. The same holds true for Uganda.

In Tanzania, during the *Ujamaa* period, foreign banks, for example, were nationalised or closed down their financial activities. They have returned to Tanzania, as is documented in the LL of downtown Dar es Salaam and in affluent areas such as Oyster Bay, as well as in industrial areas such as Mwenge.[15] South Africa (e.g. mining sector, banking, breweries and trade) and especially China (building and infrastructure projects, banking, hotels, supermarkets and more) are other global players that leave traces in the linguistic cityscape. Both monolingual English and/or Chinese texts can be found (see Figure 8.16a for a bilingual version of a menu). To quote another example, road construction companies, including the Austrian STRABAG and the Japanese Konoike, are represented in Dar es Salaam and its linguistic cityscape. They are also present in up-country construction projects building the road connecting Korogwe and Mombo. There, the STRABAG company logo (seen in Figure 8.16b) is displayed next to the road under construction.

The global impact on the LL of Tanzania, Uganda and Rwanda is manifold, but is not further discussed in this chapter for reasons of space and in anticipation of further LL documentation research.

(a)   **(b)**

Figure 8.16 Foreign origin texts: (a) bilingual menu poster of Chinese-owned Palm Beach Hotel and Casino in Dar es Salaam and (b) Austrian STRABAG logo and road construction near Mombo

8.6 Summing Up and the Way Forward

This chapter focused on LLs that have been traced in the three east African countries of Tanzania, Uganda and Rwanda. In all these countries, the authors conducted field research, which also included LL documentation and data analysis, with particular reference to African languages. Some of the results that illustrate African cityscapes and LLs in urban agglomerations were presented above. In so doing, the point of departure was the almost complete lack of earlier contributions in this field focusing on the sub-Saharan region in general and east African neighbourhoods in particular, as pointed out initially. In addition, in view of the underprivileged position of African languages in most sub-Saharan countries, the selection of Tanzania and Rwanda, on the one hand, and Uganda, on the other hand, was deliberate. Thus, in the former countries, powerful and well-established national languages, that is, Swahili and Rwanda, are found, while in Uganda the English language is at the top of a language hierarchy which, with its retention of a non-African official language, is typical for the majority of sub-Saharan states. In the latter case, but also in Rwanda (for French alongside English), the prestigious (non-African) languages are mostly known by the elite, middle-class people as well as the political and economic establishment.

As demonstrated in the LL examples and discussion above, the use of national vs. foreign languages is an ideological and symbolic act, which is emphasised in the official language policy and is an expression of power relations. Moreover, commercial interests and value-attribution/profit-driven cases were identified in the LL. It was argued that local and foreign business people and companies have understood the value of using African languages to address their potential customers by presenting their products on big billboard advertisements, posters and the like.

In the African ecologies discussed here, English and French (imposed by the British or Belgian administration prior to independence) have become local in the sense that they are part of the respective country's ecology. However, English as well as French, has a different historical background and indexical load. The use of English (and French in Rwanda) is the result of language politics and language policy, which is implemented in a top-down process that shapes the LL countrywide and especially in urban neighbourhoods. It was found that in the east African context, English is far less used as a lingua franca owing to the lack of proficiency by the majority of people, especially those who live in rural areas and regional towns. The extensive use of English on official and non-official signs in Uganda and, to some extent, Tanzania, plus French in Rwanda, and elsewhere, is due to its high prestige.

Billboards in non-African languages displaying advertisements or commodities for sale by shop owners and service providers want to impress potential customers. The text is produced in the language that addresses a particular target group that can afford the advertised product or service. For others, being exposed to the English/French-dominated LL remains rather abstract and good for window shopping. Nevertheless, as argued above, it is not strange to find texts (especially advertisements) in English and/or French, even at the grassroots level, because this approach suggests that something is of better quality and has an international reputation exceeding local standards.

As presented above, the impact of past and present language policies in sub-Saharan Africa has shaped the orientation and priorities of LL research in the three east African countries (and elsewhere in sub-Saharan Africa). Against this background, the empowerment of African languages, which is reflected in the cityscape and LL, was discussed. In this respect, the extraordinary contribution by Tanzanian authorities to change the LL of the country in response to the political and socioeconomic ideals of the *Ujamaa* period must be stressed again. As a result of the commitment of the then Tanzanian leadership, the prestige of Swahili and its position in the country in official and formal domains was substantially consolidated. This achievement was discussed to a large extent in this chapter, both from the top-down and grassroots perspective.

As for the way forward, it is assumed that a broader and ethnographic approach could benefit the study of LLs in the African context. In this regard, it seems to be appropriate for a more comprehensive documentation of sub-Saharan Africa to expand LL studies to include semiotic aspects. It is further assumed that both quantitative and qualitative analyses are complementary for appropriately capturing ongoing processes in the African context. Quantitative data contextualises language use and adds to our understanding of factors that are prominent in African countries. Moreover, the understanding of how people perceive their situation and what they actually do with languages is also important for analysing, for example, identity negotiation in the given public/social space mirrored in the LL.

In addition to the documentation of cityscapes and urban areas, the countryside, which was not covered in this chapter, should be focused on as well. It is expected that the use of national languages and other ways of LL shaping is more prominent than in urban areas. Similarly, the presence and role of the non-African official language(s) in the rural LL would be another interesting object of study.

Future research should also take into account issues such as mobility, which is characteristic of many late-modern multilingual societies, also in the African context (Stroud & Mpendukana, 2009) or language use of international corporations in Africa in the light of globalisation, including the indexical use of English, as conducted by Lanza and Woldemariam (2012) in Ethiopia. In the latter context, the concept of global cities in their relevance to Africa would be another attractive theme for research and discussion. Suffice it to conclude here with the wish that more LL studies be conducted to properly take into account the linguistic reality which, on the one hand, sheds light on the official approach to languages and, on the other hand, shows grassroots responses and initiatives.

Acknowledgements

The authors thank an anonymous reviewer of this chapter for their constructive comments and editorial input. Further, they wish to acknowledge the assistance by the language editors K. Finnegan (final version) and Ch. Haussmann (pre-final version). However, the views expressed in the chapter are entirely those of the authors.

Notes

(1) A modest beginning was the 4th Linguistic Landscape Workshop in Addis Ababa, Ethiopia (22–24 February 2012), where the Ethiopian situation was mainly focused on. For our own research results, see, for example, Legère (2012, 2015), Rosendal (2009, 2011). However, in fact, the majority of LL contributions focus on regions in other parts of the world.

(2) See Mysorekar (2014: 7) who states: 'Every year 60 million more people become city dwellers. In developing countries this means mostly unplanned urban growth.'

(3) Source of figures for Nigeria and Cameroon: 'Ethnologue' (Lewis *et al.*, 2016), for Tanzania: Languages of Tanzania Project (LoT) (2009) and section 8.2.1 below, for Uganda, see section 8.2.2 below.

(4) The country existed as German East Africa and Tanganyika for the mainland part and Zanzibar for the Indian Ocean islands of Zanzibar and Pemba before independence in 1961 and 1963, respectively.

(5) Swahili original (*Vibao vyote vya majina ya Ofisi au Wizara na kadhalika viwe vimeandikwa kwa Kiswahili*).

(6) Such as bank deposit and withdrawal slips, passport applications, forms at post offices, etc.

(7) These documents are said to be still in current use (p.c. Prof. Hermas Mwansoko, Director of Culture, Ministry of Information, Culture and Sports, 12 February 2010; Dr Sewangi, Secretary General, BAKITA, March 2015). In 2010, the then Minister of Information, Culture and Sports, G. H. Mkuchika, delivered a speech in parliament, where referring to these documents, he summarised as a reminder the government's position regarding the use of Swahili in official and formal domains (see Mkuchika, 2010).

(8) An exception to this assessment is Polomé (1980) quoting both Brauner (1975) and Legère (1975), who reported on the development at UDSM.

(9) On top of their first language, which is used to speak to members of the ethnic community they belong to.

(10) The lower part of the Swahili text dealing with contact information is, from a linguistic perspective, a fine piece of evidence relating to documenting and disseminating corpus development results. There are Swahili equivalents of English terms such as 'fax' > Swahili *nukushi*, replacing the English loan *faksi*, or *tovuti*, meaning 'home page'.

(11) Dr Magufuli was the candidate of the ruling party CCM and became the Tanzanian president as of November 2015.

(12) However, it should be noted that the standard slogan of the telecom company MTN is distributed in English.

(13) It is interesting to note on the lower left the polished plate, dating back to the early 1960s, which marks the UK's funding for the building. In 1974, when the FASS name was replaced by Swahili, that is, *KITIVO CHA FANI NA SAYANSI ZA JAMII*, this version was written on a plank and not on a polished plate. This text authenticates the then empowerment of Swahili at UDSM, which was initiated by the *Ujamaa* policy and implemented after the August 1974 Kawawa Directive (see above).

(14) Courtesy of Ch. Bwenge, as a copy from Bwenge (2013).

(15) For example, Barclays Bank's use of English and Swahili on posters, see Bwenge (2013: 286).

References

Androutsopoulos, J. (2007) Bilingualism in the mass media and on the internet. In M. Heller (ed.) *Bilingualism: A Social Approach* (pp. 207–230). London: Palgrave Macmillan.

Ben-Rafael, E., Shohamy, E., Amara, M.H. and Trumper-Hecht, N. (2006) Linguistic landscape as symbolic construction of the public space: The case of Israel. *International Journal of Multilingualism* 3 (1), 7–30.

Blommaert, J. (2005) *Discourse. A Critical Introduction*. Cambridge: Cambridge University Press.

Blommaert, J. and Maly, I. (2014) *Ethnographic Linguistic Landscape Analysis and Social Change: A Case Study* Working Papers in Urban Language and Literacies 133. Tilburg: Tilburg University.

Brauner, S. (1975) Swahili an der Universität Dar es Salaam. *Zeitschrift für Phonetik, Sprachwissenschaft und Kommunikationsforschung* 28 (3/4), 331–341.

Bwenge, C. (2013) Maendeleo ya Kiswahili nchini Tanzania: Mapitio ya mtazamo wa Mekacha juu ya kauli za Nyerere [The development of Swahili in Tanzania: A review of Mekacha's position regarding Nyerere's comments]. In K. Legère (ed.) *Bantu Languages and Linguistics. Papers in Memory of Dr. Rugatiri D. K. Mekacha* (pp. 169–186). Bayreuth: Bayreuth African Studies Series.

Gardner, H. (2016) China wants to drop 'foreign, strange' names. *US Today Weekly* 26 March, 1 and 3A.

Juffermans, K. (2015) *Local Languaging, Literacy and Multilingualism in a West African Society.* Bristol: Multilingual Matters.

Kress, G. and van Leeuwen, T. (1996) *Reading Images: A Grammar of Visual Design.* London: Routledge.

Ladefoged, P., Glick, R. and Criper, C. (1972) *Language in Uganda.* London: Oxford University Press.

Lanza, E. and Woldemariam, H. (2012) Indexing modernity: Branding in the linguistic landscape of Addis Ababa. 4th International Workshop on Linguistic Landscape, Addis Ababa University, 22–24 February 2012, unpublished conference paper.

Legère, K. (1975) Zum Verhältnis zwischen dem Swahili und anderen tansanischen Sprachen. *Zeitschrift für Phonetik, Sprachwissenschaft und Kommunikationsforschung* 28 (3/4), 342–348.

Legère, K. (2012) Swahili and English in Dar es Salaam: Bill boards, shop signs and homepages. 43rd Annual Conference on African Linguistics, Tulane University New Orleans, 15–17 March 2012, unpublished presentation.

Legère, K. (2015) SUV spare tyre covers and Swahili in Dar es Salaam, Tanzania. LL7. University of Berkeley, 7–9 May 2015, unpublished presentation.

Legère, K. and Rosendal, T. (2015) National languages, English and social cohesion in East Africa. In H. Coleman (ed.) *Language and Social Cohesion in the Developing World* (pp. 75–91). Colombo, Sri Lanka: British Council/Deutsche Gesellschaft für Internationale Zusammenarbeit GmbH.

Lewis, M., Paul, G., Simons, F. and Fennig, C.D. (eds) (2016) *Ethnologue* (19th edition). Dallas: SIL International.

Languages of Tanzania Project (LoT) (2009) *Atlasi ya Lugha za Tanzania* [Atlas of the Languages of Tanzania]. Dar es Salaam: University of Dar es Salaam.

Lyall, S. (2017) A global city, at a crossroads. *The New York Times, International Weekly* (in collaboration with *Süddeutsche Zeitung*), 21 April, 1 and 4.

Mkuchika, G.H. (2010) Kauli ya Serikali kuhusu matumizi ya Kiswahili katika shughuli rasmi za Serikali [The Government position regarding the use of Swahili in official Governmment interactions]. Unpublished handout of a speech in parliament. Dodoma: Parliament of the United Republic of Tanzania.

Mysorekar, S. (2014) Future development will be urban. *Development and Cooperation* 41 (7), 274.

Neumann, G. (2016) Erwachende Löwen. *Wiener Zeitung* March 5/6, 33–34.

Nyirindekwe, J.-P. (1999) Les problèmes de planification linguistiques au Rwanda. Bachelor's thesis. Butare: Université Nationale du Rwanda.

Pennycook, A. (2010) *Language as a Local Practice.* London: Routledge.

Polomé, E.C. (1980) Tanzania: A socio-linguistic perspective. In E.C. Polomé and C.P. Hill (eds) *Language in Tanzania* (pp. 103–138). London: International African Institute/Oxford University Press.

Rosendal, T. (2009) Linguistic markets in Rwanda: Language use in advertisements and on signs. *Journal of Multilingual and Multicultural Development* 30 (1), 19–39.

Rosendal, T. (2011) *Linguistic Landshapes. A Comparison of Official and Non-official Language Management in Rwanda and Uganda, Focusing on the Position of African Languages.* Language Contact in Africa/Sprachkontakt in Afrika. Cologne: Rüdiger Köppe Verlag.

Rwanda (2005) *Census 2002.* 3ème recensement général de la population et de l'habitat du Rwanda au 15 août 2002. Characteristiques socio-culturelles de la population. Analyse des resultats. Kigali: Ministère des Finances et de la Planification Economique/Commission Nationale de Recensement/Service National de Recensement.

Rwanda (2008) *Statement on Cabinet Resolutions of 8 October 2008.* Kigali: The Prime Minister's Office in charge of Cabinet Affairs.

Scollon, R. and Scollon, S. (2003) *Discourse in Place: Language in the Material World.* London: Routledge.

Seargeant, P. (2009) *The Idea of English in Japan: Ideology and the Evolution of a Global Language.* Bristol: Multilingual Matters.

Stroud, C. and Mpendukana, S. (2009) Towards a material ethnography of linguistic landscape: Multilingualism, mobility and space in a South African township. *Journal of Sociolinguistics* 13 (3), 363–386.

Tanzania. Ofisi ya Rais [Tanzania. President's Office]. (1974) *Matumizi ya Lugha ya Kiswahili katika Ofisi za Serikali* [The Use of Swahili in Government Offices] (=*Waraka wa Utumishi na. 1 wa 1974* [Staff Circular no. 1 of 1974]). Dar es Salaam.

UNHCR (2016) *UNHCR Sub-Saharan Africa*, available at http://www.unhcr.org/africa.html (accessed 29 November 2016).

Uganda (2006) *Constitution of the Republic of Uganda.* Reprint of the 1995 Constitution including The Constitution (Amendment) Act, 2000, Act N0. 13 of 2000, Act No. 11 of 2005 and Act No. 21 of 2005. Kampala: The Republic of Uganda.

Vertovec, S. (2006) The emergence of super-diversity in Britain. *COMPAS Working Paper.* Oxford: Oxford Centre on Migration, Policy and Society.

Vertovec, S. (2007) Super-diversity and its implication. *Ethnic and Racial Studies* 30 (6), 1024–1054.

9   Slogans as Part of Burkina Faso's Linguistic Landscape during the Insurrection in 2014

Sabine Diao-Klaeger and Rosalie Zongo

In this chapter, we analyse slogans from the demonstrations that led to the abdication of Burkina Faso's president, Blaise Compaoré, in 2014, which were either written on signs shown during the protest marches or (more or less) eternalised as graffiti on the walls of Ouagadougou (capital of Burkina Faso). We focus on the intertextual references and text models that the protesters use to express their ideas: historical ones, mostly (revised) slogans from the Sankara era (*Révolution burkinabè* in the 1980s), and more recent ones, for example, allusions to the so-called Arab Spring and other political events in nearby countries (such as the Ivory Coast). Reference is also made to a more abstract libertarian background, by using a revolutionary rhetoric. Metaphors from the semantic field of viral and other diseases and puns with abbreviations also play an important role in the protesters' repertoire.

9.1 Introduction

During the mass demonstrations in Burkina Faso from January to October 2014 against the modification of article 37 of the Constitution – and therefore against the Compaoré regime – the demonstrators used a multitude of slogans, predominantly written in French but also in the national languages Mooré and Dioula (see Section 9.2.2 for a short presentation of the sociolinguistic situation in Burkina Faso) and even in English, during several marches organised in Ouagadougou and other parts of the country. These written slogans are part of the 'texte sémiotique qu'est la ville' (Klaeger, 2007: 169), the linguistic landscape, and therefore constitute a sociolinguistic urban phenomenon. We consider this 'political genre of resistance', along with Shiri (2015: 240), as a 'legitimate form of LL, ephemeral and difficult to capture and study as it might be'.

We can find these slogans as:

(1) graffiti on urban walls, buildings and monuments (most of which, but not all, produced during the demonstrations), with the potential to remain on these surfaces as a permanent trace of protest. The graffiti forms part of the city's

transitory linguistic landscape[1] – that is, as long as it lasts or is permitted to last. It is decidedly more than just a private message; cf. Riout *et al.* (1990: 12) who emphasise that 'le graffiti n'est pas un simple griffonage privé', but written on public walls, 'pour être lu, vu […]; il assume toujours une fonction sociale'.

They can also be handwritten or typewritten on:

(2) posters, banners and T-shirts worn during the demonstrations. These slogans are transitory and mobile – Sebba (2010) calls them 'discourses in transit' – because they are written on surfaces that only temporarily form part of the urban linguistic landscape and are not geographically fixed. They seem deemed to become lost, but no: these messages are retained on social networks and in journalistic articles on the internet, and through this are part of a 'cybernetic' urban linguistic landscape, permanent in a virtual way – and thus maybe even longer lasting than the graffiti on walls.

These messages, whatever surface they are written on,[2] are spontaneous signs of activism, an expression of direct democracy. Our research interest lies in the investigation of the choice of the historical[3] and contemporary references, the texts and models, that is the intertextual repertoire the authors use for emphasising their values. We are thus presenting a qualitative analysis of the slogans, giving us insight into the common knowledge and the system of values and references (Goffman, 1975: 165) of the demonstrators.

Our analysis is essentially based on samples of slogans written on posters, banners and T-shirts observed during the demonstrations in 2014, and on political graffiti found on surfaces in Ouagadougou. To underline certain points of our argument, we added slogans dated before 2014. We formed our corpus (167 photos) by exploiting social networks, for example, Facebook (we only used sites that are freely accessible, without needing to be registered) and journals on the internet relating to events in Burkina Faso; we completed it with photos that we took ourselves in Ouagadougou in February 2015. All photos taken from websites were retrieved in December 2015.

The chapter is structured as follows: first, we briefly discuss the sociopolitical history of Burkina Faso, from its independence until recent events, to provide an understanding of the sociopolitical background leading to the demonstrations in 2014 (Section 9.2.1); we also describe the sociolinguistic situation of the country (Section 9.2.2). We then define the term *slogan* (Section 9.3). Afterwards (Section 9.4), we analyse the slogans produced during the demonstrations in Burkina Faso, classifying them into four different categories: (1) those with a revolutionary reference in general and/or a Sankarist[4] reference in particular (Section 9.4.1); (2) those which make reference to current/foreign political facts/events (Section 4.2); (3) those which use the metaphor of a virus/an illness (Section 9.4.3); and (4) those with abbreviations (Section 9.4.4). The chapter ends with a conclusion (Section 9.5).

9.2 Brief Sociopolitical History and Sociolinguistic Situation of Burkina Faso

9.2.1 Sociopolitical history

In January 1966, a general strike led to the abdication of Maurice Yaméogo, the first president of Upper Volta (as Burkina Faso was then called), after the independence in 1960. A military general, Sangoulé Lamizana, succeeded him. Starting with his reign, the country underwent several *coups d'état* until the arrival of Captain Thomas Sankara. In August 1983, Sankara took over officially, also by a coup. His best friend and political companion, Blaise Compaoré, played a special role in these events.

Sankara, a talented orator and charismatic leftist leader (up to today called 'Africa's Che Guevara'[5]), tried to implement his vision for the country. He renamed it *Burkina Faso* ('land of the upright/honest people'), a word composed of the Mooré lexeme *burkina* ('honest person') and the Dioula lexeme *faso* (*fa* 'father', *só* 'country'). His initiatives included, among others, fighting for self-sufficiency, forestation, women's rights, healthcare, mass alphabetisation and fighting against corruption. He wanted to get rid of the neocolonial system by gaining real (economic) independence for Burkina Faso. Sankara was not only upset with the pre-established governmental order in Africa, but also with the ancient colonialists whose hegemonic influence was still far too present in the management of its ex-colonies. After having 'given' independence to these countries, a mafia-like network was established: the so-called *Françafrique* (cf. e.g. Verschave, 1998).

During this Burkinabe Revolution – as it is called – Sankara and his comrades used certain rhetorical procedures, that is, slogans, such as for example, the well-known *La patrie ou la mort, nous vaincrons!* or revolutionary constructions with *à bas [xx]*. We analyse these in detail in Section 9.4.1.

Sankara was killed only four years after his accession to power, during a *coup d'état* on 15 October 1987 – under the command of his best friend, Blaise Compaoré. However, his visionary ideas have survived his death despite all the attempts by the Compaoré regime to forget about them. They are still present and popular among the younger generation in Burkina Faso and beyond, as we will see in Section 9.4.1.

After his *coup d'état* in 1987, Compaoré installed a facade democracy. For a long period, he succeeded in calming down his people, despite several popular demonstrations especially during the second decade of his regime: the murder of the journalist Norbert Zongo and three of his companions in 1989 caused protests; in 2006, students marched and asked for better living and studying conditions; in 2008, there were mass demonstrations for a price cut of first-necessity aliments. In 2011, the entire country became active between February and May in the course of the Arab Spring,[6] and this sequence of upheavals was accompanied by various mutinies of soldiers.[7]

In this context of social tension, Compaoré's mandate gradually came to an end, and according to Article 37 of the Burkinabe Constitution, he could not be a candidate for his own succession. In order to maintain his lifelong power, he prepared, in 2014, to change the constitution (for the third time in his reign).

In October 2014, a huge group of the Burkinabe people (joining political parties of the opposition), the youth in particular, took to the streets to protest against this project. These movements of people who had already previously taken part in citizens' initiatives, such as the *Balai citoyen* and the *Collectif anti référendum (C.A.R.)*, informed and sensitised the population regarding the urgency and necessity of being politically active. As a result of this, numerous well-organised mass demonstrations took place across the whole country, representing all social groups (without ethnic distinction): private- and public-sector workers, craftsmen, merchants, pupils and students, pensioners, political men and women and so on. It is this period that we are discussing in this article.

On 31 October 2014, Compaoré abdicated. Elections took place in November 2015, the current (2018) president is Roch Marc Kaboré.

9.2.2 Sociolinguistic situation

'Ethnologue' currently counts 71 languages in Burkina Faso.[8] French is the country's official language (cf. Article 35(1) of the Constitution).[9] It is used as language of instruction (from primary school to university), in administration, politics, justice and in the media (with the exception of radio broadcasting – here the national languages also play an important role, cf. Balima, 2015: 185; Balima & Frère, 2003). About 20 to 25% of the people are francophone[10] and are functionally literate in French. Even for those Burkinabe, French is, in most cases, not their L1. About 70% of the population has a proficiency in at least one of the four quantitatively most important national languages, that is, Mooré, Fulfulde, Gulmancema or Dioula (for detailed figures, cf. Bougma, 2010).

The fact that (1) French is the language of instruction, that (2) only few of the national languages are standardised, and that (3) the political discourse at a national level is pursued in French, explains why most of the slogans in our data are written in French.

9.3 Slogans: Functions and Definitions

Producing slogans on signs or spraying graffiti can be seen as part of what Tilly (1986: 541) calls the 'repertoire d'action collective'. As we have already pointed out in the introduction, an active remembrance exists: the authors use known concepts and modify these in their individual styles. Slogans are thus transmitted between (political) actors and can easily change their medium:

> [L]e fait que l'énoncé soit écrit plutôt que proféré (dans une manifestation par exemple) ne compte pas. Il est d'ailleurs probable que cet énoncé, comme la majorité des slogans politiques, ait été utilisé à l'oral comme à l'écrit. (Fraenkel, 2007: 2)

Other authors concentrate more on the form/content of slogans; see, for example, Domínguez (2005: 267, quoting Reboul 1975: 42) who defines the term *slogan* as follows:

> J'appelle slogan une formule concise et frappante, facilement repérable, polémique et le plus souvent anonyme, destinée à faire agir les masses tant par son style que par l'élément d'autojustification, passionnelle ou rationnelle, qu'elle comporte: comme le

pouvoir d'incitation du slogan excède toujours son sens explicite, le terme est plus ou moins pejoratif.

Domínguez considers slogans as designed to involve the masses; Klaeger (2007) emphasises the fact that '[un slogan doit] exprimer, en quelques mots, tout un programme politique (social, culturel), et viser en même temps un public (particulier?). Le message devrait alors, pour frapper, être formulé de manière originale, provocatrice, gaie, et/ou expressive' (Klaeger, 2007: 175) and thus may be formulated to reach (only) a certain part of the population.

9.4 Slogans in our Data

9.4.1 Slogans with a revolutionary reference in general and/or a Sankarist reference in particular

This type of slogan essentially expresses a categorical refusal of a given situation, an action a person wants to accomplish physically or morally, or a system somebody wants to be established. Here, we predominantly find slogans written in an injunctive form and introduced with the adverbial phrases *down with* (*à bas*) or *no to!* (*non à!*). The Académie Française dictionary defines *down with* as a 'cri d'improbation, marquant l'hostilité' (Académie Française, 1992: *bas*). The online dictionary *L'internaute* explains its roots as follows: 'Cette locution porte ses origines dans les manifestations populaires. Elle revendique la mort d'une personne ou le changement de quelque chose, d'un régime, d'une idée, d'un principe' (http://www.linternaute. com/expression/langue-francaise/14716/a-bas/).

Down with! is abundantly used by Sankara during the revolutionary period, when he is focusing on knocking down the anti-revolutionary entity. He uses it for example in his famous speech at the General Assembly of the United Nations on 4 October 1984. He ends his speech as follows:[11]

A bas la reaction internationale!
A bas l'impérialisme!
A bas le néocolonialisme!
A bas le fantochisme!
Gloire éternelle aux peuples qui luttent pour leur liberté!
Gloire éternelle aux peuples qui décident de s'assumer pour leur dignité!
Victoire éternelle aux peuples d'Afrique, d'Amérique latine et d'Asie qui luttent!
La patrie ou la mort, nous vaincrons!
Je vous remercie.

Sankara also uses the construction *down with* during encounters with the Burkinabe population via the call-and-response technique,[12] which has a binary structure where the orator formulates the first part of a slogan and spurs on his public to respond. This ritual genre is amongst other genres typical of gospels (reverend–parish) and work songs (foreman–workers) in the African-American discursive tradition. Sankara employs this as an opening or closing ritual in his speeches. He gives the refuted element as 'call' while the audience replies 'down with' in response (e.g. Call: *Imperialism!* Response: *Down with!*), or vice versa.

First, let us turn to some examples with the adverbial phrase *down with*:

Example 9.1 (without photo)
DOWN WITH BLAISE (*A bas Blaise*), alluding to Compaoré himself. On multiple signs and graffitied walls, he is addressed by his first name (sometimes as 'Blaise', sometimes as 'Blaiso', giving it an even more familiar touch).

Example 9.2 (Figure 9.1)[13]
DOWN WITH! THE IMPOSTORS WHO WANT TO MODIFY ARTICLE 37

A BAS!

LES IMPOSTEURS

QUI VEULENT MODI

FIER L'ARTICLE 37

Figure 9.1 A bas! Les imposteurs
Source: http://demain2015.blogspot.de/2013/12/communi ation-politique-au-burkina-faso.html

Here we can see the textual representation of the call-and-response technique. The author uses two different colours (orange: A BAS!; white: LES IMPOSTEURS...) for the two different parts of the binary structure; he underlines the exclamatory character by using an exclamation mark after DOWN WITH.

Example 9.3 (without photo)
DOWN WITH LA FRANÇAFRIQUE! (*A bas la Françafrique!*)

By making reference to *Françafrique*, the demonstrators show that they want their claims to not just be considered as local, Burkinabe ones. They want them to be seen in a pan-African, international perspective, and they want them to be historically situated in a postcolonial context (cf. Section 9.2). Next, we will turn to some slogans with *no to*:

Example 9.4 (without photo)
NO TO THE SENATE! NO TO A REFERENDUM! NO TO THE REVISION OF ARTICLE 37! NOT ONE STEP WITHOUT THE PEOPLE! (*Non au sénat! Non au referendum! Non à la révision de l'article 37! Pas un pas sans le peuple!*)

First, the author expresses his explicit refusal of the maintenance of Compaoré's power through the gradual accumulation of steps enabling the president to achieve his aims. In his last sentence, he quotes one of Sankara's most famous sayings, 'Pas un pas sans le peuple', a slogan that unfortunately loses its rhetorical force when you translate it into English.[14] In French, the repetition of the homonyms {pas} (grammatical morpheme of negation) and {pas} (lexeme meaning 'step') not only creates a rhetorical effect by the repetition; the negation even gains in power when we bear in mind the evolution of the French language, where the lexical morpheme {pas} has grammaticalised into the obligatory negation particle {pas}. In the Middle Ages, speakers used *pas* as an optional element to reinforce the negation particle *ne*; at the end of the grammaticalisation process (in the 16th/17th centuries), *pas* had become obligatory (cf. Klump, 2007: 140–147).

Example 9.5 (Figure 9.2)

NO!! TO THE REFER[END]*UM*[15]*! NO TO LIVELONG POWER!! NO!! TO WEAK COUNTRIES' STRONG MEN! BLAISO! YOU ARRIVED AT YOUR TERMINUS!! BLAISO! BUGGER OFF!!*

- NON!! AU REFER[END]UM!!

- NON AU POUVOIR A VIE!!

- NON!! AUX HOMMES FORTS

    DES PAYS FAIBLES!

- BLAISO! Tu es à ton terminus!!

- BLAISO! DEGAGE!!

Figure 9.2 Non!! Au Référendum
Source: http://www.matierevolution.fr/spip.php?article3460

The use of the antithesis *WEAK COUNTRIES' STRONG MEN* symbolises the paradox reality of rich and powerful local African political leaders in internationally powerless poverty-stricken African countries in general and Burkina Faso in particular. This expression alludes to Blaise Compaoré's words at the first US–Africa Leaders' Summit in August 2014, in Washington (Champeaux, 2014, interview with Compaoré):

> Il n'y a pas d'institution forte s'il n'y a pas [...] d'homme fort. L'Amérique a dû traverser des épreuves. Je vois la ségrégation raciale, je vois l'esclavage... Pour la suppression de ces pratiques, il a fallu des hommes forts. Il n'y a pas, aussi, d'institutions fortes s'il n'y a pas une construction dans la durée.

With these words, Compaoré considers himself implicitly as a 'strong man' and defends his desire to ensure his lifelong position as president – an institution is only strong if it is built to last. Compaoré formulates this as a riposte to Barack Obama's condemnation of tyrants who enrich themselves, during his first trip as US president to Africa, in 2009: 'Africa doesn't need strong men, it needs strong institutions.'[16]

The protester in Example 9.5 says *NO* to strong men leading weak countries and thus underlines in an ironic way the paradox between the 'strong man' and the miserable conditions in which his people live. He denounces the fact that Compaoré failed to end the extreme poverty in Burkina Faso. According to a report by the United

Nations Development Program (UNDP, 2014), Burkina Faso occupies one of the bottom five places in the Human Development Index (HDI).

The last part of the protester's sign addresses Compaoré directly as a person: he uses his first name (as already mentioned, *Blaiso* is even more familiar than *Blaise*) in a vocative expression and alludes to his inevitable destiny, the near end of his reign: *BLAISO, you arrived at your terminus!!* The term *terminus* stands for 'dernier arrêt, dernière gare ou station d'une ligne de transport' (TFLi: terminus). In this context, it is metaphorically used to designate an 'end point' ('point d'aboutissement', TFLi: terminus), a point of no return for Blaise Compaoré. Incidentally, the term *terminus* occurs quite often during the demonstrations. We would like to present just two examples, without further commentaries.

Example 9.6 (Figure 9.3)

NO TO LIVELONG PRESIDENCY. DON'T CHEAT ON THE RULES OF THE DEMOCRACY GAME. STOP MANIPULATING MY CONSTITUTION! DON'T EVEN DREAM OF A CONSTITUENT! 2015 TERMINUS BLAISE COMPAORÉ, banner of the FRC (*Front de Résistance Citoyenne*)

NON A LA PRÉSIDENCE A VIE
NE TRICHE PAS AVEC LES RÈGLES DU JEU DÉMOCRATIQUE!
NE TOUCHE PAS A MA CONSTITUTION!
NE REVE MEME PAS A UNE CONSTITUANTE!

2015
TERMINUS
BLAISE COMPAORE!

Figure 9.3 Non à la présidence à vie

Source : http://lafriquepuissancemondiale2050.ivoire-blog.com/archive/2014/10/28/images-d-unejournee-de-revolte-populaire-contre-blaise-comp-452112.html

Example 9.7 (Figure 9.4)

TERMINUS COMPAORE, graffiti on a wall in Ouagadougou

Figure 9.4 Terminus Compaoré

Source : http://internacional.elpais.com/internacional/2014/11/21/actualidad/1416597932_3786451.html

We would briefly like to return to the last line of Example 9.5, which reads: *Blaiso dégage*. The slogan *Blaise dégage/Blaiso dégage* is one of the most prominent during the demonstrations. The 'dégage' slogan obviously has become a 'battle cry ... across several events in Africa' (for further details cf. Ben Said & Luanga, 2016: 78).

After this digression caused by the explications of the references to *strong men*, the lexeme *terminus* and the 'battle cry' *dégage*, we return to other examples where Sankara is directly quoted.

Example 9.8 (Figure 9.5)

   MISFORTUNE TO ALL THOSE WHO GAG THEIR PEOPLE. POWER TO THE PEOPLE

Figure 9.5 Malheur à ceux qui bayonnent leur peuple
Source: http://www.droitlibre.net/l-insurrection-populaire-au-burkina-faso-inspire.html

   The first part of the banner quotes a speech Sankara made on 21 April 1982 (two years before he became president) in Ouagadougou,[17] in which he declares his demission as state secretary and denounces the reigning elite who are exploiting the poor and who are keeping the population stuck in poverty: *MISFORTUNE TO ALL THOSE WHO GAG THEIR PEOPLE.*

   The second part of the slogan, *POWER TO THE PEOPLE*, is, needless to say, not an invention of Sankara, but plays an important role in his revolutionary discourse. During the revolutionary period from 1984 to 1987, the following slogan was broadcast on national television before every edition of the daily TV news: 'Gloire au people, pouvoir au people, honneur au people, au genie libéré [...]' (cited in Dubuch, 1985: 49).

Example 9.9 (Figure 9.6)

   FATHERLAND OR DEATH, WE WILL WIN! is *the* Sankarist slogan and is represented on multiple surfaces in Ouagadougou. Here it can be seen on a wall in front of the *Maison du Peuple* (further right but not completely visible on the photo it says *Blaise, dégage!*, which means, as mentioned before, 'Blaise, bugger off!').

LA PATRIE OU LA MORT

NOUS VAINCRONS

Figure 9.6 La patrie ou la mort, nous vaincrons
Source: Sabine Diao-Klaeger

Example 9.10 (Figure 9.7)
   SHOOT – MY FATHERLAND OR MY DEATH

TIREZ

Ma Patrie ou ma Mort

Figure 9.7 Tirez – Ma patrie ou ma mort
Source: http://lefaso.net/spip.php?article61692

The young man in Figure 9.7 has written the injunction *SHOOT* on his T-shirt, added a target and the 'personalised' Sankarist slogan *My Fatherland or my Death* [my emphasis]. His photo circulates on several social networks and he became one of the 'heroes' of the popular insurrection.[18]

His revolutionary clenched fist and the injunction written in plural form address first and foremost the security forces, and second Blaise Compaoré himself. His gesture may be considered as an homage to Sankara, not only because he uses his personal interpretation of the slogan *FATHERLAND OR DEATH*, but also, implicitly, because he is making reference to the idea that 'l'esclave qui n'est pas capable d'assumer sa révolte ne mérite pas que l'on s'apitoie sur son sort' in Sankara's speech at the UNO on 4 October 1984 (cited above).

9.4.2 Messages making references to current/foreign political facts/events

Example 9.11 (Figure 9.8)

> *BLAISE COMPAORE GIVE UP THE POWER – 'THE BLACK WINTER' – DON'T TOUCH MY ARTICLE 37*

BLAISE COMPAORE
QUITTE LE POUVOIR

L'HIVER NOIR

TOUCHE PAS A MON
ARTICLE 37

Figure 9.8 Blaise Compaoré quitte le pouvoir
Source: http://226infos.net/?p=2167

Compaoré is directly addressed here; the protester demands him to abdicate by using an injunctive construction. The *'BLACK WINTER'* implicitly refers to the Arab Spring. The Burkinabe Revolution is thus contextualised as part of the sequence of insurrections in the Arab countries, and at the same time as a possible beginning of a series of insurrections in sub-Saharan ('black') Africa; and as we are in October, of a 'black winter'. The Burkinabe insurrection is not just a local event, but, as already mentioned above, it should be considered as a pan-African issue.

The author of this sign has written his message into the silhouette of Burkina Faso.

Example 9.12 (Figure 9.9)

> *EXCELLENT MEDIATOR! The people is taken as hostage of hunger… When should a mediation end the hunger?*

Figure 9.9 Excellent médiateur!
Source: https://laurentgbagbo.wordpress.com/2011/05/01/burkina-faso-blaise-compaore-manoeuvre-et-diviselopposition/burkina-faso-le-despote-blaise-compaore-en-fuite-au-grand-dam-d-alassane-ouattara-et-nicolas-sarkozy/

During his reign, Compaoré gained a reputation as an excellent 'mediator' or 'facilitator' between conflicting parties and warring factions in the sub-Saharan region and beyond, especially during the Ivorian, Malian and Togolese crises.[19] He was also considered as a negotiating partner for the liberation of Western hostages held by terrorists in the Sahel. It is this second point the slogan alludes to: *The people is taken as hostage of hunger.* The last part of the message, *When should a mediation end the hunger?* contains a pun in the French version, based on the homophony of *fin* ('end') and *faim* ('hunger').

The two following messages are formulated as a final warning to Compaoré. In order to emphasise this, the authors refer to movements going on in other African countries at the same time (or just before), where the stubbornness of the heads of state led to a tragic end.

Example 9.13 (Figure 9.10)
   DON'T RUSH STRAIGHT AHEAD! IT'S NOT CORN! IT'S WALL!

Figure 9.10 Fonce pas tout droit
Source: http://226infos.net/?p=2167

This message is difficult to understand if one does not have the corresponding political background information. Laurent Gbagbo, during the Ivorian election campaign in 2010, uses the slogan 'There is nothing (difficult) ahead of us! It's (only) corn',[20] implying that the ones (the persons, but also the problems) he is facing are nothing; they 'can be eaten' as if they were corn, that is, they can be defeated. This metaphorical expression symbolises the ease and certainty of achieving the political aim: Gbagbo's victory, in his vision, is more than evident. The protester in Example 9.13 transforms the slogan and turns it in the inverse direction. He addresses Compaoré directly and warns him by using an injunction: *DON'T RUSH*

STRAIGHT AHEAD, because "there is not corn but wall" (he imitates the Français Populaire Ivoirien/Burkinabe, by omitting the article), an insurmountable obstacle ahead that will hurt and stop you.

Example 9.14 (Figure 9.11)

> *THEY WERE STRONG MEN… Blé 'the machete' – Colonel Khadafi – 'Ahead of us is corn' – Yeah! Yeah! Yeah! ATTENTION…!*

ILS ETAIENT DES HOMMES FORTS...

Blé
"la machette"

Colonel
KHADAFI

"Devant c'est maïs"

Hey! Hey! Hey! N'GAOW…!

Figure 9.11 Ils étaient des hommes forts…
Source: http://226infos.net/?p=2167

This banner shows the tragic (political) end of different autocratic political leaders: Muammar Gaddafi, killed in 2011; Laurent Gbabgo, still under trial for crimes against humanity in The Hague, and his co-accused, Blé Goudé, one of his ministers.

Here we see once again the 'strong men' already mentioned in Example 9.5. Every name (in Gbagbo's case, the quote of his slogan during the election campaign already mentioned above; in Blé Goudé's case, his nickname 'machete' – he got it because he incited teenagers to use machetes to solve the problems between them) is accompanied by photos, showing the 'strong men' at the height of their powers and at the moment of their defeat. The photo at the centre of the banner represents the addressee of the message – Blaise Compaoré – without being explicitly named, looking worried (gesture: fingers at his temple), with thought bubbles leading to the others. The author ends with a warning written in Mooré: *Hey Hey Hey! ATTENTION!*

9.4.3 Messages using the metaphor of a virus or illness

Our next example is a piece of graffiti on a wall in Ouagadougou, a statement in the form of a complete predicative sentence – untypical for graffiti.

Example 9.15 (without photo)

> *BLAISE IS A VIRUS (Blaise est un virus)*

Mayer and Weingart (2004: 8–9) speak of 'a viral topos' in an 'epidemical logic' (they refer to Singer, 1993), booming in the 1980s (with the discovery of HIV) and afterwards. The source of this metaphor is to be found in the domain of biosciences, but this does not necessarily mean that the term represents a precise 'reality', anticipating its metaphorical use (for further discussions, cf. Mayer & Weingart, 2004).

In the collective imagination, a virus is something that acts as a parasite on its host and damages its interior. Burroughs (2005 [1970]: 304) summarises its function as follows: 'A virus must parasitise a host in order to survive. … In most cases this is damaging to the host. The virus gains entrance by fraud and maintains itself by force'.

It is difficult to get rid of a virus, as it is clever, working in secrecy, at the same time strategically – and it is able to mutate. It spreads; it nests everywhere (cf. the 'clan' Compaoré, his 'nepotism'). He is a threat to society and makes it sick.

The following example already becomes more concrete: the virus is named. Compaoré is compared to or equated with Ebola. These examples are shorter than Example 9.15: in Example 9.16, the author does not use a predicative sentence. They only put Compaoré on the same level as Ebola by using the metalinguistic sign =.

Example 9.16 (Figure 9.12)
   BLAISE = EBOLA

Figure 9.12 Blaise = Ebola
Source: http://www.journaldumali.com/article.php?aid=9266

What Kreuzer (1986) determines when referring to graffiti is also true for banners: graffiti should be short and concise, which means that they often use equations, formulas and numbers.

Example 9.17 (Figure 9.13)

BLAISE

EBOLA

45↓15

Figure 9.13 Blaise Ebola
Source: Sabine Diao-Klaeger

In Example 9.17, the equation between Compaoré and Ebola is implicit. They are put together on a surface, in different colours.[21]

Ebola represents the 'latest' pandemic at this moment (October 2014), and has been very present in the media worldwide. Luckily, in Burkina Faso there is no infection registered. At the same time, the number of people suffering from HIV in Burkina adds up to 107,700 and those suffering from AIDS is up to 3800.[22] However, Compaoré is not compared to HIV/AIDS in the slogans during the demonstrations – simply because Ebola is *the* virus that sub-Saharan Africa is suffering from at that moment, and therefore the biggest danger to the country and the sub-region. The metaphor works as a virtual threat.

Example 9.18 (Figure 9.14)
>*BLAISE COMPAORE IS OUR WORST EBOLA. THE PEOPLE IS IN DANGER. LET'S DISINFECT*

In a complete predicative sentence, Compaoré is not only compared to Ebola, he is *OUR WORST EBOLA*. With this hyperbole, the climax of danger is reached. The use of the possessive pronoun *OUR* personalises the virus: it is a virus that attacks the people of Burkina Faso. The Burkinabe have to become active and get rid of it through a *DISINFECTION*, i.e.: 'Opération d'hygiène qui vise à éliminer de quelque chose les agents infectieux et les germes pathogènes qui s'y trouvent', and in the figurative sense, '[l]utte contre une certaine corruption morale' (TFLi: désinfection).

Figure 9.14 Blaise Compaoré est notre pire Ebola

Source: http://blog.citizenside.com/2014/12/burkina-faso-le-peuple-africain-a-compris-que-le-pouvoir-lui-appartient/)

Example 9.19 (Figure 9.15)

BLAISE = EBOLA [TOMORROW IS PREPARED TODAY, EVERYBODY FOR A CLEANER OUAGA]

Figure 9.15 Blaise = Ebola. Demain se prépare

Source: https://matsutas.files.wordpress.com/2015/06/ouaga3.jpg

The choice of the surface that Example 9.19 is written on is particularly interesting. It is one of the signs in Ouagadougou (in its short form 'Ouaga') that invites the citizens not to throw their waste everywhere. The government is using these signs to fight against uncontrolled dumping sites, a serious problem in the capital. The author of the message *BLAISE = EBOLA* considers that the country should get rid of the president to have a better future, to become 'cleaner'.

Example 9.20 (Figure 9.16)

   BURKINA FASO'S EBOLA – KICK EBOLAISE OUT OF BURKINA

ebola

   DU BURKINA FASO

BOUTER
EBOLAISE
HORS DU BURKINA

Figure 9.16 Ebola du Burkina Faso

Source: http://www.dailymail.co.uk/news/article-2816001/Burkina-Faso-s-President-steps-27-years-power-following-wave-violent-protests.html

In Example 9.20, Compaoré's head is represented by the <o> in <ebola>. His name is hidden in the slogan *KICK EBOLAISE OUT OF BURKINA*, in the portmanteau word *EBOLAISE*, a blend of *BLAISE* and *EBOLA*. In Example 9.18, 'we needed a disinfection'; here, the virus Compaoré is simply 'kicked out' of the country. It is a reference to a pan-African campaign against polio, initiated by Nelson Mandela in 1996 and then further developed by the WHO, Rotary International, the CDC and UNICEF. *Kick polio out of Africa* is the slogan of this campaign. The week before the World Cup in 2010 started, a football was passed along 22 African countries in order to symbolically kick polio out (cf. Figure 9.17; https://kickpoliooutofafrica.wordpress.com).

Figure 9.17 Kick polio out of Africa

Source: http://www.humnews.com/hum-photo-shop/preventable-diseases/

In Example 9.20, as we already noted, Compaoré, with his head replacing the ball, is 'kicked out'. This football metaphor is an English one; in French, this metaphor with the source domain football is a priori not used, but the verb *bouter* ('to kick') is used in the expression 'bouter les Anglais hors de la France' ('kicking the English out of France'), passed on from Joan of Arc.

We shall have a look at two more photos before we close this section, going from viruses to diseases. Figures 9.18 and 9.19 were taken in 2011 and 2013 respectively and show that at that time, it was not Ebola that people considered the worst disease.

Example 9.21 (Figure 9.18)
   24 YEARS OF COMPAOROSE ARE ENOUGH!

[sign in the centre at
the bottom below]

24 ANS DE
COMPAOROSE
ÇA SUFFIT!

Figure 9.18 24 ans de Compaorose ça suffit!
Source: http://lefaso.net/spip.php?article41835

The French suffix {-ose} is found in medical terms, in 'constructions de noms de divers processus pathologiques et de maladies' (TFLi: -ose). Compaoré is thus designated as a dangerous disease that has – compare with the sign on the left in Figure 9.18 – to be kicked out of Burkina Faso. It is also common to refer to Compaoré as the *CANCER* of Burkina Faso.

Examples 22 and 23 (Figure 9.19)
   (22) BLAISE Compaoré BURKINA'S CANCER; (23) BRIBERS, DEFRAUDERS, PREDATORS

[sign on the left]   [sign on the right]
CORRUPTEURS   BLAISE Compaore
DETOURNEURS   CANCER DU Burkina
PREDATEURS

Figure 9.19 Blaise Compaoré cancer du Burkina / Corrupteurs, Détourneurs, Prédateurs
Source: http://koaci.com/burkina-faso-manifestation-historique-contre-pouvoir-compaore-89158.html

Figure 9.19 serves as a transition to our next and last category, abbreviations.

9.4.4 Abbreviation as a rhetorical means on the signs

Playing with abbreviations means here 'un remplacement partiel ou total de la forme pleine [...] par une forme altérée, souvent burlesque, partageant les mêmes initiales' (Pires, 2007: 294). In Example 9.20, we encounter 'à la fois un décodage ironique du sigle et une analyse ironique du parti en question' (Calvet, 1980: 117). In order to recognise the word play as such, a topographic highlighting of the reanalysed letters is necessary. In Example 9.23, the letters CDP, the name of Compaoré's party, *Congrès pour la démocratie et le progrès*, are lined on the vertical axis, written in red and in bigger letters than the rest of the words written on the horizontal axis. By the *défigement* (a pun based on set phrases, cf. Lecler 2006) of the abbreviation CPD, the protesters define the characteristics of Compaoré's party: its members are *BRIBERS, DEFRAUDERS, PREDATORS.*

Example 9.24 (Figure 9.20)
   ASSOCIATIVE FEDERATION FOR LOOTERS OF PUBLIC PROPERTY

Fédération Associative
pour Pilleurs de
Biens communs
FEDAP/BC

Figure 9.20 Fédération Associative pour Pilleurs de Biens communs
Source: http://www.zoodomail.com/spip.php?article5837

In Example 9.24 (the photo was taken during the demonstrations in January 2014), the FEDAP/BC (*Fédération associative pour la paix et le progrès avec Blaise Compaoré*) is modified into the *ASSOCIATIVE FEDERATION FOR LOOTERS OF PUBLIC PROPERTY.*

Example 9.25 (Figure 9.21)
   I WANT THE CHANGE, SO I AM ABCDEF – ANTI BLAISE, CHANTAL, DJAMILA ET FRANÇOIS

Example 9.25 shows a pun with the first letters of the alphabet that creates a formula against Compaoré. The slogan is based on the ABC approach of HIV/AIDS campaigns in sub-Saharan Africa: A for *abstinence*, B for *be faithful* and C for *(use a) condom.* If you want to stay healthy, you have to obey the ABC. If you want to change Burkina Faso, you have to obey the ABCDEF, which means you have to be Against (anti) Blaise, against Chantal (his wife), against Djamila (their daughter) and against François (Blaise's brother); the letter <e> represents the conjunction 'and' (*et*).

Je veux le changement, alors je suis

ABCDEF
ANTI BLAISE, CHANTAL, DJAMILA ET FRANÇOIS

Figure 9.21 Je veux le changement, alors je suis ABCDEF
Source: http://news.aouaga.com/h/20439.html

9.5 Conclusion

We analysed only a small sample of the messages written on signs or 'eternalised' (more or less) as graffiti during the demonstrations in 2014 (or before) in the city of Ouagadougou. First and foremost, we were interested in the choice of references (historical and current) and the text models the protesters used to express their revolutionary ideas and values. We have seen that during the demonstrations against Compaoré, references to slogans of Thomas Sankara were abundant, and that referring to Compaoré as a virus or a disease was another way of expressing the protesters' anger.

We thus presented several 'categories' of examples and neglected a whole series of others, such as the ones written in Mooré or other national languages; these will constitute material for further analysis – here, we present just one example (representing a bilingual sign with the Mooré message translated literally in French).

Example 9.26 (Figure 9.22)
BUGGER OFF! IF IT'S BUGGERED OFF, IT'S BUGGERED OFF!!

Looge!

sẽn yẽb

yẽbame!

DEGAGES

Si c'est

baisé, c'est

baisé!

Figure 9.22 Looge!
Source: http://cadtm.org/Burkina-Faso-d-une-revolution-a-l

Notes

(1) Referring to this concept, see for example Hanauer (2012) on the transitory linguistic landscape of political demonstrations in Pittsburgh, Rubdy (2015) on graffiti commemorating the 26/11 Mumbai terror attacks or Shiri (2015) on protest signs of the Tunisian Revolution.

(2) It could be of interest to analyse whether the fact that they are written on mobile or fixed surfaces has an influence on the linguistic form and/or content of the slogans. To do this, however, is not our aim in this chapter.

(3) Cf. Pavlenko (2010: 133) who underlines that 'the linguistic landscape is not a static but a diachronic process'; it is evident that the historical dimension helps to understand ongoing social and linguistic processes.

(4) Thomas Sankara was a revolutionary leader and president of Burkina Faso from 1983 to 1987; cf. Section 9.2.1.

(5) See, for example, BBC News: http://www.bbc.com/news/world-africa-27219307 (accessed 30 April 2014). See also Shuffield's documentation on Sankara, broadcast by ARTE under the French/German title 'Thomas Sankara. L'homme intègre/Der Che Schwarzafrikas' ('Thomas Sankara. The Upright Man/Black Africa's Che') (Shuffield, 2006).

(6) For an analysis of protest signs during the Tunisian Revolution, see Shiri (2015).

(7) For an overview of the events of 2011 in Burkina Faso, see Chouli (2012).

(8) See: https://www.ethnologue.com/country/BF (accessed 5 May 2017).

(9) See: http://www.accpuf.org/images/pdf/cm/burkinafaso/031-tf-txt_const.pdf (accessed 3 August 2016).

(10) The Observatoire de la langue française (OLF, 2014) estimates 22% of the population as francophone, Bougma (2010) counts 25,19%. The figures depend on the definition of who counts as 'francophone': a person with passive and/or active, oral and/or written competences? At what level of competence, etc? We cannot further discuss the question in this chapter (cf. Diao-Klaeger, 2015 and 2018).

(11) The full original text can be consulted at http://www.lafauteadiderot.net/Discours-de-Thomas-Sankara-a-l-ONU (accessed 13 May 2017); a video of the speech is available at https://www.youtube.com/watch?v=5fHIi2mSpMs (accessed 13 May 2017).

(12) 'spontaneous verbal and non-verbal interaction between speaker and listener in which all of the statements ('calls') are punctuated by expressions ('responses') from the listener' (Smitherman, 1977: 104).

(13) This is a photo taken during the demonstrations in 2013.

(14) A web page dedicated to Thomas Sankara (http://thomassankara.net/?lang=de, accessed 13 May 2017) uses the following statement in its subtitle: 'Nous préférons un pas avec le peuple que dix pas sans le peuple!'.

(15) Correction made on the poster, barely visible on the photo.

(16) See: http://www.sundaytimes.lk/090712/International/sundaytimesinternational-03.html (accessed 2 May 2016). For more details, see also Zouré (2014).

(17) The complete discourse can be consulted at http://www.shenoc.com/Thomas_Sankara.htm (accessed 13 May 2017).

(18) See also, for example, http://lefaso.net/spip.php?article61692 (accessed 2 January 2016).

(19) See also, for example, Pompey (2009) and N'Diaye (2013).

(20) 'Y a rien en face! C'est maïs'. Cf. a YouTube video showing him dancing during the election campaign to the corresponding song, available at https://www.youtube.com/watch?v=wq1A7cKpXOA (accessed 2 January 2016).

(21) The 45↓15 illustration seems to be the signature of the sprayer (one can see it in different locations in Ouagadougou) – unfortunately, we do not know more about this.

(22) See: https://www.cia.gov/library/publications/the-world-factbook/geos/uv.html (accessed 29 March 2016).

References

Académie Française (1992) *Dictionnaire. 9e édition. Tome 1 (de A à Enzyme)*. Paris: Librairie Arthème Fayard & Imprimerie nationale.

Balima, S.T. (2015) Radios et dynamique des langues française et locales au Burkina Faso. In M. Drescher (ed.) *Médias et Dynamique du Français en Afrique Subsaharienne* (pp. 183–191). Frankfurt: Peter Lang.

Balima, S.T. and Frère, M.-S. (2003) *Médias et Communications Sociales au Burkina Faso.* Paris: L'Harmattan.

Ben Said, S. and Luanga, K.A. (2016) The Discourse of protest: Frames of identity, intertextuality and interdiscursivity. In R. Blackwood, E. Lanza and H. Woldemariam (eds) *Negotiating and Contesting Identities in Linguistic Landscapes* (pp. 71–83). London: Bloomsbury.

Bougma, M. (2010) Dynamique des langues locales et de la langue française au Burkina Faso: Un éclairage à travers les recensements généraux de la population (1985, 1996 et 2006). Rapport de recherche de l'ODSEF. Québec: Université de Laval. See https://www.odsef.fss.ulaval.ca/sites/ odsef.fss.ulaval.ca/files/odsef_rrmbougma2010._18022010_110928.pdf (accessed 22 July 2016).

Burroughs, W. (2005) The Electronic Revolution. *Ubuclassics.* See https://www.swissinstitute. net/2001-2006/Images/electronic_revolution.pdf (original work published in 1970) (accessed 5 February 2016).

Calvet, L.-J. (1980) *Les Sigles.* Paris: Presses Universitaires de France.

Champeaux, N. (2014) Blaise Compaoré: 'Pas d'institutions fortes, sans une construction dans la durée'. *RFI* 7 August 2014. See http://www.rfi.fr/emission/20140807-blaise-compaore-histoire-usa-pas-celle-afrique (accessed 2 January 2016).

Chouli, L. (2012) *Burkina Faso 2011. Chronique d'un Mouvement Social.* Lyon: Éditions Tahin Party.

Diao-Klaeger, S. (2015) Le français dans le monde: Afrique. In C. Polzin-Haumann and W. Schweickard (eds) *Manuel de Linguistique Français* (pp. 505–524). Berlin/New York: de Gruyter.

Diao-Klaeger, S. (2018) *Diskursmarker. Eine Studie zum gesprochenen Französisch in Burkina Faso.* Tübingen: Stauffenburg.

Domínguez, F.N. (2005) La rhétorique du slogan: Cliché, idéologie et communication. *Bulletin Hispanique* 107 (1), 265–282.

Dubuch, C. (1985) Langage du pouvoir, pouvoir du langage. *Politique Africaine* 20, 44–53.

Fraenkel, B. (2007) Actes d'écriture: Quand écrire c'est faire. *Langage et Société* 121 (122), 101–112.

Goffman, E. (1975) *Stigmate.* Paris: Éditions de Minuit.

Hanauer, D. (2012) Transitory linguistic landscapes as political discourses: Signage at three political demonstrations in Pittsburgh, USA. In C. Hélot, M. Barni, R. Janssens and C. Bagna (eds) *Linguistic Landscapes, Multilingualism and Social Change* (pp. 139–154). Frankfurt: Peter Lang.

Klaeger, S. (2007) La Croix-Rousse n'est pas à vendre – graffitis politiques sur les murs de Lyon. In C. Bierbach and T. Bulot (eds) *Les Codes de la Ville. Cultures, Langues et Formes d'Expression Urbaines* (pp. 169–200). Paris: L'Harmattan.

Klump, A. (2007) *Trajectoires du Changement Linguistique. Zum Phänomen der Grammatikalisierung im Französischen.* Romanische Sprachen und ihre Didaktik 8. Stuttgart: Ibidem.

Kreuzer, P. (1986) *Das Graffiti-Lexikon. Wand-Kunst von A bis Z.* München: Wilhelm Heyne.

Lecler, A. (2006) Le défigement: un nouvel indicateur des marques du figement? *Cahiers de praxématique* 46, 43–60.

Mayer, R. and Weingart, B. (2004) Viren zirkulieren. Eine Einleitung. In R. Mayer and B. Weingart (eds) *VIRUS! Mutationen einer Metapher* (pp. 7–41). Bielefeld: Transcript.

N'Diaye, I. (2013) La méthode du 'médiateur' Blaise Compaoré, récit de la négociation d'avril 2012 à Ouagadougou, témoignage. *Bamako*, 11 July 2013. See https://blogs.mediapart.fr/bruno-jaffre/blog/290713/la-methode-du-mediateur-blaise-compaore-recit-de-la-negociation-d-avril-2012-ouagadougou-temoignag (accessed 5 January 2016).

OLF (2014) *La Langue Française dans le Monde.* Paris: Nathan.

Pavlenko, A. (2010) Linguistic landscape of Kyiv, Ukraine: A diachronic study. In E. Shohamy, E. Ben Rafael and M. Barni (eds) *Linguistic Landscape in the City* (pp. 133–150). Bristol: Multilingual Matters.

Pires, M. (2007) Le détournement de sigle: Le cas de CPE. *Langage et Société* 121 (122), 289–303.

Pompey, F. (2009) Compaoré: Profession médiateur. *Jeune Afrique*, 30 November 2009. See http://www. jeuneafrique.com/199828/politique/compaor-profession-m-diateur/ (accessed 2 March 2016).

Riout, D., Gurdjian, D. and Leroux. J.-P. (1990) *Le Livre du Graffiti.* Paris: Éditions Syros Alternatives.

Rubdy, R. (2015) A multimodal analysis of the graffiti commemorating the 26/11 Mumbai terror attacks: Constructing self-understandings of a senseless violence. In R. Rubdy and S. Ben Said (eds) *Conflict, Exclusion and Dissent in the Linguistic Landscape* (pp. 280–303). Basingstoke: Palgrave Macmillan.

Sebba, M. (2010) Discourses in transit. In A. Jaworski and C. Thurlow (eds) *Semiotic Landscapes* (pp. 59–76). London: Continuum.

Smitherman, G. (1977) *Talkin and Testifyin. The Language of Black America*. Detroit: Wayne State University Press.

Shiri, S. (2015) Co-constructing dissent in the transient linguistic landscape: Multilingual protest signs of the Tunisian Revolution. In R. Rubdy and S. Ben Said (eds) *Conflict, Exclusion and Dissent in the Linguistic Landscape* (pp. 239–259). Basingstoke: Palgrave Macmillan.

Shuffield, R. (2006) Thomas Sankara. L'homme integer/Der Che Schwarzafrikas. Documentation ARTE. See https://www.youtube.com/watch?v=MTzA9bDU6TY (accessed 2 January 2016).

Singer, L. (1993) *Erotic Welfare. Sexual Theory and Politics in the Age of Epidemic*. London/New York: Routledge.

Tilly, C. (1986) *La France Contestée. De 1600 à nos Jours*. Paris: Fayard.

TLFi (Trésor de la langue française). *Online dictionary*. See http://atilf.atilf.fr.

UNDP (2014) United Nations Development Program 2014.

Verschave, F.-X. (1998) *La Françafrique. Le Plus Long Scandale de la République*. Paris: Stock.

Zouré, A. (2014) Blaise Compaoré répond à Barack Obama: 'Il n'y a pas d'institutions fortes sans hommes forts'. *Burkina 24*, 6 August 2014. See http://www.burkina24.com/2014/08/06/blaise-repond-a-barack-il-ny-a-pas-dinstitutions-fortes-sans-hommes-forts/ (accessed 23 March 2016).

10 Investigating the Bilingual Landscape of the Marshall Islands

Isabelle Buchstaller and Seraphim Alvanides

While research on linguistic landscapes (LL) is fast becoming a mainstay of social science research, little of this inquiry has been conducted in the Pacific region. The small Pacific island states are particularly interesting because many are involved in a struggle for their right to the landscape (to paraphrase Lefebvre, 1968). This chapter reports on interdisciplinary research in the Republic of the Marshall Islands (RMI), which has recently proposed a bilingual strategy for public signage. We report our empirical findings on language use in the LL of the RMI at the cusp of this new language policy, as well as our research methods, which aim to make our findings accessible to local stakeholders. By feeding our results back to the relevant authorities, we hope to inform language policy strategy in this ongoing struggle for ethnolinguistic identity construction.

10.1 Introduction

The Republic of the Marshall Islands (RMI) is a small island state in the North Pacific. English and the indigenous language, Marshallese, are recognised as official languages. But while Marshallese continues to enjoy vigorous use as a spoken medium amongst most of the fifty three thousand inhabitants (EPPSO, 2012; Lewis *et al.*, 2016), it has long been denied visibility in the public domain. This is because the spread of English has 'marginaliz[ed the language] ... by dislodging [it] from important public domains such as higher education, business' and indeed the linguistic landscape (Ferguson, 2012: 480, see also Phillipson, 1992, 2003; Philippson & Skutnabb-Kangas, 1997, 1999). American linguistic hegemony in the island state, however, is not without contestation. In summer 2015, the RMI government took several language management decisions which aim to 'protect ... [the] indigenous language' (Hélot *et al.*, 2013: 18), 'recover [some of] ... the formal functions [it] had lost and at the same time [spread it] ... into those social sectors, within its own territory, where it was not [used] ... before' (Torres, 1984: 59–60). More specifically, the new language management strategy includes a teaching policy as well as a bilingual policy for the linguistic landscape. These top-down management decisions are part of an ongoing process of cultural revival, which emphasises the role of Marshallese as 'a symbol of identity and of cultural heritage' (Dunlevy, 2013: 57). What this effectively means is that language use in the LL of the RMI is symptomatic of the ongoing struggle for ethnolinguistic vitality and identity construction. In the context of the Marshall Islands, the signs that make up the LL are therefore 'not just indexical or symbolic but politically and ideologically motivated', indexing and affirming the relationship between English and Marshallese zones of influence and power (Rubdy, 2015: 7).

This chapter reports on a cross-disciplinary study on language choice in Majuro, the capital of the Marshall Islands. Drawing on quantitative variationist as well as geographical methods, our analysis aims to explore the factors that condition language choices in the LL. Since the proposed language management strategy is explicitly bilingual, working towards the coexistence of the indigenous language and the global language English, our chapter focuses on the occurrence of bilingual signs. Overall, thus, our research addresses three research gaps. First, we investigate how the public expression of indigenous linguistic identity is facilitated or hindered by space in relation to the English language hegemony. Secondly, we identify factors that have an impact on the implementation of the newly proposed Bill #85, which may have a bearing on future policy decisions. Thirdly, our research addresses a methodological gap of LL by combining quantitative methods drawn from the variationist paradigm combined with geospatial and visualisation methods from geography. Apart from providing the tools for undertaking the research and communicating our findings, our mixed methods approach allows us to make our findings accessible to a wider audience, including policy makers in the RMI.

10.2 The Struggle about the Linguistic Landscape of the RMI

The ethnolinguistic identity of a linguistic group depends on the right of this group to manage the use of their language across all domains. By virtue of its indexical nature, the LL can therefore display the linguistic diversity of a territory (Gorter & Cenoz, 2015; Rubdy, 2015); it can equally result in 'marginalisation and erasure, with the effect that (the) minority language(s) struggle(s) for visibility and representation' (see Marten et al., 2012; the papers in Rubdy & Ben Said, 2015 inter alia). This is because an ethnic group, such as the Marshallese, can have very strong language use in private domains and yet 'fail in their efforts to achieve some measure of socio-political and socio-economic success as an ethnolinguistic group. As a result, their language identity is threatened' (Garcìa, 2012: 90). One way to strengthen the ethnolinguistic identity of minority language groups is to actively engage in a variety of language planning activities to acquire power over their language rights. This includes 'deliberate efforts to influence ... [linguistic] behaviour ... with respect to the acquisition, structure and functional allocation of their language codes' (Cooper, 1989: 45).

As is the case in 'all polities in the Pacific Basin region.... English has official status' in the RMI, which it shares with Marshallese (Baldauf & Nguyen, 2012: 627). Until quite recently, the Marshall islanders have failed to contest the hegemony of the English language. But in the summer of 2015, the government of the Marshall Islands proposed a language policy that aims to strengthen the ethnolinguistic vitality of the Marshallese language within the RMI by increasing its domains of use

(Kallen, 2010). Adopting a two-pronged action plan, the government proposed the following two measures:

- An educational policy reform increases the use of Marshallese instruction at all levels of secondary school (Johnson, 2015). The new language policy aims to 'facilitate the development of functional bilingualism [in Marshallese and English] … by providing conditions under which all children will develop the ability and confidence to communicate for a range of purposes in both languages' (Ministry of Education (MoE), 2015: 3).
- On 21 August 2015, legislation was introduced by the minister of education and the head of the Customary Law and Language Commission to make all signs in the LL bilingual Marshallese – English. This new bilingual language policy for the linguistic landscape aims to increase the visibility of the local language in the public domain. More specifically, Bill #85, introduced to the Marshallese parliament on 28 August 2015, requires all 'public notices and … public signs, press notices, publicity campaigns, advertisements and exhibitions [to] … include both Marshallese and English languages' (Marshall Islands Journal 28 August 2015). Importantly, this bill includes a corpus planning element, which stipulates that 'all use of the Marshallese language … comply with the spelling system as endorsed by the Marshallese Language Orthography (Standard Spelling) Act [2010]' (Marshall Islands Journal 28 August 2015). Translators will be trained in this orthography by the College of the Marshall Islands under the supervision of the highest language regulatory body of the RMI, the Customary Law and Language Commission (see Sallabank, 2012: 106–107).

Both of these language planning initiatives have been hotly debated, both in the press (Marshall Islands Journal, 2015) as well as in the RMI more widely. In the context of the RMI, the writing on the wall has thus become a battlefield of linguistic visibility (Jaworski & Thurlow, 2010); the LL of the Marshall Islands is an important arena for the struggle for linguistic self-determination. But while language planning is by its very nature 'future oriented' (Rubin & Jernudd, 1971: xvi), to date, there are no data available on the extent to which the Marshallese language, and particularly the bilingual signs which are the expressed goal of the language policy reform, are represented in the semiotic ecology of the RMI.

Crucially, an analysis of the LL in the Republic of the Marshall Islands needs to be cognisant of the fact that the ecology of the RMI consists of three entirely different landscapes. Three northern atolls (Bikini, Enewatok and Rongelap, see Figure 10.1) are officially uninhabited since they were evacuated before and after the nuclear tests from the 1940s until the 1960s (Barker, 2013). We classify them here as such even though some people have since moved back to settle on the contaminated islands (EPPSO, 2012; Barker, 2013).[1]

Most of the rest of the RMI are rural and seascapes with small tightly-knit communities that live off subsistence farming, fishing and copra making. The semiotic ecology in these areas relies less on textual messages (Banda & Jimaima, 2015) and more on ecological signposting, which, due to the small and narrow landmass of the atolls, is mostly based on references related to the water (Spennemann, 2000). The

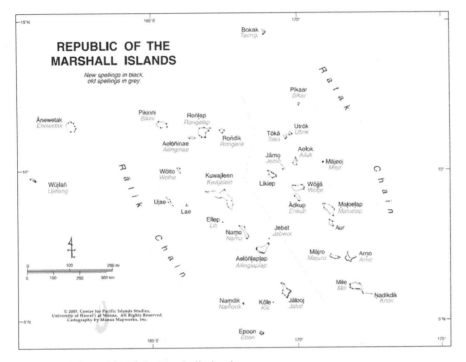

Figure 10.1 The Republic of the Marshall Islands
Source: Center for Pacific Island Studies, University of Hawaii at Manōa, 2005

iconic stick charts which map the currents and swells between the islands, encode the way in which Marshallese seafarers have schematised their environment for centuries (see Figure 10.2).

The RMI encompasses two larger settlements situated on the atolls of Majuro (population 27,797) and Kwajalein (population 11,408). Our research focuses on the urban area in the capital atoll of the island state, Majuro, where the majority of textual signs are located. We therefore follow Ben-Rafael *et al.* (2006: 11) in zooming in 'on those parts of the cities that have prolific [textual] LLs ... where the major commercial activity takes place and the principal public institutions are located'. In particular, we focus on the eastern most densely populated areas of Majuro (Rita, Delap, Uliga and Djarrit, see Figure 10.3), which tend to be labelled 'urban' by local demographers and the local publication (EPPSO, 2012; Johnson, 2015). We refer to these areas collectively as the 'Majuro conurbation' with a population of around 17,000. As a cut-off point, we used 'the bridge', an emic ecological boundary which divides the populous industrial and residential areas of the eastern side from the much less densely populated, more rural areas of the west.

Our research thus falls into the small but increasing strand of research that examines the LL of small towns (Bhatia, 2000; Kotzé & du Plessis, 2010; Moore & Varantola, 2005).

Figure 10.2 Marshallese stick chart

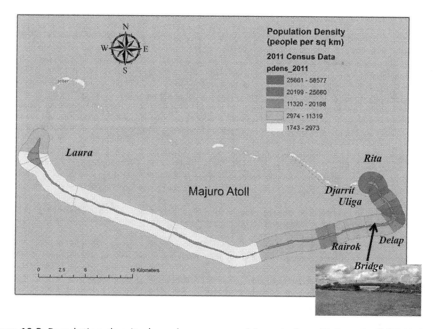

Figure 10.3 Population density (people per square kilometre) on Majuro Atoll (2011 Census available from EPPSO http://rmi.prism.spc.int/ Mapping © The Authors)

10.3 Methods

Since the foundational study by Landry and Bourhis (1997), LL research has investigated the use of written language in the public domain. But while the field has long focused on 'language of public road signs, advertising billboards, street names, place names, commercial shop signs and public signs on government buildings' (Landry & Bourhis, 1997: 25), more recently, LL research has increasingly broadened its remit towards the analysis of all kinds of symbolic practices such as, increasingly, non-textual visuals, images and objects, as well as voices, music and olfaction. This approach is captured in Scollon and Scollon's (2003) concept of 'semiotic landscape' (see also Jaworski & Thurlow, 2010; Chapter 4).

Our research considers geosemiotics in a narrower sense (Scollon & Scollon, 2003). We explore language choices on textual signs in the Majuro urban conurbation. The analysis is based on all permanent and semi-permanent signs that were readable from the main road and the smaller backstreets, including 'transient signage, as found in graffiti, ... posters, [permanent advertisements and signs that were clearly long-term use of initially] short-term signs and stickers' (Kallen, 2010: 53). As a rule of thumb for inclusion into our data pool, we asked ourselves whether we would expect a certain sign to be at the same place about a month later (see Scollon & Scollon, 2003).

The data were collected using a walking narrative methodology with a local informant who also helped us translate the bilingual/Marshallese signs (see Banda & Jimaima, 2015 for a similar approach). Over the course of one month, we took photographs of all instances of 'languaging' (Garcìa, 2012), that is, the written practices that contribute to the social construction of public space in the RMI.[2] This resulted in a corpus of almost 2500 photographs of signs as varied as shop signs, advertisements[3] (including 'repurposed' materials such as the display of wrappers for commercial purposes in shop windows, see Banda & Jimaima, 2015: 654), official governmental notifications, decorative signs, but also signs such as *No parking* or *No spitting* that some residents placed in front of their driveway. The analysis presented here is based on the totality of (semi-)permanent textual signs found in the Majuro conurbation between 21 July and 21 August 2015.

As Hélot *et al.* (2013: 18) have recently pointed out, 'linguistic landscapes are the mirror of our complex societies and our search for their interpretation can only be born out of cooperation between scholars from different disciplines using different methodologies'. Our analysis draws on state of the art geospatial methods, combined with quantitative sociolinguistic analysis. More specifically, we would like to argue that geographical information science can contribute very useful information to the analysis of linguistic landscapes, especially if we investigate the interactions between linguistic and social practice in space. In our research we developed methods for capturing the interplay between geographical, social and linguistic spaces through georeferencing photographs, coding them for a range of parameters and visualising the spatial and the contextual information with the use of static and interactive maps. This section illustrates the methodologies we developed for our project.

10.3.1 Geospatial methods and analysis

Tagging photographs with GPS coordinates in order to georeference and over-lay their locations on maps can be a painstaking process if undertaken manually after the data collection. Such a manual process would involve identifying the exact location of each photograph on a map by relating them to features on the ground with known coordinates or satellite images and aerial photographs using a tool such as OpenStreetMap or Google Maps. Fortunately, many professional cameras and most smartphones and tablets are equipped with Global Positioning System (GPS), which means that the exact geographical coordinates of the camera location (rather than the subject) can be recorded together with a timestamp of the photograph. From our pilot work we concluded that a more accurate (to less than 10 cm) method is to connect a professional GPS tracker to a camera or smartphone, but this was not necessary for the geographical accuracy required by linguistic landscapes research (usually a couple of metres). For our research, we used the same iPad device throughout the fieldwork with geotagging turned on, having compared its accuracy with other GPS-enabled devices. The photographs taken during each day were automatically downloaded and backed up on a cloud server with their date-timestamp as unique identifier.

Coding the photographs with contextual information can also be completed during or after the fieldwork. This process is more challenging than taking the pho-tographs, because despite careful planning prior to the fieldwork, both the coding scheme and the inclusion/exclusion criteria tend to develop during the process of data collection. For example, the fieldworker might decide that certain subjects are inap-propriate for inclusion or adopt an additional criterion half way into the collection process. Coding the data in the field (i.e. adding contextual information to each photograph during the fieldwork with the use of apps that can record typed-in attri-butes after each photograph is shot) is advocated by recent crowd-sourcing projects (see Wrisley, 2016). But this might not be feasible in some instances, that is, in unsafe or ephemeral environments such as the analysis of the LL of demonstrations (Hanauer, 2015; Seals, 2015) or indeed when daytime and/or light conditions may be limited. In our project, we decided against real-time automated recording of contex-tual information because of time constraints. Recording information for each pho-tograph in the field would have introduced a considerable delay that would not allow us to complete the survey of the study area. We thus resorted to collecting the pho-tographs and taking notes for situations that had to be looked at more carefully after the fieldwork, such as signs in Marshallese or other languages that we had to trans-late later.

Once the fieldwork was completed and the photographs uploaded, georeferenced and checked for inconsistencies or duplications, we coded each photograph for con-textual information. For this purpose we developed a graphical user interface (GUI) using the Python programming language that allowed us to see each photograph and enter linguistic information in the relevant fields stored in a database (as illustrated in Figure 10.4). The database was then exported into a spreadsheet with the date-timestamp of each photograph as unique identifier, the geographical coordinates

Figure 10.4 GUI for entering contextual information: LL Image Viewer (© The Authors)

and the contextual information as separate columns for further processing using the statistical package R and for mapping using geographical tools. The results of statistical analysis are discussed in the next section, while we are focusing here on the three methods for mapping georeferenced data and visualising spatial analysis results.

10.3.2 Visualising spatial data

10.3.2.1 Google Maps

Visualising the locations of georeferenced photographs as point markers overlaid on top of land maps can be a straightforward process in widely available tools such as Google Maps, as shown in Figure 10.5. This is useful for inspecting the study area coverage or for checking if the photos have been georeferenced correctly. Coding attributes (such as different languages) can also be shown with different colours or symbols, but there is little flexibility and control over the way these attributes are displayed using Google Maps. Furthermore, Google Maps does not offer straightforward functionality for dynamically linking the marker symbols displayed on the map with the underlying photographs, thus making the visualisation of the individual photographs cumbersome.

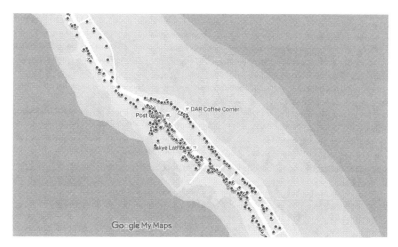

Figure 10.5 Simple visualisation of locations of photographs (as points) on top of a map of the Majuro study area

10.3.2.2 Geographical Information System (GIS)

Geographical Information System (GIS) is specific software developed for manipulating, visualising, analysing and mapping complex geographical data sets and processes. Such systems are widely used by geographers and spatial analysts and they offer a high degree of control; however, they can be intimidating for non-specialists owing to the large number of options and tools available. Software such as the proprietary ArcGIS by ESRI or the free and open source QGIS by OSGeo are capable of state-of-the-art spatial analysis techniques and professional output production. Although it can be personalised using script programming languages, such as Python, GIS demands a high level of technical skill and specialisation from both the analysts as well as the end users. In addition, the outputs are generally static maps, rather than dynamic visualisation interfaces for communicating results (see Barni & Bagna, 2009). For these reasons, we decided to display and analyse our data using more bespoke methods, which we will discuss in the next section.

10.3.2.3 Custom-made dynamic visualisations

After extensive experimentation, we adopted a custom-made approach for producing dynamic visualisations of the underlying data, photographs and spatial patterns for our project. The main benefits of this approach are twofold. First, it offers a way for bringing together our interdisciplinary expertise for a project that requires both highly technical geographical skills and sophisticated visualisation tools beyond simple static maps. Secondly, we had to think ahead about how to communicate the results of our analysis with policymakers in the RMI, for whom our results hold great interest. Since it would be unreasonable to expect them to have technical knowledge for operating a GIS, we implemented a user-friendly and intuitive mapping website developed in JavaScript, a programming language for creating interactive content that can be accessed seamlessly across different computer platforms and

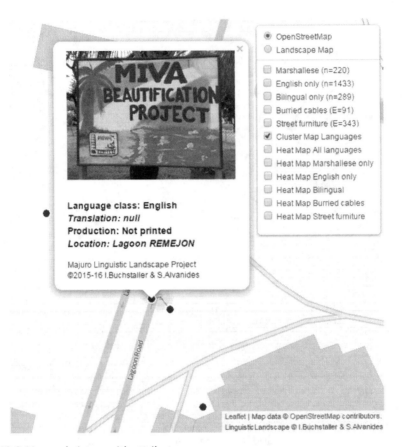

Figure 10.6 Map and picture with attributes

web browsers. This approach required a relatively high level of programming skills for JavaScript coding and for converting the various data sets into the appropriate format for visualisation. But since the output is a dynamic website where potential users can access the generated maps and photographs using most of the major web browsers, it does not require any technical skills from the range of end users we are targeting with our research findings.

The website allows not only mapping the locations of the photographs in various views (marker points, clustered symbols, heatmaps[4]) but it also gives the user the opportunity to display each photograph and the related database attributes (see Figure 10.6). Another advantage of this approach is that it allows quick visual inspection of consistency in coding and it has served as a quality check for our statistical output.

The major benefit in terms of the outreach component of our research is that the user can – depending on their needs and interests – select content by using tick boxes, zooming in/out of the map and clicking on the marker-symbols. This method generates very rich and extremely fast visualisations, even on low-capacity internet connections (see Figure 10.7a–c).

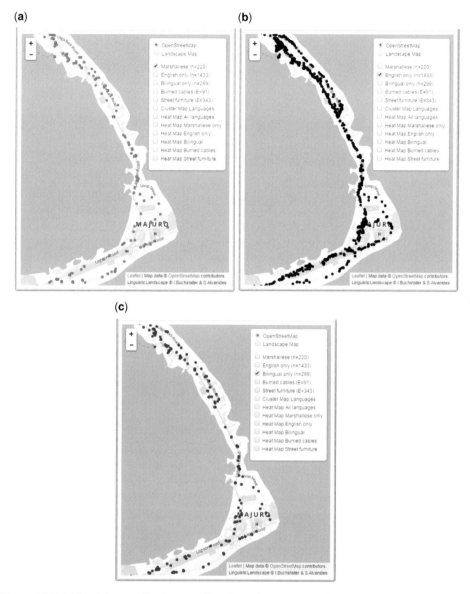

Figure 10.7 (a) Partial map of Majuro Atoll with marker symbols of Marshallese only; (b) partial map of Majuro Atoll with marker symbols of English only; and (c) partial map of Majuro Atoll with marker symbols of bilingual only

The outcome of this geovisualisation allows new insights into the geographical distribution of the languages across the LL in the RMI. As can be seen in Figure 10.7a–c, there are no spatial patterns for bilingual signs, which are distributed across the LL in the same spatial areas as English signs. However, as we have explored in Buchstaller and Alvanides (2017), Marshallese signs are distributed slightly differently across space, occurring mainly in the ocean side of the island. While we will discuss these findings in more detail below, we would like to note that this dynamic mapping tool allows the stakeholders of the Marshallese language policy to explore the areas – and indeed the signs – in which the language policy has been, or has not yet been, implemented.

10.4 Sociopolitical Determinants of Code Choice in the Linguistic Landscape of the RMI

Let us now examine how the RMI 'public space is symbolically constructed' via semiotic choices on the textual signs that line the Majuro traffic arteries (Hélot *et al.*, 2013: 18). In the summer of 2015, around the time Bill #85 was proposed, the LL in the urban conurbation of Majuro Atoll contained 2420 signs (consider also Buchstaller & Alvanides, 2017). As Table 10.1 illustrates, the textual ecology of the RMI was heavily dominated by English: English-only signs make up a staggering 76% of all signs in our data. Note in this respect that, for a nation that is situated in the middle of the Pacific and with the third largest ship registry in the world (Roussanoglou, 2015), the majority of which are flags of convenience (https://www.hg.org/article.asp?id=31395), other languages are surprisingly under-represented in the LL of the RMI. Most signs in the 'other' (and 'other-English bilingual') category are Chinese, which is to be expected given that the RMI harbours a significant (if unaccounted for in the census) Chinese minority (Johnson, 2015; see Figure 10.8).

The few residual 'other language' signs are difficult to generalise and can be exemplified by a Japanese sign at a decommissioned bar, a Hebrew plaque demarcating the Israeli consulate, a seemingly forgotten Korean children's play station and a decommissioned Japanese bar (see Figures 10.9 to 10.11).

Marshallese, the indigenous language of the islanders, is severely under-represented in the LL of the capital atoll. Overall, the Marshallese language is present in only 21% of all signs, including Marshallese-only (9%) and Marshallese-English bilingual signs (12%; see Figures 10.12 and 10.13). Elsewhere (Buchstaller & Alvanides, 2017), we have shown that monolingual Marshallese signs are also geographically and socially highly circumscribed; they are rarely found in commercial and industrial areas, occurring instead in residential zones and are predominantly

Table 10.1 Distribution of signs by language in the Majuro LL

Language	N	%
English	1844	76
Marshallese	221	9
English-Marshallese bilingual	291	12
Other	28	1
Other-English bilingual	36	2
Total	2420	100

Figure 10.8 Chinese-English sign

bearing messages from governmental and private individuals. What this effectively means is that, due to a history of colonialisation and continued cultural hegemony, 'the linguistic landscape [in the RMI is not a] visible marker of the ethnolinguistic groups living within … [the] administrative or territorial enclave' (Landry & Bourhis, 1997: 34). More specifically, the language used in the LL of the RMI does not 'symbolise … the people, [or] represent … them' (Fishman, 2006: 92). Quite the contrary, the Marshallese language has been effectively pushed out of its own ethno-cultural territory.

Figure 10.9 Hebrew sign

Figure 10.10 Korean sign

Marshallese-English bilingual signs, the declared language policy strategy of the RMI, make up merely 12% of all signs in the Majuro conurbation (Figure 10.13). At the time we conducted our fieldwork, the proposed language policy encoded in Bill #85 was thus far from being reflected in practice, making its rapid ratification and application all the more pressing (Dunlevy, 2013; Fishman, 2006; Sallabank, 2012). Note in this respect that the highest proportion of bilingual signs can be found among those issued by the government. Other sign-posters, on the other hand, such as administrative and commercial agents, tend to use much fewer of the bilingual signs that are the target of the Marshallese language policy.

Figure 10.11 Japanese sign

Figure 10.12 Marshallese sign

As pointed out by Robichaud and De Schutter (2012: 132), linguistic landscapes are 'contexts of choice' in the sense that code selection among a pool of possible language options can be understood as the outcome of political, social and ideological forces that have an impact on publicly visible signage. The following sections therefore aim to examine the factors that affect the 'structured diversity' (Fill & Mühlhäusler, 2001: 4) of code choice in the LL of the RMI. While we have discussed the factors that condition the occurrence of Marshallese signs elsewhere (Buchstaller & Alvanides, 2017), in this chapter we concentrate on sociopolitical conditioning

Figure 10.13 Marshallese-English bilingual sign

Figure 10.14 Balanced bilingual sign

and the spatial distribution of Marshallese-English bilingual signs, the declared language policy strategy of the RMI government. Also, we consider the relationship between the two languages contained within the same sign, including the salience of the language (Kress & van Leeuwen, 2006) and the translation status of the sign (Backhaus, 2007).

Salience in the LL was defined as the visual prominence of a language (see Feng & O'Halloran, 2015), including its size, focus, colour and positionality on the sign. Following Kress and van Leeuwen (2006), we considered a language to be more salient if it was printed in a larger font and/or in capitals, produced in a more vibrant colour or if it was otherwise highlighted. We also followed the authors' rationale that – given the left-to-right and top-to-bottom bias of the Roman script in which both Marshallese and English are written – the language that is read first (i.e. on the top and on the left) is the most visually salient.

Figure 10.14, a political poster, illustrates a typesetting strategy that allows the emitter of the sign to avoid giving prominence to one language over another by reproducing the information in inverse order in both languages. As Table 10.2 reveals, the vast majority of the Marshallese-English bilingual signs that constitute LL of the Majuro conurbation are biased towards one language over the other. Balanced signs – in which both represented codes are equally prominent – are by far in the minority in the RMI (with 8%).

Signs in which one language is more salient than the other are almost equally distributed, with Marshallese dominating in 45% of all cases and English only

Table 10.2 Salience of different languages on Marshallese-English bilingual signs

Balanced		Marshallese		English	
N	%	N	%	N	%
24	8	130	45	136	47

marginally more with 47%. Note in this respect that the bilingual policy for the LL proposed in Bill #85 is vague regarding the visual prominence of the languages involved. While we do not know whether the issue of code salience was left open intentionally, it is nevertheless enlightening to compare different emitter groups in terms of their preferred representation of the two languages on bilingual signs. Private individuals make up the lion's share of balanced signs (58%), and thus come closest to visually represent the equitable participation of codes at the core of the proposed RMI language policy. The signs produced by the Marshallese government on the other hand tend to bias one language over the other. Crucially, the Marshallese government leads all other groups of emitters in the production of Marshallese-dominant signs (with 39%).[5] By giving visual preference to their own ethnolinguistic identity, the RMI government thus asserts their right of linguistic 'appropriation of space' (Jabareen, 2015: 174).

Finally, we examine the translation status of the messages contained on bilingual signs in the Majuro conurbation. All Marshallese-English signs (N = 291) were classified according to the relationship between the two languages in terms of the content encoded on the sign. Our analysis follows Backhaus (2007, see also Reh, 2004), who differentiates between cases in which the information given in one language is a complete translation of the content given in another one ('homophonic' signs, as in Figures 10.15 and 10.16) and cases whether one language translates the content given in the other but provides additional information so that only part of the information is translated ('mixed signs' as in Figure 10.19). A third, very frequent, category were signs which contained parallel messages in the sense that the information encoded in one language was entirely different from the information given in the other

Figure 10.15 Homophonic: complete translation

Figure 10.16 Homophonic: complete translation

Figure 10.17 Polyphonic signs: parallel messages

Figure 10.18 Polyphonic signs: parallel messages

('polyphonic signs' in Backhaus' typology). Figure 10.17 illustrates a typical sign of this category, where the overall message is given in English followed by *kom(m)ol* (thank you) in Marshallese. Another typical illustration of this category are political campaign posters, where the factual information is given in English and the slogan encoding the political message is provided in Marshallese (Figure 10.18).[6]

A quantitative analysis of bilingual signs in the LL of the RMI across these three translation categories (exact translation, additional information in one language, parallel messages) is given in Table 10.3. Overall, our findings show that signs with the same message in both languages are in the minority in the RMI public landscape, amounting to only about a quarter of all textual sign postings ($N = 78$; 27%).

Almost half of all signs contain parallel but different messages (45%) and a further 28% have partially overlapping information. What this effectively means is that in the vast majority of all textual messages in the RMI LL, one part or the message might not be understood by sections of the potential readership. Hence, even in the few cases where the Marshallese language is indeed represented in the LL – recall that only 12% of all signs are Marshallese-English bilingual – the translation

Figure 10.19 Mixed sign: translation of the content plus additional information in one language

Table 10.3 Translation status of bilingual Marshallese-English signs

Exact translation: homophonic signs		Polyphonic signs: parallel different message		Mixed signs: partially overlapping	
N	%	N	%	N	%
78	27	131	45	82	28

strategy chosen in the production of these signs makes part of their content inaccessible and therefore results in 'passive exclusion' (Thistlewaite & Sebba, 2015: 27ff.).

The language policy strategy proposed in Bill #85 does not specify the translation status, stating merely that signs must 'include both Marshallese and English languages' (Marshall Islands Journal, 28 August 2015). We can therefore only speculate that the target strategy of the RMI government is indeed the production of homophonic translations. Note in this respect that cross-tabulation between the translation strategy used and the emitter of the sign reveals that government-issued signs are not preponderantly homophonous (only 23% of all government-issued signs give the same information in both languages). The overwhelming strategy in governmental signs is partially overlapping translation (65%), which contains information that excludes certain ethnolinguistic groups. The group of emitters who produce the highest ratio of homophonic signs are large commercial enterprises (such as oil refineries, shipping and handling companies, with 47% of all Marshallese-English bilingual signs) followed by non-governmental authorities (such as the World Bank or the local fishery board, with 31% of all signs). Further refinement to specify the translation status of signs in Bill #85 will thus be needed.

The emitter of the sign is important also because of a methodological conundrum we faced during the fieldwork stage of our project. The Marshall Islands are subdivided into smaller areas called *wātos*, which are traditional units of land inheritance and landownership that stretch from the lagoon to the ocean side (Figure 10.20; see Barker, 2013). While *wātos* are not always demarcated via spatial boundary markers, when they are, these signs are always bilingual with Marshallese represented on one side and English on the other – as can be seen in Figures 10.21 to 10.24. Our quantitative, photo frame-based analysis could not capture the bilingual nature of these *wāto* signs in one single geocoded photograph owing to their back-to-back arrangements. But it is interesting to note that the local landowners provide an ethnolinguistically viable bottom-up strategy for homophonous translations which predates – and could be seen as an indigenous model – for the LL of the RMI.

10.5 Conclusion

'Language is the symbol of ethnic identity "par excellence"' (Garcìa, 2012: 81). And while LL research has demonstrated that LLs are an important arena where political and social struggles take place, 'the hierarchies of the linguistic market are largely determined by the mundane fact of the economic and political, or military, dominance' (Alexander, 2006: 241). In this chapter, we explore the LL in the Republic

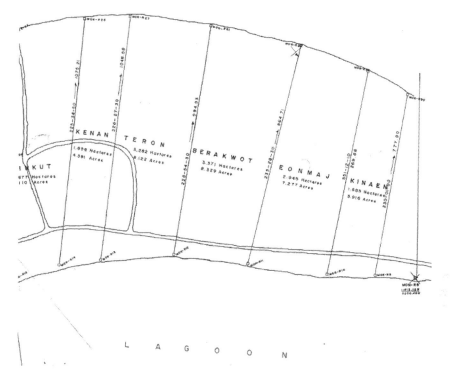

Figure 10.20 Map of *wāto* boundaries in Majuro

Figure 10.21 Mweno *wāto*, English side

Figure 10.22 Mweno *wāto*, Marshallese side

of the Marshall Islands, a country which has long been denied the opportunity to express its linguistic identity in the public domain owing to sustained US hegemony. Our analysis documents the semiotic landscape of the RMI at the cusp of a new language policy which impacts fundamentally upon the LL. At its core, the newly proposed Bill #85 aims to ensure the coexistence of the indigenous language and the

Figure 10.23   Kinaen *wāto*, English side

Figure 10.24   Kinaen *wāto*, Marshallese side

global language English both in the educational sector and the LL. The proposed language management measures in the RMI therefore epitomise the battle of the Marshallese to conquer their own territory linguistically.

Since language policy research is aimed at problem solving, and thus inherently future-oriented, our research provides important facts about the distribution of languages in contested space prior to the ratification of the bill. Also, we are trialling human geographical models that allow us to share information about the status quo, as well as about the impact of these changes. The use of bespoke interactive cartographical tools allows us to make our results available to the stakeholders in the ongoing process of language policymaking. But apart from ease of dissemination to populations halfway around the globe with varying technical skills and limited access to proprietary software licences, the methods we described in this chapter have also been immensely useful as a tool for our own analysis.

Our research finds that at the cusp of Bill #85, the proposed language policy is not being reflected in the LL with Marshallese-English bilingual signs only making up 12% of all signs. And while these bilingual signs are widely distributed across space, they are clearly socially niched. Whereas the government's declared language policy strategy finds an expression in their textual contribution to the LL – the signs produced by the government make up the majority of bilingual signs – other emitter groups do not adhere as readily to the proposed bilingual strategy for the LL. In terms of the visual representation and translation status of the codes represented on the individual signs, on the other hand, it is private individuals or indeed large commercial enterprises and non-governmental authorities who come closest to an equitable representation of languages, whereas the RMI government seems to symbolically assert their right of linguistic 'appropriation of space' (Jabareen, 2015: 174) by prioritising the Marshallese language.

Acknowledgement

We acknowledge the generous support of the German Research Foundation (DFG) and Northumbria University at Newcastle (UK).

We would like to thank Kennedy Kaneko and Siyao Wang for help with translating Marshallese and Chinese signs. Thanks also to Karl Fellenius, The Wellness Center team, Nik Willson and Dr Irene Taafaki.

Notes

(1) The very low number of inhabitants (Bikini, $N = 9$; Enewatok, $N = 664$; Rongelap, $N = 79$), combined with the fact that access is restricted to US army personnel and/or researchers with special permission, makes LL research near impossible in these areas.

(2) While originally the term *languaging* was related to the cognitive processes of language learning, it has also been applied to language policy, in particular to the 'negotiating, resisting, empowering of … the speech [and language use] of [an] ethnic community [by] language managing' (García, 2012: 85–86, 91).

(3) Since the attribution of a text to a specific language can be especially dubious for brand names, we discarded all signs containing only brands names from our analysis. Thus, a sign stating 'Mitsubishi' was not included into our corpus whereas signs such as 'Asahi draft beer super dry' or 'Vaseline Soft & Smooth' were included.

(4) Heatmaps are the output of calculating the concentration of points (where pictures were taken) within a specified distance and representing this concentration as a continuous surface across space. Darker areas on the heatmap depict a higher concentration of pictures of a specific kind (a certain language in our case).

(5) Note, however, that while the RMI government produces much fewer English-dominant signs than all other emitter groups, these still amount to 36% of all their signs.

(6) This category also contains signs that contained (semi-)permanent code-switches where the language switched from Marshallese into English and vice versa. This was often the case for signs advertising foods or other commodities for which there is no word in the Marshallese language, such as ice(cubes) and betel nuts.

References

Alexander, N. (2006) Socio-political factors in the evolution of language policy in post-Apartheid South Africa. In M. Pütz, J. Fishman and J. Neff-van Aertselaer (eds) *'Along the Routes to Power'. Explorations of Empowerment through Language* (pp. 241–260). Berlin: Mouton de Gruyter.

Backhaus, P. (2007) *Linguistic Landscapes: A Comparative Study of Urban Multilingualism in Tokyo.* Clevedon: Multilingual Matters.

Baldauf, R.B.J. and Nguyen, H.T.M. (2012) Language policy in Asia and the Pacific. In B. Spolsky (ed.) *The Cambridge Handbook of Language Policy* (pp. 617–638). Cambridge: Cambridge University Press.

Banda, F. and Jimaima, H. (2015) The semiotic ecology of linguistic landscapes in rural Zambia. *Journal of Sociolinguistics* 19 (5), 643–670.

Barker, H. (2013) *Bravo for the Marshallese.* Belmont: Wadsworth Cengage Learning.

Barni, M. and Bagna, C. (2009) A mapping technique and the linguistic landscape. In E. Shohamy and D. Gorter (eds) *Linguistic Landscapes: Expanding the Scenery* (pp. 126–140). New York: Routledge.

Ben-Rafael, E., Shohamy, E., Amara, M.H. and Trumper-Hecht, N. (2006) Linguistic landscape as symbolic construction of the public space: The case of Israel. *International Journal of Multilingualism* 3 (1), 7–30.

Bhatia, T. (2000) *Advertising in Rural India: Language, Marketing, Communication and Consumerism*. ILCAA Study of Language and Cultures of Asia and Africa Monograph Series 36. Tokyo: Tokyo University of Foreign Studies.

Buchstaller, I. and Alvanides, S. (2017) Mapping the linguistic landscapes of the Marshall Islands. *Journal of Linguistic Geography* 5 (2), 67–85.

Cooper, R. (1989) *Language Planning and Social Change*. Cambridge: Cambridge University Press.

Dunlevy, D. (2013) Linguistic policy and linguistic choice: A study of the Galician linguistic landscape. In C. Hélot, M. Barni, R. Janssens and C. Bagna (eds) *Linguistic Landscapes, Multilingualism and Social Change* (pp. 53–68). Frankfurt: Peter Lang.

EPPSO (Economic Policy, Planning and Statistics Office, Republic of the Marshall Islands) (2012) Republic of the Marshall Islands 2011 census report. See http://www.spc.int/prism/images/census_reports/Marshall_Islands_Census_2011-Full.pdf (accessed 20 June 2015).

Feng, D. and O'Halloran, K. (2015) The visual representation of metaphor: A social semiotic approach. In M.J.P. Sanz (ed.) *Multimodality and Cognitive Linguistics* (pp. 99–114). Amsterdam: John Benjamins.

Ferguson, G. (2012) English in language policy and management. In B. Spolsky (ed.) *The Cambridge Handbook of Language Policy* (pp. 475–498). Cambridge: Cambridge University Press.

Fill, A. and Mühlhäusler, P. (2001) Introduction. In A. Fill and P. Mühlhäusler (eds) *The Ecolinguistics Reader* (pp. 1–9). London: Continuum.

Fishman, J. (2006) *DO NOT Leave Your Language Alone: The Hidden Status Agendas Within Corpus Planning in Language Policy*. Mahwah, NJ: Lawrence Erlbaum Associates.

García, O. (2012) Ethnic identity and language policy. In B. Spolsky (ed.) *The Cambridge Handbook of Language Policy* (pp. 79–99). Cambridge: Cambridge University Press.

Gorter, D. and Cenoz, J. (2015) Translanguaging and linguistic landscapes. *Linguistic Landscape* 1 (1/2), 54–74.

Hanauer, D. (2015) Occupy Baltimore: A linguistic landscape analysis of participatory social contestation in an American city. In R. Rubdy and S. Ben Said (eds) *Conflict, Exclusion and Dissent in the Linguistic Landscape* (pp. 207–222). London: Palgrave.

Hélot, C., Barni, M., Janssens, R. and Bagna, C. (2013) Introduction. In C. Hélot, M. Barni, R. Janssens and C. Bagna (eds) *Linguistic Landscapes, Multilingualism and Social Change* (pp. 17–24). Frankfurt am Main: Peter Lang.

Jabareen, Y. (2015) Diversity as a concept of urban rights: The right to space production and the right to necessity. *Proceedings of the Workshop Boundaries and Bridges, the Dynamics of Urban Diversity* (pp. 165–180). Bonn: Alexander von Humboldt Foundation.

Jaworski, A. and Thurlow, C. (eds) (2010) *Semiotic Landscapes: Language, Image, Space*. London: Bloomsbury.

Johnson, G. (2015) *Idyllic No More. Pacific Island Climate, Corruption, and Development Dilemmas*. Create-space Independent Publishing Platform.

Kallen, J. (2010) Changing landscapes: Language, space and policy in the Dublin linguistic landscape. In A. Jaworski and C. Thurlow (eds) *Semiotic Landscapes: Language, Image, Space* (pp. 41–58). London: Bloomsbury.

Kotzé, C.-R. and du Plessis, T. (2010) Language visibility in the Xhariep – A comparison of the linguistic landscape of three neighbouring towns. *Language Matters* 41, 72–96.

Kress, G. and van Leeuwen, T. (2006) *Reading Images: The Grammar of Visual Design*. London: Routledge.

Landry, R. and Bourhis, R.Y. (1997) Linguistic landscape and ethnolinguistic vitality: An empirical study. *Journal of Language and Social Psychology* 16 (1), 23–49.

Lefebvre, H. (1968) *Le Droit à la Ville*. Paris: Éditions Anthropos.

Lewis, M.P., Simons, G.F. and Fennig, C.D. (eds) (2016) *Ethnologue: Languages of the World* (19th edition). Dallas: SIL International.

Marshall Islands Journal (2015) *Bill #85 Introduced*. 28 August.

Marten, H., Van Mensel, L. and Gorter, D. (2012) Studying minority languages in the linguistic land-scape. In D. Gorter, H. Marten and L. Van Mensel (eds) *Minority Languages in the Linguistic Landscape* (pp. 1–18). Basingstoke: Palgrave Macmillan.

Ministry of Education (2015) *Marshall Islands Public School Language Education Policy*. Republic of the Marshall Islands.

Moore, K. and Varantola, K. (2005) Anglo-Finnish contacts: Collisions and collusions. In G. Anderman and M. Rogers (eds) *In and Out of English: For Better, for Worse?* (pp. 133–152). Clevedon: Multilingual Matters.

Phillipson, R. (1992) *Linguistic Imperialism*. Oxford: Oxford University Press.

Phillipson, R. (2003) *English-Only Europe?* London: Routledge.

Phillipson, R. and Skutnabb-Kangas, T. (1997) Linguistic human rights and English in Europe. *World Englishes* 16 (1), 27–43.

Phillipson, R. and Skutnabb-Kangas, T. (1999) Englishisation: One dimension of globalisation. In D. Graddol and U.H. Meinhof (eds) *English in a Changing World* (pp. 19–36). Oxford: The English Book Centre.

Reh, M. (2004) Multilingual writing: A reader-oriented typology – with examples from Lira Municipality (Uganda). *International Journal of the Sociology of Language* 170, 1–41.

Robichaud, D. and De Schutter, H. (2012) Language is just a tool! On the instrumentalist approach to language. In B. Spolsky (ed.) *The Cambridge Handbook of Language Policy* (pp. 124–146). Cambridge: Cambridge University Press.

Roussanoglou, N. (2015) Marshall Islands ship registry on track to become second largest, first among Hellenic ship owners. *Hellenic Shipping News*. See http://www.hellenicshippingnews.com/marshall-islands-ship-registry-on-track-to-become-second-largest-first-among-hellenic-ship-owners/ (accessed 17 October 2016).

Rubdy, R. (2015) Conflict and exclusion: The linguistic landscape as an arena of contestation. In R. Rubdy and S. Ben Said (eds) *Conflict, Exclusion and Dissent in the Linguistic Landscape* (pp. 1–24). London: Palgrave.

Rubdy, R. and Ben Said, S. (eds) (2015) *Conflict, Exclusion and Dissent in the Linguistic Landscape*. London: Palgrave.

Rubin, J. and Jernudd, B. (1971) Introduction: Language planning as an element in modernization. In J. Rubin and B. Jernudd (eds) *Can Language Be Planned?* (pp. xiii–xxiv). Honolulu: The University Press of Hawaii.

Sallabank, J. (2012) Diversity and language policy for endangered languages. In B. Spolsky (ed.) *Cambridge Handbook of Language Policy* (pp. 100–123). Cambridge: Cambridge University Press.

Scollon, R. and Scollon, S.W. (2003) *Discourses in Place: Language in the Material World*. London: Routledge.

Seals, C. (2015) Overcoming erasure: Reappropriation of space in the linguistic landscape of mass-scale protests. In R. Rubdy and S. Ben Said (eds) *Conflict, Exclusion and Dissent in the Linguistic Landscape* (pp. 223–238). London: Palgrave.

Spennemann, D. (2000) The Sea – The Marshallese World. *Albury*. See http:/marshall.csu.edu.au/Marshalls/html/culture/SeaNavigation.html (accessed 17 October 2016).

Thistlewaite, J. and Sebba, M. (2015) The passive exclusion of Irish in the linguistic landscape: A nexus analysis. In R. Rubdy and S. Ben Said (eds) *Conflict, Exclusion and Dissent in the Linguistic Landscape* (pp. 27–51). London: Palgrave.

Torres, J. (1984) Problems of linguistic normalization in the Països Catalans, from the Congress of Catalan Culture to the present day. *International Journal of the Sociology of Language* 47, 59–62.

Wrisley, D. (2016) Linguistic landscapes at scale: Affordances and limitations of a mobile data collection approach. Paper presented at the 37th LAUD Symposium April 4–7, 2016. Landau: University of Koblenz-Landau.

11 Linguistic, Ethnic and Cultural Tensions in the Sociolinguistic Landscape of Vilnius: A Diachronic Analysis

Irina Moore

Using a multimodal diachronic linguistic landscape analysis, which advocates a historicised and spatialised approach to the study of a city's sociopolitical landscape, this chapter attempts to analyse the dynamics of sociolinguistic changes in Vilnius, the capital of Lithuania, before the establishment of Soviet rule and after its collapse in 1991. Drawing on the sociocultural geography of Vilnius and urban studies, the chapter analyses how written languages interact with the physical features of the cityscape to construct new memory landscapes and express ethnic tensions and nationalising policies resulting from ideological power change. Such a qualitative approach emphasises the importance of the sociohistorical context and leads to a greater understanding of identity and sociocultural transformations. By examining the history of this multicultural city through the lens of linguistic landscape analysis, it is possible to obtain a deeper understanding of its different ethnic narratives and tensions.

11.1 Introduction

This chapter presents an attempt to analyse the post-Soviet processes in Vilnius, the capital of Lithuania, by examining Soviet language policy and practices in the city and their reflection in sociocultural landscapes before the establishment of Soviet rule and after its collapse. De-Russification and language shift in the post-Soviet space provides an opportunity for diachronic analysis and is helpful for investigating the here-and-now linguistic landscape (LL) data in the context of historical developments and earlier language practices. The context of de-Sovietisation in the Baltic states also calls for an interpretation of the LL concept, which takes into account the cultural and physical landscape (Czepczyński, 2008; Herrschel, 2007), including monuments and everyday items, and their placement in time and space. By adopting a diachronic framework for the analysis of 'semiotic landscape' data (Jaworski & Thurlow, 2010), this chapter aims to investigate the sociocultural landscape of Vilnius from two different perspectives. One examines language practices and the historical-cultural heritage from a diachronic angle, while the other examines their current state. These perspectives together shape historical linguistic and cultural ties and reveal the roots of modern developments.

The chapter begins with a brief discussion concerning the processes of Russification and Sovietisation in the Lithuanian context. It examines how these processes shaped the development of national resistance and nation-building, which led to the declaration of independence in 1991. Strong attachment to the national language and the metaphor of its displacement in Soviet times became key elements in self-identification and the strict policy of titular monolingualism.

The diachronic analysis of the Vilnius LL in Section 11.2 illustrates that the centrality of language in Lithuanian identity can be traced historically to the anti-Russian Insurrection of 1836. It also suggests that the Lithuanian Awakening in the 19th century was further developed by the nationalising strategies of the Lithuanian government in the interwar period. These strategies were shaped by the anti-Polonisation campaign and the 'Vilnius Question', which resulted in 'thick' (Spolsky, 2002) language policies and a forced Lithuanisation of non-Lithuanian names. Section 11.2.4 focuses on the LL of Vilnius as an element in the discourse of Soviet Lithuanian identity that links the post-war era to the nationalising drive of the interwar republic and to the Lithuanian nationalist movement of the late 19th and early 20th centuries. It argues that the linguistic and sociocultural landscape of Soviet Vilnius helps to reveal such hidden continuities. Drawing on recent works by a number of Western and Lithuanian researchers and on the archive and private photographs of the period, it asserts that the imposition of Soviet rule not only crushed Lithuanian sovereignty and repressed political freedoms, but also contributed to the demographic and social Lithuanisation of Vilnius (Davoliūtė, 2014; Drėmaitė, 2010; Kotkin, 2001; Snyder, 2003).

The transparency of data analysed in this chapter is ensured by the use of publicly available photo collections from the Lithuanian State Archive and digital private photographic and postcard collections, augmented by my own photographs. The data collection consists of a total 290 pictures. Since all the data in this investigation are selective and, therefore, limiting, the analysis is also informed by other sources, such as historical monographs, sociolinguistic studies and memoirs of the city's inhabitants.

11.1.1 Sovietisation, Russification and collective memory

To understand the post-Soviet language reforms in Lithuania, it would be helpful to clarify the term 'Russification' and to provide a brief overview of language practices in Soviet Lithuania. The term 'Russification' is generally used to refer to the effects of Russian and Soviet language policies on the population of the Russian Empire and the Soviet Union. It was 'intended to ensure state control over a diverse population' (Weeks, 2010).

As Kappeler (2004) notes, until 1980, with some exceptions, there seemed to be a common belief that the process of centralisation of power by a national government involves the suppression of the majority of the languages spoken in the national territory, and the dominance of a single language. The interwar national historiographies of Lithuania were committed to the notion that a coherent and systematic Russification of the non-Russians had been undertaken in the Tsarist Empire. 'Western specialists on Russian history also followed this pattern with some exceptions' (Kappeler, 2004: 291). However, research studies since 1980 (Altapov, 2000; Andersen & Silver, 1984; Dowler, 2001; Kappeler, 2001; Laitin, 1998; Pavlenko, 2011; Thaden, 1981; Weeks, 2010) show that Russification was not a one-way process, but a dual-course language policy, which maintained titular languages and spread Russian as an L2 and the lingua franca in the USSR. This resulted in language practices of titular bilingualism and non-titular monolingualism in many republics. Asymmetric bilingualism is often cited in research on Soviet language policies as one of the examples of Russification in Soviet republics (Hogan-Brun & Ramonienė, 2004; Pavlenko, 2008; Riegl & Vaško, 2007; Zabrodskaja, 2014). However, the extent of asymmetric bilingualism differed from republic to republic owing to historical, political and sociocultural circumstances. According to the 1989 Soviet Census, Lithuania had the lowest level of non-titular monolingualism among the Baltic republics, with an almost equal proportion of titular-Russian (37.6%) and Russian-titular bilingualism (37.5%) (USSR State Statistics Committee, 1991). As Dilāns and Zepa (2015: 633) notes, census data are not always entirely trustworthy. In 1989, on the cusp of independence, Lithuanians 'may have underrepresented their Russian competence'. Even taking this into account, the 1979 census shows that 97.7% of the population spoke Lithuanian, indicative of high levels of non-titular bilingualism (Вестник Статистики, 1980).

Fierce historical resistance against Polish and Russian domination and the incorporation of a strong element of national Lithuanian identity into Soviet historiography by the national communists prevented the displacement of Lithuanian, as illustrated below and in Section 11.2.4.

I would argue that Lithuanian and Russian existed side by side, and, to a certain extent, Sovietisation in Vilnius was accompanied by Lithuanisation of the city rather than Russification, particularly between 1953 and 1988. As Snyder (2003: 88–93) notes, Vilnius was claimed and contested by Polish, Belarusian and Lithuanian communists before being returned by Stalin to the Lithuanian Soviet Socialist Republic (SSR) in 1944. As a result, there was a major resettlement of the Polish population from Vilnius. It was increasingly populated by Lithuanians, and Lithuanian culture was encouraged. This political process was closely connected to urbanisation. The internal migration of ethnic Lithuanians from the countryside 'shot up from an all-time low of 15 percent in 1945 to reach 50 percent in 1970 and a peak of 68.1 percent in 1989' (Davoliūtė, 2013: 51). Although Vilnius saw high external migration of Russian speakers from across the Soviet Union, 'the internal migration of ethnic Lithuanians from the country was much higher, and the cities were not extensively Russified as they were in Estonia and Latvia' (Davoliūtė, 2013: 51).

The political process of Sovietisation in Lithuania was also closely related to a cultural-political campaign of indigenisation. Davoliūtė (2013: 89) distinguishes two stages. The first, Beria's Indigenisation Policy (1953), was an initiative to allow the Lithuanian leadership to 'take the nationalization of politics in their hands'. Declassified MVD (Ministry of Internal Affairs) reports from that time reveal an expectation that all Russian communists would go back to Russia, with Lithuanians taking their place

(Davoliūtė, 2013). The second stage occurred after Khruschev's Secret Speech, between 1956 and 1959. During this time, the new generation of graduates from Lithuanian universities, who represented the newly trained intelligentsia, 'were pushed to top posts at the expense of older Lithuanian and non-Lithuanian communists appointed under Stalin' (Davoliūtė, 2013: 89). This enabled a purge of Russians from their ranks by the enforcement of requirements for titular language knowledge. By 1959, the majority of people in leading posts were Lithuanians (Davoliūtė, 2013: 90).

Elements of national revival, 'albeit under the oppressive and limiting conditions of Soviet rule, fulfilled the long-held dream of Lithuanian nationalists' (Snyder, 2003: 91–93). This is often either forgotten, lost or denied in the face of the radical socio- and geopolitical changes brought about by Sovietisation. A number of researchers state that since 1940, Russian has replaced Lithuanian as the language of political and economic discourse, that its overall functionality has decreased and its spheres of use have contracted, becoming limited to home and school use (Clarke, 2006; Hogan-Brun & Ramonienė, 2003; Hogan-Brun *et al.*, 2008; Zinkevičius, 1998). This interpretation of the Lithuanian-language position, in my opinion, arises from merging the notions of Russification and Sovietisation into one concept, although a body of work exists which demonstrates that they are not the same (Davoliūtė, 2016; Remnev, 2011; Weeks, 2010; Zamascikov, 2007).

I would argue that the particular sociohistorical circumstances did not lead to a language shift and displacement of Lithuanian; on the contrary, they facilitated (unusual for a Soviet republic) language practices with high language loyalty among the titular population and high titular fluency among non-titulars. Evidence gathered from my data support the somewhat controversial statement made by Snyder that the Lithuanian language 'became, for the first time in modern history, a badge of status in Vilnius' (Snyder, 2003: 95). This is discussed further in section 11.2.4.

The merging of the Sovietisation and Russification concepts could be partially explained by the phenomenon of the post-Soviet 'official policy of collective amnesia' (Czepczyński, 2008: 109), which commonly occurred as a central part of the radical social transition and is based on the rejection of many aspects of the 'recent past'. Forgetting and remembering are ways of handling the process of nation-building in the new reality. Following independence, Lithuania went through an intense period of self-identification, which resulted in the creation of a self-image as a nation of 'innocent sufferers' (Snyder, 1995). As Davoliūtė (2013: 163) argues astutely, 'deportation became the key trope for describing all forms of suffering and oppression under Soviet rule, under the Russian empire, and even earlier'. The metaphor of displacement became central in public discourse and was extended to the key symbols of Lithuanian identity, including language. Davoliūtė explored the role of the Soviet Lithuanian intelligentsia in expanding this metaphor synchronically and diachronically, to include both those who were displaced during Stalinist deportations and those who accommodated the Soviets. For example, the Lithuanian poet Justinas Marcinkevičius was a leading member of the new Soviet Lithuanian cultural elite, and yet, in a speech delivered at the Supreme Council of the LSSR in November 1988, he made a call to declare Lithuanian the state language: 'Our language has experienced much abuse, discrimination and injustice. It is now returning home as if from deportation' (Davoliūtė, 2013: 165). This statement later became the focus of *Sajūdis* rhetoric: 'We were deported not only from our homeland but from our language' (Davoliūtė, 2013: 165). This approach to collective memory and self-identification enabled the nation to see Sovietisation as associated with the trauma of deportation and displacement and Russification as part of Soviet cultural processes without 'remembering' certain details. It served as a unifying core of the nation. These observations and my analysis of the cultural landscape allow me to use LL as a powerful diagnostic tool to challenge post-Soviet Lithuanian memory landscapes and to see what Sovietisation meant in the Lithuanian context in a different light.

11.1.2 Post-Soviet landscape sweep

The linguistic landscape 'is not a state but a diachronic process and the meaning of the present day's arrangements cannot be fully understood without considering those of the past' (Pavlenko, 2010: 133). It identifies the present-day conditions and memory landscapes as developmental paths through historical memories, practices and policies of authorities. In the aftermath of independence, all former Soviet states went through 'post-communist landscape cleansing' (Czepczyński, 2008: 109). In Lithuania, too, many symbols of the Soviet period were either destroyed or dismantled. Monuments were the first to go (Figure 11.1).

The removal of Lenin's statue (erected in 1952) was one of the first of many 'landscape sweeps'. In August 1991, it was removed by a crane to the sound of cheering crowds and became a worldwide symbol of the fall of Soviet power when the footage was shown on CNN and reported internationally. The removal of unwanted references contained in Soviet monuments was the beginning of the post-socialist landscape change. It culminated in the development of a new ideology to support nation state building efforts, in which language legislation plays an important role. To accomplish the transition to a new ideology and economy, ex-Soviet republics employed a variety of de-Sovietisation policies. In the area of language, these aimed at de-Russification and the establishment of titular languages as official state languages (Järve, 2003; Pavlenko, 2009). De-Russification is carried out by various nationalising linguistic, cultural and semiotic resources. Pavlenko (2009) highlights five processes that illustrate the change in the functions of languages in multilingual post-Soviet societies: language erasure, language replacement, language upgrading and downgrading, language regulation, and the appearance of transgressive signs.

In Lithuania, the most prominent of these were language erasure and language downgrading: 'During 1990–1993, Russian language commercial and official signs, including road and street signs, were removed as being unnecessary and reminiscent of foreign occupation' (Suziedelis, 2011: 167). Figure 11.2 is an example of a bottom-up initiative of Russian language erasure, where the offending Cyrillic script was scratched from a Lithuanian-Russian street sign.

The distribution of the languages on the sign before erasure signifies the top-down language hierarchy in Soviet Lithuania. This is a reflection of a dual-course language policy in the USSR after the mid-1930s, which supported titular languages and the spread of Russian as an L2.

Figure 11.1 Removal of Lenin's statue in central Vilnius, 1991
Source: Venckus, 2013

Figure 11.2 A street sign in Vilnius where the Russian on the bottom line has been obliterated, 1991
Source: www.etoretro.ru

Erasure was a quick and cheap way to implement bottom-up manifestations of a new language policy; however, it was a temporary measure, which left material reminders. With time, such signs have been removed and replaced with official top-down Lithuanian-only signs (Figure 11.3).

Figure 11.3 Monolingual Lithuanian street signs in central Vilnius
Source: Author's photograph, 2016

An LL study conducted by Muth (2008: 143) in Vilnius concludes: 'Within 20 years, the Russian language "ceased to exist" in the public sphere, at least in its written form'. This statement is not entirely accurate. Russian is still present in public spaces in Vilnius, although it is downgraded through language ordering position, as illustrated in Figure 11.4, where a sign in a café lavatory requests clients not to throw paper into the toilet in three languages: Lithuanian, English and Russian. Russian is a part of this sign, but its position at the bottom of the sign is a feature of language downgrading (Pavlenko, 2009). Such bottom-up signs in Vilnius have very low visibility; they are usually inside commercial premises and almost never on their fronts. I must note that in other Lithuanian towns, especially those close to the Belarussian border, such as Druskininkai, visibility of Russian is much higher owing to commercial and other reasons, which are outside the remit of this chapter.

Official public signs, such as street and place names, reflect spatial power relations (Blommaert, 2013) and are sanctioned by local authorities, meaning that public space is an important political arena for the enforcement of language policies and transformation of language practices and memory landscapes. The virtual

Figure 11.4 A trilingual sign in a café lavatory in central Vilnius with Russian at the bottom
Source: Author's photograph, 2016

disappearance of bilingual Lithuanian-Russian signs in Vilnius, together with the Russian language downgrading and 'monuments sweep' are understandable core elements of nationalising processes, state building and identity renegotiation. These also contributed to the construction of public memory with the self-image as a nation of 'innocent sufferers' who were 'deported from their language' by the Soviets (see Section 11.2.4). The symbolic 're-appropriation' of the cityscape aided this process. The Soviet sculptures were dismantled and later gathered in *Grūto Parkas*, an open-air exposition of the instruments of Soviet ideology. As its website states, it provides an opportunity for Lithuanian people, visitors and future generations 'to see the naked Soviet ideology which suppressed and hurt the spirit of our nation for many decades' (http://grutoparkas.lt/en_US/outdoor-exposure). The former KGB building became a genocide victims' museum; however, it is not about the Holocaust, which is barely mentioned in its exhibition, but about the repression of Lithuanians under Soviet rule. A monument to the memory of victims of the genocide was erected nearby (Figure 11.5).

To understand why and how in the post-Soviet period the Lithuanian language assumed such a strong symbolic function in memory politics and the struggle for independent statehood, I will now turn to the diachronic analysis of the sociolinguistic landscape of Vilnius. Its importance to a variety of cultures and ethnicities is unparalleled. Over a number of centuries, it occupied a central place in the national identity of Lithuanians, Poles, Jews and Russians (Weeks, 2015: 1).

(a)   (b)

Figure 11.5 (a) A plaque at the base of the monument with the text, *Sovietinės Okupacijos Aukoms Atminti* ('In memory of victims of Soviet occupation'); (b) a sign to the entrance of the genocide victims' museum

11.2 Diachronic Perspective on the Sociolinguistic Landscape of Vilnius

11.2.1 1864–1917

A diachronic analysis of public spaces in Vilnius combined with a synchronic-descriptive approach yields a more complex sociopolitical narrative related to the process of Russification and uncovers the roots of longstanding ethnic tensions between Lithuanians, Poles and Russians, which are still evident today.

Owing to its multi-ethnic and multicultural history, Vilnius has been known under several different names: Vilna, Vilno/Wilno, Vilne and Vilnius. The city was originally called Vilna in 1323. This name was also in use when Lithuania was a part of the Russian Empire (1795–1914) as a result of the partition of the Polish-Lithuanian Commonwealth in 1793. Sociopolitical connotations of different names became particularly important in the first half of the 19th century, after two failed insurrections against Russian rule. The name Vilna became associated with Russia after the Insurrection of 1831, which aimed to restore the Polish-Lithuanian Commonwealth and the dominance of the Polish elite. Polish was declared the state language from 1698. During Polish dominance, the city's name was Wilno (or Vilno). However, another name, Vilne, was used by the second largest ethnic group of the town, Lithuanian Jews. Statistics from the Russian Empire estimated the Jewish population to constitute 42.3% of the city's population after the city's incorporation into the empire. 'Vilnius in the early nineteenth century was a small, provincial, and principally Polish Jewish city' (Weeks, 2015: 23).

The Insurrection of 1863 sought an independent Lithuanian state and rejected both Polish and Russian power and culture. The name Vilnius became associated with the Lithuanian national reawakening and 'occupied a central place in national identity, as the capital of Lithuanian Grand Duchy and the future capital of a Lithuanian nation-state' (Weeks, 2015: 2).

The Tsarist's response to the insurrections was harsh. Vilnius University, the centre of Polish culture, was closed in 1831. Official mention of the words Poland and Lithuania was not allowed after the Insurrection of 1863. This could be considered as the start of consistent Russification reforms. The Lithuanian Press Ban was imposed, which forebade all Lithuanian-language publications in the Latin alphabet; it was in force until 1904. All schools with Lithuanian language of instruction were closed (Stražas, 1996). Officially, speaking Polish and Lithuanian in public was forbidden (Figure 11.6).

'Street signs were in Russian and even shops were required to have Russian signs or to have Russian inscriptions at least as large as those in other languages' (Weeks, 2004: 3). It is not surprising that my corpus of archive photographs from this period supports the above statement and shows that the Russian language dominated public signage in Vilnius (Figure 11.7).

The majority of signs in my corpus are commercial. Figure 11.7b shows two coffee houses opposite one another (*Kofejnya*) and a bakery (*Bulochnaja*). Figure 11.7a is a rare example of an official sign depicting a military hospital (*Vojennyi Gospital*). Russian dominates the signs, although there are several signs in Russian and French (e.g. *Coiffeur*, *Hôtel Italia*, *Entrée*), which illustrate the francophone tendencies of pre-revolutionary Russia.

The 'Russianness' of the city was also accentuated by the newly erected Russian architectural monuments. One, to Count Muravyov, was erected in 1898. He was a Russian imperial statesman, who crushed the Insurrection of 1863. As Weeks (2004: 3) notes, he was cordially detested by Poles, but 'was a hero who defended state order with sometimes cruel but necessary measures'. Another major monument, to Catherine II, was erected in the main square adjacent to the city's main Catholic cathedral in 1904 (Figure 11.8). It was under her reign that the Polish-Lithuanian Commonwealth was partitioned in the 18th century; Russia acquired the larger part.

This 'analytic arrangement of space' (Certeau, 1985), together with linguistic signage, produced a landscape of power, which now could be analysed as a socio-cultural 'artefact' of its time. 'Vilna has become a Russian city not only by its

Figure 11.6 A public sign in Russian during the Lithuanian Press Ban: 'Speaking Lithuanian is strictly forbidden'
Source: Lithuanian Press Ban, 2016

(a)  (b)

Figure 11.7 (a) A Russian sign, 'military hospital', 1872; (b) a street with Russian commercial signs, 1870

Source: www.humus.livejournal.com

geographic location but also by its internal life' (Dobriansky, 1904: 120). However, this hegemonisation through spatialisation produced only 'a very thin and fragile Russian veneer' (Weeks, 2004: 4), which intensified Russian/Polish/Lithuanian tensions even further. Weeks (2004) analyses a number of documents from the Russian

(a) (b)

Figure 11.8 (a) Monument to Muravyov; (b) the unveiling of the monument to Catherine II

Source: www.etoretro.ru

State Historical Archives, which reported that Poles dominated the organs of urban self-government in Vilna. On the other hand, the Lithuanian Press Ban and the thick policy of linguistic and cultural Russification had a two-fold effect on the comparatively small and politically passive Lithuanian population. During this time, a number of illegal Lithuanian-language periodicals emerged, urging resistance to Russian assimilation and to reunification with Poland. This helped to identify language as central to the national Lithuanian identity (Clarke, 2006).

In response to the defeat of Russia by Japan, the ban on Lithuanian-language publications was lifted, as a concession to the local population in an attempt to gain their support. The first Lithuanian daily newspaper was published in 1905. The Lithuanian language made an appearance on some public signs, mostly in a bilingual combination with Russian, or with Polish (Figure 11.9).

Figure 11.9a shows a private Lithuanian school with a bilingual Russian-Lithuanian sign: 'Private Lithuanian two-year school and evening classes'. In Figure 11.9b the caption at the top is one of the first signs I managed to find where the name of the city is given with a Lithuanian spelling, Vilnius, on the right. The scene on the card is described in Polish and in Lithuanian: 'Summer theatre in the Bernadine garden'. The distribution of languages on both pictures indicates the position of Lithuanian (on the right) as the second language.

Nevertheless, these relaxation measures and the 1905 Revolution in Russia intensified the demand for ethnic-national rights and led to the major event in the history of the Lithuanian national movement, the Great Conference of Vilnius, which pressed for an autonomous Lithuanian national state with Lithuanian as the sole official language. This was achieved on 16 February 1918, when the creation of the

(a)   (b)

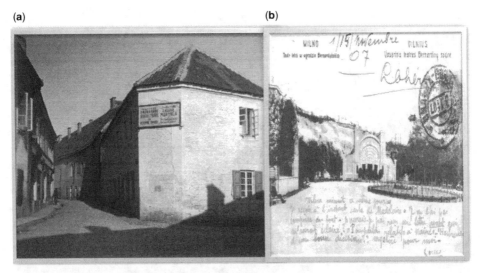

Figure 11.9 (a) Private Lithuanian school with a Russian-Lithuanian sign, 1912; (b): A Polish-Lithuanian postcard, 1907
Source: www.smolbattle.ru, www.mestai.net

Republic of Lithuania was declared, following the collapse of the Russian Empire (Clarke, 2006).

Between 1915 and 1918, the city was occupied by the German army, which had defeated the Russian forces. These three years saw a great 'landscape sweep', which accompanied the power change. The withdrawing Russian army took with it the symbols of its dominance, the monuments of Catherine II and Muravyov. Many street signs were torn down or defaced, and shop signs were painted over or had their Russian components removed (Weeks, 2004). The German language replaced Russian as the language of new power and dominance. Photographs from this period show a variety of signs, which make the linguistic landscape of Vilnius resemble a palimpsest, signs being continually changed and overwritten in different languages. The photographs taken in 1915 depict the addition of German to the public signage of the city and they often co-exist with earlier monolingual Russian signs, as illustrated by Figure 11.9, where an imposing German sign on a hostel for German soldiers (*Deutsches Soldatenheim*) hangs next to commercial Russian signs. Street names were translated from Russian into German without being renamed. For example, the main street in Vilnius before 1915 was called *Георгиевский проспект* ('George Avenue'), and this became *Georgstrasse*, as is seen in the caption in the top right-hand corner of Figure 11.10.

The military hospital sign shown earlier in Figure 11.7a changed from Russian to German (Figure 11.11).

By the end of 1917, Vilnius had lost its Russian veneer and became a German-Polish city. It was a German administrative centre, with German schools and a German daily newspaper. Lithuanian did not feature prominently, either on official

Figure 11.10 The main street of Vilnius in 1915 with monolingual Russian and German signs
Source: www.etoretro.ru

Figure 11.11 A German military hospital sign in 1916
Source: www.mestai.net

or private signs. However, some signs did contain Lithuanian as well as German, Polish and Yiddish. These signs threatened residents with deportation, confiscation and even shooting for transgressions against German regulations, which forbade trade in grain in an effort to ensure grain supplies for the troops (Weeks, 2004).

Population statistics may also explain why Lithuanian was so little used. The 1897 census carried out by the Russian Empire indicated that Lithuanians made up only 2.1% of the city's inhabitants; the German census of 1916/17 confirmed this figure (Демоскоп, www.demoscope.ru).

11.2.2 1918–1939

Although Lithuania declared independence in February 1918, Vilnius continued to be a contested territory between Lithuania, Poland and Russia. Poles put forward demands for greater cultural autonomy and expressed a desire to re-unite with Poland. As a result, 'the nationalizing Lithuanian state restricted Polish religious services, schools, Polish publications, and Polish voting rights' (Fearon & Laitin, 2006: 4). Another action of the Lithuanian government aimed at the increased use and visibility of the titular language was a forced Lithuanisation of non-Lithuanian names (Lumans, 1993). During 1919, the power in the city changed four times: Lithuanian-Polish-Russian-Polish. Finally, Lithuania and Russia signed a treaty in

July 1920, in which Moscow recognised Vilnius as Lithuanian territory occupied by Poland. Lithuania took the city back by military force. By October 1920, Vilnius was under Polish control once again. It was incorporated into Poland in 1922. 'Vilna was now officially transformed into Wilno' (Weeks, 2004: 19). The city remained under Polish control until 1939.

The Lithuanian government moved to a temporary capital in Kaunas and embarked on an explicitly nationalist policy. The first steps in implementing the national cultural policy were very practical, such as establishing Lithuanian schools and introducing compulsory education in Lithuanian. The development of cultural and literary movements was another way of nationalising the masses. Folk culture became the business card of the nation, representing it abroad, and memory politics based on the cult of medieval dukes and Middle Ages became mainstream in the national discourse. These were useful in proving that Lithuania was a 'historical' nation and were valuable for cultural self-representation (Davoliūtė, 2013; Weeks, 2015). The Vilnius campaign was an important part of this memory-building and nationalising process. Kaunas was seen as a city without history and was not considered to be the true capital. 'The Vilnius Question grew into a national obsession and a campaign to retake the city … in tandem with the glorification of Lithuania's medieval past' (Davoliūtė, 2013: 27).

Although many Lithuanians had never been to Vilnius, and their claims to it were based on history, not demography, the Union for the Liberation of Vilnius was formed in 1925, which became the most powerful civic organisation in the country (Weeks, 2015). Literary and visual representation of the city became the core of the campaign. Numerous poems and postcards representing the key icon of the city, the medieval castle of Gediminas, linked it to the original history of the nation. Symbolic Vilnius passports were issued to every schoolchild by the Liberation Union and made it 'a symbol of belonging to the nation' (Davoliūtė, 2014: 188). The Lithuanian national idea born in the 19th century had now developed into innovative mass communication tools of a nationalising interwar movement.

Meanwhile, the city remained under Polish control (until 1939). Hegemonisation is strongly connected to the process of spatialisation, when space is equivalent to representation of power and the production of ideological closure (Laclau, 1990), particularly in the context of temporal dislocation. The city was constantly 'dislocated' by opposing powers during the interwar period and the production of an ideological closure via spatial representation was a way of producing a picture of the dislocated world as somehow coherent and stable (Czepczyński, 2008). It is apparent from the diachronic analysis of the sociocultural landscape in Vilnius during these years that Polish 're-spatialisation' of the city was as important a tool in the consolidation and stabilisation of the Polish rule as the closure of 266 Lithuanian schools between 1936 and 1939, the ban on the activities of Lithuanian cultural organisations (Fearon & Laitin, 2006), and the re-opening of a Polish university, which was restored in 1919 with a new name, *Uniwersytet Stefana Batorego*. One of the photographs from my data taken in the 1930s (Figure 11.12) shows the same building as in Figure 11.7a and Figure 11.11, but by then it had become the University Hospital and the name was in Polish. This is a good illustration that supports my earlier statement,

Figure 11.12 Vilnius University Hospital in the 1930s with a Polish sign
Source: www.mestai.net

that memory landscapes are developmental paths through historical memories, practices and policies of authorities.

By 1919, a witness account stated that all street signs in Vilna were in Polish, while in Kaunas, the second city of Lithuania, they were multilingual (Lithuanian–Polish–Yiddish) (Weeks, 2004). Many streets were renamed, including the main street, illustrated earlier in Figure 11.10. The Germans simply translated the earlier Russian name, but the Polish authorities renamed it after the national poet Mickiewicz (Figure 11.13a).

The Polish identity of the city was further consolidated during the 1920s and 1930s. My corpus from this period shows new developments along Mickiewicz St, such as the modern Jabłkowski Brothers department store and various other commercial outlets. Figure 11.13b shows a monolingual Polish sign along the façade of one of the shops, *Tanie Pończochy* ('Cheap Stockings'). Numerous Polish publications emphasised the Polish nature of the city. New factories were built, and Polish radio had its first broadcast in 1927. Although there were also limited broadcasts in Lithuanian and Belorussian, Polish became the dominant language of the sociolinguistic landscape of Vilnius. The urbanist Kevin Lynch (1960) noted that the particular visual quality of the urban landscape plays an important role in the process of representation. People understand their surroundings by forming mental maps with five elements: paths (e.g. streets and transport), edges (walls, buildings), districts, nodes (intersections, focal points) and landmarks. By 1939, these mental maps of the Vilnius inhabitants were firmly associated with the Polish language. For example, the Jabłkowski Brothers department store was opened in Vilnius in 1919 and by 1939 had become a well-known Vilnius landmark. It was even featured on the cover of a

(a)   (b)

Figure 11.13 (a) The main street in 1930 with a Polish caption ('Adam Mickiewicz St.'); (b) a monolingual Polish sign, *Tanie Pończochy*, in 1938 ('Cheap Stockings')
Source: www.mestai.net

fashion magazine published in Vilnius (Figure 11.14a). Another example of Polish cultural landscape at the time was its public transport. The first motorised autobuses were purchased in 1926 and by 1930 ran along three routes (Weeks, 2015). All signs indicating bus routes and information at bus stops were in Polish (Figure 11.14b).

(a)   (b)

Figure 11.14 (a) A cover of Moda fashion magazine featuring Jabłkowski Brothers' winter collection; (b) local bus with a Polish route sign at a bus stop with Polish information in 1937
Source: www.en.wikipedia.org, www.mestai.net

Figure 11.15 Bilingual Polish-Yiddish signs, 1930
Source: www.mestai.net

Memoirs from this period depict Vilnius as a Polish city, although they aknowl-edge the Jewish, Russian and Lithuanian presence (Obiezierska, 1995). My data contain a number of photographs showing Yiddish alongside Polish on shop signs. Taken in the Jewish quarter, they indicate that most Jewish merchants 'preferred to use both Yiddish – and, as required, Polish – in their shop signs to underline the Jewish character of their business' (Weeks, 2015: 148). The name of the Jewish owner in Figure 11.15 is in Polish and Yiddish on the sign above the door. Vertical signs between the windows advertise the goods available for sale in Polish at the top of the signs *obuwie* and in Yiddish at the bottom שיך ('shoes').

Demographic data also support the fact that, for the first time, a single ethnic group, Poles, could claim a majority in this historically multi-ethnic city during the 1920s and 1930s. Weeks gives the following figures from the Vilnius statistical annual review of 1937: almost 66% of the city's population was Polish, 28% were Jews, less than 5% were Russian or Belorussian and less than 1% were Lithuanian (Weeks, 2015: 243).

11.2.3 1939–1944

The start of World War II brought yet more changes to Vilnius. As a result of the Molotov-Ribbentrop Pact, the Red Army took over the city in September 1939 and it was transferred to Lithuania. In return for this 'gift', Lithuania accepted the sta-tioning of Soviet troops in its territory. The Lithuanian army entered Vilnius display-ing a victorious slogan 'Vilnius inhabitants welcome Lithuanian Army' (Figure 11.16a). However, 'Lithuanian soldiers were astonished that they could not

(a)   (b)

Figure 11.16 (a): Lithuanian army enters Vilnius in 1939 with the slogan *Vilniaus gyventojai sveikina Lietovos Kariuomenę* ('Vilnius inhabitants welcome Lithuanian Army'); (b) a shop front with a Lithuanian sign *'Siuvejas'* ('Tailor') in 1940

Source: www.en.wikipedia.org, www.antraspasaulinis.net

communicate with the local population, and officers were forced to resort to French and German to ask for directions' (Snyder, 1996: 47). Despite this, official Lithuanian propaganda spoke of liberating the city and restoring its Lithuanian identity (Snyder, 1996: 47). By spring 1940, 'a full 490 streets received new names, though the changing of street signs lagged behind' (Weeks, 2015: 160).

Poles were dismissed from local government (Davoliūtė, 2013; Snyder, 2003). Lithuanian made an appearance on shop signs and various private businesses (Figure 11.16b). Stefan Bathory University was re-opened in 1940 as Vilnius University, with Lithuanian as the language of instruction (Liekis, 2010). Other Lithuanisation measures included the abolition of the Polish Złoty, removal of Polish books from shops, and closure of Polish schools and organisations (Bauer, 1981; Piotrowski, 1997).

The process of 're-Lithuanisation' lasted until June 1940, when the Soviet Army took over Lithuania. A month later, the Lithuanian Soviet Socialist Republic was established. The first year of Soviet rule was accompanied by mass arrests, which spared no nationality. About 19,000 'anti-Soviet socially harmful' individuals were deported during the first month (Grunskis, 1996: 23). The targets for deportation were not selected on the basis of ethnicity, as the deportees were roughly representative of the population as a whole – Lithuanians, Poles, Jews and Russians (Balkelis, 2005; Davoliūtė, 2013). Weeks (2015: 164) notes that Lithuanian commentators speak of 'genocide' against their nation by the Soviets, but some Polish researchers maintain that NKVD (People's Commissariat for Internal Affairs) worked with the Lithuanian security forces (*saugumas*) in the deportation of thousands of Poles, Lithuanians and Jews. These repressions were one of the reasons why many Lithuanians welcomed the German invasion. They hoped the Nazis would see them as allies and help to restore

(a)   (b)

Figure 11.17 (a) A Nazi flag on Vilnius Cathedral, 1941; (b) a banner across the main street, 1942: *Deutsches Soldatentheater* ('Theatre for German soldiers')
Source: http://antraspasaulinis.net

independence. This hope was short-lived, as the Provisional Government of Lithuania was not recognised by the Nazis. They formed their own civil administration – the *Reichskommissariat Ostland*. Lip service was paid to Lithuanian cultural affairs. Vilnius University continued its work until 1943. Lithuanian theatre and literature expanded under the German occupation. Newspapers were printed in German and Lithuanian, but not in Polish (Weeks, 2015). This provided steady employment for many Lithuanian writers. They formed a platform for a propaganda campaign, emphasising the nationalist sentiment of an idyllic rural life and folk culture, which happened to conform to the image of pastoral utopia promoted by the Nazis. This 'pastoral bliss' and idealised vision of Vilnius without Soviet Communists was supposed to emphasise the return of Vilnius to its native culture, although Lithuania's sovereignty was trampled (Davoliūtė, 2013). However, the photographs from this period leave no doubt about the real power landscape of Vilnius under the Nazis. Czepczyński (2008: 45) writes that the 'capacity of social actors to actively impose and engage their cultural productions and symbolic systems plays an essential role in the reproduction of social structures of domination'. 'Symbolic capital', whether it is an image of the dream city as a guarantor of statehood, or a power over the landscape, expressed in the form of Nazi banners, flags, symbols and German-language public notices (Figure 11.17a, b), is a crucial source of power.

The holder of symbolic capital imposes power and creates a socio-political hierarchy. Lithuanians were favoured by Nazi policies as minor allies. Most of the city administration remained Lithuanian, and 'Lithuanian names and companies dominated a type-written telephone book drawn by the Nazi occupiers' (Weeks, 2015: 173). Poles had few rights; Jews had none. In July 1941, an order was issued stating that all Jews must wear a special patch on their back (Figure 11.18a); subsequently,

(a)

(c)

(b)

Figure 11.18 (a) Jewish women with 'J' patches on their backs, 1941; (b) Jews in Vilnius under the escort of a Lithuanian collaborator, 1941; (c) gates to a ghetto in Vilnius guarded by a Lithuanian and German guards, 1942

Source: www.de.academic.ru

they were ordered to wear the yellow Star of David instead. They were forbidden to walk along the main streets or to use telephones and radios. Having incorporated thousands of Lithuanian volunteers into its ranks, the German military rule *Einsatzkommando* began a massive elimination of Jews. This time 'the targets were defined explicitly in terms of their ethnic and religious identity' (Davoliūtė, 2013: 38). Many Poles suffered the same fate. As they continued underground anti-German resistance, their mass arrests began in 1942. Polish memoirs and literature on the Holocaust in Lithuania stress the cruelty of Lithuanians and their collaboration with the Nazis (Figure 11.18b, c). Reports from the Lithuanian security police at the time and recent research corroborate this fact (Cesarani, 1996; Dawidowicz, 1979; Hilberg, 2003; Snyder, 2003; Weeks, 2015).

The above photographs leave no doubt about power distribution in social discourse and the position of each ethnic group; however, by 1943 nobody was safe. As the Red Army progressed westward, the Nazis began brutal liquidation of the Vilnius ghettos and the slaughter of the civilian population. Thousands of Lithuanians and Poles were sent as forced labour to Germany or murdered.

11.2.4 1944–1991

By the time the Red Army retook the city in 1944 and the Lithuanian SSR was re-established, the city's pre-war population was reduced by 50%, its Jews virtually exterminated (Snyder, 2003; Weeks, 2015). Although it remained mainly Polish by ethnicity, 'Stalin decided that Vilnius was to be Lithuanian' (Snyder, 2003: 88).[1] First, the name of the city was changed to Wilnius (the transliteration of Lithuanian), then between 1945 and 1946 '170,000 ethnic Poles were "repatriated" to Poland in the context of the post-war population exchanges negotiated among the Allies and to the Lithuanian countryside' (Davoliūtė, 2013: 43). Vilnius became the capital of Soviet Lithuania and would never again be challenged by Poles (Weeks, 2015).

The Soviet period in Lithuania has been extensively researched, both in post-Soviet Lithuania and in the West. Two opposing views are evident. On the one hand, recent historico-political and sociolinguistic research evaluates this period as the second Soviet occupation, characterised by cultural Sovietisation and linguistic Russification, which 'once again presented the Lithuanian nation with a challenge to the survival of its identity' (Clarke, 2006: 165). This analysis reflects the fact that Sovietisation was imposed by force and provoked armed resistance, whose centre moved to the countryside. It became known as the 'forest brothers' and was crushed by Soviet political repressions and mass deportations, resulting in 5% of the population being sent to the Gulag. 'In popular and official Lithuanian memory today, the Soviets were nothing less than agents of genocide' (Davoliūtė, 2014: 180). As discussed in Section 11.1.1, these tragic events became the focus of collective identity and national memory in post-Soviet Lithuania.

On the other hand, a number of researchers have recently tried to establish a link between the development of Soviet Lithuanian identity and the nationalising drive of the interwar republic, and the early Lithuanian nationalist movement which highlights the national character of Lithuanian Sovietisation (Davoliūtė, 2013, 2014, 2016; Snyder, 2003; Weeks, 2015).[2] Davoliūtė (2013: 176) argues that the problem with the first approach is that it does not explain the 'paradoxical' co-existence of national and communist discourses in Soviet Vilnius, that it ignores 'any sensibility towards the social and cultural legacy of that period'. As an alternative, she draws 'on the "new imperial history" to contextualise Lithuania after World War II as an "imperial situation" – a heterogeneous space of conflicting memories and political, social and cultural experiences created by forced and momentous geopolitical, demographic, and social changes' (Davoliūtė, 2013: 177). From this perspective, the Soviet rule in Vilnius could be seen not only as a repressive regime, but also as a catalyst of transnational and transcultural processes which brought demographic and linguistic Lithuanisation.

Weeks (2015: 233) also maintains that the weakest aspect of studies supporting the first approach is that they almost exclusively portray this period as an era of repression 'with very little discussion of the economic growth, cultural development, and major physical changes in Vilnius during these four and a half decades'.

In his provocative book *The Reconstruction of Nations*, Snyder (2003: 91) asks the following question: 'How did Wilno, a city with a tiny Lithuanian minority under Polish rule in 1939 become Vilnius, the capital of a Lithuanian nation-state, in 1991?' He argues that the Soviet policies of Polish resettlement were made by people who understood the history of nationality and opened political and physical space for the re-creation of Vilnius as a Lithuanian city in two ways. It not only changed the demographic balance, but also engineered a major sociological change. 'Poles became in Lithuania what they had never been – a peasant nation ... Lithuanians had become what they had never been: an urban nation. Their language became, for the first time in modern history, a badge of status in Vilnius' (Snyder, 2003: 95).

Weeks (2015) supports this discussion, also emphasising the population shift as one of the major factors in the post-war developments in Vilnius. He notes that Nazi and early Soviet repressions during 1939–1947 emptied the city of its 'original population and repopulated [it]', mostly with Lithuanians from the countryside (Weeks, 2015: 239). This, as was mentioned in Section 11.1.1, prevented extensive Russification and allowed the authorities to build a city which 'was simultaniously Soviet-socialist and Lithuanian' (Weeks, 2015: 239).

In the first decade of Soviet rule, the number of secondary schools quadrupled and a comprehensive Lithuanian-language education system was established. It had more titular language instruction than ever before. The first history of the Lithuanian language was published in English. It was written by a graduate of Soviet-era Vilnius University (Weeks, 2015: 239). The processes of indigenisation and Khruschev's Thaw (the period from the early 1950s to the early 1960s) contributed to the success of Lithuanian literature and arts, and solidified the Lithuanian identity of Vilnius.

The analysis of my data from this period supports the second view, and reveals a picture of Soviet Vilnius, where 'language was a mark of distinctiveness for Lithuanians under Soviet rule' (Snyder, 2003: 97). The photographs from the late 1940s and early 1950s contain predominantly Lithuanian signs. Among these are political signs typical of the era, such as election banners displayed at a polling station and banners carried during the Soviet May Day and October Parades (Figure 11.19), and everyday photographs of streets with various public buildings, such as Vilnius Railway Station, the central telegraph and post office (Figure 11.20).

(a)   (b)

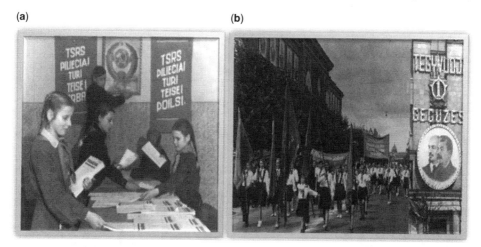

Figure 11.19 (a) Lithuanian banner: *TSRS Piliečiai turi tiesę į darba* ('Citizens of LSSR have the right to work') on the left and *TSRS Piliečiai turi tiesę į poilsi* ('Citizens of LSSR have the right to rest') on the right, 1950; (b) Lithuanian banner in the background: *Dėkojame draugui Stalinui už mūsų laimingą vaikystę* ('We thank comrade Stalin for our happy childhood') and on the right *Tegivuoja 1 Gegužės* ('Long live May 1st'), 1950's

Source: www.archyvai.lt, www.truelithuania.com

(a)   (b)

Figure 11.20 (a): Vilnius Railway Station, 1950; the words on the building are in Lithuanian: *Geležinkelio Stotis* ('Railway Station'); (b): Vilnius Central Post Office, 1958; the words on the front top corner (enlarged on the right): *Paštas* ('Post Office')
Source: www.archyvai.lt

These photographs illustrate what Snyder (2003) calls the post-war bow of the Russian to the Lithuanian language. If we compare the sociolinguistic landscape of Vilnius in Imperial Russia with the landscape during Soviet times, my earlier argument, that some post-Soviet researchers tend to equate the concepts of Russification and Sovietisation, becomes clear. Sovietisation is a far more encompassing and complex process than Russification. A number of authors argue that the strength of national communism and a compromise between Lithuanian communists and intelligentsia[3] opened an opportunity to pursue the same nationalising project as the interwar regime, but with better resources and more elaborately articulated (Davoliūtė, 2013; Weeks, 2015). The key formula of Soviet nationality policy, to be national in form and socialist in content, was used by them to focus public discourse on a construction of Lithuanian ethnic identity via the restoration of key monuments connected to the medieval past of Lithuania. For example, the restoration of the Castle of Gediminas, an important state and historic symbol of Vilnius built by the grand Duke of Lithuania in 1323, was identified as a national priority as early as 1945. This echoes the representation of the city as the symbol of national history in the interwar period, discussed in Section 11.2.2. Much of the Old Town of Vilnius was also preserved, escaping radical Soviet plans for its reconstruction. It is interesting to note that Soviet Lithuanian authorities followed the same pattern of neglecting the cultural heritage of the great manors, seen as the remnants of Polish culture, by the interwar authorities.

Lithuanian folk song and sports festivals were also a representation of socialist reconstruction, but they closely resembled the tradition of mass festivals during the interwar period (Figure 11.21). The first such festival was organised in 1924.

(a) (b)

Figure 11.21 (a) A sports parade, 1950; (b) folk song and dance festival, 1966
Source: www.archyvai.lt, www.strana.lenta.ru/lithuania/lilak/htm

Lithuanian and Soviet narratives are tightly intertwined in the messages of these mass cultural events, aiding the formation of a new collective sense of Soviet Lithuanian identity.

The sports parade depicted in Figure 11.21a is a typical example of the cultural events which emphasised the socialist cultivation of youth as an ideal of a bright Soviet future. The name of a famous Lithuanian basketball club, *Žalgiris*, is proudly displayed on participants' T-shirts, and the background is dominated by a banner with the LTSR (Lithuanian Soviet Socialist Republic) coat of arms in the middle and the words *Tarybų Lietuva* ('Soviet Lithuania'). However, the prominence of Lithuanian and the absence of Russian suggests that the titular language was at the same time the main instrument of Sovietisation and promotion of Lithuanian nationalism with an aura of Soviet legitimacy. The same goes for Figure 11.21b, showing a folk song and dance festival where all information is given in Lithuanian, although the LTSR coat of arms has pride of place in the centre. Such festivals started in August 1924 and were restarted in Soviet Lithuania in 1945. 'They contained a strong element of staged nationalism and continuity with mass identity politics developed during the interwar period' (Davoliūtė, 2013: 68).

The sociopolitical landscape of Vilnius in the 1950s and 1960s was dominated by Soviet symbols prominently displayed throughout the city in the form of the new Soviet Lithuanian coat of arms, Soviet Lithuanian flag, Soviet slogans and monuments, which conveyed the Soviet message in Lithuanian. Even non-political labels on goods were in Lithuanian, but also demonstrated the republic's participation in the process of Soviet economic integration by the inclusion of LTSR – *Lietovos Tarybų Socialistinė Respublika* (Lithuanian Soviet Socialist Republic) (Figure 11.22). The only hints of its Soviet character are circled in red: LTSR and a small word in Russian, ГОСТ, which refers to the Soviet standardisation system of goods.

(a)

(b)

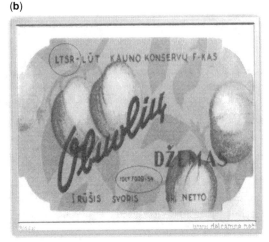

Figure 11.22 (a) A matchbox, 1956: *Tarybų Lietuvos Spartakiada* ('The Spartakiad of Soviet Lithuania)'; (b) a jam label, 1954: *Obuolių džemas* ('Apple jam')
Source: www.delcampe.net

By the late 1950s, Vilnius had its share of Soviet monuments, including a statue of Lenin, but many Lithuanian writers, composers and communists were also commemorated, as Weeks' analysis of how Lithuanian communists established Vilnius as the Soviet Lithuanian capital reveals. Many streets were renamed after communist leaders, but an even larger number lost their historical Polish names and assumed Lithuanian ones (Weeks, 2008).

By the mid-1960s and beyond, Moscow authorities often used Lithuania 'as a showcase for the achievements of Soviet science, culture and industry, and by implication the Soviet nationalities policy' (Davoliūtė, 2013: 108). Khrushchev's Thaw enabled Lithuanian intelligentsia to participate in Soviet cultural exchange trips and travel outside the USSR. This brought new European trends into Lithuanian architecture, which were reflected in the cityscape. A new distinct Soviet Lithuanian style won international recognition and the first All-Union Lenin prize for architecture in 1974 for the design of a new microdistrict Lazdynai (Синочкина, 2008). Equally, Lithuanian writers, musicians and actors began to enjoy recognition outside their republic and many of them became stars of Soviet cinema and theatre.

The sociocultural landscape of Vilnius continued to be national in its nature, but the official Soviet policy of bilingualism meant that official documents such as birth, marriage, divorce certificates and degree documents contained Lithuanian and Russian. Street signs and most shop fronts were also in two languages, with the titular language displayed first (Figure 11.23).

However, the policy was not strictly imposed and many photographs depict Lithuanian signage only (Figure 11.24).

Hogan-Brun *et al.* (2008: 68) state that the Russification policy of the 1950s and 1960s did not aim at the rearrangement of the language environment, but from 1978

(a)   (b)

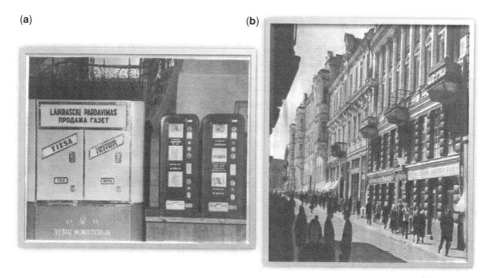

Figure 11.23 (a) Newspaper and postcard vending machines with bilingual Lithuanian-Russian signs, 1960; (b) a street in central Vilnius with bilingual Lithuanian-Russian shop signs, *Vinas – Вино* ('Wine') and '*Pieno Kavinė – Молочное Кафе*' ('Milk Bar'), 1966
Source: www.miestai.net, private archive

it was strengthened, and the Russian language and its speakers were favoured in all three Baltic republics. The authors go further and declare that 'cultural and educational policies were geared to destroy the native language/medium educational system as the basis of national identity'. It is true that since 1961 the so-called 'second

(a)   (b)

Figure 11.24 (a) A trolleybus stop with information in Lithuanian, 1977; (b) a snack bar in central Vilnius with Lithuanian signage, 1970s
Source: www.etoretro.ru

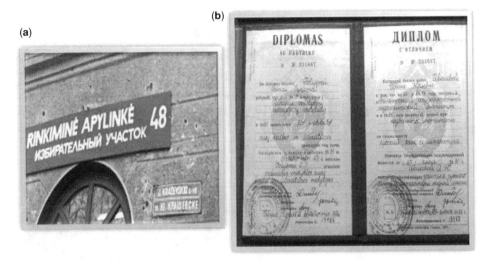

Figure 11.25 (a) A bilingual street sign and a temporary polling station sign; (b) a bilingual degree document

Source: private archive, 1979, private archive, 1981

mother tongue' campaign was gathering strength and resulted, in the late 1970s, in increased bilingualism among titular speakers and growing visibility of Russian in the sociolinguistic landscapes of Soviet cities. However, as mentioned earlier, the implementation of central policies had local peculiarities in each republic and such overreaching statements should be issued with caution. In her article, Pavlenko (2008) gives counter-evidence for the above statements. She notes that Russian speakers were not socially privileged and many schools across the republics offered bilingual education – Russian was studied as an L2 in titular schools and titular languages were studied as an L2 in Russian schools (Pavlenko, 2008). The discussion concerning the compromise between Lithuanian communists and intelligentsia, mentioned in Section 11.2.4, also contradicts the above view. It asserts that Lithuanian poetry and prose enjoyed notable successes, and Vilnius University became a haven of Baltic studies (Davoliūtė, 2013; Snyder, 2003).

My data also do not support the thesis of 'titular language destruction' in Lithuania. Figure 11.25 illustrates the continuous 'bilingualisation' of public spaces in Vilnius in the 1970s and 1980s, but detects no increase in their Russification. In fact, the patterns of language positioning and use remain similar to those of the 1960s and 1970s. In most top-down controlled locations the signs are bilingual, with Lithuanian on the top or on the left, and Russian as an L2 on the bottom or on the right.

Similarly to the previous decade, there is also evidence of monolingual Lithuanian signs, which indicate that the policy was not strictly followed (Figure 11.26).

Another interesting point made by a number of researchers with regard to late Russification policies, is the increasing prestige of Russian in various public domains (Clarke, 2006; Hogan-Brun *et al.*, 2008). Indeed, by the late 1980s, Russian became a language of interethnic communication and was widely spoken

(a)   (b)

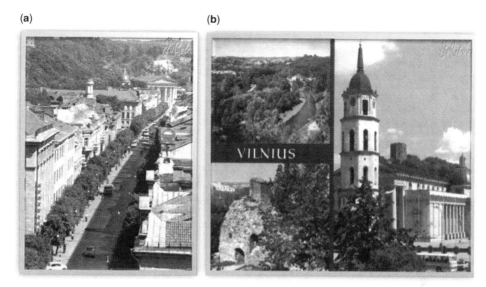

Figure 11.26 (a) A monolingual shop sign (along the corner of the building on the left) in Lithuanian: *Audiniai* ('Fabrics') on the main street of Vilnius, 1981; (b) a postcard with an inscription in Lithuanian only, 1980s

Source: www.etoretro.ru

across the USSR. Its use and knowledge were required in new functional areas of the economy and industry in terms of inter-republic cooperation and state planning and control. Nevertheless, its hegemony and use in prestige areas differed from republic to republic. Lithuania was the only republic in the Baltics where the ruling organs of the Communist Party operated in the titular language, not Russian. Hogan-Brun *et al.* (2008: 70) acknowledge this fact, but without explaining how this was possible in the light of the 'thick' Russification policies they discussed earlier. The only statement they make is that Lithuania was 'an exception' (Hogan-Brun *et al.*, 2008: 70).

As discussed in Section 11.1.1, by 1959 the majority of people in the leading posts of the local Communist Party were Lithuanians and a titular language knowledge requirement was in place for such positions, as well as for various other functionaries and administrators. Also, the strength and cohesion of national communists was ensured by its leadership. A. Sniečkus, the First Secretary of the Lithuanian Communist Party since 1927, had considerable authority in Moscow and was trusted by Stalin. He remained unchallenged in Soviet Lithuania until his death in 1972 and 'appears to have shielded Lithuania from excessive interference from Moscow' (Davoliūtė, 2013: 88). In contrast to communist elites in other republics, the Lithuanian communists 'were never purged and maintained an unusual level, by Soviet standards, of corporate autonomy in their affairs, especially as concerns cultural and economic matters' (Davoliūtė, 2013: 89).

My data contain a number of photographs depicting official meetings of the Lithuanian Communist Party. These and other photographs confirm the wide

(a)   (b)

Figure 11.27 (a) An official communist meeting with a partially visible slogan in Lithuanian: *Komunizmo Salygose* ('In Communist Conditions'), 1961; (b) 16th Congress of the Lithuanian Communist Party with a Lithuanian banner: *LKP* ('LCP – Lithuanian Communist Party'), 1971
Source: www.virtualios-parados.archyvai.lt

spheres of influence of the Lithuanian language, from shop fronts to the congresses of the Communist Party (Figure 11.27).

As we can see, the city in the 1970s and 1980s was very different from earlier periods analysed in this chapter. The diachronic approach to analysing its socio-cultural landscape illustrates that Soviet Vilnius had a mixed identity. It was 'primarily Lithuanian and Soviet, but also Russian inasmuch as the Soviet Union presupposed Russian and Lithuanian bilingualism' (Weeks, 2015: 209). The Jewish and Polish identities had virtually disappeared. My data contain very few images connected with Polish and Yiddish, mostly left on some religious and historical buildings as structural parts of their architectural design. There are also rare reminders of the city's multicultural past in the form of tourist information plaques, such as the one depicted in Figure 11.28. It is a trilingual sign commemorating the Great Synagogue of Vilna, which was damaged during World War II and pulled down in 1957.

Soviet and Lithuanian identities coexisted in the form of a bilingual cityscape in tandem with selected elements of national culture and history, but the privileged position of the Lithuanian language 'was evident at the university, in the academy of sciences, in the majority of research institutes, in the mass press' (Weeks, 2015: 191) and even in the local organs of the Communist Party. Weeks calls this situation a 'bilingual cultural hegemony', which led to the development of a modern nationalising movement through physical reconstruction of the city. It also facilitated the key role of Soviet Lithuanian intelligentsia together with the LCP in shaping public discourse in Soviet times. This, in its turn, transformed this hegemony into the modern independent Lithuanian state.

Figure 11.28 A rare example of a modern monolingual Lithuanian-English-Russian sign, 2016
Source: Author's photograph

11.3 Conclusions

The importance of Vilnius to different ethnicities makes it an ideal case study for diachronic analysis of its symbolic and physical appropriation. LL was used as a polyhedral tool to reveal how Polish, Russian, Soviet and Lithuanian states implemented their national symbolic politics. As we have seen, landscape revolutions go behind the political transformations, and can be fatal and turbulent, resulting in 'soft' (propaganda, culture and education) and 'hard' policies (repression, prohibition of certain languages … and genocide) (Weeks, 2015: 3). On the one hand, I was able to establish the surface picture of language repositioning and changes in language practices via the synchronic-diagnostic and combined historical diachronic analysis. On the other hand, an extra-linguistic semiotic analysis enabled us to investigate how written languages interact with the physical features of the cityscape to construct new memory landscapes and expose the roots of modern developments. The strict policy of titular monolingualism in modern Lithuania and the displacement metaphor in Soviet times became key elements in the city's national face and ethnic self-representation. The diachronic analysis of Vilnius LL illustrated that the centrality of language in the Lithuanian identity can be traced historically to the Polish and Russian linguistic and cultural domination, and the displacement metaphor to the cultural politics during the interwar period. Displaced from Vilnius to

Kaunas, the Lithuanian government focused on the Vilnius Question as the central part of its nationalising campaign.

The analysis of the linguistic and sociocultural landscape of Soviet Vilnius as an element in the discourse of Soviet Lithuanian identity helped me to reveal the links between the post-war era and the nationalising drive of the interwar republic. This approach enabled me to challenge the post-Soviet Lithuanian memory landscapes and see what Sovietisation meant in the Lithuanian context in a different light. The decades of Soviet rule are widely regarded as dominated by 'the grinding process of Russification, but these generalisations are only partially accurate' (Weeks, 2015: 239).

Using LL as a powerful diagnostic tool, I illustrated that Sovietisation did not only brutalise the nation and attempt to mould its identity according to Soviet ideology, but also aided the demographic, linguistic and cultural Lithuanisation of the city. It appears that Sovietisation involved considerably more than the imposition of oppressive external rule. It shaped the development of national resistance and nation building, which allowed the local communists and intelligentsia to facilitate the creation of a Soviet identity with a Lithuanian national nuance. They gained an exceptional level of cultural autonomy and followed the intellectual traditions of the interwar period, which later resurfaced in the cultural movement against Soviet rule, *Sajūdis*, and eventually led to the declaration of independence in 1991. These social transformations are often either forgotten or deeply buried in post-Soviet collective memory.

My diachronic analysis of sociopolitical, cultural and memory discourses of Vilnius may be limited and even controversial, but I believe that it has thrown some light on certain blind spots. As Davoliūtė (2013: 4) argues, the period between 1940 and 1990 was declared 'legally inoperative, politically illegitimate … and culturally inauthentic'; therefore, 'it says nothing of the role of Lithuanians in the direction and management of the Soviet regime'.

Notes

(1) For the reasoning behind this decision, see the discussion in Snyder (2003), which argues that Stalin had more to gain by giving the city to the Lithuanians.
(2) For an analysis of recent work by Lithuanian scholars on the topography of Soviet Vilnius, see Davoliūtė (2014).
(3) See Snyder (2003) and Davoliūtė (2013) for a discussion of the arrangements between Lithuanian communists and intelligentsia to preserve Lithuanian culture.

References

Altapov, V. (2000) *150 Iazykov i Politika: 1917–2000* [*150 Languages and Politics: 1917–2000*]. Moscow: KRAFT + IV RAN.
Andersen, B. and Silver, B.D. (1984) Equality, efficiency, and politics in Soviet bilingual education policy, 1934–1980. *The American Political Science Review* 78 (4), 1019–1039.
Balkelis, T. (2005) Lithuanian children in the Gulag: Deportations, ethnicity and identity memoirs of children deportees, 1941–52. *Lithuanus* 51 (3), 40–74.
Bauer, Y. (1981) *American Jewry and the Holocaust*. Detroit: Wayne State University Press.

Blommaert, J. (2013) Semiotic and spatial scope: Towards a materialist semiotics. In N.B. Pacher (ed.) *Multimodality and Social Semiotics* (pp. 29–38). Oxford: Routledge.

Certeau, M. (1985) Practice of space. In M. Blonski (ed.) *On Signs* (pp. 122–145). Baltimore: Johns Hopkins University Press.

Cesarani, D. (1996) *The Holocaust in Lithuania – Dina Porat – The Final Solution – Origins and Implementation.* London: Routledge.

Clarke, T. (2006) Nationalism in post-Soviet Lithuania. In L.W. Barrington (ed.) *After Independence: Making and Protecting the Nation in Postcolonial and Postcommunist States* (pp. 162–187). Michigan: University of Michigan Press.

Czepczyński, M.A. (2008) *Cultural Landscapes of Post-Socialist Cities: Representation of Power and Needs.* Aldershot: Ashgate.

Davoliūtė, V. (2013) *The Making and Breaking of Soviet Lithuania.* London: Routledge.

Davoliūtė, V. (2014) Postwar reconstruction and the imperial sublime in Vilnius during late Stalinism. *Ab Imperio* 1, 176–203.

Davoliūtė, V. (2016) The Sovietization of Lithuania after WWII: Modernization, transculturation, and the lettered city. *Journal of Baltic Studies* 47 (1), 49–63.

Dawidowicz, L. (1979) *The War Against the Jews.* New York: Bantam Books.

Dilāns, G. and Zepa, B. (2015) Bilingual and multilingual education in the former Soviet. republics: The case of Latvia. In E. Wright, S. Boun and O. García (eds) *The Handbook of Bilingual and Multilingual Education* (pp. 632–644). Chichester: Wiley Blackwell.

Dobriansky, F. (1904) *Staraya i Novaya Vilna [Old and New Vilna].* Vilna: Syrkin.

Dowler, W. (2001) *Classroom and Empire: The Politics of Schooling Russia's Eastern Nationalities, 1860–1917.* Montreal: McGill-Queen's University Press.

Drėmaitė, M. (2010) Naujas senasis Vilnius: Senamiescio griovimas ir atstatyma 1944–1959 metais. In G. Jankeviciute (ed.) *Atrasti Viliu: Skiriama Vladuii Dremai* (pp. 183–201). Vilnius: Vilniaus Dailės Akademijos Leidykla.

Fearon, J.L. and Laitin, D. (2006) Lithuania narrative. See https://www.stanford.edu/group/ethnic/Random%20Narratives/LithuaniaRN1.3 (accessed 17 March 2016).

Grunskis, E. (1996) *Lietuvos Gyventoju Tremimai, 1940–1941 ir 1945-53 Metais.* Vilnius: Lietuvos Istorijos Institutas.

Herrschel, T. (2007) *Global Georgaphies of Post-Socialist Transition: Geographies, Societies, Policies.* London: Routledge.

Hilberg, R. (2003) *The Destruction of the European Jews.* New Haven: Yale University Press.

Hogan-Brun, G. and Ramonienė, M. (2003) Emerging language and education policies in Lithuania. *Language Policy* 2 (1), 27–45.

Hogan-Brun, G. and Ramonienė, M. (2004) Changing levels of bilingualism across the Baltic. *International Journal of Bilingual Education and Bilingualism* 7 (1), 62–77.

Hogan-Brun, G., Ozolins, U., Ramonienė, M. and Rannut, M. (2008) Language politics and practice in the Baltic States. In R.B. Kaplan (ed.) *Language Planning and Policy in Europe* (pp. 31–193). Bristol: Multilingual Matters.

Järve, P. (2003) Language battles in the Baltic states: 1989–2002. In F.G. Daftary (ed.) *Nation-building, Ethnicity and Language Politics in Transition Countries* (pp. 73–106). Budapest: IGI Books.

Jaworski, A. and Thurlow, C. (2010) *Semiotic Landscapes.* London: Continuum.

Kappeler, A. (2001) *The Russian Empire: A Multiethnic History.* Harlow: Longman.

Kappeler, A. (2004) The ambiguities of Russification. *Kritika: Explorations in Russian and Eurasian History* 5 (2), 291–297.

Kotkin, S. (2001) Modern times: The Soviet union and the interwar conjuncture. *Kritika: Explorations in Russian and Eurasian History* 2 (1), 111–164.

Laclau, E. (1990) *New Reflections on the Revolution of our Time.* London: Verso.

Laitin, D. (1998) *Identity in Formation: The Russian-speaking Populations in the Near Abroad.* Ithaca: Cornell University Press.

Liekis, S. (2010) *1939: The Year that Changed Everything in Lithuanian History.* Amsterdam: Rodopi.

Lithuanian Press Ban. See http://en.wikipedia.org/wiki/Lithuanian_press_ban (accessed 4 October 2016).

Lumans, V. (1993) *Himmler's Auxiliaries: The Volksdeutsche Mittelstelle and the German National Minorities of Europe, 1993–1945.* Chapel Hill: University of North Carolina Press.

Lynch, K. (1960) *The Image of the City.* Cambridge: The Technology Press and Harvard University Press.

Muth, S. (2008) Multiethnic but multilingual as well? - The linguistic landscape of Vilnius. See http://www.biecoll.ub.uni-bielefeld.de (accessed 25 August 2016).

Obiezierska, H. (1995) *Jedno Zycie Prywatne na tle Zycia Narodupolskiego w Wieku XX.* Wilna: Bydgoszcz: Towarzystwo Milosnikow.

Outdoor Exposure. Sovietiniu skulpturu musiejus. See http://grutoparkas.lt/en_US/outdoor-exposure/ (accessed 25 October 2016).

Pavlenko, A. (2008) Multilingualism in post-Soviet countries: Language revival, language removal, and sociolinguistic theory. *International Journal of Bilingual Education and Bilingualism,* 11 (3/4), 275–313.

Pavlenko, A. (2009) Language conflict in post-Soviet linguistic landscapes. *Journal of Slavic Linguistics* 17 (1/2), 247–274.

Pavlenko, A. (2010) Linguistic landscape of Kyiv, Ukraine: A diachronic study. In E. Shohamy, E. Ben Rafael and M. Barni (eds) *Linguistic Landscape in the City* (pp. 133–150). Bristol: Multilingual Matters.

Pavlenko, A. (2011) Language rights versus speakers' rights: On the applicability of Western language rights approaches in Eastern European contexts. *Language Policy* 10 (1), 37–58.

Photos of old Vilnius. See http://www.etoretro.ru (accessed 12 October 2016).

Piotrowski, T. (1997) *Poland's Holocaust.* Jefferson: McFarland & Company.

Remnev, A. (2011) Colonisation and 'Russification' in the imperial geography of Asiatic Russia: From the nineteenth to the early twentieth centuries. In U. Tomohiko (ed.) *Asiatic Russia: Imperial Power in Regional and International Contexts* (pp. 102–128). Abingdon: Routledge.

Riegl, M.V. and Vaško, T. (2007) Comparison of language policies in the post-Soviet union countries on the European continent. *Annual of Language and Politics of Identity* 2 (1), 33–45.

Snyder, T. (1995) National myths and international relations: Poland and Lithuania, 1989–1994. *East European Politics and Societies* 9 (2), 317–343.

Snyder, T. (1996) Memory of sovereignty and sovereignty over memory: Poland. *Lithuanian and Ukraine, 1939–1999.* See http://www.chtyvo.org.ua (accessed 26 October 2016).

Snyder, T. (2003) *The Reconstruction of Nations, Poland, Ukraine, Lithuania, Belarus 1569–1999.* New Haven: Yale University Press.

Spolsky, B. (2002) Language policy, practice and ideology. In E. Ben-Rafael (ed.) *Identity, Culture and Globalisation* (pp. 319–325). Paris: The International Institute of Sociology.

Stražas, A. (1996) Lithuania 1863–1893: Tsarist Russification and the beginning of the modern Lithuanian national movement. See http://www.lituanus.org/1996/96_3_03.htm (accessed 26 October 2016).

Suziedelis, S. (2011) *Historical Dictionary of Lithuania.* Lanham: Scarecrow Press.

Tada ir Dabar (2003) See http://antraspasaulinis.net (accessed 26 October 2016).

Thaden, E. (1981) *Russification in the Baltic Provinces and Finland, 1855–1914.* Princeton: Princeton University Press.

Venckus, D. (2013) A one way ticket to the revolution. See http://www.daivavenckus.com (accessed 11 October 2016).

Vilno in 1870s (2014) See http://humus.livejournal.com (accessed 6 October 2016).

Virtual Exhibition Soviet Culture. Office of the Chief Archivist of Lithuania. See http://www.archyvai.lt (accessed 6 October 2016).

Weeks, T. (2004) *From 'Russian' to 'Polish': Vilna-Wilno 1900–1925.* Washington: The National Council for Eurasian and East European Research.

Weeks, T. (2008) Remembering and forgetting: Creating a Soviet Lithuanian capital. Vilnius, 1944–1949. *Journal of Baltic Studies* 39 (4), 517–133.

Weeks, T. (2010) Russification/Sovietization. See http://www.ieg-ego.en/weeks-2010-en (accessed 2 October 2016).

Weeks, T. (2015) *Vilnius between Nations 1795–2000*. Northern Illinois University: Northern Illinois University Press.

Zabrodskaja, A. (2014) Tallinn: Monolingual from above and multilingual from below. *International Journal of the Sociology of Language* (228), 113–129.

Zamascikov, S. (2007) Soviet methods and instrumentalities of maintaining control over the Balts. *Journal of Baltic Studies* 18 (3), 221–234.

Zinkevičius, Z. (1998) *The History of the Lithuanina Language*. Vilnius: Mokslo ir Enciklopediju Leidybos Institutas.

Демоскоп (Demoscope) See http://www.demoscope.ru (accessed 10 October 2016).

Синочкина, Б. (2008) *Литва*. Vilnius: Artlora.

СССР, Ц. С. (1980) *Вестник статистики*. Москва: Гостстатиздат.

Комитет по статистике СССР, U.S. (1991) *Население СССР: По данным Всесоюзной переписи населения 1989*. Москва: Финансы и статистика. (USSR State Statistics Committee).

12 Attitudes towards Visual Multilingualism in the Linguistic Landscape of the Ruhr Area

Evelyn Ziegler, Ulrich Schmitz and Haci-Halil Uslucan

This chapter presents findings from an interdisciplinary research project, *Signs of the Metropolises: Visual Multilingualism in the Ruhr Area/Germany*, which investigates the occurrence, regional distribution, function, production and perception of visual multilingualism in representative neighbourhoods of the cities of Essen, Dortmund, Bochum and Duisburg. In a multifaceted research design using a mixed-method approach that combines data on visual multilingualism with urban socio-logical data and metalinguistic data on language attitudes (collected via semi-standardised on-site interviews and multilingual telephone interviews), the research project addresses the following questions: Does the diversity of languages reflect the diversity of the urban population, that is, the settlement pattern of ethnic groups in the Ruhr Area characterised by a north-south divide? Does the perception of visual multilingualism mirror the north-south divide? What are the dominant patterns of argumentation used by informants with and without a migration background in favour of and against visual multilingualism? How are the languages and varieties perceived and evaluated by majority and minority groups?

12.1 Introduction: Project Design and Research Objectives

The following observations take as their basis an understanding of the linguistic landscape (LL) as described by Shohamy and Gorter (2009: 4), which comprises much more than a mere description and stocktaking of the various ways in which visual multilingualism in the public space is expressed and disseminated:

> it [= LL] contextualizes the public space within issues of identity and language policy of nations, political and social conflicts. It posits that LL is a broader concept than documentation of signs; it incorporates multimodal theories to include also sounds, images, and graffiti.

Characteristic of this approach is not only the very broad understanding of what constitutes potential subject matter for LL research, but also its endeavour to achieve a deeper understanding of the subject matter by emphasising the importance of the relationship between analysis and contextualisation (sociosymbolically and sociopolitically). The recently established journal *Linguistic Landscape* (published by John Benjamins), provides this approach with a platform for extended and more detailed research, particularly regarding the significance, perception and evaluation of multilingualism. As the online introduction to the journal states:

> In this day and age languages surround us everywhere; languages appear in flashy advertisements and commercials, names of buildings, streets and shops, instructions and warning signs, graffiti and cyber space. The dynamic field of LL attempts to understand the motives, uses, ideologies, language varieties and contestations of multiple forms of 'languages' as they are displayed in public spaces.[1]

The following observations pay heed to this inclusive understanding of potential subject matter. They reflect an LL that considers graffiti a legitimate focus and that does not refer solely to 'external' multilingualism, that is, the coexistence of several languages, but also to 'internal' multilingualism, that is, varieties of one language (Wandruszka, 1975: 326f.). In keeping with this concept, variety-specific forms of expression (in particular with regional, youth and colloquial linguistic features) are included in order to present a comprehensive picture of the forms of linguistic expression that create a specific LL, and to determine how they stand in relation to one another, both quantitatively and qualitatively.

This chapter will focus on findings obtained in the research project *Signs of the Metropolises: Visual Multilingualism in the Ruhr Area*.[2] The *Signs of the Metropolises* project is a cooperative project that brings together linguists, urban sociologists and integration researchers with a social-psychological focus. By working across disciplinary boundaries, we aim to gain a better understanding of the specific shaping of the Ruhr Area's LL in its spatial, social and ideological contexts.

The Ruhr Area is a metropolitan region in North Rhine-Westphalia, Germany, with approximately 5.3 million inhabitants. As one of Germany's major migrant regions, its history of migration goes back to the 19th century. The development of coal mining and the steel and iron industries increased the demand for workers, which resulted in several waves of labour migration (cf. Friedrichs, 1996: 133–172):

(1) The first wave of labour migration, from 1871 to 1914, brought migrants largely from the east of the German Reich and Poland.
(2) In the second wave of labour migration, beginning in the late 1950s and ending in 1973 with the 'recruitment ban' (*Anwerbestopp*), migrants, known then as 'guest workers' (*Gastarbeiter*), came predominantly from southern European countries such as Italy, Greece, Turkey, Yugoslavia, Spain and Portugal.
(3) A third wave of migration began in the late 1980s with (a) the arrival of ethnic German immigrants (*Aussiedler*) from Eastern Europe, that is, Poland and the former USSR, and (b) a growing number of asylum seekers.

During the last 10 years, the Ruhr Area has seen an increase in poverty-driven migration from Bulgaria and Romania and a large influx of refugees from Syria. In sum, these migration waves have resulted in 'super diverse'[3] cities and neighbourhoods (Vertovec, 2007) and particular settlement patterns. These settlement patterns have led to residential segregation, 'meaning the degree of unequal distribution of the resident population over the territory of a city in terms of social status characteristics (social status of residential areas), of family forms and life styles (family status), and in terms of the ratio of Germans to immigrants' (Strohmeier & Bader, 2004[4]). A key feature of residential segregation in the Ruhr Area is the north-south divide along the A40 motorway, the so-called 'social equator', which divides the cities into ethnically diverse and less diverse, poor and less poor, educated and less educated (Kersting *et al.*, 2009).

The research design of the *Signs of the Metropolises* project pays attention to these spatial and social characteristics of the Ruhr Area by investigating from a multidisciplinary perspective the connection between cultural and ethnic diversity, patterns of settlement and visual multilingualism. To examine the specific shaping of the LL in the Ruhr Area systematically, a cross-sectional study was undertaken in the cities of Duisburg, Essen, Bochum and Dortmund. In order to collect comparable data, two neighbourhoods were chosen in each city along the A40 'social equator'. The following neighbourhoods were selected:

- one urban neighbourhood each north of the A40 with a high concentration of non-German residents and an ethnically heterogeneous background (Duisburg: Marxloh; Essen: Altendorf; Bochum: Hamme; Dortmund: Nordstadt); and
- one urban neighbourhood each south of the A40 with a medium concentration of non-German residents and an ethnically more homogeneous background (Duisburg: Dellviertel; Essen: Rüttenscheid; Bochum: Langendreer; Dortmund: Hörde).

These neighbourhoods were also selected on the basis of their amalgamation of residential areas with trade and commerce. The final selection criterion was the inclusion of the following infrastructural units: main station, citizen advice centre, one day-care centre per neighbourhood and one cultural institution per city.

The project focuses on internal and external forms of visual multilingualism and asks how the occurrence of regional varieties and minority and majority languages in the Ruhr Area shapes and distinguishes public spaces. In a multifaceted research design using a mixed-method approach that combines data on visual multilingualism with urban sociological data and metalinguistic data on language attitudes (collected in semi-standardised on-site interviews and multilingual telephone interviews) and that allows for both extensive and precise insights, the project addresses the following issues:

- Does the diversity of languages reflect the diversity of urban population, i.e. the settlement pattern of ethnic groups in the Ruhr Area?
- What are the functions assigned to visual multilingualism with respect to type of discourse (commercial, transgressive, infrastructural, regulatory, artistic, commemorative)?
- Does the perception of visual multilingualism mirror the north-south divide?
- What are the dominant patterns of argumentation used by informants with and without a migration background in favour of and against visual multilingualism?
- How are the languages and varieties perceived and evaluated by majority and minority groups?

The following hypothesis is generated from the questions above:

> Informants living in the neighbourhoods north of the A40 perceive visual multilingualism not only more often, but also express a more positive attitude towards it owing to their higher amount of exposure to visual multilingualism.

12.2 Occurrence and Distribution of Visual Multilingualism in the Ruhr Area

Androutsopoulos (2014: 84) states: 'LL data collection is typically carried out in a vast urban environment that cannot be surveyed exhaustively'. This, however, is exactly what we attempted, by limiting ourselves to few well-defined areas typical of the whole Ruhr region.

The eight above-mentioned urban neighbourhoods in the four biggest cities in the Ruhr region were selected according to population sociological criteria. These precisely defined areas were fully documented; each individual sign ($N = 23{,}195$) in the public space was photographed. In addition, in each of these cities the linguistic and semiotic landscapes (again, outdoor only) were completely photographed at a central station, a tourist attraction, a citizen's office and two children's day-care centres ($N = 2{,}309$). All areas together amount to a total area of more than half a square kilometre.

This extremely large corpus of 25,504 geocoded digital photographs, taken from September 2012 to December 2013 in the cities of Duisburg, Essen, Bochum and Dortmund, forms the basis of the *Signs of the Metropolises Database*. The photographs stored in the online database are linked to a map of the Ruhr Area to show the distribution and density of visual multilingualism. The image database also provides metadata for the following categories according to Scollon and Scollon (2003) and Backhaus (2007): choice of language/variety, type of discourse (e.g. commercial, regulatory, transgressive, commemorative), type of name (e.g. institution, shop, gastronomy, toponym), information management (e.g. complete, partial, extended), appearance, typography (e.g. Antiqua, Grotesque, Fraktur, handwritten) and size. This tagging system allows complex search strategies to analyse sociolinguistic and geographical aspects of visual multilingualism.

Table 12.1 shows which languages are the most visible in the Ruhr Area.

Of all language occurrences in our material, 90.4% were distributed among three languages: German (66%), English (20%) and Turkish (4%). Together, French, Italian and Spanish accounted for another 4% of all texts. All other languages accounted for considerably less than 1% each. Likewise, signs, stickers and posters that were written in colloquial or regional rather than standard German accounted for less than 1% and have been grouped together under the heading 'non-standard'.

The occurrence of visual multilingualism in the Ruhr Area was then analysed to ascertain to what extent it demonstrated a north-south divide along the A40 'social equator', that is, whether in the neighbourhoods north of the A40 with greater ethnic diversity, languages other than German, in particular migrant languages, occur more frequently than in the neighbourhoods south of the A40. In the four northern

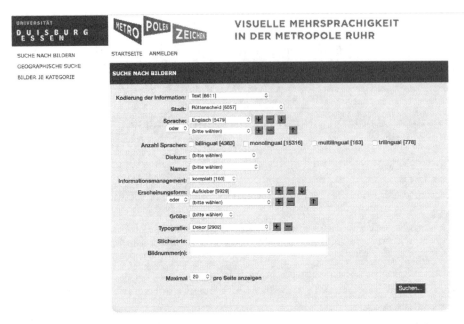

Figure 12.1 Screenshot of the *Signs of the Metropolises Database and tagging categories*

Table 12.1 Percentage of visible languages in the Ruhr Area ($N = 27,265^5$)

Language	Frequency	%
1 German	18,053	66.2
2 English	5483	20.1
3 Turkish	1122	4.1
4 French	429	1.6
5 Italian	379	1.4
6 Spanish	286	1.0
7 Arabic	185	0.7
8 Latin	157	0.6
9 Polish	143	0.5
10 Non-standard	111	0.4
11 Dutch	100	0.4
12 Chinese	77	0.3
13 Japanese	76	0.3
14 Russian	64	0.2
15 Greek	53	0.2

districts, there are less monolingual (53.4% vs. 57.7%), less monolingual German (44.3% vs. 49.3%) and slightly less monolingual English (0.6% vs. 0.7%) texts than in the southern districts, but more monolingual Turkish texts (2.3% vs. 0.2%). In the north, German (64.1% vs. 67.1%), English (18.1% vs. 20.5%), French, Italian and Spanish (together 2.7% vs. 4.9%) are less frequent than in the south; in the case of Turkish again, it is the other way around (9.1% vs. 1.6%). Young migrant languages are more strongly represented in the north, English and other Western European languages in the south.

Figure 12.2 shows the distribution of the ten most common languages in the representative neighbourhoods.

As the coloured circles of various sizes indicate, the hypothesis is generally borne out that greater population diversity is reflected in greater language diversity. The map in Figure 12.2 also shows that German, English and Turkish are the three most visible languages in the Ruhr Area, with German appearing less often in Duisburg-Marxloh, Essen-Altendorf and Dortmund-Nordstadt than in Bochum-Hamme. For migrant languages, the quantitative analysis (c.f. Schmitz, 2017) demonstrates that in Duisburg-Marxloh, Turkish at 25.9% is the most common. A reason for this high percentage refers to the fact that just under 45% of non-Germans in Duisburg-Marxloh are Turkish citizens, and therefore there is a strong Turkish influence in the neighbourhood. Another special feature of Duisburg-Marxloh is that the shops

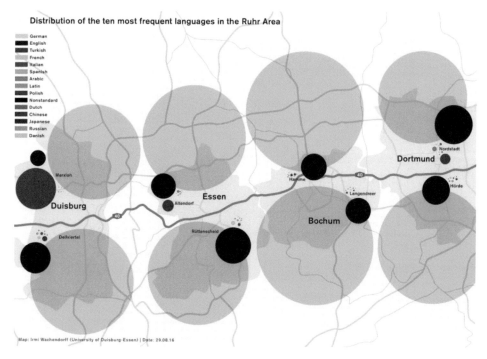

Figure 12.2 Distribution of visual multilingualism in the Ruhr Area[6]

specialise in Turkish bridal fashion, which attracts customers from far beyond the city and North Rhine-Westphalia. In Essen-Altendorf and Dortmund-Nordstadt, the number of Turkish inhabitants is just under 7%, which is still considerably higher than in Duisburg-Dellviertel (3.2%), Bochum-Langendreer (0.9%) and Dortmund-Hörde (0.9%), all of which are located to the south of the A 40. With 183 examples, Arabic is the seventh most frequent language (see Table 12.1) and is particularly visible in Essen-Altendorf and Dortmund-Nordstadt. This can be explained by settlement patterns. Residents of Iraqi nationality represent the fourth largest migrant community in Essen-Altendorf. Similarly, in Dortmund-Nordstadt many residents are Iraqi, Moroccan or Lebanese nationals.

The quantitative measurement of the relationship between language diversity and population diversity[7] draws on data provided by the statistical offices of Duisburg, Essen, Bochum and Dortmund for the eight representative neighbourhoods (using data available on 31 December 2013). The calculation is based on the Simpson diversity index (Simpson, 1949), cf. Figure 12.3.

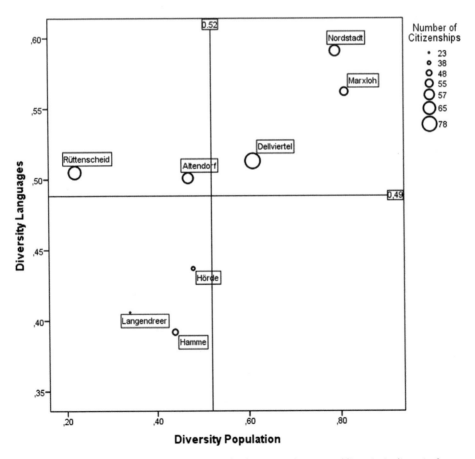

Figure 12.3 Relationship between diversity of urban population and linguistic diversity[8]

Figure 12.3 reveals three types of relationship:

- Dortmund-Nordstadt and Duisburg-Marxloh have a high level of population diversity and visible multilingualism.
- Essen-Altendorf and Duisburg-Dellviertel have a medium level of population diversity and visible multilingualism.
- Dortmund-Hörde, Bochum-Langendreer and Bochum-Hamme have a lower than average level of population diversity and visible multilingualism.

Figure 12.3 also shows that Essen-Rüttenscheid has a special status in that there is a high level of visible multilingualism although population diversity is low. This can be explained by the fact that Essen-Rüttenscheid is a gastronomic and retail magnet for the rest of the city – unlike the other neighbourhoods in our study.

The next step was to analyse in which types of discourse, that is communicative relationships, visible multilingualism in the public space is used. For this purpose, discourse types were categorised as follows (c.f. Backhaus, 2007; Scollon & Scollon, 2003): infrastructural, regulatory, commercial, transgressive and commemorative. The infrastructural category includes street signs, signs of institutional opening times (e.g. kindergartens, museums, churches, libraries), and written information on ticket machines and timetables (Figure 12.4). At 6.2% they constitute a relatively small proportion of all texts in the public space. The regulatory category applies to all signs that regulate activity in the public space, e.g. traffic signs, prohibitive signs and warnings (Figure 12.5). These account for 4.9% of all examples. The commercial type of discourse includes all forms of shop signs, advertising, and signs denoting companies, workshops and businesses etc. (Figure 12.6). This discourse category is the largest at 49%. The transgressive category (Scollon & Scollon, 2003: 149ff.) includes graffiti, tags, stickers and posters that have been sprayed, drawn or stuck

Figure 12.4 Infrastructural discourse type
Source: Essen-Rüttenscheid, Picture No. 353)

Figure 12.5 Regulatory discourse type
Source: Bochum Main Station, Picture No. 5968

Figure 12.6 Commercial discourse type
Source: Dortmund-Nordstadt, Picture No. 4094

without authorisation and illegally onto the walls of buildings, streetlights and electrical enclosures (Figure 12.7). This transgressive category of discourse makes up 38.9% of the total, making it the second largest category. Artistic signs, that is, examples that can obviously be identified as works of art (0.3%) and commemorative signs (0.1%) – including commemorative and memorial plaques – constitute the smallest group (Figures 12.8 and 12.9).

Figure 12.7 Transgressive discourse type
Source: Dortmund-Nordstadt, Picture No. 8911[9]

Figure 12.8 Artistic discourse type
Source: Dortmund-Hörde, Picture No. 2716

With regard to language choices on official signs, that is, infrastructural and regulatory, 90% of the 2,745 photos in our data are monolingual German. Only 7.7% of the official signs are bilingual. All bilingual signs include German; 89.3% of them are combined with English, followed by the language combinations German-Turkish (3.7%), German-French (2.1%) and German-Arabic (1.1%). All official trilingual signs also always include German. The most common combination in the total of 43 examples of trilingual official signs in the corpus (1.8%) is

Figure 12.9 Commemorative discourse type
Source: Dortmund-Nordstadt, Picture No. 1676

German-English-French. Most of these signs are in main stations, where this language combination is the rule (cf. Figures 12.10 and 12.11).

The rarer language combination German-Turkish-Russian is found on a garbage can reserved for paper and cardboard (Figure 12.12).

Only 0.5% of official signs exhibited four or more languages. All these signs include German and English combined with French (6x), Turkish (5x), Italian (4x), Polish (4x), Dutch (3x), Russian (2x) or Spanish (1x).

Figure 12.10 Essen main station (Picture No. 20751)

Figure 12.11 Duisburg main station (Picture No. 12128)

Table 12.2 shows the overall frequency of languages on official signs and demonstrates that English and French are the most common foreign languages.

What about language choice on commercial signs? 12,563 photos were analysed. In contrast to the official signs, only 71% of signs in the commercial category are monolingual, of which 91% are monolingual German. The dominating languages in the other 9% are English, Turkish, French, Italian and Arabic. The range of languages on commercial signs is far greater than on official signs. In total, 2991 (24%)

Figure 12.12 Bochum-Langendreer (Picture No. 5005)

Table 12.2 Frequency of languages on official signs

Language	Frequency	%[10]
German	2471	99.8
English	217	8.7
French	45	1.8
Turkish	14	0.5
Italian	8	0.3
Dutch	6	0.2
Russian	5	0.2
Other[11]	17	0.6

of commercial signs are bilingual. The most frequently combined languages on bilingual signs were as follows: 2865 signs are combined with German, 1714 with English, 506 with Turkish, 146 with Italian, 119 with French, 93 with Arabic, 89 with Latin, 77 with Polish, 61 with Spanish and 34 signs with Dutch.

This leads to the conclusion that the most common language after German on official and commercial signs is English. In the commercial category, the range of languages is – as expected – wider than in the official category. Turkish is the most frequently used migrant language, followed by Italian and Arabic.

12.3 Perception and Evaluation of Visual Multilingualism in the Ruhr Area

The study of attitudes towards languages and varieties has a long history in social dialectology and sociolinguistics (cf. Garrett *et al.*, 2003; Vandermeeren, 2005) as attitudes are considered relevant for questions of language use (choice of variants, varieties, languages), the willingness to learn new languages and the allocation of varieties/languages to communicative domains. It therefore comes as a surprise that studies on language attitudes are rather seldom in LL research. This applies especially to studies that pursue an integrated approach combining image data and data on LL attitudes as additional data. The few studies on the subject of LL attitudes are devoted to issues of perceptions of the vitality of languages (Gilinger *et al.*, 2012; Landry & Bourhis, 1997), evaluations of linguistic competencies of LL sign producers (Collins & Slembrouck, 2007) or judgements concerning the pragmatic, symbolic, aesthetic or economic value of languages on signs (Aiestaran *et al.*, 2010; Garvin, 2010; Trumper-Hecht, 2010). The preferred methods range from using questionnaires (Landry & Bourhis, 1997) via drawing of maps (Lou, 2010) to using a 'postmodern walking tour interview' (Garvin, 2010: 255) or Google Street View (Malinowski, 2010) to elicit responses. Most of these studies are restricted to qualitative approaches based on rather small sets of data.

As LL attitudes are a complex matter, the present study combines qualitative and quantitative methods to gain a deeper insight and to produce more reliable results. In a first step on-site interviews were conducted to explore how visual multilingualism is perceived and to examine the ways in which visual multilingualism is advocated for or critiqued. The on-site interviews were conducted with passers-by in the selected neighbourhoods of the cities of Duisburg, Essen, Bochum and Dortmund. In a second step and based on the results obtained from the on-site interview analysis, computer-assisted telephone interviews were conducted to reach a higher number of informants and to obtain reliable and robust results.

12.3.1 On-site interviews

Taking recent conversation-oriented developments in attitude studies into account (cf. König, 2014; Liebscher & Dailey-O'Cain, 2009; Tophinke & Ziegler, 2006, 2014), we have adopted an interactional approach to attitudes to investigate more closely how visual multilingualism is perceived and evaluated. One important advantage of the interactional approach is that it allows the elicitation of spontaneous cognitive, affective and conative[12] stances towards LL. For that reason, on-site interviews were carried out in a conversational manner in the streets of the selected neighbourhoods, providing maximum closeness to the subject matter. Potential informants were approached personally to encourage them to join the project. The interviews were structured, but they also allowed for flexibility and spontaneous adaption to the informants' responses. The following topics were covered in the interview guide: (a) general awareness and perception of community languages in the selected neighbourhoods; (b) knowledge of the neighbourhood's history and ideas for future developments; (c) evaluation of community languages; (d) relation between the visibility of languages and the social/ethnic makeup of neighbourhood residents; and (e) advantages and disadvantages, benefits and costs of visual multilingualism.

The data comprises 120 interviews,[13] that is, 15 interviews in each neighbourhood carried out mainly in German but also in migrant languages such as Turkish. The interviews vary in between 3 and 12 minutes. The interviews were conducted with 65 men and 55 women between 18 and 80 years of age. The informants had different ethnic backgrounds: 71 informants had a migration background and 49 informants had no migration background. All interviews were recorded and the sound files entered in a database for computer assisted transcription[14] and annotation to allow quantitative and qualitative analyses.

The analysis combines linguistic aspects such as patterns of argumentation, linguistic strategies, metaphors, attributions and sociolinguistic variables including ethnic group, age and gender. The results show that 73% of all informants said that they perceive visual multilingualism. A closer examination reveals that there is a clear difference between the informants interviewed in neighbourhoods north and neighbourhoods south of the A40 concerning general perceptions (see Table 12.3).

Table 12.3 Perception of visual multilingualism in the investigated neighbourhoods

Neighbourhoods north of the A40	Neighbourhoods south of the A40
Duisburg-Marxloh 100%	Duisburg-Dellviertel 60%
Essen-Altendorf 80%	Essen-Rüttenscheid 53%
Bochum-Hamme 87%	Bochum-Langendreer 47%
Dortmund-Nordstadt 93%	Dortmund-Hörde 67%

The figures show that informants living in neighbourhoods north of the A40 motorway more often perceive visual multilingualism than those living in neighbourhoods south of the A40. This result mirrors the north-south divide concerning the ethnic makeup of the investigated neighbourhoods and the distribution of visual multilingualism in the Ruhr Area (see Figure 12.2 above).

Table 12.4 shows which languages are perceived most often. The overall results reveal that Turkish is by far the most commonly perceived language, followed by English, Arabic, Italian, Russian, French and Polish (to name the languages mentioned most frequently). The discrepancy between the perceived and the factual occurrence of Turkish (4.1%), English (20.1%) and Arabic (0.7%) in the LL of the Ruhr Area (see above Table 12.1) calls for explanation. It seems that non-European languages such as Turkish and Arabic attract more attention and are thus more often mentioned than European languages such as English and French.

Our next step was to ascertain what languages are most often perceived in the investigated neighbourhoods. The results are presented in the following pie charts (see Figures 12.13 and 12.14).

The pie charts in Figures 12.13 and 12.14 reveal that in the northern neighbourhoods, more informants stated that Turkish is the language they most often perceive, followed by Arabic, English, Romanian, Polish, Chinese, Bulgarian and Spanish. In the southern neighbourhoods the informants also stated that Turkish

Table 12.4 Languages most frequently perceived

Language	Frequency
Turkish	87
English	44
Arabic	32
Italian	16
Russian	10
French	8
Polish	8
Chinese	7
Bulgarian	5
Romanian	5
Spanish	5
Kurdish	4
Greek	3
Dutch	2
Tamil	2
Macedonian	2
Other	10

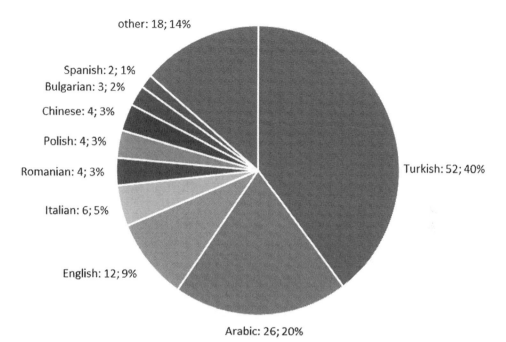

Figure 12.13 Languages most frequently perceived in the neighbourhoods north of the A40

is the language they most often perceive (but to a lesser degree), followed by English, Italian, French, Chinese, Russian, Arabic, Polish and Spanish. From this we can conclude that the north-south divide is not only central to the explanation of the occurrence of visual multilingualism in the investigated neighbourhoods, but also the key to an explanation of the differences in the perception of visual multilingualism.

When asked if multilingual signs at official institutions are a good idea, 63% of the informants agreed, 26% disagreed and 11% were undecided or did not care. A closer examination, however, reveals that informants living in the neighbourhoods north of the A40 agree more often (73%) than those living in the southern neighbourhoods (53%), where the diversity index is lower. Again, the north-south divide has an impact on the informants' responses and offers an explanation for the differences in the response behaviour of the informants.

As a next step, we examined the arguments (Niedzielski & Preston, 1999) used for and against visual multilingualism. Analysing the data in this way, we were able to group the arguments into more abstract patterns such as pragmatic argument, argument based on self-reference, feeling-at-home argument and facticity argument.

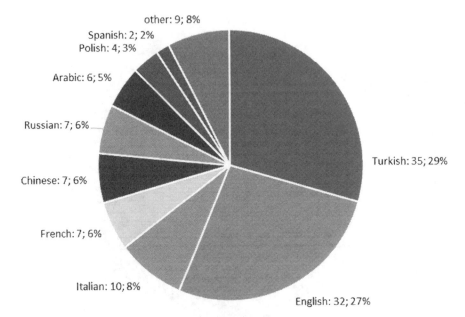

SOUTH
Perception of multilingual signs

other: 9; 8%
Spanish: 2; 2%
Polish: 4; 3%
Arabic: 6; 5%
Russian: 7; 6%
Chinese: 7; 6%
French: 7; 6%
Italian: 10; 8%
English: 32; 27%
Turkish: 35; 29%

Figure 12.14 Languages most frequently perceived in the neighbourhoods south of the A40

These are the most frequent patterns of argumentation occurring in the interviews. They can be defined as follows:

- *Pragmatic argument*: Pragmatic argumentation involves the strategy of pointing out consequences and aims, that is, the uses and functions of visual multilingualism. Central to this argumentation is the concern with orientation and barrier-free communication of public-order rules and regulations.
- *Argument based on self-reference*: This type of argumentation is based on a comparison with one's own experiences regarding visual multilingualism, for example, in a foreign country. This argumentation may be based on individual self-reference (e.g. 'I') or collective self-reference (e.g. 'we') to either refer to social groups of which the informant is a member or to increase the plausibility of the attitude expressed.
- *Feeling-at-home argument*: This type of argumentation is based on expressions of emotional involvement with a certain neighbourhood, city or region. The feeling-at-home argument indicates a relationship between place and identity by ascribing affective meaning to places.
- *Facticity argument*: This type of argumentation is based on statements that give no reasons for a certain standpoint but state mere facts or present issues and things as given. As a consequence, explicit evaluations are avoided.

- *Integration argument*: This type of argumentation is based on statements that regard visual multilingualism as an obstacle, that is, as something that hinders the process of integration, especially of linguistic integration, or as something that fosters integration.
- *Normative argument:* This type of argumentation is based on statements that refer to social norms of linguistic behaviour in given situations expected of a person or a social/ethnic group. The normative character is often expressed with the German modal verbs '*sollen*' and '*müssen*'.

The analysis of the on-site interviews reveals that informants without a migration background ($N = 71$) generally argued in favour of visual multilingualism. The types of argument listed above were deployed in the order shown in Table 12.5.

Table 12.5 shows that the most common argumentation pattern to justify a positive attitude towards visual multilingualism is pragmatic. It was often used, for example, when informants were asked if multilingual signs at official institutions such as citizen advice centres and hospitals are a good idea (see the following transcript excerpts).

Table 12.5 Frequency of patterns of argumentation in favour of visual multilingualism used by informants without a migration background[15]

Pattern of argumentation	Percentage	Frequency
Pragmatic argument	65	81
Argument based on self-reference	8	10
Facticity argument	7	9
Feeling-at-home argument	3	3

Example 12.1

das (.) find ich ganz gut (–)| ja (0.5)| ja für leute die jetzt neu nach deutschland gekommen sind| dann können die sich **vielleicht besser** (–) **orientieren** (0.6)| (DoHoe10)

English translation

I find that quite good…yes…yes… for people that have just come to Germany… then they might **be able to find their way around better**

Example 12.2

würde ja schon **barrierefreiheiten** ein bisschen ermöglichen| gerade für ausländische mitbürger vielleicht (BoLan4)

English translation

That would **help a bit with breaking down barriers** – especially for foreign residents perhaps

Informants with no migration background recognise the need for orientation and information to help migrants operate in the public space. At the same time, this act of recognition also implies an acknowledgement of the visibility of the Other, in this case the migrants. (cf. Honneth, 2003). This does not mean, however, that acknowledgement of the visibility of migrants has already become a conscious focal point of the acknowledger (i.e. the informants without a migration background).

Many informants in favour of visual multilingualism argue on the grounds of their own experiences (real or fictitious) to strengthen their argumentation. Linguistic indicators of this pattern of argumentation are self-references such as 'I' (see the following excerpts):

Example 12.3

wenn **ich** in einem fremden land bin| bin **ich** auch immer froh| wenn **ich** irgendwo (.) schilder (.) in meiner sprache sehe| oder in einer die **ich** verstehe| (DoNor4)

English translation

when I am in a foreign country – I am always glad when I see somewhere signs in **my** own language or a language that I understand

Example 12.4

wenn **ich** jetzt zum beispiel in ein fremdes land gehe| und **ich** versuche mir da irgendwie eine existenz aufzubauen| wäre **ich** schon ganz froh| wenn **ich** mich so mit öffentlichen behördengängen| so ein bisschen weiter behelfen kann| indem **ich** das auch einfach lesen könnte (BoHam11)

English translation

if for example I go to a foreign country and try to build some sort of life for myself there – I would be really happy if I had that kind of advantage when I had to go through the bureaucracy by just getting a chance to read that too

The informants thereby put themselves in the situation of being *in a foreign country themselves* and unable to understand the local language. They reinforce their positive attitude by saying that they too would be *happy* if they found signs in their own language. This pattern of argumentation, which is based on self-reference, can be interpreted as a way of recognising the language needs of migrants. Such recognition implies that informants without a migration background are able to identify with migrants. Hence, this act of identification in an *as-if* mode is the condition for recognising the need of others for acknowledgement (Honneth, 1995).

A further frequent argument in favour of multilingual signs is facticity, that is, the reference to the fact that there are many people living in Germany who do not speak German.

Example 12.5

ja gut ich mein wir haben jetzt auch sehr viele ausländische mitbürger| **die müssen ja auch sich irgendwie verständigen können** (–) (BoHam4)

English translation

Well yes – I mean we do have a lot of foreign citizens too now – **they have to be able to communicate somehow too**

Example 12.6

finde ich völlig in ordnung| (0.5) finde ich sinnvoll| (0.4) ja weil es einfach genug ähm (0.8) bürger gibt| **die ähm die eben nicht deutsch sprechen**| (DoHoe1)

English translation

I've got nothing against it – makes sense – yes because there are simply plenty of inhabitants **who just don't speak German**

Another, albeit less frequent, argument given by informants without a migration background is the feeling-at-home argument. Here, the public visibility of migrant languages is regarded as a symbol of belonging and, as the following excerpt shows, is perceived as a way of reconciling 'belonging and new home' (Uslucan, 2014).

Example 12.7

und ich finde das auch schön dass man irgendwo| auch wenn man in deutschland fuß fasst| und hier auch groß wird und (–)| sich hier verwirklicht trotzdem noch äh| (1.1)| **dieses gefühl für die heimat** hat| (BoHam11)

English translation

and I quite like it that if you gain a foothold somewhere like in Germany and growing up here – and if you do your own thing – and still have this feeling of homeliness.

What arguments do informants without a migration background use against visual multilingualism, and how frequently are argumentation patterns deployed? Table 12.6 summarises the analyses of the results.

Table 12.6 shows that the most frequent line of argument is the *normative* one in which language integration is seen as imperative for migrants. This type of argument was observed particularly frequently when informants without a migration background were asked about multilingual signs in public institutions, to which just over a quarter (25.7%) responded that they did not like multilingual signs in the

Table 12.6 Frequency of patterns of argumentation against visual multilingualism used by informants without a migration background

Pattern of argumentation	Percentage	Frequency
Normative argument	29	23
Pragmatic argument	23	18
Integration argument	12	9
Argument based on self-reference	9	7

context of stations, town halls, museums and kindergartens. They backed up their opinions with various arguments, but most frequently with the normative argument, as indicated linguistically by their use of the German modal '*sollen*' (should). They demanded that migrants 'should be able to speak German'. At times, this demand was also formulated as a condition for certain rights. See the following transcript excerpts:

Example 12.8

da halte ich eigentlich gar nichts von| ich denke **wenn man in deutschland lebt**| sollte man auch der deutschen sprache mächtig sein| (–) ne| (BoLan11)

English translation

I don't really agree with that – I think that **if you live in Germany** – you should be able to speak and understand German – no

Example 12.9

wir leben hier in deutschland| entweder lernen sie deutsch| auch lesen (—)| oder sie gehen wieder (0.8)| (BoLan14)

English translation

here we live in Germany – they should either learn German – also learn how to read – or go home again

Informants also used pragmatic arguments against multilingual signs in the context of public institutions, pointing out lack of space and confusion.

Example 12.10

äh irgendwo ist es ja auch ne (.) **ne platzfrage**| sie können sie können ja nicht da fünfzig sprachen dahinstellen und so weiter| (BoHam8)

English translation

well there's a **problem with space** too – you can't – you can't just go and put up fifty languages or so

Example 12.11

(1.1) also da **bisschen durcheinander**| (BoLan5)

English translation

well – **a bit confusing** there

The integration argument claims that multilingualism, particularly the use of migrant languages in the public space of the Ruhr Area, is an obstacle to successful integration. (Visual) multilingualism is thereby not seen as something positive but as something that gets in the way of people's willingness to learn the language of their host society and thereby inhibits integration.

Example 12.12

aber (–)| wenn man es ihnen jetzt so dermaßen vereinfacht| dass sie überall ihre sprache (vorfinden)| **dann würden die sich auch gar keine mühe machen diese sprache zu lernen|** (DoNor11)

English translation

but – if you make things so easy for them – that they (find) their own language everywhere – then **they're not going to make the effort to learn this language**

Example 12.13

äh (—)| bei mehrsprachiger beschilderung| ähm sehe ich das problem| **dass die leute nicht integrieren|** (EsAlt9)

English translation

em – multilingual signs – I see the problem **that people won't integrate**

As did the proponents of visible multilingualism, the opponents from the group of informants without a migration background also used the argument of their own experience, whether factual or potential. This is indicated linguistically by the switch from the 'I' to 'we'-perspective and the use of the first person pronoun (singular and plural), through which the informants refer to themselves, their social group or social majority. By using the modals *'müssen'* and *'sollen'* ('must' and 'should'), the informants formulate normative demands. They do not, however, address these demands to anyone concrete but to the indefinite German pronoun *'man'* (one/you).

Example 12.14

wenn wir wenn wir ins ausland gehen| dann haben **wir** auch nur die die sprache des landes| ähm (—) ähm (.) **müssen wir** damit zurecht kommen oder| also| (DoHoe15)

English translation

when we go abroad – then **we** only have the language of the country too – em – and **we have to** cope – don't we – so

Example 12.15

ich meine wenn **man** (0.4) aus dem ausland nach deutschland kommt| sollte **man** schon die äh sprache lernen| genau **wenn ich** nach frankreich gehen will| dann muss **ich** französisch lernen| wenn **ich** nach spanien gehen will| muss **ich** spanisch können| muss **ich** italienisch lernen| (DueDell11)

English translation

I mean if **you** come from abroad to Germany – then **you** should learn the language – just as **if I** want to go to France – then **I** have to learn French – if **I** go to Spain – **I** have to speak Spanish – **I** have to speak Italian

Only on rare occasions is the argument of belonging used to counter visual multilingualism. In this case, the informants refer to the opposite of 'feeling at home' by pointing out experience of alienation.

Example 12.16

ja da kommt man sich schon fast vor wie ((lacht)) **wenn man ausländer wäre**| ((lacht))| in anderer in einer in einer anderen welt| (DuDel1)

English translation

yes – sometimes you almost feel as if (laughs) **as if you are a foreigner** (laughs) – in another, another world

Example 12.17

aber andererseits (.)| fühlt man sich dann auch so ein bisschen wie so ein fremder im eigenen land ne| (BoLan11)

English translation

but on the other hand – you do feel a bit like a foreigner then in your own country

In the following, we will present the results of the interviews that we conducted with 49 informants with a migration background. The informants were allowed to choose the language of the interview. The advantage of this approach was that misunderstandings through language use were avoided and the informants were able to express their opinions and beliefs freely. Thirty-four interviews were conducted in German, 14 in Turkish and one in English.

What do the informants with a migration background think about visual multilingualism? Are they mostly in favour of it? What are the patterns of argumentation they use most often? Table 12.7 presents the frequencies and the hierarchy of the patterns of argumentation from the most frequent to the least frequent:

It is striking that informants with and without a migration background make use of the same patterns of argumentation to underpin their standpoint in favour of visual multilingualism, although the hierarchies of these patterns differ slightly. Table 12.7 reveals that the pragmatic argument is the most dominant pattern of argumentation used in both groups of informants to support positive attitudes towards visual multilingualism. As do informants without a migration background, the informants with a migration background point out concerns such as orientation (Example 12.18) and understanding, particularly with regard to the older generation (Example 12.19).

Table 12.7 Frequency of patterns of argumentation in favour of visual multilingualism used by informants with a migration background

Pattern of argumentation	Percentage	Frequency
Pragmatic argument	50%	58
Feeling-at-home-argument	17%	20
Argument based on self-reference	10%	11
Normative argument	3%	4

Example 12.18

das (.) find ich ganz gut (–)| ja (0.5)| ja für leute die jetzt neu nach deutschland gekommen sind| dann können die sich **vielleich besser** (–) **orientieren** (0.6)| (DoHoe10)

English translation

I find it good – yes for people who have just arrived in Germany – they'd maybe find it **easier to find their way around**

Example 12.19

türk ö almanca bilmeyenler için mesela| ((...)) bizim ihtiyarlar yani mesela bilmiyorlar almancayı (–) coğu|annelerimiz babalarımız bilmiyorlar| onlar için aslında çok iyi olur| (DueMar6)

English translation

Turkish is good for the people who can't speak German, for example our old folk often can't speak German for instance – my mother and father can't – it would be good for them

However, it is important to stress the fact that the second most frequent argument used by informants with a migration background is the *feeling-at-home argument*. From the perspective of recognition theory, this result can be explained by the feeling these informants have that the choice of their language means they are implicitly acknowledged and recognised in their individuality. In other words, they are recognised in their specific characteristic of not speaking German but a language other than German. This feeling of acknowledgement is, however, not conscious – indeed, a feeling of ill-ease is more likely when their language is not present – nor is the giver of this act of recognition consciously intending to do so (cf. Honneth, 2003: 10–27). This means that people subconsciously and implicitly feel their existence is being recognised through the visibility of their own mother tongue, and, on the other hand, that the person choosing to use that language is automatically acknowledging them.[16] Honneth regards this as the most elementary form of recognition. Another and more explicit facet of recognition is the experience of feeling at home, which is based on the informants' sense of recognition in their need for belonging. This is amplified when the informants resort to their mother tongue, that is, Turkish, in order to formulate their argument. This line of argument is further strengthened by the informants' frequent use of comparisons, that is, they link their experience of home to their country of origin, Turkey, and thus implicitly emphasise the tension between their old and new home.

Example 12.20

ne hissediyorum| (0.5) **türkiye gibi geliyor**| (DueMar15)

English translation

how I feel? – **as if I were in Turkey**

Example 12.21

şimdi türkçe gördüğüm bir sokakta| (0.7)| **kendimi türkiyede gibi hissediyorum|** (DoNor3)

English translation

when I see Turkish in the street **I feel as if I am in Turkey**

Example 12.22

kendimi daha iyi ifade edebildiğim için|galiba (.) ya da| kendimi| biraz| (.) böyle äm vatandan birşeyler| bulduğum için orda belki de|o yüzden| (DoNor6)

English translation

because I can express myself in Turkish better – or because I've found a bit of my home country – perhaps that's why

Example 12.23

ist ein schönes gefühl| so man sieht man| **ich äh fühle mich so wie in (-) äh meine heimat|** (BoLan5)

English translation

it's a nice feeling – so you see – **I feel as if I am at home**

The informants with a migration background also frequently use the argument based on self-reference. They highlight contexts that offer comparisons with their own experiences and – similar to the informants without a migration background – thus demonstrate that they identify with newly arrived migrants and recognise their needs (Example 12.24). A second context that is often referred to is the experience of being a foreigner in another country. Again, similar to the informants without a migration background, identification was expressed primarily in the *as-if mode*, which simultaneously emphasised that the informants themselves had successfully integrated in terms of language (Example 12.25).

Example 12.24

ja wie gesagt äh| es gibt auch äh leute|**wie ich** zum beispiel| am anfang (–) konnte **ich** gar gar kein deutsch sprechen| (EsRue1)

English translation

yes, as I said, there are people – **like me** for example – I couldn't speak any German at first

Example 12.25

ich bin ja auch froh wenn das äh| was weiß ich wenn **ich** irgendwo bin in frankreich| sagen wir mal dann steht das da auf englisch| (DueDel7)

English translation

I'm happy too when – when **I'm** somewhere in France or wherever – and then for example there's something written in English

Much more infrequent is the normative argument in favour of visual multilingualism. When it is used, the argument is either ex negativo, as in Example 12.26, or points out that multilingualism expands exposure to language in everyday situations (Example 12.27).

Example 12.26

yani hani almanyaysa sadece herşey almancadan| (—) gitmiyor| (EsAlt13)

English translation

just because we are in Germany doesn't mean that all the signs have to be in German

Example 12.27

bence normal insanları kısıtlamak bir fayda getirmez diye düşünüyorum| (DueMar10)

English translation

I think it's perfectly normal – what's the point of limiting people

What are the dominating arguments that informants with a migration background present when speaking out against visual multilingualism? The results are summarised in Table 12.8.

Table 12.8 Frequency of patterns of argumentation against visual multilingualism used by informants with a migration background

Pattern of argumentation	Percentage	Frequency
Normative argument	32	21
Pragmatic argument	23	15
Affective argument	14	9
Economic argument	9	6

A quantitative comparison with the attitudes expressed in favour of visual multilingualism reveals, however, that the majority of informants with a migration background advocate visual multilingualism in the public space – as do informants without a migration background (cf. Table 12.6). Table 12.6 also shows that, similar to informants without a migration background, the most common argument against visual multilingualism in the public space is normative, as can be seen in the following examples.

Example 12.28

halt wir leben in deutschland| so wie gesagt habe| (0.4) halt äh| **wir müssen uns ja hier anpassen**| (DueMar12)

English translation

well we're living in Germany – like I said – **we just have to learn to adapt**

Example 12.29

wer hier äh <<lachend> nach deutschland kommt> | (–) **dann soll er (.) deutsch können|** (DueDel15)

English translation

whoever (laughs) comes to Germany – **should be able to speak German**

The attitudes expressed highlight that linguistic integration is expected of migrants. The informants expressed the pressure to integrate by using the German modal verbs '*sollen*' and '*müssen*', which voice the different levels of necessity assigned to the subject at hand – here integration.

Although the informants with a migration background do present pragmatic arguments (Examples 12.29 and 12.30), their frequency is comparatively low, as is the frequency of the affective (Example 12.33) and economic (Example 12.34) arguments.

Example 12.30

erstmal finden (—)| da wo das steht| **man verliert die übersicht|** (BoLan15)

English translation

you first have to find what is where – **you get confused**

Example 12.30 refers only to the argument of the readability of multilingual signs. Example 12.31, however, combines the pragmatic with the affective argument:

Example 12.31

ähm (.) ja wenn das jetzt nur italienisch stehen würde (-)| **dann würde ich es ja nicht verstehen|** das würde mich **stören|** (EsRue9)

English translation

em – if that was only in Italian – then **I wouldn't understand it** – would I – that would **bother** me

This response goes beyond the pragmatic argument, and is based on two premises: (1) that only one language rather than German is being used; and (2) that this other language – here Italian – is not the language of the informant. In addition, the informant pronounces judgement on this situation, expressly using the German verb '*stören*', meaning 'to bother'.

The nature of an affective argument is to express subjective feelings. The following examples convey that not only the attitude towards languages is of concern but also always the attitude towards the speakers of the respective language. It becomes apparent that the relationship among migrant groups is not without tension and that there are problems running through the ethnic groups.

Example 12.32

finde ich unfair| die werden bevorzugt behandelt die türken (0.7)| (DueMar13)

English translation

I don't think it's fair – they get special treatment the Turks

Example 12.33

manya| (0.5)| almanyadayım hissediyorum|ama başka dilde gördüğüm zaman o zaman| (0.5)| kendimi yabancı hissediyorum|(—) äm| äm| rusca| äm| fransızca ingil| (DoNor3)

English translation

when I see a language other than German I feel like a stranger – a foreigner – Russian French English

The economic argument against visual multilingualism and the highlighting of costs occur very infrequently.

Example 12.34

die höheren betriebskosten| weil die faulen maler oder beschilderer da mehr zeit dann brauchen| ja um diese sachen da anzubringen| (BoHam15)

English translation

higher overheads – because the lazy painters or sign people then need more time to put these things up

Apart from being asked to evaluate multilingualism and give reasons for their opinions, informants were also asked which languages they thought should be present on institutional signs. The informants' responses are summarised in Table 12.9.

Table 12.9 shows that when a decision had to be made regarding which language should appear alongside German on signs in public institutions, 44% of informants chose English. The other most commonly cited languages are Turkish (20%), followed by French (15%) and Arabic (10%).

12.3.2 Telephone interviews

Alongside face-to-face interviews, telephone interviews were conducted with 1000 people over the age of 18, 500 of whom had no migration background (No MB), 300 of whom had a Turkish migration background (Tr MB) and 200 of whom had an Italian migration background (It MB). The cohort without a migration background had an average age of 59, with an Italian background around 56 years, and with a Turkish migration background just under 44 years. We asked the respondents to indicate their age with respect to six groups: 18–24 years; 25–34 years; 35–44 years; 45–54 years; 55–64 years and over 65 years; afterwards we classified them. Besides the onomastic access through an electronic telephone register, the respondents were asked to indicate their citizenship

Table 12.9 Preferred languages on signs

Language	Frequency	%
English	53	44.2
Turkish	43	35.8
French	18	15.0
Arabic	12	10.0
Spanish	8	6.7
Italian	7	5.8
Greek	5	4.2
Polish	5	4.2
Russian	5	4.2
Bulgarian	4	3.3
Chinese	3	2.5
Other	15	12.5

(Italian, Turkish etc.), their country of birth (Italy, Turkey) as well as the county of birth of their parents.

Table 12.10 shows the pattern that emerged when the cohort was divided according to gender.

Whereas in the groups without a migration background and with a Turkish migration background the majority of informants were female, in the Italian cohort males formed the majority. In the Italian group, 76% were born in Italy; 67% of the Turkish group were born in Turkey.

The questions for the telephone interview were trilingual and the informants were able to switch languages (e.g. from Italian into German) during the interview.

Acceptance: Not every language enjoys the same value and status, as pertinent studies in other parts of Germany have already demonstrated (Gärtig *et al.*, 2010). In view of this, we asked the informants to attach a value to various languages (Tables 12.11 and 12.12).

Table 12.10 Distribution of informants according to gender and origin (percentages in columns)

Gender		Origin			Total
		No MB	It MB	Tr MB	
Male	n	189	134	129	452
	%	37.5	63.5	42.4	44.4
Female	n	315	77	175	567
	%	62.5	36.5	57.6	55.6
Total	n	504	211	304	1019
	%	100	100	100	100

Table 12.11 Question C.6 Different languages enjoy different status. In your opinion, how valued are the following languages in Germany in general: very, quite, not very, not at all? (percentages in rows)

Language	Very	Quite	Not very	Not at all	Don't know	No comment	Mean value
Arabic	2.1	4.8	35.8	49.4	7.0	1.0	3.44
Chinese	6.1	16.0	33.1	34.5	8.7	1.6	3.07
German	93.4	3.4	0.6	0.5	1.0	1.1	1.06
English	85.6	9.9	1.5	0.5	1.8	0.8	1.15
French	48.2	30.0	13.5	3.9	3.1	1.2	1.72
Italian	35.2	33.0	19.8	7.3	3.5	1.2	1.99
Turkish	19.1	25.4	30.8	19.4	3.1	2.1	2.53

*Mean value on a scale of 1 = Very to 4 = Not at all; excluding 'Don't know' and 'No comment'. The higher the mean value, therefore, the lower the prestige.

It is apparent that after German, English enjoys very high status. The informants' mother tongue or language of origin is given approximately the same status as French (1.93 vs. 1.89) for the overall population. Although Polish migrants have historically shaped the Ruhr Area, Polish is not held in high regard. But the languages that are assigned the least value are Arabic and Chinese, both of which are also considered 'visually alien', since they are not written in Latin script.

It becomes clear, however, that when informants were asked to give their personal opinion, they attached considerably greater value to certain languages than they did when they were assessing overall attitudes in Germany. On an individual level, informants consider themselves more 'tolerant' towards foreign languages than the

Table 12.12 Question C.6.1 With regard to your own personal opinion, how highly do you regard the following languages? (percentages in rows)

Language	Very	Quite	Not very	Not at all	Don't know	No comment	Mean value
Arabic	24.2	13.7	22.4	34.5	4.0	1.1	2.71
Chinese	19.3	12.2	21.8	41.3	3.5	1.9	2.90
German	90.6	5.8	1.5	0.6	0.5	1.1	1.11
English	76.2	14.1	3.3	3.8	1.5	1.1	1.33
French	50.5	19.3	14.4	12.8	1.9	1.1	1.89
Italian	48.7	20.4	15.1	13.3	1.3	1.2	1.93
Dutch	34.1	20.9	20.2	20.8	2.7	1.3	2.29
Polish	27.1	15.0	26.5	27.0	2.9	1.5	2.56
Spanish	39.5	22.7	17.5	16.8	2.1	1.5	2.12
Turkish	50	16.9	14.9	14.3	2.6	1.5	1.93

*Mean value on a scale of 1 = Very to 4 = Not at all; excluding 'Don't know' and 'No comment'. The higher the mean value, therefore, the lower the prestige.

anonymous 'general public'. Turkish, for example, enjoys a much higher status on the personal level. This is due to the fact that one-third of the informants have a Turkish background, but they are aware that in general Turkish is not held in high esteem in Germany.

When the language evaluation is split up according to migration background, a clear pattern of partisanship emerges, which is also typical for the social construction of ethnic identity: people assign greater value to languages and linguistic communities to which they feel a personal affinity (Table 12.13).

While informants of Turkish origin consistently placed greatest value on German (mean value = 1.08) with Turkish a close second (mean value = 1.11), informants of Italian origin placed greatest value on Italian (mean value = 1.24), followed by German (mean value = 1.26), while they gave French a lower ranking (mean value = 1.67). A cross-comparison reveals that informants of Turkish origin attached greater prestige to Italian (mean value = 2.59) than vice versa; informants with an Italian background are more sceptical of Turkish (mean value = 2.72). The differences between the three groups (German, Italian, Turkish) were highly significant ($p < 0.05$). It is also noteworthy that Arabic enjoys a considerably higher status among informants with a Turkish background than among German informants or informants with an Italian background. It is possible that those of Turkish origin feel a certain cultural affinity to Arabic, for example in Islamic symbols (halal symbols, etc.). Moreover, some informants with a Turkish background were perfectly capable of interpreting Arabic symbols due to their own place of origin (the inhabitants of some Turkish towns on the borders of Syria

Table 12.13 Question C.6.1 With regard to your own personal opinion, how highly do you regard the following languages? (mean values)

Language	Origin						Total	
	No MB		It MB		Tr MB			
	Mean value	N	Mean value	N	Mean value	N	Mean value	N
Arabic	2.95	481	2.78	184	2.28	302	2.71	967
Chinese	2.96	480	2.66	183	2.96	301	2.90	964
German	1.06	500	1.26	200	1.08	303	1.11	1003
English	1.22	498	1.40	192	1.48	303	1.33	993
French	1.66	496	1.67	192	2.41	301	1.89	989
Italian	1.81	494	1.24	199	2.59	301	1.93	994
Dutch	1.94	496	2.43	183	2.78	299	2.29	978
Polish	2.33	493	2.67	181	2.87	300	2.56	974
Spanish	1.95	492	1.74	189	2.64	302	2.12	983
Turkish	2.14	494	2.72	184	1.11	301	1.93	979

*Mean value on a scale of 1 = Very to 4 = Not at all; excluding 'Don't know' and 'No comment'. The higher the mean value, therefore, the lower the prestige.

and Iraq also speak Arabic) or Islamic socialisation, and so they did not regard Arabic as 'foreign'.

The lower value that migrant groups attached to English can probably be traced to their poor English skills: whereas approximately 79% of informants without a migration background said they could speak English, approximately 52% of informants of Turkish origin and only 47% of informants of Italian origin could speak English.

The final data we wish to present indicates the extent to which the existence of public signs in migrant languages conveys the feeling of being at home and belonging (Table 12.14).

When the categories 'strongly' and 'quite strongly' are taken together, it becomes clear that in both groups of migrant origin well over half of the informants (54% to 59%) felt a sense of belonging through the existence of signs in their language of origin. The comparison on a mean value level shows that this tendency was significantly higher for migrants with a Turkish background than for those with an Italian background (mean values: 2.31 vs. 3.02; $p < 0.00$).

It is cognitively not very demanding to decode and interpret signs, and their existence therefore encourages the feeling of being in a familiar environment. On the other hand, approximately one-fifth of informants explicitly denied that signposting in the language of origin has anything to do with dimensions of belonging.

Table 12.14 Question D.1. How strongly does the existence of signs in your language of origin give you the feeling of being at home in Germany? (percentages in columns)

		Origin		Total
		IT MB	TR MB	
Very strongly	n	62	116	178
	%	29.4	38.2	34.6
Quite strongly	n	52	63	115
	%	24.6	20.7	22.3
Not very strongly	n	29	57	86
	%	13.7	18.8	16.7
Not at all	n	42	64	106
	%	19.9	21.1	20.6
Don't know	n	17	3	20
	%	8.1	1.0	3.9
No comment	n	9	1	10
	%	4.3	0.3	1.9
Total	n	211	304	515
	%	100.0	100.0	100.0

12.4 Conclusion

Our studies of the existence of visual multilingualism in the Ruhr Area have shown that the larger the population diversity, the greater the diversity of visible languages in the individual city neighbourhoods (with the exception of Essen-Rüttenscheid). In particular, we have been able to confirm the hypothesis that the neighbourhoods north of the A40 displayed greater visual multilingualism than those south of the A40. With regard to the contexts in which visual multilingualism occurred, it was revealed that the dominating discourse types were commercial and transgressive, which means that the frequency of multilingualism in these types of discourse are considerably greater than in the infrastructural, regulatory and commemorative discourse categories.

The data collected during on-site interviews regarding perception and evaluation reveal that here again the north-south divide plays a crucial role. The two main findings are that informants living in neighbourhoods north of the A40 motorway are not only more aware of visual multilingualism in the public space, but that they also hold more positive attitudes towards it. Moreover, our analyses show that the most common reasoning by those in favour of visual multilingualism is the functional and pragmatic argument; those opposed to visual multilingualism, on the other hand, most frequently give normative arguments to justify their rejection. These tendencies apply to informants both with and without a migrant background.

The results of the telephone interviews indicate that informants both with and without a migrant background widely accept multilingualism in the public space and regard it as an enrichment. One critical observation, however, is the persistence of a certain scepticism towards Polish and Arabic in the public space. In view of the fact that one of these languages (Polish) has actually long been established in the Ruhr Area and the other (Arabic) has to be seen in the light of recent refugee migration as the major migrant language of the future, urgent action is needed (e.g. more Arabic on signs in the public space), not only to make it easier for new migrants to find their way around, but also to increase acceptance of these languages and of those who speak them. Furthermore, the results of this study are not only notable in sociolinguistic terms, but also carry considerable political and application-oriented implications in terms of local integration policies and urban planning. The results support the demand for shaping the public space with more multilingual signs and labels. This would both promote the integration process of migrants and their feeling of being at home in Germany and underline the normality of multiculturalism in modern societies for the local communities.

Notes

(1) See https://benjamins.com/#catalog/journals/ll/main (accessed 4 October 2016).
(2) The *Signs of the Metropolises: Visual Multilingualism in the Ruhr Area* project is funded by the Mercator Research Center Ruhr (GZ MERCUR: Pr-2012-0045, from: 1 August 2013 to 15 January 2017) and is a cooperative project between the University of Duisburg-Essen and the Ruhr-University Bochum (Director: Evelyn Ziegler, University of Duisburg-Essen, cf. Cindark & Ziegler, 2016; Schmitz, 2017; Schmitz & Ziegler, 2016; Ziegler, 2013).

(3) The term 'super diverse' refers to the diversificaton of diversity in terms of ethnic and national backgrounds, cultural practices, religion and migration experiences. According to official statistics, 186 nationalities are counted in the Ruhr Area (cf. Reuschke *et al.*, 2013: 10).

(4) Online document. See https://difu.de/publikationen/demographic-decline-segregation-and-social-urban-renewal-in.html (accessed 4 October 2016).

(5) Many of the 25,504 photographs in our database do not show any recognisable language, but tags or pictures only. On other pictures you can see texts in different languages. We counted the occurrence of each language. This resulted in 27,265 individual text occurrences.

(6) Many thanks to Irmi Wachendorff (student assistant in the Metropolenzeichen project at the University of Duisburg-Essen) for creating the maps.

(7) Compare also, Peukert (2013).

(8) Many thanks to David Gehne (research assistant for the Metropolenzeichen project at Ruhr-University Bochum) for the diversity-index calculation and the corresponding diagram.

(9) This sticker imitates the North Face Logo. The words on the sticker '*The Nordstadt. Dem Spießer sein Alptraum*' (The Nordstadt: nightmare of the petit bourgeoisie) are a self-ironic reference to the image of Dortmund-Nordstadt, both with regard to content and expression. In terms of expression, the self-irony is contained in the switch from the English definite article to German and in the possessive construction composed of a dative phrase combined with the possessive article. This construction is considered to deviate from the grammatical norm and is highly stigmatised and seen as a mark of low education. In colloquial German, however, it is a very common construction and a very typical – though not exclusive – feature of the Ruhr German variety (cf. Ziegler *et al.*, in print).

(10) Over 100% in total due to languages occurring more than once on multilingual signs.

(11) Others: Arabic (3), Spanish (3), Korean (3), Latin (2), non-standard (1), Portuguese (1), Czech (1), Danish (1), Swedish (1), language unclear (1).

(12) The 'conative' aspect refers to the tendency or disposition to act in certain ways towards something (cf. Lasagabaster, 2004: 400).

(13) The interviews were conducted by the following student assistants: Nilgün Aykut, Sebastian Opara, David Passig, Michael Wentker and the student intern Yvette Rode.

(14) The interviews were transcribed according to the GAT 2 transcription system using the conventions for minimal transcription; see Selting *et al.* (2009).

(15) Remaining categories have been omitted from the table as their numbers were too small.

(16) In a similar vein, Landry and Bourhis (1997: 27) point out: 'Having one's own language enshrined on most private and government signs should contribute to the feeling that the in-group language has value and status relative to the other languages in the sociolinguistic setting'.

References

Aiestaran, J., Cenoz, J. and Gorter, D. (2010) Multilingual cityscapes: Perceptions and preferences of the inhabitants of the city of Donostia-San Sebastian. In E. Shohamy, E. Ben-Rafael and M. Barni (eds) *Linguistic Landscape in the City* (pp. 219–234). Bristol: Multilingual Matters.

Androutsopoulos, J. (2014) Computer-mediated communication and linguistic landscapes. In J. Holmes and K. Hazen (eds) *Research Methods in Sociolinguistics: A Practical Guide* (pp. 74–90). New York: John Wiley.

Backhaus, P. (2007) *Linguistic Landscapes: A Comparative Study of Urban Multilingualism in Tokyo.* Clevedon: Multilingual Matters.

Cindark, I. and Ziegler, E. (2016) Mehrsprachigkeit im Ruhrgebiet: Zur Sichtbarkeit sprachlicher Diversität in Dortmund. In S. Ptashnyk, R. Beckert, P. Wolf-Farré and M. Wolny (eds) *Gegenwärtige Sprachkontakte im Kontext der Migration* (pp. 133–156). Heidelberg: Winter.

Collins, J. and Slembrouck, J. (2007) Reading shop windows in globalized neighborhoods: Multilingual literacy practices and indexicality. *Journal of Literacy Research* 39 (3), 335–356.

Friedrichs, J. (1996) Intra-regional polarization: Cities in the Ruhr Area. In J. O'Loughlin and J. Friedrichs (eds) *Social Polarization in Post-Industrial Metropolises* (pp. 133–172). Berlin: de Gruyter.

Garrett, P., Coupland, N. and Williams, A. (2003) *Investigating Language Attitudes: Social Meanings of Dialect, Ethnicity and Performance*. Cardiff: University of Wales Press.

Gärtig, A.-K., Plewnia, A. and Rothe, A. (2010) *Wie Menschen in Deutschland über Sprache denken, Ergebnisse einer bundesweiten Repräsentativerhebung zu aktuellen Spracheinstellungen*. IDS Mannheim: Eigenverlag.

Garvin, R.T. (2010) Responses to the linguistic landscape in Memphis, Tennessee: An urban space in transition. In E. Shohamy, E. Ben-Rafael and M. Barni (eds) *Linguistic Landscape in the City* (pp. 252–271). Bristol: Multilingual Matters.

Gilinger, E.S., Sloboda, M., Šimičić, L. and Vigers, D. (2012) Discourse coalitions for and against minority languages in signs: Linguistic landscape as a social issue. In D. Gorter, H.F. Marten and L. Van Mensel (eds) *Minority Languages in Linguistic Landscape* (pp. 263–280). Basingstoke: Palgrave Macmillan.

Honneth, A. (1995) *The Struggle for Recognition: The Moral Grammar of Social Conflicts*. Cambridge: Polity Press.

Honneth, A. (2003) *Unsichtbarkeit: Stationen einer Theorie der Intersubjektivität*. Frankfurt am Main: Suhrkamp.

Kersting, V., Meyer, C., Strohmeier, K.P. and Teerporten, T. (2009) Die A 40 – Der 'Sozialäquator' des Ruhrgebiets. In A. Prossek, H. Schneider, H.A. Wessel, B. Wetterau and D. Wiktorin (eds) *Atlas der Metropole Ruhr* (pp. 142–145). Köln: Emons.

König, K. (2014) *Spracheinstellungen und Identitätskonstruktion: Eine gesprächsanalytische Untersuchung sprachbiographischer Interviews mit Deutsch-Vietnamesen*. Berlin: de Gruyter.

Landry, R. and Bourhis, R.Y. (1997) Linguistic landscape and ethnolinguistic vitality: An empirical study. *Journal of Language and Social Psychology* 16 (1), 23–49.

Lasagabaster, D. (2004) Attitude. In U. Ammon, N. Dittmar, K.J. Mattheier and P. Trudgill (eds) *Soziolinguistik: Ein internationales Handbuch zur Wissenschaft von Sprache und Gesellschaft* (pp. 399–405). Berlin: de Gruyter.

Liebscher, G. and Dailey-O'Cain, J. (2009) Language attitudes in interaction. *Journal of Sociolinguistics* 13 (2), 195–222.

Lou, L.J. (2010) Chinese on the side: The marginalization of Chinese in the linguistic and social landscapes of Chiatown in Washington, DC. In E. Shohamy, E. Ben-Rafael and M. Barni (eds) *Linguistic Landscape in the City* (pp. 96–114). Bristol: Multilingual Matters.

Malinowski, D. (2010) Showing seeing in the Korean linguistic cityspace. In E. Shohamy, E. Ben-Rafael and M. Barni (eds) *Linguistic Landscape in the City* (pp. 199–215). Bristol: Multilingual Matters.

Niedzielski, N. and Preston, D.R. (1999) *Folk Linguistics*. Berlin: Mouton de Gruyter.

Peukert, H. (2013) Measuring language diversity in urban ecosystems. In J. Duarte and I. Gogolin (eds) *Linguistic Superdiversity in Urban Areas* (pp. 75–95). Amsterdam: Benjamins.

Reuschke, D., Salzbrunn, N. and Schönhärl, K. (2013) The economies of urban diversity: An introduction. In D. Reuschke, N. Salzbrunn and K. Schönhärl (eds) *The Economies of Urban Diversity: Ruhr Area and Istanbul* (pp. 1–24). New York: Palgrave Macmillan.

Schmitz, U. (2017) Linguistic landscapes im Ruhrgebiet: Internationalismus und Lokalkolorit. In L. Anderwald and J. Hoekstra (eds) *Enregisterment: Zur sozialen Bedeutung sprachlicher Variation* (pp. 163–188). Frankfurt: Peter Lang.

Schmitz, U. and Ziegler, E. (2016) Sichtbare Dialoge im öffentlichen Raum. *Zeitschrift für germanistische Linguistik* 44 (3) 469–502.

Scollon, R. and Scollon, S.W. (2003) *Discourses in Place: Language in the Material World*. London: Routledge.

Selting, M., Auer, P., Barth-Weingarten, D., Bergmann, J., Bergmann, P., Birkner, K., Couper-Kuhlen, E., Deppermann, A., Gilles, P., Günthner, S., Hartung, M., Kern, F., Mertzlufft, C., Meyer, C., Morek, M., Oberzaucher, F., Peters, J., Quasthoff, U., Schütte, W., Stukenbrock, A. and Uhmann, S. (2009) Gesprächsanalytisches Transkriptionssystem 2 (GAT 2). *Gesprächsforschung. Online-Zeitschrift zur verbalen Interaktion* 10, 353–402.

Shohamy, E. and Gorter, D. (2009) *Linguistic Landscape: Expanding the Scenery*. London: Routledge.

Simpson, E.H. (1949) Measurement of diversity. *Nature* 163, 688.

Strohmeier, K.P. and Bader, S. (2004) Demographic decline, segregation, and social urban renewal in old industrial metropolitan areas. *Deutsche Zeitschrift für Kommunalwissenschaften.* See https://difu.de/publikationen/demographic-decline-segregation-and-social-urban-renewal-in. html (accessed 4 October 2016).

Tophinke, D. and Ziegler, E. (2006) 'Aber bitte im Kontext': Neue Perspektiven in der dialektologischen Einstellungsforschung. In A. Voeste and J. Gessinger (eds) *Dialekt im Wandel: Perspektiven einer neuen Dialektologie* (pp. 203–222). Duisburg: Universitätsverlag Rhein-Ruhr.

Tophinke, D. and Ziegler, E. (2014) Spontane Dialektthematisierung in der Weblogkommunikation: Interaktiv-kontextuelle Einbettung, semantische Topoi und sprachliche Konstruktionen. In C. Cuonz and R. Studler (eds) *Sprechen über Sprache* (pp. 205–242). Tübingen: Stauffenburg Verlag.

Trumper-Hecht, N. (2010) Linguistic landscape in mixed cities in Israel from the perspective of 'walkers': The case of Arabic. In E. Shohamy, E. Ben-Rafael and M. Barni (eds) *Linguistic Landscape in the City* (pp. 235–251). Bristol: Multilingual Matters.

Uslucan, H.-H. (2014) Ubi bene, ibi patria? Türkeistämmige Migranten in Deutschland zwischen Beheimatung und Heimweh. In J. Klose (ed.) *Heimatschichten, Anthropologische Grundlegung eines Weltverhältnisses* (pp. 347–364). Wiesbaden: Springer Verlag.

Vandermeeren, S. (2005) Research on language attitudes. In U. Ammon, N. Dittmar, K.J. Mattheier and P. Trudgill (eds) *Sociolinguistics/Soziolinguistik: An International Handbook of the Science of Language and Society* (pp. 1317–1332). Berlin: de Gruyter.

Vertovec, S. (2007) Super-diversity and its implications. *Ethnic and Racial Studies* 29 (6), 1024–1054.

Wandruszka, M. (1975) Mehrsprachigkeit. *Öffentlicher Vortrag.* See http://ids-pub.bsz-bw.de/ frontdoor/index/index/docId/1330 (accessed 4 October 2016).

Ziegler, E. (2013) Metropolenzeichen: Visuelle Mehrsprachigkeit in der Metropole Ruhr. In:*Zeitschrift für germanistische Linguistik.* 41 (2), 299–301.

Ziegler, E., Schmitz, U. and Eickmans, H. (2017) Innere Mehrsprachigkeit in der *linguistic landscape der Metropole Ruhr.* In P. Gilles, H. Christen and C. Purschke (eds) *Räume – Grenzen – Übergänge* (pp. 347–374). Akten des 5. Kongresses der Internationalen Gesellschaft für Dialektologie des Deutschen (IGDD). *Zeitschrift für Dialektologie und Linguistik – Beihefte.* Band 171. Stuttgart: Steiner.

Index